There are several historical accounts of the Treaty 7 agreement between the government and prairie First Nations but none of these are from an Aboriginal perspective. The elders of each nation have, however, maintained an oral history of events, passing on from generation to generation many stories about the circumstances surrounding Treaty 7 and the subsequent administration of the agreement. *The True Spirit and Original Intent of Treaty 7* gathers this "collective memory" of the elders to provide unique insights into a crucial historical event and the complex ways of the Aboriginal people.

The True Spirit and Original Intent of Treaty 7 is based on the testimony of over eighty elders from the five First Nations involved in Treaty 7 – the Bloods, Peigan, Siksika, Stoney Nakoda, and Tsuu T'ina. Their recollections highlight the grave misconceptions and misrepresentations of the two sides, due in part to inadequate interpretation and/or deliberate attempts to mislead. The elders consistently report that the treaty as they understood it was a peace treaty, not a surrender of land, and that they had agreed to "share" the land with the white newcomers in exchange for resources to establish new economies – education, medical assistance, and annuity payments.

The book provides both a historical overview of Treaty 7 and an analysis of the literature on treaties generally and Treaty 7 specifically. It makes clear that different agendas, different languages, and different world views affected each side's interpretation of events.

This review of the events and interpretations surrounding Treaty 7 takes place at a time when indigenous peoples all over the world are re-evaluating their relationships with imperial powers. It was undertaken in good faith in the hope that it will begin a dialogue that can alter the dominant discourse of Euro-Canadian society, which has been so damaging to Aboriginal people.

TREATY 7 ELDERS AND TRIBAL COUNCIL
Walter Hildebrandt is director of the University of Calgary Press.
Dorothy First Rider is a member of the Blood Tribe and a graduate of the University of Regina/Saskatchewan Indian Federated College.
Sarah Carter is professor, Department of History, University of Calgary.

McGill-Queen's Native and Northern Series
Bruce G. Trigger, Editor

The True Spirit and Original Intent of Treaty 7

Treaty 7 Elders and
Tribal Council
with Walter Hildebrandt,
Dorothy First Rider,
and Sarah Carter

McGill-Queen's University Press
Montreal & Kingston • London • Chicago

ISBN 978-0-7735-1521-5 (cloth)
ISBN 978-0-7735-1522-2 (paper)
ISBN 978-0-7735-6637-8 (ePDF)

Legal deposit third quarter 1996
Bibliothèque nationale du Québec

Reprinted 1997, 2005, 2013, 2017

Printed in Canada on acid-free paper that is 100% ancient
forest free (100% post-consumer recycled), processed
chlorine free

McGill-Queen's University Press acknowledges the support
of the Canada Council for the Arts for our publishing
program. We also acknowledge the financial support of the
Government of Canada through the Canada Book Fund for
our publishing activities.

All illustrations are from the Glenbow-Alberta Archives,
with the exception of the photograph of David Laird
(Provincial Archives of Manitoba) and the sketch
of James ("Jimmy Jock") Bird
(Montana Historical Society Archives).

Canadian Cataloguing in Publication Data
Main entry under title:
The true spirit and original intent of Treaty 7
(McGill-Queen's native and northern series,
ISSN 1181-7453 ; 14)
Includes bibliographical references and index.
ISBN 978-0-7735-1521-5 (cloth)
ISBN 978-0-7735-1522-2 (paper)
ISBN 978-0-7735-6637-8 (ePDF)
1. Canada. Treaties, etc. 1877 Sept. 22.
2. Indians of North America—Canada—Treaties.
3. Indians of North America—Canada—Government
relations—1860–1951.   4. Indians, Treatment of—
Canada—History—19th century.   I. Hildebrandt,
Walter.   II. First Rider, Dorothy.   III. Carter,
Sarah, 1954—   IV. Series.

E92.T78 1996   971'.00497   C96-990059-7

Cover painting by Henry Standing Alone.
The spiritual leaders of the Blood people depicted in this
painting are (left to right) Pat Weasel Head, Dan Weasel
Moccasin, Mark Old Shoes, and Willie Scraping White.

Contents

Foreword

GREGG C. SMITH

Executive Director, Treaty 7 Tribal Council

In the past we have heard about treaties from legal experts, politicians, anthropologists, and historians, but we have never heard from the elders of Treaty 7 in a comprehensive way. The primary aim of this book is to provide an opportunity for the elders to speak. For this reason the book has been organized so that the elders speak first in Part 1. Analysis of what they have to say and comparison with what others have written then follows in Part 2.

What motivated the elders to come forward and give their stories was the need to educate both members of their own tribes and also the descendents of the newcomer society. The Blackfoot-speaking tribes begin their explanation of what the treaty means by explaining the concept of *inistsi* or peacemaking. It is a concept that is also understood by the Nakoda Stoneys and Tsuu T'ina as a broad process of peacemaking or of forging new relationships. For the Canadian treaty makers, Treaty 7 was something that was more narrowly a legal agreement, later interpreted to have been a land surrender. The written text of the treaty did not encompass the spirit and intent of the whole treaty-making process. For the elders of Treaty 7, the treaty was an agreement that was to benefit both sides in a substantial way. Each side had to bring something substantial to offer to the other. The elders say that the Treaty 7 people's offer to share the land with the newcomers has been of greater benefit to the government side than it was to the First Nations. The promises have not been properly fulfilled.

There appears to be substantial unanimity in what the elders have said about Treaty 7. Elders from each of the tribes agree that Treaty 7 was first and foremost a peace treaty; they do not remember ever being told that the Treaty 7 First Nations had agreed to a land surrender. This unanimity does not mean that there is always complete agreement on all issues relating to the treaty, and there might also be dissident opinions among members of the Treaty 7 First Nations. What the unanimity shows is that a broad spectrum of elders from each of the First Nations are in substantial agreement. Their agenda is not a political one or a legal one, but rather they seek to educate people about what their ancestors told them. The elders all agree that there is a fundamental problem with the written treaty because it does not represent the "spirit and intent" of the agreement that was arrived at at Blackfoot Crossing in September of 1877.

In closing, I would like to acknowledge the assistance of task force members who helped with the administration of the project. Members of the task force included Les Healy of the Blood tribe, Hugh Crow Eagle of the Peigan tribe, Alex Crow Child of the Tsuu T'ina tribe, Fred Breaker of the Siksika tribe, and Dave Bearspaw, Tina Fox, and Frank Crawler of the Stoney tribe. Thanks also go to Nigel Bankes of the College of Law at the University of Calgary for reading the manuscript and making many useful suggestions. The research directors of the Stoney tribe, Ian Getty, and Blood tribe member Annabelle Crop Eared Wolf also provided technical support and advice on the project as a whole. And finally I thank Dorothy First Rider, who was with the project from the beginning, for her commitment to the completion of the project.

Preface

CHIEF ROY WHITNEY
Portfolio Holder and Chairman, Treaty 7 Tribal Council

In 1877, at Blackfoot Crossing in Alberta, an agreement was reached between five of the First Nations and the Canadian government. This was known as the Treaty with the Blackfoot, Treaty 7. The purpose of this review of Treaty 7 is to determine the "original spirit and true intent" of the treaty as related to us by our elders. A number of non-Native writers and historians have written on the subject, but very little exists that presents the point of view of the people who represent the First Nations of Treaty 7: the Bloods, the Peigan, the Siksika (Blackfoot), the Stoney, and the Tsuu T'ina (Sarcee). Fortunately, the oral tradition of our nations has preserved many accounts of the circumstances surrounding the making of Treaty 7 and the subsequent fulfilment of the treaty.

The treaty review process was begun in 1991. A major aim of this project was to gather the "collective memory" from the elders of Treaty 7. Our research director, Dorothy First Rider, was given the task of defining and carrying out a treaty review process that would not only gather valuable material from the elders but would produce a manuscript for publication. The project was an ambitious one, demanding a great deal from the elders, who were consulted many times through its course. But the elders were committed to devoting their energies to an undertaking that they unanimously agreed was important. During the workshops, they often spoke eloquently about the need to gather information on the treaty so that subsequent generations of our own people would have a better understanding of the actual event that took place at Blackfoot Crossing in 1877.

Many elders were worried that if this project were not carried out, some of our history would be irrevocably lost. Unfortunately, in the course of the treaty review, a number of our most knowledgeable and respected elders passed away. This recording of our history will pay homage to their memory. A primary concern of our elders was to preserve the history of Treaty 7 for our own children and to have the information used in our schools. It is also our intention to let non-Native peoples know about the original intent of the treaty as opposed to the written text of Treaty 7. It is clear that many people have serious misconceptions about what Treaty 7 was about. One need only look at the continuous misrepresentation of the Native point of view in the Canadian media to see that there is a serious need to educate and inform people about this important event in our history. Many of these misconceptions continue to have a damaging effect on the attempts of Native peoples to define ourselves in the face of the newcomer society, which will not listen to or only selectively hears what we have to say about our history. The need for us to tell our own history on our own terms is self-evident. According to our elders, the time has come to tell our side of the Treaty 7 history.

The treaty review began with a process whereby representatives from each of the nations of Treaty 7 met to define the project and decide on its objective. Elders from each of the nations were interviewed in their own language. This allowed each elder to feel at ease and comfortable with both the situation and the interviewer. The use of their languages permitted the elders to express themselves more accurately than they otherwise could have. The verbatim interviews were then translated into English. This interviewing process was undertaken over a two-year period. The third year of the project was devoted to writing. Three years proved to be a short time to complete this ambitious program of interviewing, analysis, and writing. Throughout the writing process, the project historian, Walter Hildebrandt, worked in close consultation with the research coordinator, Dorothy First Rider, and the elders.

The resulting book is divided into three parts. Part 1 presents the testimony of over eighty elders from the Treaty 7 First Nations: Bloods, Peigan, Siksika, Stoneys, and Tsuu T'ina. Part 2 is an analysis of academic writing on the Canadian treaties generally and on Treaty 7 specifically. Part 3 presents brief biographies of the elders, interviewers, translators, and researchers who participated in this treaty review project.

Part 1 consists of four chapters. Chapter 1 briefly summarizes the events at Blackfoot Crossing as described in the oral history of the elders. Chapters 1 through 4 focus on specific issues that emerged out of the treaty negotiations. Chapter 2 examines the social, political, and religious beliefs of each nation, and explains the land-use patterns and international relations of the Treaty 7 First Nations. Of particular interest in this chapter are the Blackfoot elders' memories relating to the Lame Bull Treaty of 1855. Chapter 3 focuses primarily on Treaty 7 itself: what it meant to the First Nations and what the elders understand was promised by the Crown. Specific issues are highlighted: problems with translation; the clash between written and oral histories; the role of the North-West Mounted Police; mineral or sub-surface rights; the actual making of the treaty; and the land boundaries promised to the First Nations. Chapter 4 focuses on post-treaty life. The evidence of the elders is significant in that it sheds light on the institutions and mechanisms that were put in place to implement agreements reached at Blackfoot Crossing. Specific sections deal with government policy, the missionaries, industrial and residential schools, reserve life, purported land surrenders, and the issue of surveys.

In summary, a number of conclusions arise from the testimony in Part 1. Of most importance is the conclusion that Treaty 7 was a peace treaty rather than a land surrender. The Treaty 7 nations all said that what was discussed and agreed to was a peace treaty between themselves and the Canadian government. The First Nations agreed to share the land with Canadian new-comers in return for the Crown's promises, which entailed an-nuity payments, education, medical care, ammunition, assistance in farming and ranching, and assurance that we would be free to continue to hunt as we always had. All of the First Nations elders said that their people did not give up the land; in fact concepts such as "surrender" and "cede" had been untranslatable to them. What is clear from the elders' testimony is that our people would allow newcomers to farm and to use the topsoil of the land. Our elders from each of the nations were adamant that there was no discussion of surrendering the land.

There was also unanimity among the elders concerning trans-lation problems at Blackfoot Crossing. Historic records have left the impression, for example, that missionary Reverend John McDougall spoke Stoney and that the translator Jerry Potts was a fluent Blackfoot speaker, but our elders had a different view. According to the Stoney elders, McDougall spoke some Cree but not Stoney and he was not able to communicate directly to most of the Stoneys. Elders of the Blood, Peigan, and Siksika tribes say that Potts was a very ineffectual translator. He was unable to understand the legal and formal English that he was expected to translate into the Blackfoot dialects. Important matters that would have a lifetime impact on the Treaty 7 First Nations were never related to them at the time the treaty was made.

Another unacknowledged fact relates to the evidence provided by the elders concerning government policies, such as those embodied in the Indian Act. This act was already in place when the treaty was made, but its effects were never explained to the elders. Elders stated that the Indian Act was in direct contradiction to terms of the treaty. Some of them also spoke passionately about the restrictiveness of subsequent policies such as the pass system and the permit system. Many elders recalled the underfunded programs and the ineffectual farm instructors and self-serving Indian agents. Details of illegal land surrenders and improper surveys were described by the elders, and they remembered how rations were used to influence decisions on reserves.

It is important to appreciate all of the treaty-making process that occurred in 1877 at Blackfoot Crossing. The discussions on each of the terms of the treaty took place among the chiefs, headmen, medicine men, and spiritual leaders. These discussions were conducted with sacred prayers and the singing of ceremonial songs. It is within this cultural and spiritual context that our forefathers arrived at their understanding of the meaning of the sacred treaty.

Part 2 begins with a general discussion of the historical background of Treaty 7. Indian policy of the seventeenth and eighteenth centuries is outlined, and the historical context of early treaties in Canada up to and including the Robinson Treaties is explored. Government Indian policy of the nineteenth century is presented through an analysis of the numbered treaties made during the 1870s in the Northwest. A detailed examination of Treaty 6 precedes the analysis of Treaty 7 to draw attention to their similarities and differences.

Part 2 contains a narrative of the events leading up to Treaty

7. This narrative, presented in chapters 5 and 7–9, has been constructed from the primary sources as well as from some secondary sources. The primary sources, which contain the major participants' versions of the treaty, are analysed in detail. The participants included Commissioner David Laird, Commissioner James Macleod, Father Constantine Scollen, Reverend John McDougall, and land trader Richard Hardisty. The work of Hugh Dempsey, who has written extensively on leaders such as Red Crow and Crowfoot as well as on Treaty 7, is also examined. The treaty itself is reproduced in chapter 6.

In chapter 10 the work of academics whose studies have either generally or specifically touched on Treaty 7 is analysed. This includes the work of Sakej Youngblood-Henderson, John Taylor, John Tobias, Sarah Carter, Jean Friesen, Richard Price, Doug Sprague, Noel Dyck, and George Stanley.

A number of conclusions emerge from an analysis of the primary and secondary sources as well as from the academic studies. Probably most significant is the fact that agreements that leaders of the First Nations thought would be included in the treaty were omitted and some issues that were never discussed were included. Indeed, a majority of the academic analysts agree with the elders that a land surrender was never discussed.

The Canadian authorities were anxious to sign a treaty with the tribes of southern Alberta for a number of reasons. The presence of Sitting Bull's Lakota at Wood Mountain made the potential for an alliance between the Lakota and the Blackfoot a real threat to settlement. The fighting between the Nez Percé people and the US Army in 1877 similarly concerned Canadian officials, who feared the arrival on Canadian soil of tribes that had successfully done battle with the US Army. Furthermore, White traders and missionaries were putting pressure on the Canadian government to sign a treaty as quickly as possible because they feared violence if settlers came to these territories without treaties being in place. The Blackfoot had limited contact with fur traders or missionaries before the 1870s and thus were seen as being volatile and unpredictable. For these reasons, academics such as John Taylor question whether an issue as controversial as a land surrender was ever raised for discussion.

At each stage of this Treaty 7 project, meetings were held with elders and representatives of the five nations. Long discussions

ensued to help clarify meaning and resolve problems of translation. This volume thus represents a collective effort rather than
one that can be attributed to only a few individuals. It is a remarkable achievement for five nations representing three distinct
language groups to produce such a book.

However, we recognize that there may be problems with what
we have produced. For example, meanings may not be accurately
conveyed where there are no Blackfoot, Nakota, and Tsuu T'ina
(Dene) words that correspond to English words or concepts –
or the reverse. More generally, First Nations peoples have expressed the belief that our languages represent a significantly
different world view from that of the newcomers, one that cannot be glibly translated without an understanding of the context
and environment in which the languages were created. "Verb-
centred" Native languages and "noun-centred" European languages arose out of radically different contexts and environ-
ments. As Sakej Youngblood-Henderson has recently pointed out
in an article, these fundamentally different languages are not
compatible with simple translation.

What has become abundantly clear is that in 1877 two peoples
with mutually exclusive world views attempted to communicate
with each other as they negotiated Treaty 7. We would like to
register the caveat that much work still needs to be done before
either side can be effectively understood by the other. A process
of things unfolding has always been a part of the Native world
view, and perhaps it could become part of the Euro-Canadian
world view as well. Perhaps our next task should be to translate
the treaties into Native languages to draw attention to the many
specific and general problems that exist in representing languages
and world views.

Finally, this review of Treaty 7 is taking place at a time when
indigenous peoples all over the world are revisiting the documents they made with imperial powers. In the colonial era, newcomer societies portrayed, then treated, indigenous populations
with contempt, as people lesser than themselves. They insisted
that indigenous peoples were victims of inferior cultures that
were destined to disappear. This has not happened. In fact, in
the post-colonial era, especially since the 1960s, a time when
dominant societies seem more accommodating and more willing
to listen, indigenous peoples have taken bold steps to assert

themselves. Treaties were originally the starting point for the process of defining the Aboriginal peoples' relations with new-comers, and they continue to be what our peoples regard as our Magna Cartas, as the place where we articulated just how we would live with the newcomers and just how we would share the land with them.

We undertook this review in good faith to begin a dialogue that will hopefully alter the dominant world view of European society, which has been so damaging to indigenous people in Canada and throughout the world.

Map 1 Locations of Northwestern Plains Nations ca. 1870
over Modern Boundaries

Map 2   Area of Treaty 7 and Traditional Territory
of the Blackfoot Confederacy

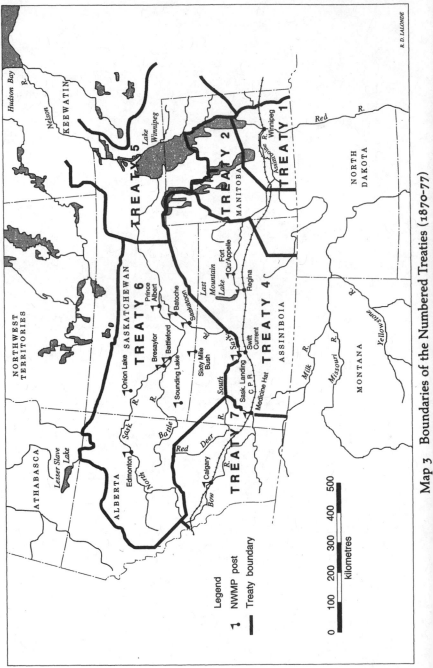

Map 3   Boundaries of the Numbered Treaties (1870-77)

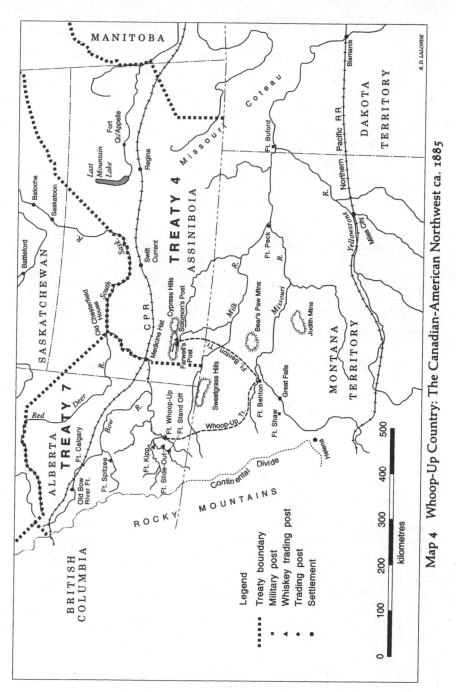

Map 4   Whoop-Up Country: The Canadian-American Northwest ca. 1885

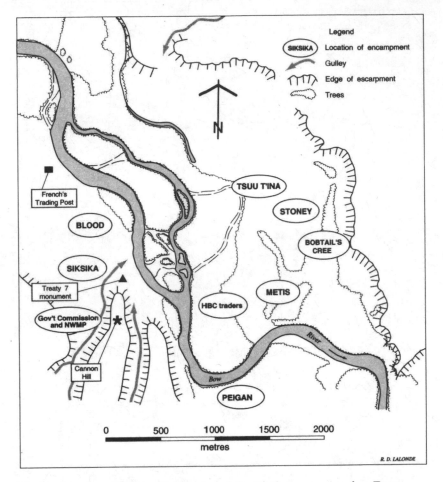

The largest tribes at Treaty 7, the Bloods and the Siksika, were camped on Treaty
Flats along with the Government Commission and the NWMP. The Tsuu T'ina were
camped just across the Bow River. The Stoneys were camped to the east of the Tsuu
T'ina. Bobtail's Cree were farthest east. The Cree were present not to sign Treaty 7
but rather to sign an adhesion to Treaty 6 negotiated a year earlier at forts Pitt and
Carlton. The tribes of the Blackfoot Confederacy, aware of numerous massacres in
previous years, feared that if negotiations broke down they might be attacked. The
Peigan were therefore strategically placed behind the NWMP and the commissioners.
Along with the Peigan were war parties from each of the other tribes, prepared to
attack if necessary. Just across the river were the Métis and the traders, who were
there to sell their goods to the tribes once the treaty had been completed and payments made to them.

Map 5   Position of Parties at Blackfoot Crossing, September 1877

Otsistsi Pakssaisstoyiih Pi
(the year when the winter was open and cold)

WILTON GOODSTRIKER

Among all First Nations people, there is and has always been a recording of significant events in our history. Our ancestors were just as anxious to leave a record of their story as we are today. I wish that somehow we could let them know that we have remembered, but then again, they probably knew all along that we would.

The stories have been recorded in many forms, through our winter-counts, on the land, but most importantly in the minds and spirit of our people. In these ways, the stories have been passed down from one generation to another throughout the ages. Throughout this document, we will share the various methods that the First Nations people of Treaty 7 used to record our history.

In the winter-counts of the First Nations of the Treaty 7 area, the year 1877 is referred to as *otsistsi pakssaisstoyiih pi** (Blackfoot – the year when the winter was open and cold). Among the other nations, it is known as "the year when there was great hunger," "the year when the long rains did not come," "the year of star-

---

* Blackfoot is an oral language, and over the years several Blackfoot dictionaries have been produced. For consistency in this book, we will use Don Frantz's *Blackfoot Dictionary of Stems, Roots and Affixes* (Toronto: University of Toronto Press, 1995), second edition, unless otherwise noted. This choice is not intended to raise Frantz's dictionary as a final authority for usage, since each Blackfoot tribe has its own legitimate dialect and usage.

vation and hunger," or "the year when the first snow was late." In any event, to our people it was to be a year which was not going to be normal. To the elders, something was going to be wrong.

It was also the year that a treaty (Treaty 7) was entered into between the First Nations people of this area and the representatives of the Queen of Britain. Interesting is the fact that the treaty did not make its way onto any of the winter-counts of the First Nations people. However, the memory of that occasion is vivid among our people, and the story has been told many times among Niitsitapi (the real people) throughout the years since that time. This story is about *istsist aohkotspi* (the first time that we received gifts and money) at Soyooh pawahko (ridge under water) or Blackfoot Crossing. In our languages there is no word for treaty; the event is simply referred to as *istsist aohkotspi* or *iitsinnaihtsiiyo'pi* (the time when we made a sacred alliance). Among our people, there are several ways to make an alliance and we will examine these closely in the hope that the reader will come to understand the complex ways of our people. The alliance process of the First Nations played a major role at Blackfoot Crossing.

The memory of a people is made accurate with the help of ceremony. This memory is a precious gift among our people.

The Story

"Sit here my child, and watch me close as I prepare the sacred smudge. I will then tell you a story. The reason I will use the smudge is so you will never forget that which I will share with you. And in time, when it is your turn to share, you will share with your children exactly as I will share with you. In this way, things will never change." – Sa'ksisakiaaksin (Laurie Big Plume)

Laurie Big Plume went on to tell me many stories. I remember one time when he told me that "The Christian story always begins with 'In the beginning.' Our story, if we were to write it down, would start with 'Before the beginning.'" I asked him at one point, "How old are our ways?" and he replied, "The ways of the White people are a child compared to our ways."

History has been documented in many ways, and in large part what we know of the past is dependent on information gained through archaeology and to some extent anthropology. Among our people, oral history is perhaps the most accurate. Our people's memory goes back to the beginning of time and in some respects beyond. Our story has come through seven ages, the last one being referred to as *i'kookaiksi* (the age when the people used tipi designs). We are still in this age and will be for as long as the people use the tipi design. This era dates back some five hundred years, and it will be the one that we will concentrate on for the purposes of this document. It is an era that saw the coming of the horse, of the immigrant nations to our land, and of new ways to a people.

One must keep in mind the history of a people when attempting to understand their perspective, their spirit and intent, in their dealings with the newcomers. This story will take you into the world of the First Nations. We will share our history, our alliance process, and our ceremony as they pertain to the treaty. Constant through the ages have been the use of ceremony and the need to document our history accurately. The latter has been done by way of marking in some way on the land, in our wintercounts, and, in all cases, in the oral history, which has been the most accurate method.

Let's begin with a brief walk through our history of alliances. Alliances have always been common to our people. There were alliances for trade, for cohabitation of territory. *Innaihtsiini* are sacred alliances of peace between individuals, families, and nations. These alliances find their beginning in the sacred ways of the Plains people, and they go back for thousands of years. Each year one would still witness these in our sacred ceremonies.

For the purposes of this introduction, concentration will be given to alliances beginning in the 1600s and going on into the 1800s.

Early in the 1600s there was a trade alliance between the Cree and Assiniboin, acquired from the early Hudson's Bay Company (HBC) traders in the east. The HBC traders then wanted to trade directly with the Blackfoot, and in their records, they indicate that their first encounter with Blackfoot in their own territory was in 1691. The horse was acquired from the Kootenay/Salish, the Cheyenne, and the Shoshone tribes, who previously had acquired these from the southern tribes who traded with the Spanish traders. During this era, the need for guns and horses dramatically expanded the trade among First Nations.

The 1700s saw a further expansion of trade among the Plains tribes, and with the use of the horse, trading now was occurring over great distances. This era saw the establishment of formal trade centres among the First Nations people, with many of the tribes hosting trade and acting as middlemen/agents for the trade.

The Nakoda (Stoney) were contacts for trade with the Shuswap and Kootenay tribes to the west of the Rockies. The trade centre was located near where the present town of Banff is situated. The Nakoda also facilitated trade with their relatives the Assiniboin. The Shoshone were facilitating very active trade to the southwest with Kootenay/Salish, Flathead, Nez Percé, Ute, and Yakima. This trade saw several trade centres operating: one, called Helena, near the present city of Idaho Falls, another near what is now Missoula, and others near present-day Kalispell and at Waterton Lakes.

In the east, the Mandan/Hidatsa people were agents for traders from the east. This trade centre was located near the present site of Bismarck, North Dakota. South of the Black Hills was the trade centre of the Arapaho and Cheyenne, and they were contacts for the Comanche, Kiowa, Pueblo, and Apache nations. Blackfoot trade with the Sioux was initially through the Mandan and Arapaho centres; however, at a later date there was direct trade with them.

La Vérendrye, an early French fur trader, was perhaps the first to witness a well-organized trade alliance between the Blackfoot, the Assiniboin, and the Cree. This was in 1734. He had ventured into the area in 1730, and that same year he had witnessed a gun battle between the Shoshone and Peigan. In 1738 he witnessed a similarly well-established trade alliance between the Blackfoot and others utilizing the Mandan trade centre. This was at the mouth of the Heart River. History books also mention trading among the Blackfoot, Sarcee (Tsuu T'ina), Assiniboin, and Cree nations in 1754. In 1785, near Waterton Lakes, the Kootenay brought horses to the Blackfoot in trade for guns which the Cree had acquired for the Blackfoot from traders on the Saskatchewan River. The Kootenay were unable to acquire guns from their Spanish trade contacts, as it was at that time against the law for Spanish traders to provide guns to the Indians. Not until the early 1800s did the American traders realize that the trade of guns would enhance their trade relations with the nations of the upper Missouri.

In the late 1700s, due to an incident involving two young boys in which one was killed, the Assiniboin and the Blackfoot became fierce enemies. This happened near the present site of Gleichen. This was one of the stories which resulted in direct trade being made with former contacts of the Assiniboin.

Trade alliances, as one can see, were well established by the 1600s and the 1700s, and trade covered virtually the whole of the continent. The rearrival of the horse simply made for more frequent trade among the First Nations. Trade centres were marked on the land by stones and on nearby rocks and cliffs. These would indicate who were to use these sites and on whose territory they were situated. Some of these markings were in later years mistaken for medicine wheels. Many of these trade centres in later years were to become the sites of the new trading posts and forts.

Alliances for purposes of trade were oftentimes "gentlemen's agreements" between leaders and were respected while trade was occurring. However, they were not binding once trade was completed. Alliances of peace between nations were a different matter.

ALLIANCES OF PEACE

These alliances were binding for all time. Peace accords between leaders and elders were sealed with ceremony in the traditional ways and the promise to peace was made to the Giver of Life; thus, they could never be broken once made. Many of these alliances exist among the Plains people and are still intact. A record of many of them are on the land and in our winter-counts, and our elders will ensure that these are not forgotten. Take time to sit with our elders, and they will share.

In 1810 there was a meeting between the Bloods and the Sioux in the Cypress Hills to establish peace between the two nations. At that time, the reason for a peace was so that they might share hunting territories. It was decided that the Cypress Hills would be the boundary point, with the Sioux to the east and the Bloods to the west.

In the early 1830s, Seen From Afar, then leader of the Bloods, made a peace alliance with the Mandan near Bismarck, North Dakota, and as a result of the alliance he brought back a medicine pipe as a gift. That pipe is still among our people.

There is a record of trade alliances and ceremonies in 1826 at the Black Hills among the Blackfoot, Bloods, Sarcee, Sioux, Gros Ventres, Cheyenne, and Arapaho nations. These alliances are marked on the land.

As a result of the earlier alliance with the Arapaho in the Black Hills, some of the Blackfoot/Blood/Peigan/Sarcee lodges stayed with the Arapaho. In 1851 explorers among the Plains tribes noted about ten lodges of our people among the Arapaho. Also around that time, some of our people were trading with Sioux and witnessed the talks surrounding the Laramie treaty.

In 1855 our people were present at a "peace treaty" initiated by US government authorities to facilitate trade and peace among the Blackfoot. This was to be termed the "Lame Bull" Treaty, after a Peigan leader who was a signator of the proceedings. The Bloods present were Seen From Afar, Father of Many Children, Bull Back Fat, Many Spotted Horses, Calf Shirt, Rainy Chief, and Medicine Calf. This treaty was very quickly broken by the authorities and left a bad impression on our leaders.

Ten years later, in 1865, our people were again summoned to peace talks at Fort Benton, and these talks were attended by Blackfoot, Peigan, Bloods, and Gros Ventres. The treaty provided for $50,000 in annuities for twenty years, but it was never ratified in the US Congress, another lesson in treaty making with the newcomers.

The year 1868 saw further talks surrounding the Laramie treaty, and again Bloods were present to witness the proceedings. Along with the Blood contingent were Alexander Culbertson and Naato isttsi ksiinaa, his Blood wife.

By this time there was a strong alliance between the Sioux and the Bloods, and a meeting was held to discuss the rapid encroachment of outsiders on territories they now shared for hunting. At this meeting, held at the Cypress Hills, there was tremendous gift giving between the two nations. The Bloods received the big drum, the long knife, the whip and whistle, the headdress, the Crow belt, and all the ceremonies attached to these gifts. These and the ceremonies are all still among our people. When you witness the traditional celebrations, you will see these.

The winter of 1870–71 saw a peace alliance between the Cree and Blackfoot nations. This was the result of a devastating battle that resulted in tremendous loss to the Cree. This battle was near the present site of Lethbridge. In April of 1871, a message sent by the Cree chief "Sweet Grass" to Governor Archibald stated the following: "Make provisions for us against years of starvation. We have had great starvation the past winter, and the smallpox took away many of our people ... We have made peace this winter with the Blackfeet." In 1873, after peace had been established, the Blackfoot chief Crowfoot adopted the Cree Poundmaker as his own son. This alliance was held in the Sand Hills.

In 1873 the North-West Mounted Police (NWMP) was established. The force was renamed the Royal North-West Mounted Police (RNWMP) in 1904, and in 1920 the Royal Canadian Mounted Police (RCMP). The year 1874 saw the arrival of the Mounted Police into Blackfoot territory, and as a token of their friendship the war chiefs extended their welcome. The leader of the police, James Macleod, was given the Blackfoot name of Stamikkso'to-kaani (Bull Head) by a Peigan war leader of the same name. A way to bestow one of the highest honours and tributes was to give one's own name. (At a later date, Major Irvine was to receive Innii stamik – Buffalo Bull.) With this kind of reception, the police asked if they could winter there (present-day Fort Macleod). They were granted permission for one winter, and it's been a long winter.

The year 1875 saw a major meeting between the Bloods, Blackfoot, Peigan, Sarcee, and Mounted Police. The leaders petitioned Macleod with their concerns: they felt that the police were facilitating White and half-breed settlement of their lands. Macleod had earlier promised the leaders that he was not there to take away their lands. He had also promised to protect the buffalo from White slaughter and had said that he was not in favour of a treaty. The following year he was to change his mind.

Soon after, in the same year, there was a major meeting among the nations of this territory to discuss the rapid encroachment of settlers into the area. This meeting took place in the Hand Hills.

In the spring of 1876, the Bloods, Blackfoot, Peigan, and Sarcee held a meeting with the Sioux. This meeting took place in the Sand Hills north of Cypress. It was an alliance of peace again. A short while later, Sitting Bull, in honour of the occasion, named his son "Crowfoot." In July of the same year, another meeting was held between these nations to reaffirm their alliance of peace. The issue at this time was the possibility of the "Blue Coats" (the US Army) crossing the "medicine line" and coming into the territory to make war with the Sioux. It was decided that if the "Red Coats" (the NWMP) fought on the side of the Blue Coats, the Plains nations would unite. As far as it being a great alliance against the White people, this was something the newspapers had started. What's new?

August of 1867 saw another peace alliance between the Blackfoot, Cree, Nakoda, and Assiniboin. This meeting was held at the Cypress Hills. In 1877 there was a reaffirmation and celebration of the alliance between Crowfoot and Sitting Bull. This meeting was held at the Sand Hills. That same year saw the alliance of peace between our nations and the Queen's representatives at Blackfoot Crossing. The promises again were to be quickly broken.

The winter of 1879–80 saw an attempted alliance at the request of Louis Riel with our nations. Jean-Baptiste L'Heureux was an interpreter at these talks and our nations refused to participate in Riel's plans. Sitting Bull was present, and he too refused to participate in the plans. These talks were held east of the Cypress Hills.

The year 1883 saw a meeting at the Cypress Hills between our nations and Big Bear of the Cree. These talks concerned the trains going through the territory.

The same year saw a reaffirmation and celebration of the alliance between the Bloods and Sitting Bull. This took place at Wood Mountain following Sitting Bull's confinement at Fort Randall.

In 1885 the alliance between the Blackfoot and Little Pine of the Cree was made. This meeting took place at Blackfoot Crossing. As a result of this alliance, Father Lacombe panicked and consequently wrote to the authorities asking for more troops. His letter can be found in his papers and his memoirs.

In all the alliances that were made, the only ones broken were the ones with the newcomers. The First Nations people would never break a sacred alliance, and the alliances made with other First Nations still hold to this day. They are reaffirmed and celebrated each time the people come together, and our young people are taught to know these and respect them, for they are great promises to the Giver of Life. They will last as long as the sun will shine and as long as the rivers will flow.

STORYTELLING

Storytelling is a great gift among our people. A requirement among our people is for young children to spend much time with grandparents. It is the responsibility of grandparents to teach legends and stories and the ways of our people. In this way a closeness develops between the very young and the old. Our people do not believe in old-age homes.

I was a small child when I witnessed my first storytelling session among the old ones. Those present were my grandfather Many Fingers, Old Man Rabbit, Shot Both Sides, Low Horn, and Old Black Plume. For several days they shared stories, legends, and history. There was always great care in correcting each other when there was error found in one of the accounts. In this way, when everybody left for home, they all left with the same story to be retold at another time. For many years I have heard these stories, and they remained unchanged. It is in this way that our history and heritage have been accurately handed down through the ages. Because our languages are not written, we rely heavily on the oral traditions and on the winter-counts. Among our elders, it is only when individuals could recount stories without error that they were allowed to teach history. When young people were present at these storytelling sessions, they weren't allowed to make noise or be up walking around. From an early age, the young were taught to be careful listeners. A great deal of tenderness and gentleness was required when talking to young people. The elders would talk to the young ones in a low voice, sometimes so low and gentle that the children would think that they were dreaming. In this way a child would never forget.

The teaching of history among our people was given to everyone. Only a select few, however, were privy to sacred teaching, and throughout our recent documented history, this is the information which has been absent. The elders were very careful in the sharing of this kind of information. For the first time, and under the close authority of the elders, this document will attempt to shed some light on those areas which pertain to the events at Soyooh pawahko (ridge under water or Blackfoot Crossing).

SWEETGRASS

The sweetgrass with its three strands represents a harmony which is necessary between the Giver of Life, all that lives, and Mother Earth. It is a harmony which cannot be deliberately imbalanced or separated by man. This is common knowledge among the buffalo people, the Plains tribes. It was this understanding that our leaders and elders took with them to the talks at Blackfoot Crossing in 1877. This was the harmony which for some reason to this point has not been mentioned in the official accounts of Treaty 7. From an early age each young person is taught about this gift of the Giver of Life, and throughout one's lifetime, many times one will experience the ceremonies where it is used. It is a ceremony that played a major part in the talks at Blackfoot Crossing.

THE SACRED SMUDGE

The sacred smudge is a ceremony given to Niitsitapa (the real people) by the Giver of Life. Along with this precious gift there are spiritual laws which govern the use of the smudge: it is used only when there are very important issues to be discussed, the issues cannot be of a negative nature, and spiritual guidance is asked for so that all that will be discussed will be treated with the highest regard for honesty. The sacred smudge is often used in the teaching of sacred information so that the one being taught will never forget. The person teaching or sharing the information will also ask for spiritual guidance, so that he or she will share in exactly the same way as they were taught themselves. When using the smudge, the people present are conducting themselves with the knowledge that the Giver of Life is witness to the proceedings. The smudge is used for cleansing first of all the participants and then the area or environment where the ceremony is being conducted so that everything will be done in a clean and pure way. The ceremony is as old as time and can never change in process because it is a sacred gift to all First Nations.

The ceremony itself is a prerequisite to the use of the sacred pipe.

THE STORY OF BLACKFOOT CROSSING

Many stories have been told surrounding the events which took place at Blackfoot Crossing in the fall of 1877, but seldom from the perspective of the First Nations people themselves. In many cases, vivid accounts have been solicited from our people as to the happenings during those few days in September, but noticeable is their reluctance to mention the ceremony attached to the participation of the First Nations. In some instances, the reluctance comes from their not wanting to share that which is sacred; in others, they were not privy to the information. On the part of historians and academics, the reason is oftentimes an ignorance of the complex ways of a people they simply do not know. Thus, in various published accounts, the occasions that involved ceremony are often recorded inaccurately or it is indicated that no record exists of what took place. A good example of this kind of reference is found in documents of the officials at Blackfoot Crossing. The officials simply reported that on the evening of the twentieth there appeared to be much joy and singing well into the night. In actuality, there were prayers and ceremonies in each of the camps of the various nations. This had been going on for several days, and the purpose was to seek guidance as the nations prepared to discuss important issues pertaining to their survival. By that time, all of the various nations were well informed about the deceit that their neighbours to the east and south had experienced at the hands of government and military officials. Many treaties had been entered into, and in most cases, the promises made had been broken over and over. It was common knowledge that the newcomers were not honest people. Before we go into the actual events and talks at Blackfoot Crossing, there is one more ceremony that needs mention, as it was probably the most important ceremony of this occasion. This ceremony took place in the few days prior to the actual discussions of the treaty.

There is a ceremony known to our people as *kano'tsississin* (where everybody smokes ceremony). At times it has been referred to as the "big smoke." It was one of the few ceremonies

that brought together all those affiliated in some way with the
sacred smudge – elders, medicine pipe holders, members of
sacred societies, leaders, and war leaders. One requirement was
that those in attendance would bring with them their pipes and
knowledge of sacred songs and prayers. The elders conducted
the ceremony. They played a key role even in the everyday lives
of the people. Important decisions affecting the people were
never made in the absence of or without consultation with the
elders. The ceremony was, and is, held during the winter moons
of our people or, if we use the new calendar moons, from September to March. It began at sundown and ended at sunrise
and lasted throughout the night. One could hear the songs and
prayers, which are as old as time, with each of the participants
asking for guidance in whatever was going to happen. Many of
the people in attendance would have their faces painted with
sacred ochres to protect them from anything that would be negative in nature. Throughout our recorded history, this painting
of the faces has been erroneously termed "war paint." Among
our people, there is no such thing as war paint. As with all ceremonies, the sacred smudge was at the centre of all activity. Prior
to any pipe being used, the first requirement was to place the
sweetgrass on some coals, and in doing this, you would ask the
Giver of Life to guide you in what you will say and that you
will only hear good things. The pipe would then be taken and
again you would ask the Giver of Life to give you courage and
strength as the stone of the pipe is strong and that you will
talk straight (honestly) as the stem of the pipe is straight. You
would then ask the same of those who would join you in smoke.

At Blackfoot Crossing, the ceremony was initiated on the advice of Father of Many Children, who had been present at the
signing of the Lame Bull Treaty of 1855. On his urging, the
ceremony would give protection against the authorities' apparent
disregard of the provisions in the American treaty and the subsequent starvation and hardships of the people. By this time,
Father of Many Children was a respected elder and teacher
among his people. Many of the participating leaders at Blackfoot
Crossing were medicine pipe holders. Each of the five nations
had beaver bundles as well as medicine pipes at the time.

Not surprising is the fact that in 1991 the chiefs of Treaty
7, on the advice of their elders, initiated this whole treaty review

project by participating in the same ceremony. Their teaching had remained constant in the ways of their people. The songs which were heard were the same songs as those heard in September 1877. This ceremony has remained unchanged throughout the ages, and it is still very much in use today. The chiefs, in authorizing this review, felt that it was important to document the stories of their elders so that, for generations to come, those who would read the story would somehow get a much better understanding of the spirit and intent of the First Nations people with respect to their participation in Treaty 7.

These, then, were some of the ceremonies held in those few days in September of 1877. The sad note is the fact that no descriptions of them found their way into the official accounts of the time. Perhaps those who were responsible for the recording had viewed ceremony as a small detail, insignificant and not worth mention in official documents. To the First Nations people, this was the spirit of the whole process. Only ceremony could seal an accord that would last "as long as the sun would shine, and as long as the river would flow." I once asked Dan Weasel Moccasin where this expression came from. His response was, "The term 'as long as the sun shines and the rivers flow' comes directly out of the way of the pipe. The way of our people is the way of the pipe. Since then there is much sadness each time there is effort to renege on promises they feel were made to them upon a sacred oath."

It is also interesting to note that the elders refer to this year (1995) as "the year when the winter was open." Some will say it's coincidence, others will say that there is a message in this.

The event known as *ist'sist aohkotspi* (the first time we received gifts and money) took place from September 16 to September 26, at Soyooh pawahko in 1877. In this document, the story will be told first of all according to the First Nations' understanding of these talks and then according to the report of the commissioners. The reader will easily discover the unfortunate misunderstandings, due partly to inadequate interpretation and/or a deliberate attempt to mislead. Whichever the case may be, there was tremendous distance between the two perspectives. There is an old saying that every story has three sides – yours, mine, and the facts. To gain insight into the discussions at Blackfoot Crossing, let's first meet some of the key players and then look at those who were responsible for interpreting to the First Nations. Who were these people who in a few days would change history forever?

Stamikkso'tokaani (Bull Head), Colonel James Farquarson Macleod

James Farquarson Macleod was born in Scotland on the Isle of Skye in 1836. At the time of Treaty 7, he would have been a young forty-one years of age. He had been appointed assistant commissioner of the North-West Mounted Police three years earlier, in June of 1874, when he was thirty-nine years old.

Macleod was the son of Captain Donald Martin Macleod of the 25th Imperial Regiment. When James was still a young child, his family moved to Toronto, Ontario. After his early schooling in Toronto, he attended Upper Canada College in that city. Following this, he undertook his undergraduate studies at Queen's College in Kingston, Ontario, graduating with a bachelor of arts degree, and then studied law at the same college. After being called to the Ontario Bar in 1860, he operated a law practice in Bowmanville, Ontario. On the influence of his father, he joined the militia, the Volunteer Field Battery in Kingston. With his law degree, it didn't take him long to advance his career, and by 1867 he had been promoted from major to colonel. He joined the Red River Expedition as brigade major in 1870. Decorated with the Orders of St Michael and St George, he then joined the North-West Mounted Police. He was posted to Red River, where he was given charge of acquisition of oxen, Red River carts, and supplies and the employment of half-breed drivers, guides, and interpreters. All of these would be required for his next assignment, which was to go west to solidify the efforts of Parliament in the North-West Territories. In 1873 he was in command, and in June of 1874, after his appointment as assistant commissioner of the NWMP, he headed west with his troops.

Because he was unfamiliar with the country, he became hopelessly lost, eventually ending up in Fort Benton, Montana. This was where he changed his guides, now to include Jerry Potts, who according to the local people was very capable as a guide. Macleod and his troops then were guided into the heart of Indian territory around Fort Whoop-Up. After his arrival into Blackfoot territory he eventually was given the name Stamikkso'tokaani

(Bull Head) by the Peigan. He established Fort Macleod in 1874. Before the Treaty 7 talks began, he was appointed commissioner of the North-West Mounted Police, on July 22, 1876. In 1880 he gave up his command of the force and became a magistrate of the North-West Territories. In September of 1894 he died in Calgary at the age of fifty-eight years.

Mi'k ai'stoowa (Red Crow), Clan and War Leader of the Mamio-yiksi (Fish Eaters), the Kainawa Clan, the Bloods

Red Crow was born in 1830 to Kiaayi siksi namm (Black Bear) and Handsome Woman. He was a nephew of Piinakkoyim (Seen From Afar), a leader and war chief who had taken part in the treaty of Otahkoi iitahtaa (the Yellowstone, or Lame Bull, Treaty of 1855), a peace and trade treaty with the American authorities. One of his teachers and advisers in the ways of a warrior and leader was Rainy Chief, who was also present at the American treaty negotiations.

The leaders of the now five nations of Treaty 7 were well versed in the failures of previous treaties with the newcomers to these territories. They already had well-defined alliances with each other on the plains. The leaders were all in their mid-forties, and in accordance with our customs, were not allowed to make important decisions without close consultation with their elders, in other words, with m aahsowaawaiksi, their grandfathers. This custom is consistent among all Plains tribes.

Mi'k ai'stoowa aahkoiyinnimaani (was a medicine pipe holder) and knew well the sacred ways of his people. His uncle Piinak-koyim was involved in the first alliance, forged at what is now known as Bismarck, with the Sioux nation for trade purposes. Mi'k ai'stoowa was a key figure in a subsequent alliance with Stamiksoopi (Sitting Bull) for the sharing of hunting territories, made necessary because of the diminishing buffalo herds. This alliance took place at what is now known as Cypress Hills. According to Sioux elders, the two peoples had great mutual respect for each other, particularly with regards to ceremonies. The Sioux had sent a pipe requesting a joint Sun Dance, but unfortunately the messenger was intercepted near Fort Walsh, as there was fear on the part of the British and American authorities of a great alliance forming for purposes of war against the newcomers. The subject had been discussed at some point, and Mi'k ai'stoowa had responded that his people would not get involved at this time, as Maohksisoka'simiiksi (the Red Coats) had been good to his people. However, if the Red Coats were to join the O'tsskoinnakkiiks (the Blue Coats), Mi'k ai'stoowa would have no choice but to fight on the side of Stamiksoopi.

Because of the earlier alliance with the Sioux, the Blackfoot's and Tsuu T'ina's relationship with their relatives the Nakoda (Stoney) became closer. The Nakoda, for trade purposes, had been the facilitators of trade among the Blackfoot with the Kootenay and Shuswap nations west of the Rockies.

Mi'k ai'stoowa was a statesman and a well-respected leader of his people for many years. He died on August 28, 1900. Before his death he made it clear who was to succeed him as leader, his adopted son, Ma ko'yoo piss to kii (Crop Eared Wolf). Sometime prior to this, he had been asked about his position on lands and surrenders. In response he had picked up grass with his left hand and dirt with his right hand, and as he held up his left hand, he said, "This you can have"; then, holding up his right hand with the dirt, "This is for me and my people forever." Likewise, when Crop Eared Wolf was on his deathbed and was choosing who was to succeed him as leader, he said to his minor chiefs, *"Piino wa a'paihkahtakiik"* (Don't ever sell your land). All our leaders have been well instructed by their teachers in their stewardship responsibilities for the land. They would never knowingly sell or give away their land. According to the spiritual laws of our people, this is a responsibility given to us by Iitsipa' itapiiyo'pa (the Giver of Life).

Issapo'mahkikaaw (Crowfoot)

Crowfoot was born in 1830 to Isttoa'ni (Packs/Carries a Knife), a Blackfoot, and Ahkiap sai pi ya wa (Attacks Toward Home), a Blood, whose father was Scabby Bull. He was five years old when he was taken to the Blackfoot tribe (called the Siksika). He survived the diphtheria epidemic of 1836 and the smallpox epidemic of 1837, which reduced the tribe by six to seven thousand people. It was later discovered that the smallpox had originated on the steamer *St Peters* which was owned by the American Fur Trading Company of Fort Benton. Issapo'mahkikaaw was a member of the Kanattsomitaiksi (All Brave Dogs) society.

His trade allies were the Plains Cree and the Mandan to the east. To the west, through the Nakoda, they were the Kootenay and Shuswap. White trading was mostly with the Hudson's Bay Company at Fort Edmonton and Rocky Mountain House. To the south, through the Bloods and Peigan, it was with the people at Fort Benton.

Crowfoot was renowned during his warrior days. He was given special powers as a war chief and this earned him much respect from his enemies. His predecessor as war chief and leader was Three Suns, who taught him much in the ways of a warrior and, eventually, a leader. During Crowfoot's tenure as leader, he saw the return of smallpox in 1869. This was the epidemic that took the life of Seen From Afar of the Bloods and almost wiped out the Tsuu T'ina (Sarcee).

During his lifetime Crowfoot was believed to have had ten wives. One of these was a sister of Red Crow of the Bloods, and this made for closer ties between the two leaders. Crowfoot was Red Crow's brother-in-law (*ostamoohkowai*), and they were almost exactly the same age. In the ways of the Plains tribes, there was tremendous respect between in-laws. In 1873 Crowfoot adopted Poundmaker of the Plains Cree and taught him the Blackfoot language.

In 1874 he saw the building of a whiskey fort at Blackfoot Crossing. In 1875 he was at the meeting among the Blackfoot, Bloods, Peigan, and Tsuu T'ina with regard to the ever increasing encroachment of White settlers into the territory of these nations. The pipe was used. The summer of 1877 saw a peace alliance between Crowfoot and Sitting Bull of the Sioux Nation. Again a pipe was used to solemnize the occasion, which took place in the Sand Hills north of the Cypress Hills. This particular alliance is often mistaken in history books as an alliance for purposes of war. It is well known among our people that it was for purposes of peace between two nations that were now to share hunting territory.

Crowfoot died on April 25, 1890. He was sixty years old.

Kiaayo ko'-si (Bear Child), Jerry Potts

Jerry Potts was the best known of the half-breed scouts and guides of the North-West Mounted Police. He was born in 1840 at Fort McKenzie, Montana Territory. His father, Andrew Potts, was a Scot clerk of the American Fur Company, and his mother, Naamopia (Crooked Back), was a Blood woman of the Siksinnokaiksi (Black Elks) band. The story goes that his father was accidentally killed by a Peigan who was apparently trying to get even with another employee of the fort who had swindled him in trade. The swindle had involved the sale of buffalo robes to the White employee, who had reneged on payment. Jerry at this time was still a small child. He was left to be raised first by a notoriously cruel trader by the name of Alexander Harvey and then by Andrew Dawson, a Scot who was later nicknamed the "Last King of the Missouri." Harvey, an employee of the American Fur Company, was well known for killing many Indian people at the trading post. Jerry learned English from Dawson and some Blackfoot from his mother. He was an accomplished hunter and became very familiar with the territory and the people as he alternated between the two worlds. Between the years 1869 and 1884, he worked for various traders of furs and whiskey, in Montana and what is now known as Alberta. In 1870 he was a participant in the battle between the Blackfoot and the Cree. He survived that battle and returned to Montana Territory in 1872. It is said that the reason he left the area of Whoop-Up was his disgust at what whiskey was doing to his people and his family. After the liquor had caused the death of his mother and half-brother, he broke ties with the whiskey traders.

After the North-West Mounted Police found themselves in Fort Benton, it was clear that they needed more competence in their guides, and Jerry Potts was pointed out to them as a capable candidate. He was somewhat reluctant because of his former ties to the whiskey traders and his drinking, but after much coaxing he accepted. This was in 1874, he was thirty-seven years old, and he led the NWMP to Fort Whoop-Up. It is reported that over his lifetime Potts had four wives and many children. He was one of the interpreters at Blackfoot Crossing in 1877. At the onset of the talks, he was the first of the interpreters to attempt to explain the reason for the negotiations. It was soon discovered that he had been drinking extensively during this time and that he was having extreme difficulty in making the situation clear to the chiefs. On Wednesday, the 19th of September, the chiefs requested that he be no longer used as an interpreter. He continued to work with the Mounted Police until his death in 1896.

History books indicate that he died as a result of tuberculosis, and some say it was cancer. He was buried with full military honours at Fort Macleod.

James Bird

Bird was a trader among the First Nations at the time and, just prior to the treaty talks, he was well known as a whiskey trader. Among the traders, he was known as "Jimmy Jock"; in the whiskey trade, he was referred to as "Jimmy Jug"; to the Blackfoot, he was *aottakkiiwa* (the giver of intoxicants). He had limited knowledge of the Blackfoot language and was asked by the commissioners to interpret the discussions of September 19. Like Potts, he had difficulties, and at that point Jean L'Heureux was asked by the police to assist.

Ikkakssi (The Short One), Jean-Baptiste L'Heureux

L'Heureux was born near St Hyacinthe, Quebec, in about 1825. He studied for the priesthood, but before completing his studies, he was involved in some criminal activities and was expelled. He went west to the Montana gold fields in about 1859. After being in that area for only a short period, he began wearing a cassock that he'd made, and passed himself off as a priest at the Jesuit mission on the Sun River. The truth was eventually discovered, and after he was caught in homosexual activities, he went into the wilds by himself. He was starving when the Blackfoot took him in. He moved to their camps and drifted northward into Alberta, where he went to the St Albert mission. He succeeded in convincing the Oblates that he was a priest, and by the time news of his true identity came from Montana, he had been seen so often with the priests that the Indians never could be convinced he was an impostor. L'Heureux then moved to Crowfoot's camp and remained with the Indians until they settled on their reserve. During this time he performed marriages, baptized children, and performed all the rites of a priest. He also acted as interpreter and scribe for the chiefs. In about 1880 L'Heureux became interpreter for the Indian department but was dismissed in 1891 because he continued his religious work. Throughout his life he was a controversial figure, despised and distrusted by many fur traders, considered both an asset and embarrassment by the Oblates, and received by the Blackfoot with the mixed emotions they had for crazy people. After his dismissal from his interpreter's position, he became a recluse near Pincher Creek and finally died in Lacombe Home near Calgary on March 19, 1919.

Father Constantine Scollen

Father Constantine Scollen also helped with interpretation, particularly when the commissioners communicated with the Cree who were present. Father Scollen could understand a little Cree, having spent some time with this nation, but no Blackfoot. The previous year he had indicated to the authorities that the Blackfoot had wanted a treaty with the Queen's representatives. In fact, what the Blackfoot had wanted was a meeting to discuss the rapid encroachment of newcomers into their territory. There had been nothing said about a treaty. The 1875 petition of the Blackfoot chiefs had been transcribed by Jean-Baptiste L'Heureux.

John McDougall

John McDougall, a missionary at Morleyville, also provided some assistance in the interpretations. His family had originally established a mission among the Cree in Edmonton and thus he knew some Cree. The people he was interpreting for were the Nakoda (Stoney) Nation, but he could not speak their language and the manner by which he communicated to these people is unclear.

Both Father Scollen and John McDougall had been recruited as agents by the commissioners in the previous years to prepare the First Nations peoples for the upcoming treaties. In September of 1876 Father Scollen expressed his assessment of the situation in a letter to the governor of Manitoba:

Although they are externally so friendly to the police and other strangers who now inhabit their country, yet underneath this friendship remains hidden some of that dread which they have always had of the white man's intention to cheat them; and here, excellent Governor, I will state my reason for believing that a treaty should be concluded with them also at the earliest possible date ...

Your most humble servant, Constantine Scollen. Priest, O.U.I.

P.S. – I am also aware that the Sioux Indians, now at war with the Americans, have sent a message to the Blackfeet tribe, asking them to make an alliance offensive and defensive against all white people in the country. C. Scollen (Scollen Papers, Provincial Archives of Alberta)

As we all know, there was never a great alliance against White people.

Given this group of interpreters, it becomes extremely difficult to imagine how effective communication took place between the commissioners and the chiefs.

THE INTERPRETATION PROBLEMS

Most of the First Nations languages are very descriptive and thorough in composition; consequently, much is lost in attempts to translate them accurately – in this case into English. The First Nations languages are verb-centred, while the English language is noun-centred. This alone would make literal translation extremely difficult. For example, the English "Good morning" in the Blackfoot language would be something like "*Nitsotamiitapoh sokimhsi anoohk ksiskanotonii ni tootatsiopi*," which would mean literally, "It makes me feel really good in meeting you this morning." The point to be understood here is that the translation process failed at Blackfoot Crossing. The official reports on the narrative that took place at Blackfoot Crossing indicate that the commissioners spoke at great length in reading the official documents to the chiefs in English and that then the interpreters were called upon to translate their presentation in full. However, the official records of the narrative indicate that the chiefs were only given one-sixth of the presentation of the commissioners. Consequently, the Blackfoot expression "*Anahka aipoihka iipitsinnim aniistoohpi*" (The person speaking has choked considerably that which is spoken) is often used in the Blackfoot elders' stories about the narrative that took place at Blackfoot Crossing.

Such was the apparent difficulty facing the interpreters at Blackfoot Crossing.

We still do not have words in many of the First Nations languages for some of the English-language terminology used at Blackfoot Crossing. Terminology such as the following would have been difficult to translate:

Great White Mother – Because the First Nations of this area had absolutely no concept of imperial systems, the closest that the interpreters would have come to this term would have been *nina'waakii* (the woman leader) or *kitoomhk skapiwksistsinon* (our great big white mother).

Reserve – In the Blackfoot language there is still no word for reserve; today one would simply say "our lands" or "Native lands."

Mile – The term *ni'taa'si* now describes a mile; however, it only came into our language in the early 1900s with the establishment of mission schools.

Square – This term and its meaning had no place in the ways of the Blackfoot Confederacy, maybe a circle but not a square. The word now used, *iksisttoyisi*, again only found its way into the language in the 1900s.

Canada – The story is that this word comes from a Cree word. The Blackfoot had no word for Canada, only a word for the territory of their nation, which extended into present-day Montana. Today one would say *"amsskaa poohtsi"* (the lands to the south) or *"aapa'ttoh soohtsi"* (the lands to the north).

Treaty – There was not a word for "title," as this was a foreign concept. The new word *issksskomootsspi* (to be given a parcel of land) was developed in the 1950s. This was provided for in the Indian Act.

Surrender – There was no word for surrendering or relinquishing of title to land. We are one with the land. Is it possible to give or relinquish part of one's self?

These difficulties with interpretation and terminology would have made for a trying day, and it is no wonder several of the interpreters resorted to intoxicants. Today we would like to ask the most proficient Blackfoot speakers to translate the entire text of those talks, but so far there is no one able to do so.

The above dilemma, coupled with the entirely different agendas of the chiefs and the commissioners, would have made for communication chaos. On the part of the chiefs, their agenda was very specific: they wanted the encroachment of newcomers controlled, they wanted the buffalo protected, and they wanted the American traders controlled. These problems had resulted in tremendous hunger in the previous several years. Among the Plains tribes, many alliances of peace were already in place to accommodate their hunting and survival needs. Newcomers within their territories added a new twist to the situation. The chiefs realized that an alliance was necessary to bring things under control. They went to Blackfoot Crossing intent on an alliance of peace, to safeguard their territory and to protect their way of life. This would last for as long as the sun will shine, and as long as the rivers flow.

The commissioners, on the other hand, also had a specific agenda: their task was to extinguish all Indian title to land and to facilitate settlement of the Northwest by placing Indians on reserves.

When one compares the two perspectives as well as the different understandings of the narrative that took place, it is apparent that although each side had voiced its concerns, neither had heard the other. Every once in a while, one finds in history books evidence of this major misunderstanding.

Never before has the story been told. Our elders have carried, in their hearts and spirit, their story through some five generations since the treaty. Hope among our people is truly a great gift, and our elders say that now is the time to tell the story. Now is the time that people will listen. For a long time people had no ears.

Someone once asked, "What is an elder?" Neither age nor gender plays a role in the definition of an elder. Elders are the teachers of wisdom and traditions because they know the secrets of life; they have walked that path. They know the way to inner peace, which is one of life's ultimate goals. They know not anger, nor spite. They are the ones who would tell you that among the great values in life the most precious are spirituality, compassion, and honesty. As young children they witnessed the deliberate attempts by newcomers to destroy their entire way of life. They were called heathens, savages, and obstacles to progress. They saw their ceremonies banned. As children they were separated from their parents, and later their own children were taken away and they were told that this was civilization. For five generations they have witnessed dysfunction in their families and they can only cry in silence, because they know why it happened. They are the ones who continue to serve against tremendous odds. They pray each day that their children would listen to their advice. Throughout all, the elders are the ones who never lose hope, the ones who will say, "Tomorrow is a new day, things will get better. Come sit here my child and I will tell you a story."

My grandfather, Many Fingers, was the adopted son of Crop Eared Wolf, and Crop Eared Wolf was the adopted son of Red Crow. My grandfather told me the story that was told to him, and many times I have heard the elders tell the same story. *Istsist aohkotspi* (the first time we received money and gifts) was simply an alliance of peace between our people and the representatives of the government. *Kaaksinnaihtsiimottsiimayaawa* (we only formed a kinship with them); *ihtsiksittoyii yaawa* (for this, they made promises). Our people were there for ten days.

My grandfather told me that *innaihtsiinni* (our alliance- and kinship-forming process) comes from the ways of the sacred societies, the buffalo societies. When this way is used, it lasts for all time because the promise is made to the Giver of Life. It is the time when people adopt each other as parent and child and as brothers and sisters. From that time on, there will be no anger or dishonesty between those who adopt each other. When this way of making alliance is undertaken, there is great gift giving. In times of war, when one party suffered tremendously and wished for peace, it would sometimes use this way and would approach the aggressor and offer gifts. From then on, there would be no more anger between them. An agreement of this kind cannot be broken. It is the highest form of making peace. The government people came to us in this way and they brought gifts. They wanted us to stop our wars, especially against the White people.

Before our people went to Soyoo pawahko (Blackfoot Crossing), Stamikkso'tokaani (Macleod) had told our leaders that the
meeting would be at *aka aapiioyis* (the place of many houses),
Fort Macleod. The police told us that if we agreed not to fight
anymore, the government would give us money, food, and gifts.
When Sspitaa (The Tall One, Laird) came, he told us that Stamikkso'tokaani had not told the truth and that the first meeting
would be at Soyooh pawahko and after that the meetings would
be anywhere we wanted them to be. We were told that if we
didn't agree, we would not receive these gifts. Kiaayo ko'si (Bear
Child, Potts) was our ear that time. Our people reluctantly agreed
to travel to Soyooh pawahko. Some of our people were away
hunting in the lands to the south and east for the winter supply
of meat. Buffalo were hard to find in those days. The White
people and the half-breeds were hunting and chasing them away.
For two winters, there had been much hunger. Our leaders were
going to tell the government people to help us chase these people
away. The Giver of Life gave us the buffalo. We travelled for
three days. We hunted along the way.

When we arrived at Soyooh pawahko, there was much gladness
because some of the people we had not seen in a long time.
Many pipes and stories were shared. This place was a place of
prayer; many times they had the sacred ceremonies there. The
people brought their sacred bundles, these are not left
unattended.

Red Crow was born around 1830 into the Fish Eaters clan of the Blood tribe. He came from a lineage of leadership that included his grandfather, Two Suns, and his father, Seen From Afar. Early in life Red Crow distinguished himself as a warrior with successful raids against the Crow, Cree, Assiniboin, Shoshoni, and Nez Percé.

Red Crow assumed leadership of the Fish Eaters in 1869 when his father died of smallpox. He led his people through some of their most difficult times. The free flow of whiskey across the border wrought havoc on people already demoralized by disease and the loss of the buffalo – their staple for survival. Red Crow thus welcomed the arrival of the Mounted Police, who had come to put an end to the whiskey trade.

During these years Red Crow successfully brought a number of clans together under his leadership, which made him an important participant in the 1877 negotiations at Blackfoot Crossing. No treaty could have been negotiated without his presence and approval. Furthermore, his friendship with Colonel Macleod quite likely contributed to the successful conclusion of the negotiations.

Later Red Crow was bitterly disappointed that Macleod did not do more to see the treaty provisions enforced. He became a vehement spokesman for the Bloods and also helped resolve differences among his own people. Red Crow was a strong advocate of education for his people and was tolerant of Anglican, Methodist, and Catholic missions even though he himself remained a traditionalist.

Red Crow himself became one of the most successful farmers on the Blood reserve, competing with local White farmers for supply contracts with the NWMP. By the 1890s he was ranching and had established a cattle herd of one hundred head. He died in 1900 on the Blood reserve.

Mi'k ai'stowa (Red Crow), head chief of the Bloods

Crowfoot was born along the Belly River around 1830 and died at
Blackfoot Crossing in 1890. He was born into the Blood Tribe, although he later came to be a chief of the Siksika. He earned his name
after bravely fighting in a battle with a Crow tribe and being wounded.
He was known as a successful warrior by the time he was twenty and
was wounded again a number of times. By 1865 Crowfoot had become
a minor chief of the Siksika, with twenty-one lodges in his band.

He came to know Father Lacombe in 1865. Lacombe had been visiting a band of Blackfoot who came under attack by the Cree. Crowfoot
arrived, routing the Cree and saving the priest and the camp. Crowfoot
was also on friendly terms with White traders. He once prevented his
own warriors from attacking and looting a Hudson's Bay Company
supply train. He also became a friend of Richard Hardisty, the trader in
charge of Rocky Mountain House.

The smallpox epidemic of 1869–70 brought great devastation to the
Siksika. A number of chiefs succumbed to the disease, and after Big
Swan's death in 1872, Crowfoot and the elderly Old Sun were the only
two main Siksika chiefs left.

Crowfoot welcomed the North-West Mounted Police when they arrived in 1874 to rid the territory of the whiskey trade. Crowfoot had
become dismayed that his people traded horses, buffalo robes, and
other valuable belongings for whiskey. In 1874 he met and became
friends with NWMP colonel James Macleod. Macleod showed respect for
the ways of the Siksika, and in return Crowfoot asked his people to
obey the laws that the NWMP had come west to enforce.

Macleod treated Crowfoot as the chief of the entire Blackfoot Confederacy, but Crowfoot had a more accurate sense of the lines of power
and was always careful to consult with all chiefs before making any decisions that affected the Siksika and the whole of the confederacy.

Crowfoot played a pivotal role in the Treaty 7 negotiations, and at
their conclusion, speaking for the Blackfoot Confederacy, he asked that
the government be charitable, that the First Nations people be provided
for, and that the police protect them "the way the feathers of a bird
protect it from the frosts of winter."

Even though Crowfoot was an enthusiastic supporter of the treaty,
he soon became disillusioned with the administration of the Department of Indian Affairs. He was dismayed both by the Indian Act and
the manner in which it was enforced. Crowfoot was suspicous of Indian agents for their often callous treatment of his people. In spite of
this, he kept his people from joining forces with Louis Riel in the Riel
Resistance of 1885.

Issapo'mahkikaaw (Crowfoot), chief of the Blackfoot (Siksika)

Ozija Thiba (Bearspaw), Stoney chief

Jacob Bearspaw was born around 1837 near Morley. He was known as the chief of the southern Stoneys and was reknowned as a warrior. The traditional territory of the southern Stoneys was along the foothills from Morley to the north to as far south as Chief Mountain. Bearspaw's stature as a warrior led the hereditary chief of the southern band to choose him as chief over his own sons. Oral tradition suggests that Bearspaw encouraged George and John McDougall to establish a mission among the Stoneys, which they did in 1873.

When Bearspaw heard a treaty was to be negotiated, he left his camp at Chief Mountain and travelled to Blackfoot Crossing. Although he was initially uncertain about signing the treaty, he was the first chief to support it. Later Bearspaw became an outspoken opponent of the regulations that limited the hunting rights of the Stoneys; he also lobbied the federal government to grant his southern band a separate reserve. Nevertheless, he remained peaceful during the 1885 Riel Resistance, and some of his men served as scouts for the North-West Field Force during the campaign.

This is the only known photograph of Bearspaw in existence.

Sitting on Eagle Tail Feathers

Sitting on Eagle Tail Feathers was head chief of the Peigan when they agreed to Treaty 7. He had become chief only the previous winter after the death of Bull Head.

Bull Head was born in approximately 1833 and died on the Tsuu T'ina reserve in 1911. He was a powerful chief and a renowned warrior. The Tsuu T'ina, or Beaver clan people, are a fragment of the Dene-speaking tribes more commonly found in northern Canada. Bull Head led his warriors on many campaigns, especially against the Cree to the west of them. He was said to have been an imposing presence, standing over seven feet tall. Bull Head came from the Big Plume family but was given his name because of his stubbornness and strong character. His exploits in war were legendary. A unique painting that depicts his war record over fifty years was produced on steer hides in 1909 and is presently housed in the National Museum in Ottawa.

In spite of his reputation as a warrior, Bull Head welcomed the arrival in the West of the North-West Mounted Police. He agreed to Treaty 7 for his people in 1877 and is remembered by Tsuu T'ina elders as having been an astute negotiator. The Tsuu T'ina stayed at Blackfoot Crossing until 1883, when they decided to have their reserve surveyed at a site just west of present-day Calgary.

Bull Head remained a traditionalist, never converting to Christianity, and was in fact opposed to allowing missionaries onto the Tsuu T'ina reserve. He is said to have had seven wives, and his son by a Cree wife, captured in battle, was adopted by Sitting Bull. Bull Head's presence was felt on the reserve long after his death. People were afraid to pass his house at night, thinking it was haunted, and made great detours to avoid it. Bull Head was said to have appeared in the flesh to his people, warning them not to sell the land that made up the reserve.

Chula (Bull Head), chief of the Tsuu T'ina

Old Sun was born in central Alberta around 1819 and died in 1897 on the North Camp Flats on the Siksika reserve at Gleichen. A revered medicine man, Old Sun was leader of one of the largest of the Blackfoot Confederacy bands, largely because of his success as a warrior. Unlike many other chiefs, Old Sun did not turn to the role of peacemaker with age but continued the life of the warrior. His wife, Calf Old Woman, was also a renowned warrior and one of the few women to take a place in the Siksika warrior society.

Old Sun was said to have received his spiritual powers from a deer during a vision quest experience. He was also known for curing blindness with a sacred amulet.

In the Treaty 7 negotiations, Old Sun, the warrior, deferred to the Siksika chief of the time, Crowfoot, but signed the treaty for his band. His followers settled north of Crowfoot's band at North Camp Flats. Old Sun himself was not much interested in farming but assumed the role of patriarch and remained a much-respected medicine man and spiritual leader. He tolerated missionaries on his reserve but never converted to Christianity himself.

Natosapi (Old Sun), head chief of the Siksika (North Blackfoot)

There is no known photograph of Jacob Goodstoney in existence, but the photograph opposite shows his son Jonas Goodstoney (far right) with a group of chiefs and missionaries. John McDougall is seated on the far left.

Jacob Goodstoney was born in the 1820s in a hunting camp at the source of the Brazeau River and died at Morley in 1885. Goodstoney was a warrior and hunter, and the last in the line of dynastic chiefs of the northern band of the Stoneys. He was among the last of the Stoney warriors to travel across the mountains through the Athabaska Pass to launch raids on the tribes of the British Columbia interior.

Though a warrior in his early years, Goodstoney was remembered as being a peacemaker in his later years. He was converted to Christianity by the Reverend Robert Rundle and remained a good friend of John McDougall throughout his life. Goodstoney was fluent in the Cree language and his name was conferred on him by the Rocky Mountain Cree, who held his peacemaking abilities in high esteem.

Jacob Goodstoney signed Treaty 7 for his band, referred to in official records as Jacob's Band. In the years immediately following the signing, a rift developed in his band between those willing to make the best of reserve life and those who found the new way of life too restrictive. Many were frustrated by trying to farm on what turned out to be poor land for agriculture. The band's name has changed a number of times over the years. Since 1990 it has been called the Wesley Band, after Chief Peter Wesley.

Jonas Goodstoney (seated, far right), son of Kitchepwat
(Jacob Goodstoney), Stoney chief

John Chiniquay was born around 1834 and died around 1906. His mother was Cree and his father was said to have been a Métis. As a child he travelled with the Cree chief Maskapatoon, primarily in the territory along the Red Deer River. His name, John, was apparently given to him by the missionary Robert Rundle, who visited the tribes in the area during the 1840s. After the death of his parents, he lived with a Stoney family who hunted along the Red Deer River. He joined the band when he married the sister of Chief Jacob Bearspaw. Chiniquay was a convert to Christianity and a known peacemaker.

Chiniquay's band occupied the middle part of the Stoney territory, with Bearspaw's people to the south and Goodstoney's to the north. Chiniquay supported making treaty with the Canadian government and was a party to Treaty 7. When the time came to survey the reserve for the Stoneys in 1879, only John Chiniquay was present, and one reserve for the entire Stoney Nation was all that was surveyed. This created great dissatisfaction for those chiefs of the northern and southern bands who had not been present to explain their understanding of where their reserves were to be situated.

Chiniquay's understanding of the treaty was that the Stoneys would be aided by the government to make the transition to an agricultural way of life. Two factors frustrated the realization of this goal: first, the land surveyed for the Stoneys was not suitable for farming, and second, supplies and instruction were not forthcoming as had been expected. The Stoneys of Chiniquay's band were able to survive until the turn of the century by hunting, but game was rapidly being depleted and hunters had to go further and further afield. Chiniquay was a strong supporter of education and took a keen interest in the success of reserve schools.

John Chiniquay (Chiniki), head chief of the Stoneys

Sitting Bull

Sitting Bull's Lakota sought refuge in Canada after their defeat of Custer's army in the Battle of the Little Big Horn. Canadian and American authorities, missionaries, and traders all feared the threat that the Lakota posed; they especially feared the alliances that might be made with the militarily powerful Blackfoot Confederacy. There was thus great pressure put on the Canadian government to complete a treaty with the tribes of what is now southern Alberta. Sitting Bull is portrayed here addressing the Terry Commission from the United States, sent to Fort Walsh to persuade Sitting Bull to return.

Rainy Chief, head chief of the Bloods

Rainy Chief was born in approximately 1809 and died in 1878. He had been given a second name – White Wolf – after exposing himself to danger during a battle with Crow warriors. He was known as a medicine man but was also one of the few Blood chiefs to convert to Christianity. Rainy Chief became a friend of both Father Scollen and Father Lacombe during the 1870s. At Treaty 7 the older Rainy Chief was recognized as head chief of the northern Bloods, while the younger Red Crow was recognized as head chief of the southern Bloods.

Medicine Calf

Medicine Calf (also known as Button Chief) was an influential leader among the Bloods. He was one of the chiefs of the Blackfoot Confederacy who had also signed the Lame Bull Treaty in the United States in 1855.

Manisto'kos (Father of Many Children)

Father of Many Children was born around 1838 and died in 1897. At the time Treaty 7 was made, he was a war chief and head of a band known as the Marrows band. He agreed to the treaty on behalf of his band, which numbered 107 members at the time.

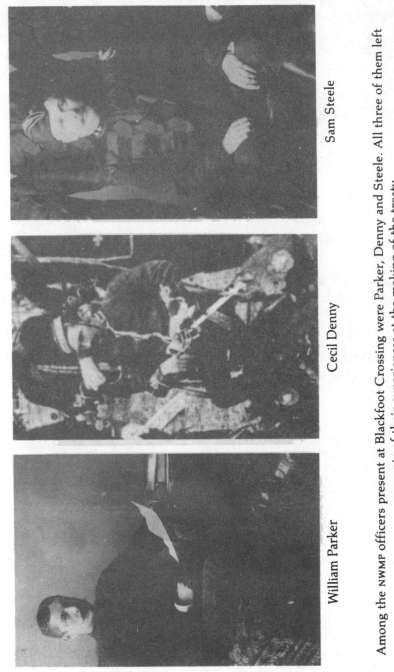

William Parker

Cecil Denny

Sam Steele

Among the NWMP officers present at Blackfoot Crossing were Parker, Denny and Steele. All three of them left accounts of their experiences at the making of the treaty.

Bobtail, Cree chief

Bobtail was chief of a band of Cree who were present at Blackfoot Crossing to sign an adhesion to Treaty 6, as the band had failed to arrive at Fort Pitt or Fort Carlton the previous year for the signing of that treaty.

David Laird was born in Prince Edward Island in 1833 and died in Ottawa in 1914. Although educated in a Presbyterian seminary, upon completing his studies he worked as a journalist, eventually becoming editor of the Charlottetown *Patriot*. He was elected to the House of Commons in 1873. Laird served as minister of the interior from 1873 to 1876 in Prime Minister Alexander Mackenzie's administration. He was appointed the first lieutenant-governor of the North-West Territories in 1876 and served until 1881. Laird became Indian commissioner for the North-West Territories, Manitoba, and Keewatin in 1898, and in 1899 he negotiated Treaty 8 for the vast area north of Edmonton. From 1909 until his death in 1914, Laird served as an adviser to the Department of Indian Affairs.

In 1876 Laird replaced Commissioner Alexander Morris as lieutenant-governor of the North-West Territories and assumed the negotiations of Treaty 7 with the tribes of what is now southern Alberta. Laird's role in negotiations remains controversial. Some historians suggest that a treaty was achieved because of mutual trust between commissioners Laird and Macleod and the Aboriginal leadership. The elders of Treaty 7 suggest that Laird and the other government representatives were not entirely honest with the First Nations, either in the treaty negotiations, the written treaty, or afterwards. It seems that Laird showed more interest in the potential of mining and settlement in the Northwest than in the welfare of the people who were occupying the land.

David Laird, government commissioner at Treaty 7

James Macleod was born in Scotland in 1836 and died in Calgary in 1894. Over his career he was employed as an army officer, lawyer, NWMP officer, magistrate, judge, and politician. After studying law and serving in the Canadian militia, he joined Colonel Garnet Wolseley's column sent west to deal with the first Riel Resistance in 1870.

Macleod's political connections allowed him to obtain a commission as a superintendent and inspector with the North-West Mounted Police, formed in 1873. In 1874 Macleod became the first assistant commissioner of the force. In that year, the NWMP moved further west, with orders to put an end to the illegal whiskey trade in Whoop-Up Country. The Cypress Hills Massacre of 1873 had exposed the vulnerability of the Canadian territory to intrusions by American traders. By October of 1874 Macleod had established a strategically positioned fort on the Oldman River. His work in putting an end to the whiskey trade came as a relief to the leadership of the Siksika, Peigan, Bloods, Stoneys, and Tsuu T'ina. A Peigan chief, Bull Head, bestowed his own name, Stamikkso'tokaani, on Macleod in tribute.

Macleod was one of the commissioners appointed to negotiate Treaty 7. A number of historians have credited much of the success of the negotiations to the groundwork laid by Macleod's fair dealings with the local tribes between 1874 and 1877. The elders of Treaty 7 suggest that his role was exaggerated.

Lieutenant-Colonel James Farquharson Macleod, government commissioner at Treaty 7

John McDougall was born in Owen Sound in 1842 and died at Calgary in 1917. He was primarily known as a Methodist missionary to prairie First Nations, but he was also an interpreter, scout, commissioner, and government agent. McDougall arrived in the West in 1860 when his father, George McDougall, was appointed to the Rossville mission at Norway House. In 1863 the two McDougalls established a mission on the North Saskatchewan River at a place they named "Victoria" (present-day Pakan). George McDougall built the first Methodist church in Edmonton in 1870, and in 1873 he and his son began a mission among the Stoneys at Morley, where John was to stay and work for many years. In 1876 George McDougall died mysteriously in a snow storm, but his son John carried on his father's mission until 1906. McDougall served as chairman of the Saskatchewan District for the Methodist Church and as superintendent of Indian missions for Manitoba and the North-West Territories. In 1885 he acted as chaplain and scout for General Strange's column as it moved north from Calgary towards Edmonton. Throughout his career he served governments in a variety of capacities, including work on several commissions, such as those on the First Nations of British Columbia and on the Doukhobors.

McDougall left behind numerous books of reminiscences describing his life on the prairies. He considered himself a pioneer and frontiersman, and was proud of his knowledge of Cree, referring to himself as nine-tenths "Indian." He worked hard to learn the language, customs, and manner of living of many Plains tribes. But there was a contradiction in his position: while he greatly admired the Plains tribes for their frontier skills, he looked down on them as "savage" and "uncivilized."

McDougall was an important factor in the making of Treaty 7, being a dogged proponent of both treaties and reserves for prairie tribes. In 1874 he accepted a commission to go among the tribes to explain the treaty process to them and encourage them to make treaties. Then, in 1877, he worked as a translator for the treaty commissioners at Blackfoot Crossing.

McDougall's role in the treaty making is controversial. A number of historians have presented McDougall as a great friend of the tribes he worked among, but some elders have suggested he might have deliberately misled the Stoneys on a number of issues, perhaps to serve his own interests.

John McDougall and family

Jimmy Bird was born around 1798 near Carlton House, Saskatchewan, and died in 1892 on the Blackfeet Reservation in Montana. Bird was a fur trader, interpreter, hunter, and guide. His mother was a Cree and his father a mixed-blood trader employed by the Hudson's Bay Company. Bird lived with his father at a variety of trading posts. He too worked for the HBC but left the company in 1821 to become a free-trader, hunting and trapping on both sides of the Rocky Mountains. In 1831 Bird became associated with the American Fur Trading Company and began to establish his enterprise with the Blackfoot-speaking tribes on the American side of the border. Throughout the next three decades Bird interpreted for explorers, missionaries, and the US government. He was said to be knowledgable in five languages in addition to French and English.

By 1877 he had returned to Canada's Blackfoot country and had gone blind. He was present at Blackfoot Crossing to interpret for the treaty commissioners. Although it has been said that Bird was trusted by both sides, some Treaty 7 elders suggested that he did not enjoy a good reputation among the Blackfoot-speaking people and that he did not translate all that was said. The elders said that Bird made a death-bed confession that he had knowingly misled Treaty 7 leaders with his translation at Blackfoot Crossing.

James ("Jimmy Jock") Bird, translator at Blackfoot Crossing

Jean L'Heureux was born in Quebec in 1831 and died at Midnapore, Alberta, in 1919. He studied for the priesthood at Trois Rivières, Quebec, but was never ordained. Sources suggest that he was expelled from the seminary for misconduct. He came west in the 1850s, and representing himself as a priest and a "missionary catechist," he worked among the Cree. In the 1860s he went to Montana to work in the gold fields but was expelled from the territory after being caught in the act of sodomy. He was also accused of fraudulently reporting gold finds and was associated with the mythical "Lost Lemon Mine." L'Heureux became a helper to Father Lacombe at the St Albert mission in the mid-1860s even though it was known that he had never been ordained. He worked as a "priest" among the Siksika, but was eventually dismissed in 1891 for giving religious instruction to children.

L'Heureux travelled with the Siksika and was responsible for transcribing the important nine-point document that was formulated at the 1875 meeting of the Blackfoot Confederacy in the Hand Hills. A general council had been called to discuss the issues to be brought forward when the treaty commissioners arrived.

L'Heureux was also present during the negotiations at Blackfoot Crossing in 1877 and assisted the commissioners by attaching the names to the X's made by the Aboriginal signatories.

L'Heureux remained on the Siksika reserve, promoting education and assisting the Siksika to lobby the government to deliver on their treaty promises. He was also engaged by the Indian department as an interpreter. L'Heureux appears to have been tolerated, even trusted, by the Siksika until his departure from the reserve around 1890.

Throughout his time among the Siksika, L'Heureux took great interest in their culture. He produced a number of articles of some ethnographic interest.

Jean-Baptiste L'Heureux (standing, left), interpreter and "priest"

Constantine Scollen was born in Ireland in 1841 and died in 1902 in Dayton, Ohio. Scollen joined the Oblates, taught in Ireland for a time and came to Canada in 1862 to the mission at St Albert, where he taught English and French. He also learned Cree and worked with Father Lacombe to produce a book of Cree grammar and a Cree dictionary. Scollen established the first mission in southern Alberta and remained there from 1873 to 1882. He worked with the people in the camp of the Blood chief Sotenna.

Scollen assisted with the signing of Treaty 6 at forts Carlton and Pitt. His knowledge of Cree allowed him to help with translation and gather information from the Cree that could assist the treaty commissioners. He was one of the witnesses to Treaty 6 and his signature appears on the treaty. It was at Treaty 6 that Scollen was asked by the minister of the interior, David Mills, to report on the character, habits, and condition of the Blackfoot Confederacy. Scollen compared the Blackfoot people unfavourably with the Cree, describing them as suspicious of White men and warlike. He recommended that a treaty be arrived at as soon as possible, citing the presence of Sitting Bull, a possible ally for the Blackfoot, as an ominous threat to peace. He also described the whiskey trade's devastating effect on the culture and morale of the Siksika, Bloods, and Peigan.

Scollen was present at Treaty 7 and remained to work among the Bloods after the treaty was signed. By 1879 he was finding the poverty and destitution on the Blood reserve alarming. He lobbied to have the government fulfil its treaty promises and suggested that the meaning of the treaty had never been made clear to the Bloods.

Constantine Scollen, missionary priest

Jerry Potts was born in Montana in 1840 and died at Fort Macleod in 1896. A mixed-blood, Potts spent considerable time with his Blood mother, but also lived much of his life at the forts and trading posts in Whoop-Up Country. He variously worked as a hunter, interpreter, scout, and guide. After his father's death, Potts was put into the custody of Alexander Harvey, a trader who mistreated the boy before deserting him in 1845. Potts was then adopted by a kindly trader, Andrew Dawson, who taught him to read and write. In his late teens he joined his mother's tribe for a time and moved between the Blood band and Dawson.

Potts lived in a violent period, acting as a hunter for various whiskey traders throughout the 1860s and 1870s. In 1870 he was involved in the Battle of the Belly River, fought between the Bloods and Cree. He fought with a group of Peigan who were allied with the Bloods in the Blackfoot Confederacy. Three hundred Cree and Assiniboin warriors died on the battlefield. In 1872 he avenged his mother's murder by shooting her killer.

After Potts met the commissioner of the North-West Mounted Police at Fort Benton in 1874, he became an important asset to the Mounties, helping them to understand the customs and culture of the local tribes. In 1874 Potts arranged for the first meeting between Assistant Commissioner James Macleod and the First Nations chiefs Crowfoot and Red Crow. He remained with the NWMP for the remainder of his days; in most of its major expeditions, the force relied on his skills as a scout and guide.

Potts, along with Jimmy Bird, served as an interpreter for commissioners Laird and Macleod at Blackfoot Crossing during the Treaty 7 negotiations. His service in this role remains controversial. Some historians argue that his understanding of many languages made him invaluable in the discussions, but the elders say that Potts had a very poor understanding of the Blackfoot dialects, no understanding of either the Stoney or Tsuu T'ina languages, and a poor grasp of English. Some elders accuse him of not translating all that was said in the speeches made by leaders on both sides. In his later years, ill with tuberculosis and still a heavy drinker, Potts became less useful to the police but he was in their employ when he died.

Jerry Potts, scout and guide

Father Lacombe

Father Lacombe was not present at Treaty 7 but was influential in persuading leaders of tribes south of Edmonton to sign the treaty. He actively advocated treaties for these tribes throughout the 1860s and
1870s.

Richard Hardisty, chief factor, Hudson's Bay Company

Richard Hardisty was present at Blackfoot Crossing during the treaty negotiations. As a trader with the Hudson's Bay Company, Hardisty was camped east of Treaty Flats, ready with company wares to sell to the tribes once the treaty was completed and treaty payments were made.

Crowfoot addressing Commissioners Macleod and Laird.
Painted by Bruce Stapleton ca. 1887.

Crowfoot meeting the Marquis of Lorne. Painted by Sydney Hall,
1881.

Stapleton's interpretation of Crowfoot speaking to the treaty commissioners (top) is copied from the similar image painted by Sydney Hall
and could not have been made from firsthand observation.

PART ONE

The Elders' Evidence

THE ELDERS OF TREATY 7
WITH WALTER HILDEBRANDT
AND DOROTHY FIRST RIDER

CHAPTER ONE

Elders' Narrative
of the Making of Treaty 7

INTRODUCTION

The events, circumstances, and promises surrounding the discussions and signing of Treaty 7 in 1877 are still shrouded in
myth, misunderstanding, and a profound sense that "sacred
treaty rights" were betrayed. No single elder from the Treaty
7 First Nations left behind a complete linear narrative of what
occurred at Blackfoot Crossing from September 19 to September
22, 1877. There are, however, many insights and stories that
taken together provide a comprehensive portrait of what happened in those four days. It is a version that differs in many
ways from the official history constructed by government officials that presently constitutes the predominant version of the
events as they took place at the signing of the treaty. Tribal elders
have different stories about the "spirit and intent" of the events
of the 1870s. These stories have been passed on from generation
to generation.

BLOOD TRIBE

The Bloods have a tradition of treaty making with other nations
referred to as *innaihtsiini*. As Louise Crop Eared Wolf explained:

Our people's concept of the treaties is entirely different from the non-
Native's point of view. Treaty, or *innaihtsiini*, is when two powerful nations come together into a peace agreement, both parties coming forward in a peaceful, reconciliatory approach by exercising a sacred oath

through the symbolic way of peace, which is smoking a sacred pipe and also through the exchange of gifts to sanction the agreement which can never be broken. The smoking of the pipe is similar to the non-Native's swearing on the Holy Bible.

To our people the sun is the symbol of power. That's why we call the sun Natosi or Powerful One. The sun is the power of growth; the river is the power of life; the grass is the power of spirituality; the mountains are the power of peace.

To further explain, Indian people's concept of treaty is one of creating a good and lasting relationship between two nations who at one time were at war with one another.

Treaty 7 was one of several treaties the Bloods entered. Our people were already familiar with the treaty process prior to the signing of Treaty 7 in 1877. They had made treaties with the Crows, Sioux, Crees, and other tribes.

In signing treaty with the Queen, they had undestood Treaty 7 as a sacred agreement. The basis of the relationship between the Blood tribe and the government of Canada is based on the treaty. Any agreements between the Bloods and the government of Canada must always be in the light of Treaty 7.

Wallace Mountain Horse also described the tradition of treaty making among the Bloods:

Well, what that treaty is all about is very important – *it is very important* – that is, *innaihtsiini* ... We Indian people, we make treaties with other tribes that we are fighting with. Well ... just like the Crow, one of our main enemies before the White people came, we were always at war with one another, Crow and Cree. We made treaty with them and to this day we are still on friendly terms with one another. There's no way a treaty that has been made can be altered. We became really friendly with one another ... So that's what the treaty means. Both parties have to agree with one another on everything that they want to make treaties on. They will sit together, they will discuss, then they will say, "We don't live like this anymore, on our side and your side." They will discuss and agree to everything, while their side of the people are listening as they are negotiating how they are going to go about the terms that they agreed upon to get back together as friendly with one another for the rest of their time. That's the way it was with the treaties. Well, the way the Canadian government approached us, they wrote the treaty or documented everything in the treaty. We had no say in anything – that's what we mean when we say they shoved that thing down our throats. They said, okay this is the way we will be from now on, now we've made a treaty. We will not fight nor disagree anymore, this is what we are going to do to prevent any more disagreements. We will do what we can to prevent trouble and keep the peace with us from here on. These agreements that we made with you, that's yours forever. The way the treaty is written, this is what you will follow, just as we've agreed on through the treaty. These are what we have promised you, this is how we will live with one another ... Okay, looking at that treaty of today, maybe more than half of those treaty agreements they set up themselves, on how we will live with one another, are not with us today. There's a very few that are still in existence. It's not us that demolished those treaties that they set up for us to go by, when we made that treaty with them.

The leaders of the treaty believed Jerry Potts's interpretation of the Crown's promises and everything else he told them, even though he spoke very poor Blackfoot: "Elders thought the treaty could be signed in good faith and that it could be further looked into in the future when they signed."

Rosie Red Crow indicated that, along with the poor translation provided by Jerry Potts, some of the Bloods gestures might have been misunderstood by the commissioners. A conversational practice of the Bloods is to continue to say "ah, ah" as a speaker is talking, not to indicate agreement with what is being said but simply to acknowledge that the person is speaking and has the floor to say his piece. Red Crow contended that the commissioners might have thought that the Bloods were agreeing to all the points that the government read to them, rather than understanding that the Bloods were simply acknowledging the commissioners' right to speak. By the fourth day, said Rosie Red Crow, the Bloods made a treaty "because the Whites spoke in a manner that pleased them," creating a feeling of trust but they did not necessarily agree with or understand the specific legal terms of the treaty content.

Elder Louise Crop Eared Wolf recalled that when Crowfoot invited Red Crow to come to Blackfoot Crossing, Red Crow consulted with Rainy Chief, an elder and chief of the northern Bloods. Both chiefs consulted with their own people about the treaty. Red Crow conferred with Seen From Afar and also with Bad Head and Medicine Calf, especially with the latter two, who had knowledge of the Lame Bull Treaty of 1855. These men told Red Crow that while that treaty had seemed generous at first, the US government soon began to ignore its terms. Red Crow preferred to make a treaty at Fort Macleod, rather than at Blackfoot Crossing, since he had established a good relationship with Colonel Macleod.

At Blackfoot Crossing the Bloods prayed, smoked their sacred pipes, and sang songs "to empower themselves and to seek guidance." But the tribes were also prepared to go to war if necessary. There was great tension at Blackfoot Crossing. Louise Crop Eared Wolf was told a story by a granddaughter of Chief Bearspaw of the Stoneys that illustrated the tension felt by the tribes. The story was told of a woman who had special powers as a "seer." This seer thought that there was going to be war because of the apprehension she felt: "She fasted and prayed for four days, so that a war would not occur. They say that her prayers and offerings were successful in that they prevented a war from occurring."

PEIGAN NATION

Peace was the main issue at treaty-time, according to the Peigan elders. Nick Smith described what happened at Blackfoot Crossing in September 1877:

What they were told was, we will make peace here with everyone. The people are here (Queen's representatives); they will put laws for us. We will use those laws with our people in our land. That's what I heard this old man say. Those people selected to sit together at Crowfoot [Blackfoot] Crossing, you see they were scattered into different areas. That's where we made peace with the Queen at Crowfoot Crossing. You will no longer live the way you were used to. You will be taken care of by the Queen and her representatives. She sent them here. The Red Coat was sent here to watch and take care of you. We will make peace with everyone and we will live in harmony with one another ...

The people did not agree on their own to everything that was planned. They only knew when they arrived at Crowfoot Crossing.

These White people will take care of you, you will receive rations as long as there is a sun, the river flows in this land. The old people said they did not give their consent right away, but it took quite a while. The old man said that people sat for a long time. They were waiting to hear from Crowfoot. It took him a long time before he came out of his lodge. He mounted his horse and rode around the encampment. That's when he spoke: "The reason I took much time to come out, I was thinking about what is going to take place. You know the White man is not being honest with the promises he is making to take care of you. I feel sorry for my children. They will no longer be able to live as they please. They will be restricted from everything." There were many things he said when he rode. Then he went to the centre and he spoke again. He spoke for a long time. You could see him pointing around, just as you see in the picture at Crowfoot Crossing.

The interpreter spoke only those things he understood. A lot of the things said were not included. The old people said there must have been words used by Crowfoot that were probably very high words. The French man probably did not understand them. Only those things he was able to interpret were written. Interpretation at Crowfoot Crossing was not good or [it was] incorrect.

They were promised, you will be cared for. I heard they were given beef as rations at the signing of the treaty. They were not very interested in the beef. They would rather have buffalo, which was their main source of food and it was taken from them. They used the buffalo for their existence in life. That's what I heard the people say. The decision to sign depended on Crowfoot's decision. These were leaders, and they looked to Crowfoot for that one decision. They all cooperated with him once he spoke. They did not agree prior; they waited on Crowfoot [because traditionally leaders were looked to for those kinds of decisions].

Now that you have signed, these are the laws that you will abide by. The old people that I heard said that it was a law to live by, and the people were not aware. They did not know that the representatives led them around as they pleased. It was a difficult time; if only the interpreter could have related in a better manner.

John Yellowhorn, hereditary chief of the Peigan, related the following account that was told to him by Small Water Child, who was living at the time of Treaty 7:

Macleod went in, sat down, and explained his reason for wanting to
see (chief) Bull Head. He said, "The Queen has sent me here to make
treaty with you. She has sent me here to keep peace amongst you people." They made friends with one another and this is when Bull Head
gave Macleod his name. Colonel Macleod told him he would give him
a uniform the same as he was wearing. Bull Head said, "No, you will
not give me this clothing. The trail you took to come here, you must
follow the same trail back. You will not sign treaty with me."

The NWMP went to these tea parties that the Indians were having.
There were Indian camps nearby where Macleod was camped and it
was here that they were holding those tea parties. Colonel Macleod
and his men greatly enjoyed these tea parties. They came in 1875, and
in 1877 the treaty was signed. There was no mention during these
years that there was going to be treaty (1875–77). All of a sudden it
was being said that there would be treaty and the place it would be
signed was at Blackfoot Crossing. Red Crow and Sitting Against the
Eagle Tails broke up camp and moved there. The Sarcee chief moved
there. To this day I do not know who this chief was. On one side
Crowfoot camped. On the other side they were camped; they were
camped for quite some time [they being the Queen's representatives].
Crowfoot was elected by the Indian people to represent them because
he was a very intelligent man. For days, the Queen's men were sent
across the river to negotiate with Crowfoot. [He] told his people, "I
will hold off as long as I can. So that we may get as much for our
people as we can." Finally he signed. The Queen's representative must
have been an east Blackfoot who came to ask Crowfoot again. He turned
his horse in the direction the sun goes, because the Indians are always
following the sun, and this east Blackfoot turned his horse around to
the Indian people and he went to all the different people and talked
to them. This is where he talked to my grandfather and my father's
mother. And this is what they heard him say, right from his mouth.
He said, "All of you people, you have all given up. The reason why
I haven't given up [is that] in the future our way of living is going to
change. We will no longer live our nomadic way of moving around. Away
in the future there will be no more hunting or living from the earth" ...

They went ahead and met for the signing. And this same east Blackfoot who spoke of the future said, "My people, I will show off to you."
He put on war paint, and he went and shook hands with Colonel Macleod. Next thing, Colonel Macleod pulled his hand back quickly. His
hand was burned on this east Blackfoot's hand. And after this they

had the final signing of the treaty. There were no chairs and no tables. Just Crowfoot and Colonel Macleod stood together. There was no writing at the signing of the treaty. All of the writings about the treaty are all recent. I feel like taking a piece of paper and making my own writing now, to say what actually took place at the signing of the treaty. That is one reason why I don't look at these recent books written about the treaty. Because they are all recent and do not say what actually happened. What was discussed at the treaty and the promises that were made by the Queen's men at the treaty, this is what I believe in, this is what I go by.

Elder Hilda Yellow Wings stated that Colonel Macleod informed the Peigan to go to Blackfoot Crossing. She also said that the Peigan trusted Crowfoot to make the right decision on the treaty. Crowfoot prayed and deliberated about the treaty: "While praying he foresaw what was going to happen to his people. He saw the river was running with blood and he took this as a warning to his people." Crowfoot rode around the camp on his sorrel horse and said it would be sad for the children of the future if they went to war rather than make treaty. With this message he obtained their agreement to the treaty.

Hugh Crow Eagle said that many people from the Blood, Peigan, and Siksika nations camped at Blackfoot Crossing beginning in the spring of 1877. Many of the people in these camps had dreams and visions about what would happen if they made treaty: "These spiritual persons prophesied through their dreams and visions and warned the leaders not to sign the treaty. Their dreams told them that they will live in poverty and the White man was going to treat them very unkindly. Indian people rely on and place great honour on their dreams. These warnings by the spiritual persons probably made the decision to sign the treaty extremely difficult." But Hugh Crow Eagle concluded that the Peigan leadership had little choice in the final analysis but to make treaty "because of what they had seen of the massacres of Indians that took place in the us." Crow Eagle said that Crowfoot camped apart from the rest of the people because of the difficult decisions he had to make. Prior to signing the treaty, Crowfoot mounted his horse and talked to each tribe about what he foresaw in the future. He advised people that there would be many changes in their way of life, mostly hard times. After he circled the camps, he went into the centre of the camps and dismounted his horse and continued with his talk."

Elder Paul Smith had been told stories about Blackfoot Crossing by Bull Head (not the chief), who was ten years old when Treaty 7 was made. Bull Head, a member of the Horn Society for most of his life, remembered that the Peigan and Tsuu T'ina were camped on the south side of the crossing, while the Siksika were on the other side of the river. The North-West Mounted Police came across the river to "speak with us, they were killing cattle to feed the camps, but ... the people did not care for the meat; instead they fed the meat to their dogs." Hugh Crow Eagle pointed out that the Peigan were camped in a valley east of Cannon Hill during the negotiations at Blackfoot Crossing. Crow Eagle indicated that that elders told him that this position was occupied by the Peigan as well as warriors from the other tribes because some of the chiefs believed there might be fighting if negotiations broke down. Massacres on both the Canadian and American side of the border left many chiefs wary of what might be a trap. The Peigan position was chosen behind the east flank of the NWMP just in case a confrontation developed.

The Peigan leaders did not know English and had no comprehension of words like "cede" and "surrender." They only understood treaties as peacemaking agreements. Jerry Potts and Jimmy Bird were the interpreters, though Bird was the main interpreter. Smith does not believe that the interpreters were able to explain such terms as "cede" effectively: "I say this because the Indian leaders would never give up the territory that they used for their everyday survival." Bull Head told Smith that the Peigan who were at Blackfoot Crossing were very hungry and that as soon as the treaty talks were over, they headed out to look for buffalo. "They went hunting for them as far as into Montana. The government did not try to stop them because they also knew that they needed the buffalo meat for their winter survival."

SIKSIKA NATION

Siksika elder Margaret Bad Boy had been told by her mother that it was Father Lacombe who encouraged the Siksika to make treaty. Her mother remembered that he was known as Big Knife to her people: "When Big Knife died, he had a black dot on his heart [chest]. The Indians believed that the black dot on his heart was there because he was not honest with the Indians about what they would lose if they made treaty. I personally saw this dot on his heart because I once viewed his body as it rested in state in Calgary."

Victoria McHugh, the wife of the late Chief Clarence McHugh, had detailed memories of the stories about the years when the treaty was made. In the years just prior to the treaty, there was considerable starvation:

We mostly hunted, gathered goods for our survival, and maintained our spiritual way of life. After the buffalo started to disappear, our way of life began to change. The buffalo was our main source of life and when it began to disappear we were in a dire situation. I believe the situation we were in helped the government to settle treaty with us more easily. The missionaries also began to Christianize us and we started to lose our spiritual way of life. We would move to the mountains close to rivers during the winters and hunted wild game. The wild game also started to deplete because we were hunting them too much when the buffalo was disappearing. Old Mrs Many Guns told me that one year they did not have enough hide material to make winter clothes. The Siksika Nation also had to eat gophers and whatever they could find to feed themselves that year. Crowfoot sent word to each tribe to consider making treaty so that it may provide them food. Stoneys did not agree with Crowfoot. Father Lacombe had a lot to do with Crowfoot being in favour of making treaty. He advised Crowfoot that if you keep asking for a lot of things, the government will not give you anything, they will just leave you to starve. I believe Father Lacombe influenced Crowfoot on what to agree on. When the missionaries started learning the Blackfoot language and living with the Indians, the Indian people started to gain their trust in them. At this time the missionaries would start talking about the treaty and say we would live with the White man peacefully. Old Mrs Many Guns used to tell me that Father Lacombe and Crowfoot would call on the people to meet together and Father Lacombe would begin to explain to them how things would be if they made treaty. All the old people were against it. Mrs Many Guns was only nine years old when she witnessed this.

Mrs McHugh indicated that from the stories she had heard

there was much dissention at Blackfoot Crossing. Old Sun, Yellow Horse, Running Rabbit, and others were against the treaty. Many leaders walked away from the negotiations on the first day and stayed away for two or three days. Mrs McHugh said that many did not trust the interpreters: "The interpreters were Jerry Potts and Jim Bird but they could not interpret well in the Blackfoot language, so they spoke Cree most of the time. Old Lady Buffalo from the Peigan Nation used to tell me that the NWMP had control over Jerry Potts but he was mostly drunk when he tried to interpret. He would just babble away and didn't make sense."

The Siksika recalled that when the commissioners came north to Blackfoot Crossing to talk about the treaty, they came with a large herd of longhorns. The Siksika set up camp along with the other tribes, including some Cree with the Bobtail band who were seeking to sign an adhesion to Treaty 6. Augustine Yellow Sun relates that Crowfoot camped two water inlets away from the police and the commissioners. When interpreter Jerry Potts was sent by Macleod to speak to Crowfoot, he was alleged to have said, "I came to get you. The tall White man [Treaty Commissioner David Laird] is going to give you people the money." Crowfoot replied, "Yes, I don't think my children should take the money. Tell that to the White man." Potts didn't say much to that and returned to tell Colonel Macleod. On his second visit, Potts told Crowfoot that there was food for all those assembled, but Crowfoot, equating gifts of food with gifts of money, replied, "I told you, we don't want to take the money." Then one of the minor chiefs, Na-ta-wo-ta-ne, was said to have told Macleod that he would take the money but Macleod answered that he would deal only with Crowfoot. By saying he would take the money, Na-ta-wo-ta-ne was agreeing to sign. Soon after this, Crowfoot agreed to talk and Macleod made preparations to conclude the treaty. Crowfoot moved his lodge across the river, the cannon went off to signal the start of negotiations, and then the beef rations were released: "Those that went to get rations were all covered in blood ... the sight was very original." The flag then went up signalling that Crowfoot had agreed to take the money. Macleod told Crowfoot that twelve bluebacks (dollars) were to be given to each person.

After some discussion, Crowfoot said that Rabbit Carrier

would announce to the people what was in the treaty. Macleod said that the participants in the treaty would "not be able to kill what roams and flies and could not sell wood and stones to Whites." Crowfoot disagreed with this and told Macleod that he would now tell him what the tribes wanted in the treaty. When the right to hunt had been settled, Macleod asked where the tribes would settle. Crowfoot immediately took land around Blackfoot Crossing, Red Crow took the Belly River, Eagle Tail Feathers took Porcupine Hills, the Stoneys took "at the Mountain." As soon as the treaty was signed, the cattle were slaughtered, although "some of the Indians didn't know the meat was to be eaten" – many did not like the taste of this meat, preferring buffalo.

Beatrice Poor Eagle, who was raised by the daughter of Crowfoot's youngest wife, said that Crowfoot was pressured into making treaty by his brother Three Bulls. Three Bulls threatened to make treaty on his own if Crowfoot would not agree.

The leaders believed they had made a peace treaty and that the Whites were going to be allowed to use the land to the depth of a plough blade. As Chief Calf put it, "Today, we only loan out one and two feet. White men could dig post holes for the fences. The ground underneath we did not loan out." One foot was for planting, another foot for post holes. To stop fighting, they agreed to $12 per year, not realizing that this was an initial payment only, for the treaty stipulated $5 as the annuity thereafter.

STONEY NAKODA NATION

The Stoneys, along with the Siksika, Bloods, Peigan, and Tsuu T'ina, were invited to Blackfoot Crossing to make a peace treaty. Former chief of the Bearspaw Nation, Bill Mclean, recalls the events surrounding the meeting at Blackfoot Crossing:

The old Stoney people tell of stories about a certain place where the Blackfoot live ... referred to as Blackfoot Crossing. Again, it was the missionaries who told the tribes when and where the treaty was to take place.

The different tribes, the Blackfoot, the Sarcees, the Peigans, the Bloods, and the Stoneys, were told when the time comes they were to gather at Blackfoot Crossing to make a peace treaty. That was why they were told to go there – to make a peace treaty. The chiefs of the Stoney tribe, there were three, were told to proceed to Blackfoot Crossing when it was time. So when it was time, the Stoney chiefs, along with many of the Stoneys, proceeded to Blackfoot Crossing. The old people say that the other tribes (the Blackfoot Confederacy) camped on one side of the Bow River and the Stoneys camped on the other side. The commissioners, along with the police and the Natives, gathered to start the treaty-making process. It is said that there were discussions on the treaty amongst the commissioners, the heads of police, and the Natives. However, the White people's side, the government people, had a pre-written document containing only their concept of what the treaty entails. They told the Indian chiefs, "This is our terms of the treaty and this is what will be in the treaty agreement." But in those days there was nobody at all from the Natives' side to translate or understand exactly the legal jargon in the treaty document. Nonetheless, the Indian chiefs had an indication of why they were there – to make a peace treaty. Even though all the various tribes were gathered at Blackfoot Crossing, all the tribes together made a single treaty.

According to a description of the circumstances that existed just before the negotiations began, one of the Stoney leaders heard the Blood chiefs say, "Our land will be taken away [so] let's kill them instead." But the Stoney leaders and other chiefs prevailed over the militants, saying that peace was good and that the fighting had to end: "Our tribal wars are depleting us. The White people are scheming to starve us, to let us go hungry. They are killing the buffalo. They have brought firewater."

Much was said by the First Nations leaders gathered, but the treaty commissioners' words were given more weight and were more completely recorded. The speeches made by Crowfoot about his willingness to share the land were recorded more fully than most other First Nations speeches. He also said, "The game are mine. Do not tell me what to do regarding wild animals." When treaties are made, both sides should be understood and recorded, say the Stoney elders. Legal language was never interpreted properly. Of the Stoney leaders, curiously, only Chief Jacob Bearspaw was quoted (or paraphrased by the interpreter) in the government minutes, whereas the words of Chief Chiniquay and Chief Goodstoney were omitted (or ignored) entirely.

Reverend John McDougall was a significant participant in the treaty negotiations according to Lazarus Wesley. In Cree (not Stoney), McDougall told them about the treaty – that money would be given out, that weapons must be laid down. McDougall told them, "Make peace and the Queen will look after you." The Stoneys agreed, saying that they would no longer fight if the police would protect them. McDougall convinced the Stoneys to attend the treaty discussions by promising, "Come to Blackfoot Crossing and you will receive money." McDougall made it sound urgent. They were told they would be fed there. Bearspaw had initially answered that he would rather fight than sign the treaty, but the Christian Stoneys said it was wrong to make war and that peace was good – it said so in the Bible. So Bearspaw was finally persuaded to give up on his idea of fighting the newcomers. The Mounties were being offered as protectors of peace, and would see to it that there was no more horse stealing and killing. In addition to promising peace through the treaty, Commissioner Laird had said, "You will live a comfortable life. I will look after you. You will not go hungry."

Elders also recalled speeches in which it was said that the Stoneys would loan the topsoil to the newcomers so that they could grow things. Some of the Stoneys did not think that the treaty was all that important and did not take it seriously: "If the land for growing wheat was all they wanted, there was no problem." If the Stoneys could continue to hunt as they always had, there was no problem. Lazarus Wesley said that the Stoneys were told that they would be taught to read and write, that there were things that were of value to many who wanted to learn English. The promises that were made in return for letting the newcomers use the land seemed attractive. The Stoneys did not mind agreeing to grow wheat, as they were told that bread "goes good with meat." The Stoneys thought it was a fair bargain, especially since there were to be no restrictions on hunting and they were to be given snare wire, hooks, guns, and ammunition. Some Stoneys felt pressured to sign when they were told that the "White man would soon flood the land." There was no discussion of giving up landownership. Because McDougall only knew Cree, he was unable to communicate the full details of the agreement to the Stoneys.

John Snow pointed out that McDougall had been given $1,500

the year before the treaty was signed to buy clothes that he was to divide up among the Stoneys. As he did this, he spoke to them about the upcoming treaty and about the importance of signing it. This largesse was undoubtedly a successful form of persuasion, especially among the Christian Stoneys.

What was written in the final treaty amounted to far less than what had been spoken about, and many things were not understood, said Snow. Many of the Stoneys had never seen a fence before and didn't understand how land was to be partitioned. Nowhere in the treaty was anything written about the two feet of topsoil that the newcomers were to be allowed to use for "growing things."

George Ear remembered that the treaty was negotiated over a period of four days and that some of the Stoneys had been eager to fight. He also recalled the story of the cannons of the North-West Mounted Police that had been brought to the Stoney village. People were offered rations of beef, but they thought it really stank. People preferred the buffalo meat and only reluctantly accepted beef as an alternative.

On the third day of the negotiations, Crowfoot met with Commissioner Laird at the centre of the encampment and told him to disarm all the cannons that were aimed at the people, saying, "If the commissioner is not willing to lay down his guns, I too will aim my guns at him." Jerry Potts went to Colonel Macleod with this message and the cannons were immediately withdrawn. After this, the Union Jack was raised and a cannon was fired signalling that the talks were beginning. Bearspaw, who had initially wanted to fight, was told that in addition to peace, he would be given money, rations, clothing, and farm machinery. These promises persuaded him to sign the treaty. George Ear says that a thousand lodges were in the encampment at Blackfoot Crossing and that the Stoneys and Cree were camped together some distance from the other tribes.

TSUU T'INA NATION

Tsuu T'ina elder Helen Meguinis thought that the treaty was really intended to keep the prairie First Nations from bothering the incoming settlers. Some of her people, like the leader Bull Head, had great trust in the Queen's assurance that their people would be taken care of. Starvation was an issue for the Tsuu T'ina. According to Hilda Big Crow, the Tsuu T'ina people had already formed alliances with some of the tribes, such as the Blackfoot, prior to treaty-time in 1877. Hilda Big Crow went on to say that "a treaty is a contract of peace with the government; Treaty 7 was a peace treaty." In 1877 the Tsuu T'ina people felt they had to enter into the treaty. "There was fear of being killed ... our people did not understand what they were agreeing to." Tsuu T'ina people had no translator or interpreter present to translate and/or interpret for them. They relied on the Blackfoot for interpretation.

Treaty promises were lifetime promises, but not all of Tsuu T'ina people were present and counted at Blackfoot Crossing. According to some of the elders, such as Dick Big Plume, the treaty was a time of annuity only. Their recollections are of a $5 treaty payment – there were no recollections of a land surrender whatsoever.

Louise Big Plume said, "The treaty was essential for the survival of the Tsuu T'ina. People did not understand the treaty – they only understood that they needed to enter into the treaty to survive." According to Louise, the treaty was made with Queen Victoria.

Hilda Big Crow, Dick Big Plume, and Louise Big Plume all recollected that the treaty specifically promised the provisions of health and education.

Elder Lucy Big Plume understood that, according to the elders, the treaty was "a promise made by the White man to keep the Indians from interfering or to keep the White man interfering into their life style." According to Lucy Big Plume, the role of the elders is to advise the chiefs (leaders): "The government explained to the tribes but we were not sure whether the interpreter interpreted the right words to the people." The Tsuu T'ina entered into treaty "because the buffalo were getting smaller and people were starving. They had to do something to keep people living." "They more or less were forced to [make treaty] for the welfare of the people." The interpretations were not good enough. "The government promised us medical [care] and education." "The Indian didn't record the treaty but it was brought down from one generation to another."

The interpreter Jerry Potts did not speak Tsuu T'ina, according to elder Maurice Big Plume. The Treaty was a contract with the White man to make peace: "We were to receive government protection, education, free medicine, free of taxation, and ammunition."

Tom Heavenfire had this opinion about the treaty: "Well, I guess the way our people look at it was that they were not going to be fighting any more wars and that education will be paid for ... [and] medicine ... Our chiefs didn't want to fight anymore because they saw that it might just wipe us out, because of the population of the White man coming west ... There were more of them coming and if we didn't sign the treaty they were going to wipe us out." He also believed that the treaty guaranteed "ammunition money every year, like the medicine chest, the treaty, the five dollars we get."

Helen Meguinis said that "back in 1877 when our chief made Treaty 7, I think they were illiterate; they did not understand and I think they had American interpretation of the treaty, whoever was interpreting. Our chief, Bull Head, when he made Treaty 7, he took it upon himself to enter into Treaty 7 on behalf of his people. Tsuu T'ina people and he had a great trust in the great white mother [as they used to call her], Queen Victoria ... They made treaty because they had great trust in the government ... that's why they signed it."

Clarabelle Pipestem stated that "after they kill all our buffalo, they were promised rations, well, they had to sign [the treaty] that time in order not to starve." According to seventy-six-year-old Rosie Runner, "Treaty was a security for food supply." Tsuu T'ina people entered into the treaty for peace as well as for food and tools, livestock, education, medication, and freedom from taxes.

CHAPTER TWO

Pre-treaty Life of Treaty 7 First Nations

SOCIAL AND RELIGIOUS LIFE

Blood Tribe

As it always had been, according to Fred Gladstone, the Bloods' advisers on spiritual matters were the elders. Dick Nice Cutter emphasized the importance of the spiritual roots in the world view of the Bloods: "They called the land Mother Earth because it brought them food ... everything connected with earth was considered sacred." The fundamental laws were the laws of nature. Society was organized around clans, which were made up of a number of families. Groups called *inaki* were responsible for law and order: "When people broke the law, they were helped so it wouldn't happen again." Various societies, such as the Horn Society, assisted people, giving them help and support in their daily lives.

Pete Standing Alone also emphasized the spiritual basis of life for the Bloods: "The land was put there by the Creator for our use, but only what we needed." It was believed that the Creator gave them the land and the land was believed to be sacred: "We pray and give thanks to the Creator." The land was not to be deliberately destroyed or damaged. The land was there to provide food for daily survival. The land for the Sun Dance was considered especially sacred and was set aside for that purpose alone.

The leaders of the Bloods were chosen on the basis of their experience and knowledge. They were also chosen for their compassion and integrity. An important quality for leadership was a willingness to help or advise anyone who asked for assistance. Leaders were not chosen for what they promised but rather for what they had done in the past. Leaders made decisions for the benefit of the whole tribe, such as when to go hunting or when to move camp.

Clans were units and resembled a large extended family. A clan would be given a name that reflected one of its characteristics.

The pipe was a sacred object for the Bloods; it was a symbol of truth. You could not tell a lie in the presence of the pipe. The pipe would be used to determine whether or not there was infidelity between a couple: "The elder would tell the couple they would have to tell the truth like the straightness of the pipe." If a person lied in the presence of the pipe, he or she would suffer in the future.

Pete Standing Alone explained that the "role of elders was to care for sacred religious ceremonies and spiritual matters such as prayer." Various societies served different needs and age groups. The Horn Society members were looked to for their wisdom and knowledge. The Horn Society decided when the Sun Dance would be. "If a woman calls a Sun Dance, it will be on the land of the clan she is from." The Sun Dances were held in mid-summer at the request of individuals and were focused on matters of importance. Other religious rituals included marriages, transfer ceremonies, and medicine pipe ceremonies.

Louise Crop Eared Wolf also emphasized the importance of the pipe: "The pipe is always used when important issues or events take place because it is held to have sacred powers that cannot be disturbed or replaced. The treaty signatories smoked the pipe with the White officials to solidify and sanction the treaty-making process according to the Indian signatories' interpretation and understanding of the treaty."

Wallace Mountain Horse spoke about the importance for the Bloods of observing "the spirituality of nature." The Bloods lived with nature: "We lived on meat and berries; there were no restrictions on our movements as we pursued these things ... we kept physically fit by moving on foot." This led the Bloods to "respect all creations."

Mountain Horse said that the Bloods chose their leaders on the basis of respect and reliability. According to the laws laid down, people were to respect one another – "Crimes like stealing were dealt with by returning the goods."

The Bloods believed that the Creator was the "life-giver." When missionaries came, they taught things about God that the Bloods already knew: "We were living the things that were in the Bible before the Whites came."

Elder Adam Delaney outlined some of the beliefs of his people:

The world is round and each society has been given the right to exist in this world within its territory. This is how the Creator had arranged it. Therefore, the traditional territory of the Blackfoot Nation was given to our people by our Creator. We respected and protected this traditional territory with our minds and our hearts and we depended on it for what it encompasses for our survival. Everything that we ever needed for our way of life and survival existed in our traditional territory, such as herbs for medicine, roots, rivers, game animals, berries, vegetables, the buffalo ... Because of the way we hold this land, I do not believe that our Indian leaders at Blackfoot Crossing gave up this territory but offered to share it with the White man in exchange for peace and friendship between each other and among other tribes.

Rosie Red Crow remembered a variety of activities that were part of the Blood way of life:

During the summer we picked berries and hunted and just before fall we dried meat; in this way we were well prepared for the winter. We knew winter was near when migrating birds began to fly south. The old people would look at the sun and when it's at a certain point it will tell them how cold the winter will be. Then they would move to the river where there are a lot of trees. We used the trees for firewood, also for shelter from the cold winter. We never moved from our winter quarters unless we were invaded by the Crees or some other tribe. I heard a story once about our warriors who were going to battle with the Crees one winter when there was a lot of snow. When our warriors tried to fight back against the Cree, they could not get past the snow because they kept getting stuck. The Crees just glided over the snow because they had these funny-looking shoes [snowshoes] and easily chased the Blackfoot away from their winter encampment. The first sound of thunder was our sign to begin to prepare for our annual Sun Dance. All owners of medicine bundles took out their pipes and smoked their tobacco that was left over from the previous year. They prayed and fasted in their sweat lodges in order that they could have a successful Sun Dance. They camped in four different places before settling camp for the Sun Dance. Ghost Dances were common during the Sun Dance. The people would sing in their lodges most of the night until the dogs started to bark, which was a sign that the ghost had come. They would then place berry soup outside their camp for the ghost to feast. Dances were held all year round by various societies. They always had "give away" but very few would have nothing to give. Feather games were also played during these dances. During the winter, the boys played a type of hockey on the river.

Peigan Nation

Spirituality for the Peigan was connected to ceremonies in which the band members began their quest for "paint." These ceremonies started with a "sweat," asserted Davis Crow Eagle: "No noise was allowed and the members painted their faces." Prayer would be considered to have been answered only when paint was found. Ceremonies were carried on for four days and four nights at the site where Crow Eagle reserve was situated. People whispered during the entire ceremony: "We were told there were sacred people there."

Ray Cross Child said leaders among the Peigan were chosen because they were able to accumulate wealth and prestige. Wealthy men would be able to have more than one wife. Success in war was also considered to be an important attribute for a leader.

Louise English contended that leaders were chosen who were "gentle and wise." She stressed that the Peigan got along with the missionaries and that the elders often followed the teachings of both the Roman Catholic and Anglican churches. She too remembers the importance of going to get paint on the Crow Eagle reserve and also recalls the significance of tobacco in healing ceremonies.

Nick Smith stated that spiritual life began with the belief that everyone belonged to the land. Leaders among the Peigan would be chosen for their courage. The Roman Catholic Church was the first to arrive among the Peigan to help those who did not know where they were headed in life. Smith recalled that at the

Anglicans' meeting the children would be fed after the service: "That's what we enjoyed, getting something to eat." Smith also told stories about the trips to Crow Eagle reserve to get paint on the grounds that were considered sacred. Spirituality has become difficult among the Peigan, contended Smith: "Today we are starting to live like the White man. Today the young people do not help one another anymore. Our lives have become very difficult."

Fred North Peigan also fondly remembered the trips to get paint at Crow Eagle reserve: "We went to get paint after the Castle River Rodeo." They stayed at the paint site for four days because this was a sacred number. "They didn't just get paint but had long ceremonies throughout the night." The Peigan would use paint every day for either ceremonies or decoration. Fred North Peigan also commented on the clans' practice of changing their names, "often humorously."

Cecile Many Guns also affirmed that getting paint was central to the spiritual life of the Peigan. The people prayed, offered cloth, and presented themselves in humility to the spirits. Buffalo rocks were used to invoke the spirit of the buffalo for a successful hunt. Incense was also used to call upon the spirits. Participants paraded to the site in a single line.

We would take our places and start slowly searching for paint, reverently striking the rocks in prayer from four sides. These rocks appear to be shining elements; then we would immediately start finding the paint ... If done with great reverence, it would almost come to you ... The reverence of praying was the principle method of obtaining paint. This paint was a very important asset to the Peigan people's culture; it was used daily in ceremonies and rituals to obtain spiritual help in health, in battles, in social gatherings, and in medicine. This is the reason it was found in all the Indians' belongings. It was a principle asset to the Sun Dance, the Blackfoot major religious ceremony.

Paint was very hard to get and "if noise were made it would disappear or turn a dirty colour." The Peigan brought paint to buffalo rocks and painted on the them: "We'd paint the rocks to show appreciation to them for their luck." At night people prayed and put on paint. They celebrated finding paint by cooking berry stew and singing the songs of the sacred societies –

"This strengthened our luck for the next day's ventures." Many Guns explained that there were many different kinds of paint; some kinds would shine and had to be baked in ashes before it was usable. Those shining rocks were also once used to make pottery. The last ceremonies organized to get paint were in the 1920s.

Cecile Many Guns also talked about the importance of buffalo rocks for the Peigan. She told the story of how people had been hungry and looking for buffalo in vain when a woman had a dream about finding the herds. She found a rock that was singing to her, telling her where the buffalo were. Such rocks could be used as charms in spiritual or supernatural ceremonies. At other times rocks were used as weapons, utensils, or toys that represented horses or other animals.

One of the most important stories for the Peigan people is the story of Napi, who lost the contest with the Kootenay people for land east of the mountains. Napi lost the game with the Kootenay and with it the land west of the mountains; he was, however, able to retain land to the east of the Rockies, which is the homeland of the Peigan. This story is important to the Peigan, stressed Tom Yellowhorn, because it is their story of origin and of their right to the land.

The pipe was also significant to the Peigan. It was smoked at ceremonies and treaties where people prayed they would become friends. Smoking the peace pipe means there are no hard feelings. The pipe ceremony is viewed as a most solemn ceremony, as it reconfirms "faith in the great spirit." Yellowhorn explains that the Creator gave them this country, gave them the light of the sun and the light of the moon: "Our Mother – the land – that's where they get all their food, from the land. All the fruit and the game they got, they get their food from the land, grass, water. So then that's why they call it Mother." The Great Spirit is believed to be the father. It is believed that the land belonged to the Peigan, since they gambled for it with Napi.

Yellowhorn described the spirituality surrounding the medicine pipe ceremony in spring: "They have it early; they used to have it the first time they hear the thunder if it is going to storm. They hear the thunder any time early in spring. Well, they used to have a medicine pipe dance almost the same day they hear the thunder. That's the time they have the big night's prayer, you know. A prayer for the coming of summer and all they ask is to have a good summer and pray for all that, you know." The medicine man for the ceremony is the one who owns the pipe. These pipes can not be replaced. Yellowhorn ended his comments on the spirituality of the Peigan by stressing, "I don't find any evil in the Indian faith."

Mrs Buffalo affirmed that the earth is where life comes from and that many prayers are made for the earth: for example, "Help our earth, our Mother." Prayers were made to wish and hope for others as well as for "our relatives to walk happily on the earth ... We pray to our Mother Earth that we may ever live good and travel in safety and always be happy." Everything that the Indians thought holy came from Mother Earth. Tobacco and berries were used in ceremonies to honour the earth's spirit: "Whenever they offered anything in sacrifice, it went back into the earth."

Siksika Nation

Frankie Turning Robe explained the origins of the Siksika on the land, saying, "At one time we were just put on the land." Societies, said Turning Robe, were the way in which social order was maintained. The pipe was considered to be a most sacred artifact: "No one can just smoke it. We cannot lie when we smoke it." Turning Robe noted that the Siksika "always had a strong and vital religion but that when the missionaries came they called down our religion."

Jim Black also confirmed that the Siksika were not treated with respect by the missionaries and Mounties in whom they had placed their trust: "Our ancestors were a trusting people. They really thought, without the knowledge that [the Mounties] were just police, that they were high officials. And those missionaries – because our ancestors had deep religious beliefs, they really believed that they were heavenly people. That is why they trusted them." But unfortunately the treatment they received from the missionaries "changed all that – the Indians lost that trust."

Stoney Nakoda Nation

Before the White man came, the Indians had everything, said Bill Mclean. Everything was at their disposal, to make a living, to camp anywhere, to use the resources of the land – that was

the aboriginal right of the Stoneys. These rights were not discussed at the treaty. The First Nations had their own systems
of government; they had prophets and elders who had knowledge
of the Creator. They had a long tradition of contact with the
land and respect for it. Spirituality for the Stoneys was bound
up with the land. The Sun Dance was a very religious ceremony:
"In the Sun Dances, they prayed to the Creator and all the creatures, the sun, the wind, the water, and all living things. They
prayed so that they can have a good life, that the future would
be good to them; it was a powerful religion. Unfortunately, the
different church denominations tried to stop it: "They said the
Native people are not praying to God but are praying to the
sun – they condemned it. But they could not squash it. The
Creator helped the Native people."

For Lazarus Wesley the right to hunt was not just a legal right
of the Stoney but was tied to spiritual beliefs about the land.
Rights that were promised were taken away when federal parks
were established and hunting was forbidden.

What they understood was the concept of the government to only turn
the topsoil and to plant seeds. They accepted that because they had
tasted bread and knew how it goes well with other food. They didn't
give away their land just for that either. The government was just allowed to use the land for growing things, not given [it]. This story
has been handed down from the people, not from any documents. The
government gave them hope of good tidings. It said it will not impose
any regulations on the wild game or their hunting.

At that time [1877] nothing was ever mentioned about cutting up
the land here and there into recreational areas and provincial parks,
etc. The government didn't tell them it will eventually be doing this.
It is because of these special areas, we can't go hunting. In the Ka-
nanaskis valley we can't hunt because it is now a park and there are
campgrounds. And at other places, too, that we used to hunt we can't
now. All those areas where we used to hunt are shut off and we can't
go anywhere to hunt. The government says you can hunt. You have
the right to hunt, but there is nowhere to hunt. It would say you can
hunt in your reserve. No one will interfere with you if you hunt there.
That is an argument it uses. The next thing left for it to do is to collect
our guns. It would be better for us to know if this is going to happen.
It is getting so that we can't even shoot a rabbit.

There is one more thing that I just remembered. The government said, "You will be supplied with snare wire, fish tackle like hooks and lines and guns, too. Whoever is the most skilful hunter will be given the gun." The people liked this, to be supplied with the mentioned things.

The Stoneys had always had respect for the land and the life it gave; ceremonies like the Sun Dance showed this:

It is a time for acknowledging their blessings and to give thanks. Just like birds of feather who make nests in the trees and sing their sweet songs, praising the Creator, so do the Indian people. They make a nest in the Sun Dance tree. They think about it as representing the Creator. They see it as a tree of life. It is a family representation and they rejoice at those Sun Dances. They rejoice during the beautiful summer season that they have survived another harsh winter. The Sun Dance was seen in this concept, to give thanks and praise the benevolence of the Creator.

Sweat lodges were used for spiritual purposes even though "the government made fun of our ceremonies, calling us Indian worshippers. It was difficult to continue the ceremonies that were banned and ridiculed." But for the Stoneys these ceremonies not only were part of a long tradition but were also joyous occasions: "I can't condemn my grandparents and say that they worshipped the devil. I can't do that," pronounced Lazarus Wesley.

Summarizing the words of the elders, translator Clarice Kootenay presented the impact of the treaty promises to the present generation: "God put us on earth in North America for us Native people to live here. We were healthy, self-sufficient, and independent people before White people came. But with the coming of the White people, everything has changed, everything has changed for the worse for us, such as their bringing diseases to the country, and we are now living on reserves." The elders described how the Stoneys had their own systems of rights and values and that through oral tradition these rights and values were passed on from generation to generation. Chiefs were chosen from those who were the most resourceful hunters. The Stoneys had their own system of governing and elders were given responsibility to preserve the spiritual concepts and knowledge of the tribes. Honoured people and title holders were given these duties.

Lily Wesley noted the stories about the mistakes Whites made as they "explored" North America, their initial mistaken belief that they had found India and the many problems they had in negotiating the land – they needed the Aboriginal people often in the early years to survive at all. Lily Wesley asserted that on religious matters there was amazing similarity between the teachings of the Christian missionaries and Native beliefs:

Look at how, today, we say the Bible or White people's religion [the beliefs the White people preach] just came recently with the White people, but the same preachings have, long before, been expounded among the Indian people. I am amazed at the similarity of the two preachings – the Indians preachings are the same as the White people's; it is amazing to know that they had already known this ...

It is really amazing to see that what is written in the Bible was already known to the Indian people. The preachings from the New Testament or the Old Testament are the same as those preached by the Indian people before the White people came. The peace pipe can be seen in the same light as we see and understand the Bible's sermon about the staff, "Thy rod and thy staff, they comfort me." What the Indian preached to the men and women, such as to teach respect to others, and how they should live all seemed as if it was taken from the Bible, yet the Bible was not introduced then. The Indian already had been preaching this concept.

Lily Wesley emphasized that there were significant differences between the early Whites and the Stoneys. She said the Stoneys found the Whites to be serious and dour. The Stoneys used the term *wasi ja* – or mourner – to refer to the Europeans with whom they first came into contact. *Wasi ja* also meant a person who was "terrible looking," someone who was covered all over with dirt, unable to take care of himself, a person who had brought a curse on himself. The Whites were also called *wasi ja* because they had beards and moustaches and "very serious faces."

Lily Wesley said that the Stoneys took the treaty seriously; an indication of this was the presence of the pipe at the treaty. But the Whites did not show the same respect for what was contained in the words of the treaty, and instead of honouring the treaty, the government took aboriginal hunting rights away.

We had our rights long before the White people came. Just like the government says our rights come from a legislated policy ... for instance, from the Commonwealth, the Indian people, too, had their own system. They had their system from which to declare their rights to the various aspects of their lives. Yes, our rights were present before the treaties. However, they don't say, "This is yours. You have specific rights to this, etc."

Because the Native people had hunted freely before and have tried to continue that practice, the Fish and Wildlife officials are trying to stop it. The government is now running the country. The White people (ranchers) have said, "I am tired of these Indians hunting everywhere, even discharging firearms on my land. Let's put a stop to this, so they won't be able to hunt anymore or to fish, etc." They are doing this because the government has given them the right to do so. We are put way behind everything.

The spiritual beliefs of the Stoneys all began with the Creator, who gave powers to the animals; these gifts were then passed on to human beings. Each person or leader (such as a chief) would have certain powers – for example, the keeper of the knife, the keeper of the whip, the keeper of the staff, and the keeper of the entrance. Under this system each person had a place, each a specific duty. The Sun Dance was the most sacred ceremony in which powers were bestowed.

God gave them something to believe in and to preach. The prayers were seen as very sacred and were respected very much. In the past the Sun Dance was a very sacred concept. The handling of Indian medicine, too, was very sacred and holy. There is a thing called *charh ga moobi* (pot drum). It is a large pot filled with Indian medicinal herbs, and stretched over it and let to dry is a rawhide. When it is beaten with a drumstick, you could hear that it is spirited by its loud sound that it is able to give. In those days these things were not missed in any way. They were guarded, not just anybody can approach them. The very young girls, especially, were kept far away from them.

The Sun Dance was very sacred. If the person making the Sun Dance makes the entrance towards the south, that person is praying to the sun. If the entrance is towards the sunrise, he/she is praying to the day [weather]. If the entrance is towards the sunset, he/she is praying to the sunset, giving thanks for the day it provided. Never has there been an entrance made towards the north. The Sun Dance tree is called "tree of life" just like it says in the Bible there is a tree of life. The Indian knew the concept of the tree of life before being exposed to the Bible. The nest made in the Sun Dance tree symbolizes a family. A woman who has been a very good wife, who always respected her husband, and who never played around behind her husband's back was given the honour to make the nest in the Sun Dance tree.

In those days the Sun Dance was a very sacred and a very honoured concept of the Indian people. God gave the Indian people a very powerful guiding belief with which to guide itself.

Other significant sacred ceremonies were related to the rattle owners:

The "rattle" is also very sacred and highly regarded. The "woman rattle" was respected very much. A woman who possesses one is treated with great respect. If there is such a woman in the presence of people, the people would caution each other: "Beware. Don't go near her." The women were highly respected. Women who have the rattle do not give it to anybody. These women were respected by all. A person who has a rattle respects her. A person who can put on a Sun Dance respects her. They were respected very much ... not just anybody can take or hold the rattle. Only a person who has a song(s) given to him by the spirits can do so, but he cannot own the rattle.

These things I have mentioned were very sacred and powerful entities of the Indian people until the Indian held the pencil. From then on these things have faded away from his life. Presently I wonder what it's like, the concept of Indian religion, of how it is being performed. The Indian people should revise this practice again, and respect it, and not play with it like a toy. Respect your Sun Dance. Only those who are given the gift to hold a Sun Dance should put one on, and only one should be performed yearly. These are my thoughts now of the Indian religion.

Spiritual beliefs pervaded every facet of Stoney life, and people with special powers would be called upon to help out in times of need. This practice was described by Joe Brown:

What I am telling you has been told to me before. Back then special powers were used to survive ... The gifted people would tell the people where to go for winter camps and this is how they survived ... like today they have satellite dishes to tell the weather ... in the same way the people before would use the powers by gathering gifted people and asking them to pray for the knowledge of where the buffalo would be ... If you were chosen to go to look for the food then you would go ... To depend on each other was the Indian law ... If one man got a kill then the whole camp or tribe would share ... today the White man has taught us to look after only ourselves.

George Ear also spoke about the traditional spirituality of the Stoney people: "The Great Spirit created the sun, stars, universe, human beings." Gifted people were then empowered by the spirits of the animals. Those with power could predict; they could tell when the cold weather was coming. These people would also tell the camp about visions. One vision told of a white god who would come, so when the White man came, some Stoneys threw away their bundles and converted to Christianity.

An elected leader of the Stoneys, Chief John Snow, said that the Whites who came in contact with Native spiritual beliefs had a fundamental disrespect for them. Whereas Indians trusted the Whites and thought they were honest, the "Whites thought of us as savages and did not respect our people. They thought they were dumb animals." Snow, who was an ordained Christian minister and also believed in "Indian ways," contended that "missionaries lied and cheated ... They criticized the Indian beliefs in the Great Spirit." The Stoneys believed that the earth was created in a way that would allow each ecosystem and each animal to survive. The Creator taught the Indian how to make a living on earth with all his creations. The Stoneys in return gave thanks with sweetgrass offerings and through other ceremonies. The Sun Dance, which was criticized by White missionaries as being a heathen form of worship, is an example: "White people think the Sun Dance is a ritual praising the sun god. But the Indian is praying to the god who created the sun." With its light the sun gives strength to everything that has grown on earth, and it gives heat to make us warm. Snow said that the Whites did not respect Indian beliefs or aboriginal rights and that fundamental to these rights was the right to hunt. These rights originated a long time ago, long before the Whites arrived. Unfortunately, "the White race has been working to overpower the Indian all along. This is especially the case when denying the Indians the right to hunt where they might choose to, to respect their aboriginal right."

Tsuu T'ina Nation

According to Hilda Big Crow, the Tsuu T'ina believed that land was owned by all. Tom Heavenfire said, "Land was to be shared by all and from this flowed the fundamental law [to] respect all things and everybody around." The earth was honoured through different ceremonies and societies and with dances like the Sun Dance, Ghost Dance, Tea Dance, and Women Round Dance. As Helen Meguinis put it, "Mother Earth was very sacred; we didn't chop down trees if we weren't going to use [them]." Land was sacred because the Great Spirit gave us the land.

Leaders of the Tsuu T'ina were elected by elders on the basis of bravery or success in the buffalo hunt and also on the basis of how they lived and the kind of knowledge they possessed that would help their people. These leaders worked in the community to help people from doing wrong.

Social organization was based on clans and societies. The Tall Hats Society had responsibility for powwows, the Shell for peacekeeping, and the Prairie Chickens for dancing. Like the clans, some societies had bundles like the beaver bundle or medicine pipe bundle. An act of bravery was required to enter some societies. The rules of these societies operated around the belief that you had to be honest with yourself in all things. Spiritual values were passed on in societies, and functions such as naming children were handled by them as well. Clans functioned on the authority of the leaders of extended families, whose decisions had to be respected. Some of the clans were the Middle House, Big Plume, Big Belly, Starlight, Big Knife, and Crowchild. Celebrations would be accompanied by feasts for the clan members.

The Pipe Society was responsible for law and order and peacemaking. Crimes were usually punished individually, with specific breaches having a given punishment – a cut nose for adultery, for example.

The last Sun Dance was held in 1892. The Tsuu T'ina still

have two bundles, the beaver bundle and the medicine pipe bundle. "At the first sound of thunder we take them out and pray with them and also at the going out of the thunder," explained Meguinis. "The Sun Dance was stopped because the missionaries intervened and said that it was too cruel to us and that we were not animals to be practising this type of cruelty to ourselves."

Helen Meguinis felt that many of the customs and traditions that the Tsuu T'ina had had in earlier times were eroded by the treaty. The right to go anywhere, for example, was limited by the Indian Act legislation.

LAND USE AND WAY OF LIFE

The First Nations that entered Treaty 7 found that their territory was now restricted to a small core of the land base they had used for the decades before the treaty. Both the Stoneys and the Blackfoot had often moved as far north as the North Saskatchewan River, as far east as Battleford, and beyond the Cypress Hills to the south. The Peigan, Bloods, and Tsuu T'ina had frequently camped in territory far to the south of the 49th parallel. This freedom of movement was now curtailed. Their survival in the prairie environment, their way of life, and their economies, whether for subsistence or for harvesting the land to acquire trade goods, were dependent on the flora and fauna of the land. Their movements thus followed the seasonal cycles. However, the presence or absence of game affected their ability to hunt and move through the prairie and foothills country. Trade patterns changed over the years as old alliances fell apart and new ones were forged. The whiskey trade also had significant consequences for tribes trading throughout Whoop-Up Country, especially in the years immediately preceding the making of Treaty 7. The economic rights of the First Nations that entered Treaty 7 had been established over many hundreds of years as the peoples moved over the land in patterns that the prairie habitat allowed.

Blood Tribe

Wallace Mountain Horse noted that the Bloods used the land from the Red Deer River to the Yellowstone River. The Bloods relied on berries and meat as their staples: "As the buffalo moved more southerly, we moved with them." Mountain Horse remembered being told of the dogs that were used for transportation and of the fur trade that provided opportunities to purchase many kinds of goods such as "pots, dishes, forks, utensils, buckets that made our lives better." But of the trade that brought alcohol to the Bloods, Mountain Horse said, "The main weapon to make friends with the Native people was to use firewater." Sadly, "life worsened after whiskey was imposed upon us" in the Whoop-Up Country era.

"Hunting was our heritage," said Dick Nice Cutter. "Everything we kill we use it all." Even the feathers were used for decoration. There were no restrictions on hunting. Nice Cutter also remembered stories about wars between the Bloods and the Cree over the territory of the diminishing buffalo herds. He said that in the early reserve years the economies changed: people grazed horses and cattle, there were good gardens of potatoes and pumpkins, and a variety of crops were harvested by sickles and threshed by hand. But in the early reserve years there were still "no restrictions on hunting."

Pete Standing Alone recalled the importance of berries and how they "stored berries for [the] long winter." The ethic of using only what was necessary prevailed in every aspect of life for the Bloods. Standing Alone also told of how the Bloods went to war to protect their territory from the Crow and Cree people.

Peigan Nation

Among the most important uses of land, according to Davis Crow Eagle, were the annual trips to get paint at Crow Eagle reserve. This paint was used for ceremonial purposes and Crow Eagle's memory of it was vivid enough that he was able to draw a map of exactly where the paint was found.

Ray Cross Child had many memories of his own experiences on the land and he could also remember the stories of others that were told to him over the years. Traditionally, the Peigan moved across the prairie following the buffalo, but when they were in critical need, even the lowly gopher became a source of food. Buffalo dung was used for fuel, and occasionally buffalo were run over cliffs in a buffalo drive. People would bury the buffalo bones and return later to eat the marrow. Buffalo hides were used for clothing and tents. People were able to live off the buffalo exclusively for a long period of time, but the establishment of the US border began to restrict access to the buffalo. Cross Child remembered being told the story of a man who had a dream about the scarcity of the buffalo - in the dream the man prophesied what would actually happen.

Prior to the horse, people moved about with dog travois. In winter the Peigan gravitated to the protection of river valleys. Along the river bottoms they were able to pursue deer with the bow and arrow as well as with the gun. Cross Child remembered in more recent times people being unable to hunt properly for food because of disease and inadequate, sometimes poisoned, rations. As well, he said, "alcohol made people die early."

Louise English recollected that much of the work done by Peigan women involved hauling water and cutting trees for wood. In the early reserve days they worked hard at tending gardens. A cow was slaughtered every Tuesday, which traditionally was ration day. In winter they worked at cutting fence posts, which were then sold to neighbouring ranchers. She fondly reminisced about the annual trips to get paint from the Crow Eagle reserve.

Elsie Crow Shoe had detailed memories about the economies of the Peigan: "Buffalo were the prime sources of life." She recalled that the women made the travois when it was time to move and that dogs were still used extensively. Buffalo and berries were the staples, while moose and elk were hunted when necessary. These latter were pursued more than deer. The Peigan hunted over a wide territory: "Our land was along the Oldman River and Porcupine Hills (they look like a porcupine) ... We used water and wood at Waterton Lakes, especially in wintertime."

The fur trade remained important for the Peigan. Elsie Crow Shoe noted that it "took them four days to get to Edmonton." Each year they bought supplies to last for the winter. They traded for tobacco and "necessaries." The traders of Edmonton were especially interested in hides. She alleged that the traders cheated the Peigan in this trade. Some of the Peigan worked for the NWMP in the early years, and "all they got in return was vegetables."

The enemies of the Peigan were the Crow people from Montana, who would often be found around Writing-on-Stone. They also fought with the Flathead people further to the south. Crow Shoe said that in winter her people would try to stay close to the buffalo. They camped "near Oldman River some winters, where wood and water was easily accessible."

Nick Smith recalled that trapping was his main source of income and that he spent most of the rest of his time hunting for food. He also worked on the reserve "for hire" and as a range rider, though he "never had an opportunity for long-term employment." But Smith remembered many stories about the past when the main staple for survival was the buffalo and when homes were made of tanned hides, berries were picked, and wild turnips were harvested. In winter children were dipped in hot springs. Life on the plains and along the foothills was difficult, and moving camp had to be given careful consideration.

Smith had known the time when people dug up buffalo bones to sell. He attested to the destructiveness of alcohol in the time when people would buy whiskey with the furs and hides. Smith said that it was "the traders who first put alcohol among the Native people." Sometimes children were not taken care of because of drinking. Smith identified the many social ills that accompanied alcohol: "Many Native people went to jail because of drinking – it was used to imprison Native people. That's the way the White man was ... There were many fatalities because of drinking ... We had to suffer with drinking just like the White man ... The alcohol we used has shortened all our lives ... People do not find partners because of drinking." All kinds of sickness came from contact with the White man and weakened the ability of Aboriginal people to cope.

Fred North Peigan recalled the trips to Crow Eagle reserve to get paint, which would be used like a "sunscreen."

Cecile Many Guns remembered that a chief at the time of the treaty took the Peigan to the Porcupine Hills so that they could be close to the timber that they had traditionally relied on from the surrounding hills. She noted that it was Jerry Potts who told the Peigan to take the land at the Porcupine Hills because of the good hunting there. Many Guns said that southeast of Pincher Creek lay "our main camping ground; we cut hay there and hauled water from the creek." There were times when the travois was still used.

The buffalo hunt was the major activity for the Peigan and

buffalo rocks were used for good luck in the hunt. Many of the stories about the buffalo hunt remain an important part of Peigan culture.

Tom Yellowhorn explained the significance of the Napi story as it relates to Peigan land and land use. Napi was interested in the land east of the Great Divide because he wanted land that was rich in fish, deer, elk, and buffalo. But Napi lost the land west of the mountains when he was defeated by the Kootenay in the ring game, but he was able to save the land east of the Rochios. After he lost the game, the Kootenay people never came across the mountains. This gave the Peigan the right to the land, for as Yellowhorn stated, "We know what the claim means." Yellowhorn recollected that his father still hunted the buffalo and lived from hunting after wild game. But the buffalo disappeared "because of the mass killing in the States." The Canadian authorities were complicit in this, according to Yellowhorn, for the "Canadian government agreed to kill buffalo off so that Indians would have no livelihood. The two governments agreed to try to kill off all the buffalo."

Yellowhorn noted that Whites also cleared the fish from all the rivers "just for sport, not really to eat." But the buffalo were really the best staple to live on, and after they were gone, the Peigan had to rely more on moose and elk for meat. Before the treaty was signed, there was a lot of whiskey trading throughout Peigan territory; furs and hides in particular were traded for whiskey.

Yellowhorn attested to the devastation of diseases at the time: "Many people died in the smallpox epidemic ... So many died they couldn't all be buried ... Also the black locust plague eating everything."

The buffalo were the staple for the Peigan according to Sally Provost. She recalled stories about the importance of buffalo jumps before the arrival of the horse: "Whole camps moved all over to hunt" even after the treaty. Everyone worked and adjusted in order to survive after the treaty: "Everyone did like cow meat when the buffalo was gone."

Women were always busy tanning hides. These hides were then taken to Edmonton to trade. On a number of occasions the Peigan fought with the Cree as they made their way to Edmonton. Dry goods, pots, knives, and axes were traded for furs and hides. Whiskey was also traded and this resulted in "a lot of killing among the Indians ... The White man just brought the liquor here – 100 percent strong stuff." Sally Provost declared: "It was good the government restricted the whiskey trade." She also recalled the devastation of disease: "Epidemics just about killed all our people ... Smallpox was real bad."

Mrs Buffalo noted that "our ancestors depended on the buffalo for everything, living and shelter ... When the buffalo disappeared the White man gave us cattle." The fur trade was a major economic activity. The furs were brought in by the men and tanned by the women. The hides and furs were then taken to Edmonton and traded for food and clothing, but "no money was given out." Eventually furs were also used to buy whiskey. Smallpox struck after the treaty was signed, said Mrs Buffalo: "Across the river from Macleod east ... some of the tipis were empty, no one was living in them. Sometimes all the people from one tipi were wiped out by smallpox. They were struck really bad."

Tom Yellowhorn recalled the economy of the whiskey-trade days. More peaceful times followed, and the Peigan were told "the Red Coats will look after you, they will clean up the whiskey traders ... They will protect you from the wrongs these whiskey traders are committing against your people."

Before the days of Whoop-Up Country, trading posts existed in the present-day locations of Edmonton, Calgary, Lethbridge, Fort Macleod, and Pincher Creek. "We did most of our trading with HBC [Hudson's Bay Company]. That is why they were so rich, because of the way they cheated the Indians," said Yellowhorn. Pincher Creek at one time was the post closest to the Peigan: "When the Indian realized the value of money the HBC pulled out of Fort Macleod, Lethbridge, and Pincher Creek, they found out they could no longer cheat the Indian ... They got rich off the Indian ... The HBC not only cheated the Indians but took their land and sold it." Many Peigan who did not know about the value of money were cheated by these unscrupulous traders.

Yellowhorn described the hardship brought on the Peigan with the reduced buffalo herds: "White people killed off all the buffalo ... White people and the half-breeds ... Indians never killed more buffalo than they needed ... Indians killed a buffalo and used almost everything from it." Then the women undertook the hard work of preparing the hides before they were taken to the HBC post. When the buffalo were killed off, the Peigan subsisted on cattle—but at first not all of them liked beef. "We were told our way of getting food and medicine had to change." Yellowhorn also remembered his father describing the epidemics that swept through the Peigan in 1860 and also in 1868–69 prior to the treaty: "There were many people who died. I think the Indian people got smallpox because they were no longer strong; they were eating White man's food." It is estimated that as many as a third to a half of the Blackfoot people died in the 1869–70 epidemic reported by Captain William Butler, including several important chiefs and leaders.

Siksika Nation

The members of the Siksika Nation also remembered the days of the fur trade. Augustine Yellow Sun told of trading with "reddish hair," which was how they referred to the traders: "We called the trading 'bush buying' because we had to go north to the bush country to trade – the bush around Edmonton or Big House ... We floated the skins across the river and exchanged goods for hides; there was no metal money." Yellow Sun stated that money was not understood. It took a long time to get to the fort, and the trade usually took place in spring. The main items gained from the trade were blankets, tobacco, ammunition, and gunpowder. On some occasions if you needed ammunition badly enough, it would be given out on credit.

Elder Margaret Bad Boy explained that the seasonal cycle for her people included going to land near Banff surrounding Castle Mountain. Here the Siksika traditionally hunted and trapped, and after the treaty was signed, they used this area to cut timber for building and also for firewood. Logs would be floated downriver. Bad Boy said that this land was never surrendered by the Siksika and that the government acknowledged this pattern of land use by the Siksika but never set aside this land for them. Beatrice Poor Eagle added: "Families would go up there and camp while the men would cut the logs and mark them each for themselves. The women would make tipi linings while they were there and took care of the cooking. The men would then throw the logs into the Bow River and push them downriver. We would camp alongside of the river and keep pushing the logs where they would clog up. At one of these times when our families went there to camp, a herd of horses went across the railroad track. One of the women went across the tracks to fetch the horses when a train came by and ran over her."

Finding the means to make money was always difficult. George Crowchief remembered that for a time in the early years the Siksika would cut logs and float them east to build houses until they were told "not to do that" by the authorities.

Siksika, like other Blackfoot people, recalled the difficult times during the days of Whoop-Up Country when their numbers were dramatically thinned. According to Frankie Turning Robe, "they signed the treaty because the whiskey trade was killing so many people."

Beatrice Poor Eagle remembered areas being used for specific ceremonies: "In early spring holy tobacco was grown. It was a big celebration and a sacred event. Everyone from all over would come – from the Blackfeet in Browning, Kainai [Bloods], and Peigans, along with Siksika. Where it was grown is around the Bassano area. It took four days to plant and then the ceremonial branches are taken by two warriors and they would take them on their horses and ride away as fast as they can and never stopping or looking back at the camp. When ceremonial branches start to break, they stop and camp until the rest of the camp reaches them and then would all go home to their camp."

Stoney Nakoda Nation

Land use by the Stoneys differed somewhat from that of the other Plains tribes in that they hunted more often in the mountains, but they too suffered when the buffalo declined, as they had always relied on their coming north onto their lands. Bill Mclean recalled stories about the chiefs' deliberations at Blackfoot Crossing:

They say a Blood chief refused to make the treaty. He said, "Our land will be taken away from us. Let's kill them all instead." However, the other chiefs said, "No, let's make the peace treaty instead. Then all this killing amongst ourselves will be put to an end. At the same time our tribal wars are depleting us; the White people are scheming to starve us – to let us go hungry. They are killing off all the buffalo. This is

how they will make us go hungry. Along with their killing of the buffalo, they have brought firewater; and with it, the firewater is in their
scheme of things for us to die off."

That is also why they went for the treaty, so that liquor will not
be made available to the Natives. That was what was said by the other
chiefs. For those reasons, to have peace amongst themselves, to end
tribal wars, and to prohibit liquor to Natives, they conceptualized that
the treaty was a peace treaty.

At the treaty talks, the White people brought their pre-written treaty
document fully understanding the terms in it. But on the other hand,
at that time, the Native people did not know anything about such things.
For this reason (lack of understanding of the foreign language, written
or spoken), interpreters were not proficient to fully comprehend legal
wordings to interpret them properly. All they did was to interpret only
parts of the wordings. But on the other hand, the government people
were well versed in the legal jargon used. On the contrary, the interpreters did not understand the legal jargon. For us Stoneys, we didn't
have an interpreter. Only John McDougall was there for the Stoneys.
They say he only knew a limited vocabulary of Cree, not very well
versed in that language. So all he did, they say, was to try and relate
only some part of the treaty terms in Cree to the Stoneys. That was
all he could do. He did not give a full explanation of the implications
of the legal wordings because he could not.

Lazarus Wesley told stories from the days of the buffalo hunt.
He spoke of Bearspaw's renown as a good buffalo hunter as well
as the tradition of sharing the hunt with all the band members.
Wesley lamented the ending of the days of the unrestricted hunt,
saying that at the treaty the government said that "the fish and
buffalo were ours." But now "it's getting so we can't even shoot
a rabbit ... our major right was to hunt but we lost that right."
Wesley remembered the trade days when trips were made to Edmonton where lynx, coyote, weasel, and other furs were traded
for guns.

Traditionally the Stoneys used the Morleyville area primarily
as a wintering site and not as a place of year-round residence.
Lawrence Ear said that after wintering in the territory around
Morleyville the bands "split up to hunt over a wide territory."
He also recalled being told about the horrors of the Whoop-
Up Country days when the Stoneys were "poisoned because

Americans added things to the whiskey ... Indians were destroyed by alcohol."

Bighorn reserve elder John Abraham told of the Stoneys who used the Kootenay Plains as a place of refuge and a place to go to die. These people were called Mountain People, and they inhabited these areas since the days of the "dog pack," prior to the mid-eighteenth century.

The difficult existence during the Whoop-Up Country days in the 1870s surfaced again and again in the stories of the Stoney elders. John Snow related how the Americans brought whiskey to the Indians and how the Indians traded their hides for liquor: "Some got drunk and gave things away." Others were poisoned by the alcohol "because the Americans added things to the whiskey ... It was during this time that the Indians suffered a great deal."

Morley Twoyoungmen recalled stories about the use of the land before the reserve era: "Even in hard winter they managed to survive and hunt for furs ... hunting for cats and other animals around Kootenay Plains." Twoyoungmen ironically reflected on the arrogance of some Europeans who came to claim the land of the Stoney: "I did not go over the ocean to claim his land."

George Ear had vivid memories of a time when the Stoney people hunted big game, a time when they used rawhide sleighs to haul goods in the mountains with dog travois and wore clothing made of fur and rawhide pelts. Wild berries were a major source of food and were stored for use during the winter months, as were dried meat, pemmican, and animal fat. For some the diet was more varied and included wild herbs, potatoes, onions and turnip. Fishing also helped the Stoneys vary the basic diet of meat and berries. Ear spoke fondly of the taste of wild potatoes baked in animal fat. But he lamented the days when buffalo were slaughtered wantonly and the times of disease: "White people brought sickness into this great land – especially the epidemic – sickness reduced the Stoney people."

Tom Labelle related the stories of pre-treaty days when the Stoneys competed with other tribes for access to fur-trading posts: "As soon as the enemies cleared out, others made approaches to the post." The Stoneys traded for ammunition, tobacco, and necessaries. He remembered that the HBC built a fort on the Bow River in 1832, but after Old Bow Fort was burned down, the company retreated to Rocky Mountain House and Edmonton. Labelle remembered stories about the many battles between the Stoneys and the Cree over the years before they made peace alliances.

The Stoneys made use of the local Saskatoon bushes in different ways. Labelle stated that branches of these bushes were used to make bows and arrows. The bushes were also a source of food.

Tsuu T'ina Nation

The Tsuu T'ina told of a similar pattern of land use for their people prior to Treaty 7. Hilda Big Crow spoke of the fur trade in beaver, bobcat, and coyote furs. These were taken to Edmonton to be traded. The Tsuu T'ina subsisted on a diet of rabbit, deer, and beaver as well as roots and berries. Finally, the Tsuu T'ina elders told of the days of the whiskey trade and the sickness brought by Europeans.

Edward Gingold described the days of the buffalo hunt and the pursuit of elk. These staples of the Tsuu T'ina were supplemented by berries, many of which were stored for consumption in winter. The conservation ethic was strong among the Tsuu T'ina. They "killed only a certain amount, never any waste."

Tom Heavenfire remarked on the importance of trapping. The furs and hides were used for clothing and tipis. He too spoke about the sacred ceremonies where offerings were made to the earth to remind his people that nothing should be wasted: "What they had to offer back to the Creator was some of the things that belonged to the animal too."

In their use of the land, the Tsuu T'ina, according to Helen Meguinis, would follow the rivers "because the buffalo have to drink from the water." Buffalo were killed for food and clothing; the meat was dried for winter use. There was not much fishing but berries in season were an important food source. Herbs, roots, and leaves were used medicinally and for food.

The Tsuu T'ina planted their own tobacco for use in the Sun Dances. The sacredness of the land affected the way the Tsuu T'ina used the land. As the tribe moved across their territory, said Helen Meguinis, the land was always respected: "You didn't take anything you didn't use. You didn't chop down a tree if

you weren't going to use it – even the leaves had spirits ... Mother
Earth was very sacred."

Helen Meguinis explained the story of the origin of the Tsuu
T'ina who entered Treaty 7:

Originally the Tsuu T'ina were part of the Dene Nation from the
North. We broke away from them a long time ago but not intentionally.
The story goes that the Dene wanted to migrate to the south. It was
during the winter when they began to migrate because all the lakes
and rivers were frozen. They were crossing this one river when a little
boy, carried by his mother on her back, began to cry for this set of
antlers that was sticking out of the frozen water. His mother agreed
and started to pound the ice with her hatchet. When she was doing
this, she did not realize that the ice was cracking behind her. Finally,
the ice cracked and gave way. She barely made it across to the other
side of the river where many of her people were. The rest of the others
were left behind and are now the present Dene of the North. Part
of the Tsuu T'ina people stayed on the prairies and the rest kept migrating south. These are the Navahos and the Apaches. When the Nav-
aho die, they bury their people with their feet facing north, so that
they can be reborn in the place where they originally came from.

INTERNATIONAL RELATIONS

Treaty making had long been a way of life for the prairie First
Nations, both through treaties signed among one another and
through treaties signed with European colonizers. Many of the
treaties between Aboriginal peoples of North America were related to the shifting alliances that came about as a result of various kinds of trade pacts and the new trade in European goods,
especially the gun. The introduction of the horse also led to shifting alliances, as various tribes manoeuvred to get access to the
horse. The Blackfoot made various alliances over the years to
keep their central position close to the buffalo herds. As the buffalo herds diminished, there was increasing conflict among those
tribes that wanted to maintain their access to the main staple
of so many of the Plains First Nations.

The Lame Bull Treaty (1855) and Jay's Treaty (1794) were two
of the most important treaties entered into by the Treaty 7 First
Nations and non-Aboriginal governments. Jay's Treaty was spe-

cifically intended to allow First Nations people the freedom to move across borders, and the Lame Bull Treaty was a peace treaty with Plains people that would allow White Americans to build railroads and maintain other transportation systems across territories where there were still very few settlers.

It was this tradition of treaty making that the Blackfoot were familiar with and that no doubt influenced how they understood Treaty 7.

Blood Tribe

Rosie Red Crow and Fred Gladstone emphasized that Jay's Treaty was an international boundary agreement that guaranteed free crossing of the border. The significance of Jay's Treaty to Gladstone was that it created an international boundary that guaranteed the Blackfoot access to their territory to the south.

The Lame Bull Treaty differed from Treaty 7 in that the Americans signed it when they were in a position of weakness on the American plains. If they had gone to war with the tribes of the American West in the 1850s, they would most certainly have been defeated. They needed a peace treaty to allow for passage across this territory. According to Gladstone, "The tribes that were dealt with at the time were more numerous in number and outnumbered the number in the army of the United States government. They were afraid of dealing with them. That is why the Lame Bull Treaty was signed." Louise Crop Eared Wolf stated: "I heard at Lame Bull Treaty the US government was very generous with its material possessions given out to those in attendance. The Indian women could hardly carry the bundle of blankets given to them." But this didn't last long. Only a few years after the treaty was made, the US government began to mistreat the Blackfoot peoples and ignored its treaty promises.

Peigan Nation

The Peigan remembered treaties being made with Indians of the plains, in particular treaties having to do with getting access to the buffalo. They viewed, for example, their conflict with Napi as having been resolved by a treaty that kept the Kootenay people on the other side of the mountains.

Sally Provost was one of the Peigan with stories about the signing of the Lame Bull Treaty: "At first we belonged to the United States. We used to put up councillors like men from down [there]. They used to give them rations, clothing, and I never did hear if they got any money. And we were all in one; [the] States used to look after us. Give us rations and clothing. And lately, these Canadians on this side, they cheat us really bad."

Siksika Nation

Augustine Yellow Sun remembered that the people who lived on the east side of the Siksika reserve were people from the United States. They received treaty payments around Yellowstone as a result of the signing of the Lame Bull Treaty. They received money and rations at the US "Many Houses."

It was Crowfoot who persuaded these Siksika to come to Canada from territory in the United States, since Canada was going to sign a treaty like Lame Bull with the Aboriginal nations in Canadian territory. There would be benefits just as there had been with the American treaty. Crowfoot told his people: "We are going to be fed. All we have to do is count our fingers for each passing day to our next food ration."

Stoney Nakoda Nation

The Stoneys made numerous treaties with neighbouring tribes over the years, especially with the Cree. The Stoney and Cree peoples were traditional enemies of the Blackfoot Confederacy. The clans would look for opportunities to steal horses and would watch for intruders into their hunting grounds. Occasionally one group would attack the other. The last full-scale battle between the Cree and Stoney-Assiniboin nations and the Blackfoot tribes took place in the early 1870s along the banks of the Oldman River where Indian Battle Park is now located in Lethbridge.

CHAPTER THREE

The First Nations' Perspective on Treaty 7

WHAT DID TREATY 7 MEAN TO THE FIRST NATIONS?

The leaders who accepted Treaty 7 believed that it was first and foremost a peace treaty. All the Treaty 7 First Nations were unanimous on this point: that through the agreement with the British Crown and the Canadian representatives, the First Nations would cease to war among themselves and that peace would be preserved between the First Nations and the Canadian authorities. Peace and order were essential for the protection of the settler populations that were to be ushered onto the prairies under various schemes initiated within the framework of John A. Macdonald's National Policy. The resulting stability in the newcomer settlements would help to realize the agricultural potential of the West that so many central Canadian explorers and politicians had desired. To some degree the peace process had already been set in motion with the arrival of the North-West Mounted Police in southern Alberta in 1874–75. Their presence and the stability they were able to establish by stopping the whiskey trade were much appreciated by the First Nations people of southern Alberta. Indeed, some historians say that Colonel Macleod became somewhat of a hero among the Blackfoot Confederacy for the authority he was able to establish in the aftermath of clearing Whoop-Up Country of the outlaw traders who had generated so much of the violence that had plagued the territory for the previous decade.

In fact, from the point of view of the elders, it was above all a peace treaty that the Canadian government had desired for this territory. Peace had not been of central importance in the other prairie treaties. The First Nations genuinely appreciated the peace and stability that was brought to the southern territory of the Canadian plains. In return, the First Nations agreed to end hostilities among themselves, promising not to interfere with the peaceful settlement of the newcomer agriculturalists who had been arriving to share the land. There was nothing said among the elders about this peace being in any way linked to giving up land; rather they viewed the peace as being of benefit to all the groups agreeing to the treaty.

In the view of the government, the most significant part of the written treaty involved the surrender of land – not peace. However, peace must have been prominent in the minds of the commissioners who set out to sign Treaty 7, since the tribes of southern Alberta, having had the least contact of any Aboriginal peoples with settler society up to this point, were thought to be a serious threat to settlement. This fact was most trenchantly underlined by Father Scollen's letter warning the treaty commissioners that these southern Alberta nations were the most "warlike" on the plains. Scollen and others were also concerned about the potential alliance between Sitting Bull's Lakota at Wood Mountain and the tribes of the Blackfoot Confederacy. Thus, it was the Canadian officials, perhaps more so than the First Nations attending the talks, who wanted to be assured of peace and who raised the issue specifically during the treaty discussions. Certainly they wanted to avoid other international incidents like the one precipitated by the arrival of Sitting Bull or the crisis produced by the Cypress Hills Massacre of 1873.

The First Nations at Blackfoot Crossing were very familiar with the treaty process. Indeed, a number of Blackfoot chiefs had signed the Lame Bull Treaty of 1855, which allowed road development into the West in return for peace with the tribes across the American plains and promised payments to those who signed. This treaty was not understood to be a land surrender but rather a peace treaty, and the tribes at the time were left to move freely over rather large territories. However, the nature of the peace agreed to under Treaty 7 was understood in different ways by the First Nations. Each nation's interpretation of the treaty – just what the peace was to achieve, and who was to benefit – depended on the historical situation that each found itself in at the treaty signing.

The Stoneys, traditional enemies of the other four nations that accepted the treaty, believed that peace meant that they would no longer be fighting with nations of the Blackfoot Confederacy and the other First Nations to whom they had been hostile at various times in the past. As understood by members of the Blackfoot-speaking nations, peace meant not only the kind of peace they enjoyed in the American territories into which their hunting territory still extended, but also the cessation of hostilities with the Stoneys and Cree, and the prohibition of the whiskey trade. But aside from these slight differences in perception, what is clear is that all the First Nations understood the agreement reached at Blackfoot Crossing to be first and foremost a peace treaty. Secondarily, it represented their agreement to share the land and its resources with the newcomers in return for a variety of compensation benefits understood to be their "treaty rights" or "treaty promises."

Blood Tribe

According to Pete Standing Alone, the Blood word for treaty, *innaihtsiini*, means that two sides must "achieve a common purpose." A treaty had to be approached with care and caution. One tried not to be aggressive when negotiating a treaty, as it was a serious undertaking and the consequence of failure might be too great. It was therefore with much gravity that Treaty 7 was pursued. Various interpretive language was used by the Blood elders to describe what the treaty meant to them and their ancestors. Fred Gladstone said that a treaty meant having peace between peoples or tribes; it was a "negotiation between two peoples." Rosie Red Crow indicated that the treaty meant that "we all agreed to be on friendly terms." Wallace Mountain Horse described the treaty process as it had affected the Bloods when they made treaty with both the Cree and the Crow peoples at various times in his memory. He reiterated that the treaty meant an agreement "not to fight anymore." Mountain Horse also discussed the significance of the role of the North-West Mounted Police in pacifying the territory of southern Alberta; this was seen as an important achievement by the Bloods. However, he lamented the fact that the recording of what was said about peace was one-sided, leaving it to look as though the land surrender was the most important issue discussed when in fact for the

Bloods peace was most important. Louise Crop Eared Wolf said that the fundamental beliefs of the Bloods would not have allowed them to give away the land: "We believed and understood [that we would] share this territory amongst each other and we also believed that the land could not be given away because of its sacredness; therefore, it did not belong to us or anybody else. The earth is just put there by our creator for only our benefit and use."

Adam Delaney stressed that surrendering land is a concept foreign to the Bloods. Treaties can be made in three situations. Payments are made between in-laws when couples marry; payments can be made between spiritual persons to break a taboo; and finally, treaties are made between nations or tribes to signify peace and friendship or to end wars.

To illustrate the Blood understanding of what happened at Blackfoot Crossing, Louise Crop Eared Wolf related the story of Red Crow: "At the signing of the treaty at Blackfoot Crossing, Red Crow pulled out the grass and gave it to the White officials and informed them that they will share the grass of the earth with them. Then he took some dirt from the earth and informed them that they could not share this part of the earth and what was underneath it, because it was put there by the Creator for the Indians' benefit and use."

Peigan Nation

According to John Yellowhorn, it was the government that wanted the peace treaty, and it was at the government's initiative that the negotiations commenced. People were told that "they would have a much better life if they made the treaty." The reoccurring theme of peace was stated rather differently by Sally Provost: "It's a sign of peace to say we accept the treaty ... they were just promising and promising, and we were going to get help for the rest of time." That was how important peace appeared to be for the government. Sally Provost also mentioned that the government wanted peace in order to "civilize the Indians." Nick Smith remembered that the main purpose of the treaty was that "we will make peace here with everyone." The "Queen's representatives will make laws for us." Unfortunately, these laws were used "to control us," and the peace that was

sued for under the guise of the government "caring for" the
First Nations was instead used to restrict and control them. The
peace meant that the First Nations' way of life would be changed,
for the officials told them, "These are the laws you will abide
by." Hugh Crow Eagle remembered his grandfather saying that
the treaty was for peace and friendship, "not only with the White
man but also with all other tribes that we may have been fighting."

The North-West Mounted Police were considered significant
not only for their past service in driving out the whiskey traders
but also for enforcing the new laws that were established. Peace
would be more complicated than simply not fighting: "You will
no longer live the way you were used to. You will be taken care
of by the Queen and her representatives. She sent them here.
The Red Coat was sent here to watch and take care of you.
We will make peace with everyone and we will live in harmony
with one another."

For Cecile Many Guns, to make peace meant "no more fighting
between anyone, everybody will be friends, everybody will be
in peace." Tom Yellowhorn noted with disappointment that the
Peigan's initial enthusiasm for the peace treaty grew into bit-
terness when the seriousness with which they took the agreement was later not reciprocated by the government. In subsequent years the Peigan were "sorry that they made this treaty."
For the Peigan the ceremony of peace making was solemn, undertaken with much gravity, especially when they smoked the
peace pipe: "They prayed that they would be friends." Yellowhorn
thought that the government officials who signed Treaty 7 were
serious as well; Macleod in particular was respected. When Macleod said that the First Nations would be thought of by the
Queen as "my children," the Peigan thought a great obligation
would be attached to so solemn and important a commitment.
But disappointment soon followed: "They thought they were
going to get money, that they'll own the land and still be free
in the country. But this [disappointment] was after, when they
found out that they had to stay on the reserves." Macleod had
convinced the Peigan that the Queen "was going to treat them
good." As Tom Yellowhorn bitterly concluded, in the wake of
the treaty "they put up the Indian Act to punish Indian people
and protect the White man." In fact, the Indian Act of 1876 had
already been enacted.

Elder Ida Yellowhorn remembered: "Long Pipe Woman said that the Peigan leaders understood the making of the treaty as a peace treaty. She said that the leaders said that we should take the White man as our children and share our land with them."

Siksika Nation

The Siksika interpreted Treaty 7 as a commitment to peace in return for government assistance. Philip Many Bears remarked that "the police were to take care of us." For Arthur Yellow Fly, the terms of the peace treaty included "no more killing, no more whiskey trafficking, no more fighting with White men and other Native tribes." The end of warfare and violence was also foremost in the mind of Josephine Weasel Head, who remembered stories about her people deciding that they "wanted to save children from bloodshed and smallpox, also to stop the fighting between tribes." Stemming the violence that accompanied the economic exploitation in the free-wheeling days of Whoop-Up Country was foremost in the memory of Frankie Turning Robe, who stated that "whiskey trading was killing people. Crowfoot was thinking of his people when he signed." In return for the Siksika's agreement to stop fighting, the Mounties were "assigned to watch over the Native people." There was to be "no more bloodshed between White and Indian."

For Augustine Yellow Sun, peace was agreed to in return for money, freedom to hunt, and rations: "The way I heard it is that treaty money was used to keep us from fighting." The government gave people $12 each for the peace agreement: "The treaty money was used as a token of peace to us at the treaty. Many material things were promised." The Siksika believed the agreement was honestly sought by the government: "We were a treaty people and really thought that we would be taken care of." But Jim Black noted that the Siksika were soon to be disappointed: "Fifty thousand dollars was given out – that was cheap compared to the land we were cheated out of."

To illustrate the point that the Blackfoot tribes had no intention of selling land, Reverend Arthur Ayoungman told a story about Crowfoot that had been related to him by Joe Crowfoot, the grandson of Crowfoot and a former chief of the Siksika himself. A few years after the making of Treaty 7, Crowfoot met with government officials in an evening meeting at his lodge, where a fire was going. Crowfoot took some earth in one hand and, throwing it into the fire, said that the earth would not burn. He then said that if he took money and threw it in the fire, it would burn and disappear. Finally he said that he would rather keep the earth because it will not burn. Ayoungman related the story to underline the contention of the Blackfoot tribes that the earth could not be sold.

Stoney Nakoda Nation

The understanding that Treaty 7 was a peace treaty is very strong among the Stoney. Lou Crawler Sr recalled that it was "a peace agreement between First Nations and Europe." The nature of the agreement, according to Carl Simeon, was explained by Chief Bearspaw: "He said he [the Stoneys] will camp and live wherever he likes and he will not kill any White man." Della Soldier believed that peace was agreed to in return for land for the Stoney "and to choose more land in the future."

Morley Twoyoungmen remembered leaders of the Stoneys asking why the NWMP cannons were pointed in a threatening manner. The chiefs said, "You talk of peace while there are guns pointing at me. This is not peace ... lay down your guns." Similar sentiments were echoed by John and Gordon Labelle. George Ear described the agreement as "a peace treaty between two races." Ear too recalled the request to turn away the cannons "if he [Commissioner Laird] really wants peace."

The Stoneys remembered discussions between their leader Bearspaw and Crowfoot: "Bearspaw told Crowfoot that there were only two options: one was to make war and fight back. But this would make things worse. Women and children will be killed. On the other hand, if we signed the treaty we would be without any worries and would be happy with each other. Crowfoot answered: 'Yes, that is why I want to make peace.'"

"Peace every day" would be valued by the Stoneys according to Joe Brown. "Before there was killing and stealing – because of the killing the treaty was made." The prospect of no more violence was a relief to all sides.

Lily Wesley contended that the peace that was agreed to was not a land surrender; it was meant to "stop the fighting." The stories Wesley remembered suggest that Whites feared an Indian war greatly, that many things were offered to secure peace and that "the White people were very persuasive using slick words." It was clearly the Whites who wanted the treaty most desperately. But according to Wesley, the Stoneys were deceived by the many promises given to get peace. The government ploy was to pacify the tribes initially with false promises so that they would not resist and talk back.

Lazarus Wesley stated that Queen Victoria was highly regarded by the Stoneys and that they solemnly agreed to stop the antagonistic practices that had existed up to that time. The treaty would stop horse stealing, and the parties agreed "not to kill each other anymore – to have peace in the land."

In summary, the Stoney attitude was "let's shake hands; as long as we live, we will not oppose each other in any way." This was the meaning that the Stoneys believed both sides understood.

For Lazarus Wesley, the treaty was a comprehensive negotiation between nations: "Countries sign treaties so as not to have war and prevent devastation." The main point of a treaty was "to make peace, to shake hands, to make promises and agreements." In return "we will no longer fight over the land because the NWMP will protect us." Wesley remembered that John McDougall, as he talked about the treaty prior to the meetings at Blackfoot Crossing, emphasized the peace that was to be gained by accepting the treaty. McDougall vowed: "We will be going to other tribes and tell the others about the [treaty] money to be given out, and that you will lay down your weapons and make peace and there will be no more animosity between the Indian people and the government's people. The government will look after you." The Methodist mission started at Morleyville in 1873 was originally set back in the forest so that it could be defended against attack. Only in 1875, when the NWMP arrived, was the mission church moved to its present location on the valley bench of the Bow River at the junction of Jacob's Creek.

The treaty meant money for Gwen Rider: "It was signed so they would receive money and to have peace." She, like a number of others, stressed that it was the government that wanted the treaty most and this was because "hostility existed between White and Native people."

Bill Mclean had perhaps the most detailed recollection of Treaty 7 as a peace treaty. Mclean remembered the significant

role that John McDougall played in talking about the treaty prior
to its signing. The missionaries talked about how a treaty would
soon be made and the Stoneys would be part of it; they told
the Stoneys about a "peace making." There had always been
tribal wars but McDougall presented an ominous picture to the
Stoneys; he talked about the government's intentions and "how
White people would flood the land." Mclean felt that the missionaries had a strategic place among the tribes and acted as
government agents, passing along messages the government
wanted to get to the First Nations people: "The missionaries told
the people when and where the treaty would be made." After
reflecting on the nature of this peace making, he concluded that
the treaty had been pre-written, even though it ought to have
been a matter of "two parties coming together discussing an
issue and coming to an agreement." Mclean, like John Snow,
thought that the Stoneys had said much more in the treaty making than was recorded; the Stoneys had been able to say what
they wanted "but no one wrote it down."

Elva Lefthand recalled that ancestors had talked of Bearspaw
having said, "If I sign this treaty, everything I say now will have
to be honoured. And there will be no more fighting. The fighting
will have to stop." For the Stoneys, peace was the most important
reason for accepting the treaty.

Tsuu T'ina Nation

Like the other five nations, the Tsuu T'ina emphasized that the
treaty was a peace treaty. Hilda Big Crow, Dick Big Plume, Louise
Big Plume, Lucy Big Plume, Helen Mcguinio, Clarabelle Pipe
stem, and Rosie Runner all echoed the words of Maurice Big
Plume, who said that the treaty meant that Native people and
Whites alike would "live as brothers and sisters in peace." The
peace, according to Tom Heavenfire, meant that the Tsuu T'ina
would be protected: "We were going to live our lives by the laws
that White people brought," laws intended to "keep peace" and
to "protect families."

WHAT WAS PROMISED?

In return for the peace that the Treaty 7 First Nations agreed
to, numerous promises were made to them by the treaty com-

missioners. Again, as with the issue of the peace treaty, there is substantial unanimity among the First Nations as to what was promised. Most prominent and repeated were promises of money, unrestricted hunting, education, and medical assistance. What emerges as significant is that the nations were asked to give the Whites access to the land for settlement but that there was virtually no discussion of surrendering the land. The five nations were to give commitments to peace and access to land in exchange for the government's many "sweet promises." Recurrent in the memories of the elders was the fact that what the First Nations had said in the treaty negotiations was left unrecorded and that what emerged afterwards was far different in emphasis from what the First Nations remembered. That they would be taken care of was the theme reoccurring throughout the elders' testimony. Overcoming the problems inherent in language translation and understanding the details concerning the government's promises are key to establishing just what the Treaty 7 First Nations understood they were agreeing to at Blackfoot Crossing.

Blood Tribe

An interesting nuance in the position of the Bloods was that they were anxious to sign because they thought the way of life of the Whites could benefit their people. Recognizing that their former way of life was no longer viable, they looked to alternatives. This is the tone of Fred Gladstone's comments: "They were promised many things to improve their way of life, since their original livelihood was taken away from them." Similarly, Wallace Mountain Horse stated: "Well, one of the things that influenced us to sign the treaties was that we found out the White man's way of life is good and that is why they want us to be with them, and we thought they wanted to share with us ... We thought the White man's way of life was O.K. ... We wanted the good life they had."

Standard phases appeared in the language of the Bloods with regard to the money promises of $12, split between an annual payment of $5 and $7 to be held for future use. Guns and ammunition were the promises that Rosie Red Crow remembered the most. Fred Gladstone stated that access to "wildlife

[was] promised as well as the freedom to roam and get food and clothing." Health care too was to be given, and as Annie Bare Shin Bone stated, "They promised to take care of us for all time."

The promises for agricultural assistance figured prominently in the statement of Pete Standing Alone as well as in that of Wallace Mountain Horse, who said that tools and agricultural equipment were to be given free of charge. Pete Standing Alone remembered the promises of "farm implements, hoes, tools for haying ... Today, we don't get the tractors and everything else we need for farming."

According to Louise Crop Eared Wolf, the Bloods were promised education, health care, and economic development "in the form of farm implements, ammunition, livestock, tools." Money and rations were also promised.

Peigan Nation

Among the Peigan, the Crow Eagle reserve emerged as an outstanding issue. According to Fred North Peigan, the reserve was on the land where they got their paint for ceremonial purposes, and this land had been promised to his people at the treaty. Nick Smith commented on the double-edged nature of some of the promises: "The Queen's men came and laid down their laws, they controlled us ... You will be taken care of by the Queen and her representatives ... The Red Coats will be sent here to watch and take care of you ... Rations ... rations stopped long ago ... Now they've broken the promises made with the land."

There was to be no end to the help the government promised according to Sally Provost, and no end to the freedom to hunt for game. Cecile Many Guns itemized the ammunition and rations that were to be given annually to the signatories of the treaty. Tom Yellowhorn recalled that there would be the introduction of all kinds of instruction.

Siksika Nation

"We were promised we would get money for the rest of our lives," stated Philip Many Bears. "We were told there would be fishing, hunting, trapping." Education, health, timber rights,

Winchester rifles, food rations, ammunition in the fall, free seed
to grow wheat and barley were the goods and services listed
by Roy Ayoungman. Arthur Yellow Fly added that the Siksika
"were entitled to free use of the land." Agricultural assistance
was mentioned by Frankie Turning Robe: "bulls, cows, ploughs,
seeds, hoes, spades, axes, and saws." Augustine Yellow Sun remembered the promises made to his people as follows: "The Tall
White Man is going to give your people money. The White man
will feed you." Victoria McHugh said, "They promised us free
medical services, free education, but they never allowed us to
go further than grade eight. Most of the promises were never
kept by the government. At first they gave us some of their
promises but it never lasted."

Stoney Nakoda Nation

According to Elva Lefthand, Bearspaw was promised that everything would be paid for by the government: "We will take good
care of you, we'll always do as you say, we'll always do as you
say, we will always listen to your words, we will always look
after you and your people, and we will always heed your words
if you sign." These were the promises that enticed the Stoneys
to sign, but an even stronger factor was their belief that they
had the "rights to live as they wished, nobody telling them how
to [live]."

McDougall again was remembered as playing an important role
in the discussions about what the Stoneys would be given. He
had said, "Come over here [Blackfoot Crossing] and you will
receive money." Gwen Rider recalled that the Stoney stories also
emphasized that there was to be an end to the liquor trade as
well as an end to horse stealing. The freedom to hunt was reiterated by Lazarus Wesley, who remembered that there were
to be no regulations on hunting and fishing: "You will not go
hungry."

Lily Wesley said that the people were given hope by the many
promises, and Clarice Kootenay said that the Queen's promise
"to look after the well-being of your people" was a powerful
incentive for the Stoneys. "You will have no worries" the people
were told according to Tom Twoyoungmen. Schooling was promised for children, and this gave hope to the Stoneys, who were
concerned about the future generations.

Continued freedom to hunt wild game was a crucial issue stressed John Snow. Also important was the promise of "law and order," which protected the Stoneys from the whiskey traders: "These laws will keep this land safe and quiet." Snow wryly alluded to the fact that more than promises were used to get the Stoneys to sign. These great promises were "greased" by incentives: "McDougall had $1,500 to buy clothes and [he gave] them to people to persuade them to sign the treaty."

Eunice Mark remembered that it was "agreed that the White man would not break his promises," and Carl Simeon recalled that the Whites agreed "to share the land." Tom Labelle said, "They were promised cattle so they can make a living." George Ear mentioned the promise of "machinery," and Joe Brown said that "the government would look after us and not lead us astray."

Tsuu T'ina Nation

Ammunition "to help feed people" was an important promise for Edward Gingold. For Tom Heavenfire, the medicine chest and education were central: "The treaty meant to our people that we were just going to live our lives and by the laws that the White people brought us and that it was going to give us a better education. More of a better life was promised."

Helen Meguinis listed the standard items: "schools, rations, land allotments, medicine chest, housing, and farm equipment." She also mentioned that the Tsuu T'ina believed that they would be able to move as they wished and as they had always done prior to the treaty, but in reality "the treaty limited the rights to move." Freedom from taxes was an issue mentioned by Rosie Runner. "Schooling and welfare" were the words used by Hilda Big Crow. "People signed because they were starving and buffalo were disappearing," said Lucy Big Plume. The government "wanted laws so people could get along." The Tsuu T'ina thought that one of their major agreements upheld that "hunting and free lifestyle [would be] ... our rights."

ORAL HISTORY, CULTURE, AND LANGUAGE ISSUES

A great number of problems arose because of the different perceptions of what was agreed to at Blackfoot Crossing. Many things have been said over the years about what was intended and what in fact was understood. Even aside from the possibility that the government deliberately misrepresented its intentions just to get the First Nations to sign, there are many areas where there was room for misunderstanding and miscommunication. Perhaps most importantly, the two sides had different cultural traditions for remembering their history. In the Euro-Canadian cultures, history was written down, whereas in the First Nations cultures, history was transmitted orally in stories passed on by the elders. It was important that these stories be accurate precisely because they were not written down. The First Nations people faced an incoming and soon-to-be-dominant culture could formally record its own discourse and that viewed the Aboriginal culture as inferior.

Another major problem at Blackfoot Crossing was the fact that no single person present could speak all of the languages of the people in attendance. Furthermore, there were fewer Métis people, who commonly spoke two or more languages, at Blackfoot Crossing than there had been at the negotiations of the earlier numbered treaties. Questions arise such as: Could all the First Nations people assembled, who represented four distinct languages, have understood the same thing when words like "surrender" or "cede" were used? This would be especially doubtful for words that did not exist in the various Aboriginal languages; the very concept of landownership, for example, was completely foreign to a number of the nations present.

The abilities of the translators are at issue for Treaty 7. For example, even though in many established histories Jerry Potts has been valorized for his work as a translator, it appears that he was not regarded as a competent translator by the First Nations people who were present. Not only was he not knowledgeable about the languages of the Bloods, Peigan, and Siksika but his ability to understand English, especially the legal and formal expressions that the commissioners were using, was limited. Furthermore, although the Reverend John McDougall later would write that he was fluent in Stoney, the Stoneys themselves said that McDougall knew some Cree but no Stoney. Also, while Jimmy Bird is remembered as a better translator than Potts, his reputation was questioned by a number of the Blackfoot speakers.

It seems that the question of language is much more at issue for Treaty 7 than for any of the other numbered treaties. It was the last of the treaties to be signed by prairie tribes and these First Nations were viewed as a greater threat to peace than any of the Plains tribes who had signed previous treaties.

It is therefore possible that the commissioners had been willing to say or promise anything to get the tribes of this last frontier to sign the treaty and that they had minimized issues of controversy. How the written words were later interpreted was not the same as the "spirit and intent" of the Treaty 7 negotiations that the First Nations would remember.

On one of the most crucial issues, whether the treaty was a surrender or an agreement to share the land, the two sides have disagreed fundamentally. The First Nations were unanimous in their understanding that the treaty signified that they were willing to share the land with the newcomers, not that they had agreed to sell or to "cede, release and surrender" it.

Blood Tribe

"We didn't write down our laws. We passed down our stories and knowledge to the younger generation." This is a most felicitous statement by Pete Standing Alone, indicating the importance of oral culture for the Bloods. The Bloods carry on such traditions to the present day and it was to the disadvantage of the First Nations that the validity of this cultural tradition was not respected by the settler society. Others, such as Priscilla Bruised Head and Rosie Red Crow, also spoke on the issue of the oral cultural traditions still carried on by the Bloods: both said that the Bloods spoke their stories and history "but did not write things down." There was great skill required to become a storyteller, and it was an honour to be responsible for stories that were to be passed from generation to generation, declared Rosie Red Crow: "In the past the stories were tricky, hard to learn, but we learned them and passed them on ... Indian songs and holy songs were not written but we learned them as they came along."

For the Bloods it is clear that they did not understand words like "cede" and "surrender" and that the meaning of many such words were never properly conveyed to them. Fred Gladstone said that they simply did not understand the words used at the time. Priscilla Bruised Head said that even the interpreters did not understand the words "cede" and "surrender," nor what was intended by them. Annie Bare Shin Bone also recalled that Potts "did not explain cede or surrender properly." The meaning of these phrases only became clear when restrictions began to be imposed, long after the treaty was made.

The Bloods were clear and consistent when they spoke of Jerry Potts. Fred Gladstone had heard it said "that Potts did not speak Blackfoot or English very well." Priscilla Bruised Head remembered that Potts had seemed to be speaking with the Peigan more than with the Bloods. Rosie Red Crow accused Potts of not giving the Bloods the "right information," adding that he spoke neither good Blackfoot nor good English. "The interpreter was telling the Bloods all the wrong things."

Rosie Red Crow had heard it said that Potts was a Mexican who had married a Blood woman and had then moved to Fort Macleod. The Bloods believed that he had never left the employ of the North-West Mounted Police because he was so valuable to them in that "he spoke a little English and a little Blackfoot ... He did not speak Blackfoot fluently." It was also emphasized that he had not had a good education – "in fact he did not have an education." Rosie Red Crow repeated what others also said: "He liked to drink and all he wanted to do is get back home ... I never heard of him respected or treated with respect."

Of all of the Bloods, Wallace Mountain Horse put the issue most strongly, saying that "the interpreters did a bad job making them [the Bloods] understand the terms of the treaty." The failure to discuss what was central to the treaty meant that there were fundamental misunderstandings: "The interpreters never gave the information out to the Native people that clearly; what information they gave out never was understood the way [it was] supposed to be. They [the interpreters] gave their own interpretations as they thought the Indian would understand; this was different from what the Indian actually understood." As Wallace Mountain Horse pointed out, it was significant that Potts was a half-breed, as "a half-breed can be thrown out of any reserve – that's why they are in a weak position and might be vengeful towards Indians." Potts spoke "very poor" Blackfoot, stressed Mountain Horse: "They all knew that the interpreters did a bad job making them understand the interpretation of the treaty."

For a knowledge of the Blackfoot language, James Bird was more highly regarded by the Bloods than was Jerry Potts. But the story among the Bloods was that in a death-bed confession to people in Browning, Montana, Bird had said, "I told a lie." Rosie Red Crow recalled that Bird hadn't said anything earlier "because he thought he would get into trouble." Because Bird might have passed on information to the Bloods that he did not know was false, the issue might not have been that he was an incompetent translator: "I don't know why he said he was lied to as an interpreter; maybe only after that he understood what happened." Rosie Red Crow, however, was adamant in her opinion that "he did not interpret correctly for us ... He was an Indian like us and he lied to us."

On the point of whether the treaty was a surrender or a sharing of the land, it is clear that the Bloods understood it to be an agreement to share the land: "Indian people understood they would just share the country – they did not understand it meant to cede or surrender the land." The Bloods understood that "the White and Indian would help one another ... Whites would share the land and help Indians live better lives ... share food and other things." They understood that both sides agreed to be on friendly terms: "To help out ... we agreed to share land if the White man shared his way of life ... but it was all a misunderstanding."

Wallace Mountain Horse suggested that, on the basis of what they were told, the Bloods believed that sharing the land was the intent of the treaty: "Potts said the White man wants to be on friendly terms with us ... We [Bloods] don't want to disagree with that; it's good to be on friendly terms ... That's how the interpretation of Jerry Potts was understood ... The White people want to be with us – sharing." There was never any discussion of surrender.

Peigan Nation

Mrs Buffalo identified the cultural differences between the Peigan and the commissioners and the translators as a significant problem: "The Indians were not familiar with writing. That was the White man's form. The White man had been writing a long time before we knew how to write." This meant that many of the points made by the Peigan were not recorded in any reports on the treaty and were not included in the text of the treaty itself. As Sally Provost said, "A lot that was asked for was left out."

The Peigan elders pointed out another factor relating to the fundamental problems of comprehension: none of the Peigan had been able to speak or understand English. Some fundamental items were simply not properly appreciated, even the promise of money. As one elder stated, "The Peigans didn't have an understanding of money."

Along with other Blackfoot speakers, the Peigan believed that Jerry Potts had been unable to provide a proper translation for them, which led to errors of both omission and commission. As Elsie Crow Shoe noted, "The interpreter misinterpreted many things, changing things around that we said." Or in Louise English's words: "They did not explain things to the Indian people ... People cheated us ... Chiefs and people signed things they didn't know ... Interpretation was no good." Nick Smith thought that much was excluded because of how little Potts understood and "only those things he was able to understand were written." Tom Yellowhorn emphasized that Potts was just a guide who was in the service of the North-West Mounted Police – he was "not a good interpreter." Smith said that Potts spoke English but had never had an education and therefore he didn't appreciate what the legal English spoken by the commissioners meant; he obviously could not communicate what he didn't understand.

A number of the Peigan said that their interpreter was Jimmy Bird and that he suffered from the same problems as Potts: even though he spoke English he had never gone to school and didn't understand the concepts that were being discussed. As Tom Yellowhorn put it, "James Bird did not go to school and was the main interpreter." John Yellowhorn also indicated that James Bird was the interpreter for Treaty 7, not Jerry Potts, also known as Bear Child.

With regard to whether the treaty meant a surrender of land or a sharing of the land, the understanding among the Peigan was that the land was to be shared. Land would be given outright to each nation and the rest was to be shared; the issue of surrender was not discussed. Cecile Many Guns remembered being told about the role of Potts; she had heard that he had made it seem as though the Peigan were getting a lot: "Jerry Potts

[Bear Child] advised Sitting Eagle where to take land – told him to ask for the foothills all the way to Porcupine Hills." As Tom Yellowhorn stated, "People didn't think they had to settle and stay on reserves ... They thought they were getting money but that they still owned land." Much of the belief that the land could simply not be given away stemmed for the history of the Peigan. They had obtained the right to occupy the land after a duel between the Kootenay people and Napi. Napi had lost the land east of the Rockies, and this land and the land along the Oldman River would be the territory of the Peigan from then on: "They didn't think the Whites could own land because they had won the land from Napi." That the land would be shared was also the impression left by Sally Provost, who stated, "It was not what they said it was going to be ... We were supposed to be free to hunt and move across the land." Hugh Crow Eagle emphasized the binding nature of a promise made by the Peigan leaders. By smoking the pipe, they had made the treaty spiritually binding.

The treaty is held to be very strong and can't be broken. Indian people have never broken their agreements to the making of the treaty as far as they understood it to be. However, the White government had continued to break their promises to the Indians. There is an important distinction why this happened. The White negotiators' intent on the making of the treaty was represented by a physical being, the Queen; therefore, their intent was weak and that is why they broke promises. The Indian leaders' intent was represented through the Creator; therefore, it was strong and binding and can never be broken with.

Siksika Nation

Though the Siksika had little specific information on the problems surrounding translation and other language-related issues, they did draw attention to some fundamental cultural differences that had become apparent in the way in which the Charcoal case was handled by the Canadian justice system. In this clash between an oral and a written culture, not only was justice not seen to be done but there was clear evidence that there was bias against the testimony of the Siksika: "Yes, White men stress their written words as the only truth. The Indian that was actually there to witness it as an observer or was actually part of the incident has his words overruled by the written word. That is how the White man treats us."

Stoney Nakoda Nation

The Stoneys had the most to say about the misunderstandings that arose as a result of basic cultural differences as well as specific problems with language and interpreters.

The Stoneys saw the First Nations' inability to come to terms with the legal language used by the commissioners as a fundamental problem. The government officials were "well versed in the legal jargon" according to Bill Mclean, but "the fundamental basis of the treaty during the legal talks was never interpreted properly. This was one of the reasons both sides failed to hear each other clearly." In reality the talks were not negotiations at all: "They told the Indian chiefs, these are our terms of the treaty and this is what will be in the treaty agreement. But in those days there was nobody at all from the Natives' side to translate or understand exactly the legal jargon in the treaty document." There was simply no shared understanding: "The only time each individual tribe was asked anything was when they were asked to select land." Certain sections of the treaty were only explained to them in a legal English that no one understood or could explain. Mclean stressed that "the concept of the treaty, 'what is meant,' was never conveyed to both sides."

The Stoneys' responses to those sections in the treaty that they had not understood or agreed with are not mentioned in official government reports. Furthermore, compounding this problem and making any resolution difficult, the points made by the Stoneys were left unrecorded in any written form. "White people recorded their own position – none of the speeches or demands made by the Natives are included ... None of the speeches are in the agreement." Gwen Rider stated: "Native people not knowing English and not knowing how to write did not record the events and discussion at the treaty ... At the time no one in the Indian community spoke English and consequently did not understand what [Treaty Commissioner Laird] said."

Basic cultural differences were central to points made by Lazarus Wesley regarding fundamental misunderstandings. The Stoneys "didn't know what they were signing ... They didn't live by the mode of signing documents ... They didn't know how to write Stoney ... They had some hieroglyphics they told stories with to indicate parts of the month; they drew flowers to indicate a hard winter." These cultural differences, then, left a gulf of misunderstanding between the two sides: "Stoneys understood about one-quarter of the document ... They didn't realize what it meant and were just anxious to get back to the mountains."

The Stoneys at Blackfoot Crossing did not understand private ownership of the land as it was understood by Euro-Canadians, especially since their own decisions were made communally and not individually.

These fundamental problems were reiterated by others in a variety of ways. Matthew Hunter asked, "Our people did not speak English – how could anything be finalized properly?" As well, "The White man only put what he wanted into the treaty; then they pretended to tell the Indian what was in it."

Joe Brown echoed these points: "Stoneys could not read, they used sign language, there were no Blackfoot-speaking people who could speak Stoney ... How could there be a person who understood Stoney, English, and Blackfoot properly?" And, finally, Brown said, "The White man put what he wanted in the treaty and told them to sign."

Doris Rollingmud also raised the problem of the clash between written and oral cultures: "Stoneys couldn't read or write." Gwen Rider stated, "Nobody spoke English well." Gordon Labelle added that there was a great imbalance between the two sides and that as a result the interpreters misinformed the Indian: "The White people were very well informed and they devised the treaty according to their benefit." Finally, John Snow said, "When the Indian first promised they would take treaty money, nobody wrote down what they said." No one recorded their side of the story.

As to whether the specific term "surrender" was mentioned or discussed, Bill Mclean said: "They did not know in the White people's language what surrender meant – they did not talk about giving anything up ... The White people [government] had placed this term in the treaty but the Natives did not know or were not aware of it, and thus did not talk about giving up anything."

The main adviser for the Stoneys at Blackfoot Crossing was

John McDougall, who throughout his writing left the impression that he was fluent in the Stoney language. But when the Stoneys were asked about his translation abilities, an entirely different picture emerged, one that suggested that McDougall had little or no understanding of the Stoney language. McDougall had commented mostly on how poor his Cree was, but the Stoneys thought he had some competence in that language. It would not be the first time McDougall's veracity would be questioned – one of his fellow missionaries once called him the biggest liar on the prairies. As Bill Mclean put it: "The Stoneys did not have an interpreter. John McDougall was there ... He had only a limited vocabulary of Cree and [was] not very well versed in that language ... so all he did was try and relate some part of the treaty terms in Cree to the Stoneys ... That is all he could do ... He did not give a full explanation of the implications of the legal wordings because he could not."

Lazarus Wesley was told that McDougall had with him a half-breed interpreter who could speak both Blackfoot and Cree but not the Stoney language, and that there were some among the Stoneys who could understand Cree: "There was no one who spoke Stoney to effectively relay the message to the rest of the Stoneys who did not know Cree ... The essence of the message was relayed to them in the Cree language ... Due to lack of proper translations, the Stoneys were not imparted on them the proper information." The consequence was that the "Stoneys did not understand the full extent of the treaty ... There was a half-breed who spoke Cree – but he did not get the full meaning of the negotiations." A similar recollection was related by Elva Lefthand, who said, "The treaty was not understood – Stoneys did not speak English ... The interpreter was a Métis, a half-Cree not half-Stoney ... Being half-Cree he spoke that language but his Stoney was very poor ... He could understand Stoney but he could not speak it ... None of the Stoney spoke English." McDougall was not trusted by many among the Stoneys, for, as Gwen Rider said, he had his own interests to take care of first: "McDougall always had his way." Archie Daniels stated, "It is thought that McDougall voiced his own ideas, not those of the Stoney."

The half-breed interpreter referred to by the Stoneys was

likely Jimmy Bird, who it was said took over the translation duties from Jerry Potts, but according to Archie Daniels, both Potts and Bird had poor reputations as translators in the eyes of the Stoneys: "The interpreter was found passed out from drinking ... The White people had bought him with lots of liquor. They couldn't wake him up, couldn't use him. He was Jerry Potts. Two days passed but he was in no condition to interpret, so it was resolved to go and get Jimmy Jock, who lived in Fort Benton, Montana, to be the interpreter." Jimmy Bird's reputation was drawn into question by the Stoneys as well: "Jimmy Jock had many common-law relationships with women." It was acknowledged, however, that he did know Cree and that he lived among the Blackfoot in Montana. George Ear had heard that the Stoneys' interpreter knew some Blackfoot and that they called him "Jimmy Jug," a humorous reference to his fondness for alcohol.

Like the Bloods and Peigan, the Stoneys made many clear statements to the effect that they had not believed they were surrendering land at Treaty 7 but rather that they had agreed to share the land with the newcomers. As Elva Lefthand stated, "Bearspaw did not give the land away ... He did not relinquish it in any way." Mark Lefthand remembered that Bearspaw had explicitly said, "I do not give up this land. I will only share it." Bearspaw had agreed that the land would be used by all to make a living. Lazarus Wesley recalled, "They did not know that they were being asked to give up their land. What they thought was that the government was only saying that they would plough the land to grow something and nothing more. They didn't know that they were giving up the land." Lily Wesley said that the Stoneys had believed "they could keep their land as long as the sun shines, and the rivers flow." Lawrence Twoyoungmen said, "There was never any talk about giving up our land."

The misunderstandings created major problems. As Lawrence Ear noted, "Two-thirds of the Stoneys took land at Morley but one-third stayed south, thinking they would have land there: for reasons of poor understanding of English they did not understand what was said. One-third stayed down south, thinking that the land down there was theirs, without knowing that the only reserve for the Stoneys was at Morley."

Tsuu T'ina Nation

What emerges definitively in the position of the Tsuu T'ina is that they did not have an understanding of the words "cede" or "surrender." In fact, these words did not exist in their language, and as Tom Heavenfire pointed out, "people did not really speak good English and did not understand the translation."

Like those of other nations, the Tsuu T'ina's stories about Jerry Potts indicate that he was not an effective translator. Potts was remembered as speaking in Blackfoot to those among the Tsuu T'ina who understood Blackfoot, but the people thought he was misleading them. "Jerry Potts was a stool pigeon," stated Lucy Big Plume. Both Maurice Big Plume and Tom Heavenfire reiterated that Potts was working for the police and the government and that he had little interest in explaining the treaty fully to the Tsuu T'ina: "Potts had good relations with the government; he got money to buy liquor from them." He had little interest in relaying the response of the Tsuu T'ina to the government, and according to Tom Heavenfire, "he did not understand what we were really saying. The interpreters didn't really interpret the English words back to the people." Clarabelle Pipestem raised the same point, that there was no reason for the interpreters to give a clear message to them; the interpreters had a "bias for the government, since the government was paying them." Tom Heavenfire remembered it being said that Potts had trouble pronouncing the names of the Tsuu T'ina people properly – never mind explaining the more complicated issues to them.

NORTH-WEST MOUNTED POLICE IN THE TREATY ERA

The role of the Canadian Mounties during discussion of the numbered treaties entailed more than just policing or enforcing the law. The Mounties also took on a military function in that they provided a military escort for the treaty commissioners. In fact, it would be fair to say that their role was essentially a military one, as in their dress and discourse they played the part of a military colour guard for the government officials present. In this capacity, they were to provoke awe among the First Nations with a show of force that would be seen by some as intimidating.

Tom Heavenfire and Helen Meguinis put it most directly when they said that the role of the police was primarily to assist White settlers and the newcomer society. Heavenfire stated that the NWMP came "to pave the way, to settle things with the Native people so that the White people will be protected." This role, according to Helen Meguinis, was also intended as an intimidating one: "The NWMP came out to keep the Indians under control so they wouldn't bother the White people ... so they had a whole bunch of soldiers present when they signed the treaty – some people were scared."

When the police first arrived in southern Alberta in 1874, they held meetings with the chiefs to find grounds on which they could agree, grounds that would help to pave the way for the treaty. They were uncertain about their safety, fearing confrontation, and thus they felt they needed to ask permission to stay in the area for their first winter, in 1874–75. Elsie Crow Shoe stated, "When the Red Coats arrived at [what would be] Macleod, they asked Bull Head if they could stay the winter. They arrived in October and asked to stay the winter ... Bull Head gave his approval but he told them to leave in spring." Crow Shoe went on to indicate that the police probably never had any intention of leaving: "They did not listen to Bull Head and instead they started building homes ... Fort Macleod was on our land ... The Red Coats never left, they stayed."

In the initial discussion Bull Head had with Macleod, he trusted Macleod and saw him as a great and honourable friend. In meetings the two held in 1875, Bull Head "told Macleod he was a great leader, warrior, and a great hunter and gave Macleod his own name." Macleod returned the honour, giving Bull Head "the Queen's own guide uniform."

John Yellowhorn also told a story about Bull Head and Macleod. As early as their first meeting, Macleod wanted to a make a treaty and he then asked to stay one winter. At the end of the meeting, "Macleod shook hands with a Blackfoot who knew the future and who burned Macleod's hand when he shook it." During that winter, MacLeod took pleasure in attending social functions with the local tribes: "Macleod and his men greatly enjoyed these tea parties."

At the negotiations, Macleod played an important role in communicating with the chiefs to a large degree because he had earned the respect of the First Nations. According to Augustine Yellow Sun, "Tall White Man [Laird] said he would give out metal things [money]" when the negotiations began, but at first Crowfoot would not take the money. The Mounties were dressed in their military finery – the "Red Coats had long knives [lances], white plumes, chains across their mouths." They used bugles, and cannons were present. When the cannons were fired, Crowfoot approached and a flag went up to signal that he was willing to accept the start of negotiations.

The role of the cannons was certainly controversial according to George Ear of the Stoneys: "The police cannons were ready and aimed at our camp when the negotiations started." At this point Crowfoot objected and said, "If he really wants to make peace, he first has to disarm all his cannons, that one facing me and aimed at me."

The peacekeeping role of the police was emphasized by some of the elders, but it was secondary to the military role they played at the treaty making. Wallace Mountain Horse stated, "NWMP came out to impose their laws, especially when the Whites outnumbered the Indians ... They were the peacekeepers ... were to maintain the laws ... Police were to reinforce the peace created by the signing of the treaties." John Snow agreed with this, stating that the "red-coated policemen quieted down the land and enforced law and order."

But a series of incidents that took place after the treaty was agreed to made many First Nations people sceptical about the sympathies of the police. Louise English remembered that the Mounties treated "drunks mean" and that the police "should be more gentle and the Indians will get along with them." Tom Yellowhorn told the story of an Indian agent who falsely claimed he'd been attacked so that the police would come out and arrest some Peigan he didn't like. There was no doubt whom the police would believe in these situations. The Siksika remembered the objectionable way the police handled cases such as the shooting of Charcoal and the arrest of A Ja Ma Na for the killing of the much despised Indian agent Frank Skyner. Instead of arresting the suspect, the police had shot dead an unarmed man.

The Peigan also had vivid memories of the cruel enforcement of the pass system only a decade after the signing of the treaty. Some Bloods were arrested for visiting the Peigan reserve: "One

Indian talked to the police and told them that they had no heart and showed no mercy for locking them up just for visiting, which was a very common procedure among us. This kind of treatment from the police to the Indian caused the Indian to lose faith and trust in the White man."

Louise Crop Eared Wolf said that the NWMP used intimidation tactics to instil fear among the Indians: "They were parading and marching around and shooting their cannons. This caused additional tension among the Indians, who were already very tense due to the mistrust of the White man at Blackfoot Crossing."

BOUNDARIES PROMISED

To this day there are still questions about the land each Treaty 7 nation claimed as its territory and about the way this land would be held. The issue of landownership and land tenure was bound up with many other issues surrounding the treaty, such as problems with translation and inadequate explanations of the terms of the treaty. All of the bands that accepted the treaty thought they would be able to continue "to use" all of the territory on which they had traditionally lived by hunting and fishing. This is evident in the challenge they made to the commissioners' initial suggestion that hunting and fishing would be restricted. All of the First Nations leaders found this unacceptable, and the government changed its position to recognize the unrestricted hunting rights that the First Nations would have across the area of Treaty 7. None of the groups at Blackfoot Crossing had a clear idea of exactly how the land would be held and how they could live on it. Most of them assumed that they could continue to live as they always had and that they would share the land with the Whites.

Blood Tribe

Annie Bare Shin Bone said that "Red Crow chose the Belly Buttes area; Crowfoot further north." Louise Crop Eared Wolf said the Blood territory was vast. The Bloods ranged as far north as areas north of Edmonton: "Our ancestors talked about these little people that looked like dwarfs running around naked. When these dwarf-like people saw the Indians they dove into the lake and disappeared. These same stories are told by the Northern Cree." The Blood territory included the Cypress Hills to the east, the Yellowstone River to the south, and the Rocky Mountains to the west.

Peigan Nation

The Peigan had a number of major differences with the federal government over what constituted the boundaries of the lands they claimed. To begin with, like other groups, they chose a broad area for their territory; this was the land over which they had traditionally moved. This area, according to Ray Cross Child, encompassed the "Oldman River, Waterton Lakes and Kootenay River, and the mountains where the Porcupine Hills end northeast of Medicine Hat." The Peigan land claims originated with their stories about Napi and the land east of the Rockies they had won from him when they defeated him in the ring game. Elsie Crow Shoe described this as being "bounded by the Porcupine Hills north, to the base of the Rocky Mountains, Crowlodge, and Waterton Lake." Cecile Many Guns remembered stories about Chief Sitting on Eagle Tail Feathers asking for land enclosed by three landmarks: "The Old Man's Playground, the Porcupine Hills, and Crowlodge Creek to Belly Buttes where there were no White people ... their main camping grounds were southeast of Pincher Creek."

Tom Yellowhorn also describes the Peigan claim as originating with the land won from the people across the mountain (the Napi legend). This included Crowlodge Country, Old Man's Playground (Livingstone area), and Porcupine Hills. "This area was as far northwest as Squaw Buffalo Jump, in the Porcupine Hills, west of Nanton, east to Lookout Buttes, north of Lethbridge, Waterton Lakes, the Waterton River. All this area, the deal was made so that Napi could occupy all these places specified by the said landmarks and that he would not cheat the Indian." The Peigan, according to Tom Yellowhorn, still know the location of the landmark for the ring game; it is beyond Livingstone north of Lundbreck.

The major area in dispute for the Peigan was the Crow Eagle reserve. This area was especially important for the Peigan in that it was the place where they gathered the paint that they used for ceremonial purposes. The Crow Eagle area has traditionally been considered part of the land they claimed, yet it has never been surveyed as such by the government. The Peigan believe they were defrauded of this traditional territory.

Siksika Nation

The Siksika boundaries were described by Crowfoot at the treaty signing. Augustine Yellow Sun indicated that Crowfoot spoke as follows: "The Blackfoot are bush-living people. We are people at the treeline in the north, and as summer approaches we move southwards where we have spent summer on the open plains. Thus we move from home to home." Crowfoot told the commissioners that the Siksika would live on the open plains around Soyooh pawahko ("ridge under the water" or Blackfoot Crossing). Exact boundaries were not discussed during the treaty negotiations. Elder Philip Many Bears remembered: "Our boundary was from the Bow River to the Red Deer River, but as the White settlers began to encroach into this area, our people slowly started to move on the south side of the track and somehow we have lost the rest of the land to the Red Deer River." Beatrice Poor Eagle recalled that the land promised was "north up to the Red Deer River toward Drumheller and south to Bassano area, along the Badlands to Milo and Arrowood and Carseland to the west. The Bow River was in between the north and south boundaries."

Stoney Nakoda Nation

There is still controversy over what land was to be chosen by the Stoneys. The three separate bands of Bearspaw, Chiniki, and Goodstoney clearly thought that they would get more land than was eventually surveyed for them. All three groups lived in distinct areas along the foothills of the Rockies, and they did not understand that they would all be placed on a single reserve at Morleyville. Morleyville had traditionally been a wintering place for some of the Stoneys and was a permanent camp site for only one of the three bands, the Chiniki.

The territorial claims of the three groups therefore differed widely. Mark Lefthand said that Chief Bearspaw chose "Chief Mountain to the south and up to Morley and beyond – all along the foothills of the mountains." Other family groups led by James Dixon chose land "around a ranch east of Eden Valley where stakes were driven to mark the land," stated Archie Daniels.

Bill Mclean reiterated the point that the Bow River Valley at Morley was just a stopping place and that the land the Stoneys chose was "from the origin of Jumping Pound Creek to the confluence of the Bow River and from the origin of the Ghost River to the confluence of the Bow – this would be our land." Gwen Rider said that the land taken by Bearspaw was "all the eastern side of the Rocky Mountains," land that started around the Oldman River and extended north.

Lazarus Wesley noted that at the time of the treaty the Stoneys also lived at the origin of the Belly River and Castle River area but that "the land chosen was bounded by the Ghost River and Jumping Pound Creek." This is what the Stoney had asked for, but Wesley indicated that McDougall only wrote down "his own ideas." The articles of Treaty 7 stipulated that the Stoney reserve would be surveyed "in the vicinity of Morleyville" where the Methodist Church started its mission in 1873 at a site chosen by the reverends George and John McDougall.

John McDougall was involved in all of the discussions relating to land but did not write down what the Stoneys said. Wesley also said that at the time the Stoneys were not aware of McDougall's hidden agenda, the "undertakings" he had made to register land for himself even before the treaty was signed. From the evidence of the Stoney elders, one can conclude that "Morley was only a wintering habitat" (according to Clarice Kootenay) and that the Stoneys chose land all along the foothills south to Chief Mountain, and that Goodstoney chose land around the Gull Lake area.

Lily Wesley said that elders had told her that the land used by Bearspaw was "bounded by the Castle River, Belly River, Crowsnest River to the Waterton Lakes – all these rivers join together on the prairies – this is the territory of Bearspaw – north of the Buck River was the area of the north people or Goodstoney people ... In harsh winters people would migrate to Morley."

The misunderstanding about the land allocations discussed at the treaty had dire consequences for the Eden Valley Stoneys according to Lawrence Ear: "Eden Valley people mostly wintered down south. One-third of Bearspaw's people stayed at Eden Valley after the treaty was signed, thinking that this was their land ... Dixon Lefthand's families stayed down south believing they had a reserve there."

Similar problems existed for the Kootenay Plains people, who had occupied the North Saskatchewan and Clearwater River area since the days of the "pack dog." They are now known as the Bighorn Stoneys – "they used the area as a place of refuge and died there ... Some have seen the remains of their lodges." As John Abraham said of his Kootenay Plains people: "Government told us to take our land and this is what we did." According to the traditional stories of the Bighorn people, their ancestors had lived on the Kootenay Plains since time immemorial.

George Ear summarized the generally recognized land-use areas of the Mountain Stoneys as follows: "Wesley [and Goodstoney] people migrated north to the North Saskatchewan River ... Bearspaw moved down to Chief Mountain area ... Chiniki stayed along the Bow River."

In conclusion, the great difficulty in resolving the differences between the Stoneys and the government over what was said about boundaries lies in the fact that "nobody wrote down what was said about the land that was claimed by the Stoneys." The oral history of the Stoney elders clearly disputes the accuracy of the official record presented by Treaty Commissioner David Laird, who was relying on the word of the Methodist missionary John McDougall. Chief John Snow hypothesized that McDougall did not really understand the way the Stoneys used the land along the foothills. Today, the Stoney elders of the three bands are still claiming additional reserve lands in their traditional lands north and south of the Morley reserve on the Bow River.

THE SIGNING OF TREATY 7

In addition to unresolved problems relating to the interpretation, translation, accuracy, and meaning of the treaty text, a great deal of controversy surrounds the actual signing of Treaty 7. Hugh

Dempsey said that Crowfoot never touched the pen with which he was to sign the treaty and that perhaps, therefore, technically the treaty remains unsigned by the First Nations of Treaty 7. What emerges from the oral testimony is that the First Nations leaders did not actually make the X's on the original treaty, but rather that the X's were made for them and they simply touched the pen with which the X's were made to acknowledge the signature as their own, thereby approving the document. This was the explanation of the process given by Augustine Yellow Sun of the Siksika: "The White man placed a piece of paper on the table and asked the Indian through an interpreter to sign ... The Indian does not write ... The White man tells them that he will give them the goods and money if he signs." The treaty commissioners simply said, "Just touch the pen." Yellow Sun then elaborated: "Now, when the Indian touches the pen, it is the same as giving his holy word [promise]. Later on it changes a little where the Indian people marked their own X's. Before that we didn't know how to use a pen signifying that we agreed with the matter that we are dealing with. After an Indian makes his mark, the White would say, 'Well, he has touched the pen. Now we will finish the deal; he has agreed.'"

Bill Mclean and Lazarus Wesley of the Stoneys are sceptical that the method of making the X's at Blackfoot Crossing was legitimate. Mclean suggested that the fact that the individual did not himself make an X leaves the signing suspect: "The Native did not make the X himself ... this is not right because the signing of a treaty between nations requires both parties to sign." Wesley also said that the signings were dubious: "They didn't sign the document themselves either. If you look at the X's made they are all done very neatly. At that time the Native people, if asked to place an 'X' on a paper, would say, 'Hey, what does that mean? What is it?' They wouldn't be able to mark it neatly because [not being used to it] their hands would be too shaky."

THE CONCEPT OF THE SQUARE MILE

The First Nations' inability to understand certain concepts makes it doubtful that they could appreciate a number of key issues. Such is the case with the "square mile," which was to be used to survey the reserves. Not only was it semantically not understood but conceptually "a mile" was not a measurement used by the First Nations. Other measurements were used by the nations present at Blackfoot Crossing.

The Stoney elders were particularly emphatic about the consequences of their people's not understanding what a square mile was, especially after it was explained to them how little land was being surveyed for them. "They did not know then," said Bill Mclean, "because a square mile is White man's language and is part of their culture. Whatever the White man measures, they measure in a straight line. That is their policy. But the Native people did not use that ... They did not understand that the government would assign land on the basis of one square mile per family of five." They would have thought that what the officials were saying about the land they would get would correspond to what they had described as the territory they wanted. Lazarus Wesley also said that the First Nations did not know what a square mile was: the expression that was used for half a mile was the phrase "as far as one can hear." Real misunderstandings arose because these measurements were not understood: "They didn't know such things as there are thirty-six square miles in a township. The terms they used to indicate a mile or half a mile evolved much later with the coming of the White people and their measurement for race tracks ... The race tracks having one mile distances, the Stoneys came up with the term 'cha wazi' for a mile and 'châ hâge chorân' for a quarter of a mile. At that time they didn't know they were to be assigned land on the formula of one square mile per family of five." Wesley added that there is no evidence to suggest that the Stoneys had ever discussed this issue or that they had agreed to such a formula; they simply told the commissioners what land they claimed. They never employed a straight measurement to indicate the boundaries of their lands; instead they referred to natural geographical features, such as the mountains and the rivers, when speaking about their boundaries: "They didn't say so many square miles or so many sections because they didn't know what those terms meant."

SHARING TOPSOIL AND MINERAL RIGHTS

The troubles that the Lakota experienced in the United States as a result of gold rushes in their territories were well known to the Treaty 7 nations, especially the Blackfoot peoples who lived close to the Lakota. To stop the intrusion of newcomers into sacred lands like the Black Hills, Sitting Bull's Lakota attempted to deny access to gold deposits. These military tactics did not succeed in the long run. In Treaty 7, the tactic that was used to prevent gold rushes and other mineral exploitation was to deny the newcomers ownership to the sub-surface minerals and metals.

The First Nations of the Northwest had long known about using oil for caulking canoes. In the eighteenth century it was the Cree who drew Anthony Henday's and Peter Pond's attention to oil deposits used by their people. The First Nations of southern Alberta were well aware of the coal-mining schemes of Alexander Tilloch Galt – one mine, in fact, had been planned for Blackfoot Crossing. The Treaty 7 First Nations viewed these developments as treaty violations.

Evidence that the Treaty 7 nations thought that they would share – not surrender – the land can be seen in their testimony about how the land was to be used. The commissioners asked for agricultural land for the incoming White settlers. It was this "topsoil," to a two-foot depth, that the Treaty 7 chiefs agreed could be used by the newcomers. The land below this was never given up, and the Treaty 7 First Nations still claim ownership of the sub-surface resources. As Rosie Red Crow of the Bloods explained, "The White people were told by the Indians that they can reside on the grass [top surface]. Now they have gone below the surface. The mineral rights, oil, everything they are taking." She also stated, "We believe that all our mineral rights were retained and the land was only to share with the White man; however, no one wrote down what we wanted and that's why our mineral rights were ignored by the White man."

Similarly Annie Bare Shin Bone said that Red Crow took some dirt and said, "This is what we will allow you to use, to give you. That was all the topsoil and the grass on the surface of the land."

Strong statements from Siksika elders also indicated that only the topsoil was to be used by the White settlers. Augustine Yellow Sun said, "The land was measured by the length of a shield [a plough blade was called a shield]. Two feet were given up – one for ploughing and two for post holes ... That's what I was told." Jim Black used the same terms as Augustine Yellow Sun to describe the land that could be used – two feet for post holes and one foot, or the length of a shovel blade, for ploughing. The rest of the earth was not sold; neither was the water or the "black rock" (coal, oil, or "the things you make nails out of [metal]"). Elder Philip Many Bears said, "I heard from the old people that were at Blackfoot Crossing that only the surface of the land was given up to share with the White people and not beneath the ground."

Elva Lefthand of the Stoneys was told that Bearspaw had said, "I will only allow you to work the ground to a depth of six inches." Bill Mclean said that Bearspaw's words on this issue were not written down but that he had said, "We will only share the surface with you." One of the commissioners is remembered to have said, "All I will do is to turn over the topsoil of the land and one foot only, to plant seeds to grow wheat for flour." Lazarus Wesley said that this is what the Stoneys understood they were agreeing to. The Stoneys were told that flour would be useful to them for making bread because bread went well with meat. It was the commissioners themselves who said they wanted one foot: "Concerning the land, the top part, to the depth of one foot was all the government was to use ... He will plant seeds to grow wheat for flour." Bearspaw was said to have replied, "If that is what he is talking about, then it should be okay. These things are good to eat with meat, etc."

John Snow also stated that the tribes only agreed to share the surface, that part of the land which the commissioners said was going to be tilled: "The Queen's representatives had stated the Crown land will be from the surface to two feet underground. The land below that belongs to the Indians. The Crown land will be tilled from half a foot to one foot. This ground which is tilled will be used to grow 'various products.' The mineral rights were never surrendered: 'Only the surface will belong to you.'"

CHAPTER FOUR

Post-treaty Life of Treaty 7 First Nations

GOVERNMENT POLICY

The Canadian government initiated a number of programs in the post-treaty era to begin to implement its promise to assist Aboriginal people to make the transition to an agricultural economy. Federal policies such as the Home Farm Plan, the Peasant Farm Policy, and Work for Rations were put in place in the 1880s to fulfil the obligations that arose out of the treaty. Many of these policies had mixed results.

The government also began to enforce the Indian Act of 1876. This act had many consequences for treaty Indians and in a number of ways worked against the gains made by the First Nations in entering the treaties. The government introduced coercive measures such as the controversial pass system of 1885. Evidence of cynically administered policies suggests that the government never intended to help the First Nations to become self-sufficient, but rather primarily intended to keep them out of the way of settlers and under control through the Indian agency system and the NWMP outpost patrols.

Blood Tribe

Wallace Mountain Horse noted that agricultural supplies were to be given according to the policies established in the treaty. These supplies were often either inadequate or not forthcoming. Rosie Red Crow recalled the humiliation of the pass system: "They also would write something for us. We would have to go to an agency and they would write for us a permit stating if we were going to the States, Brocket, or Siksika, [indicating] the number of days [allowed for visitation]; if we went beyond that, we would be jailed."

Rosie Red Crow, Annie Bare Shin Bone, and Louise Crop Eared Wolf all spoke about the restrictiveness of government policy and the role of Indian agents in the post-treaty era. Rosie Red Crow stated:

The Indian agents were very controlling. They used all types of tactics to control us, especially with a paper known to us as the "paper written in red," a type of summons used to threaten us that we will go to jail if we were to disobey their rules. For example, if a person did not obtain a pass permit to leave the reserve, the person will receive this paper, but we are not aware if anyone went to jail. We never heard anymore of the "pass or permit system" after the 1940s. The Indians, for the most part, honoured this system because the honour system is part of our culture. Also, the Indians were fearful of going to jail and leaving their families. The other instance is when a family who picked up their children from residential school fails to bring them back on time because of lack of transportation or some other reason, [this family] will be threatened with the red paper. The Indian agents treated some Indians more favourably than others, especially those that agreed with his policies and rules. No Indian was allowed to take monies that were earned by him through his farming, ranching, or labour in a lump-sum payment. The agent took the money and gave it to the Indian in a piecemeal fashion. Most of the time the Indian will not know how much he made from farm proceeds or stock sales. Most of the monies earned by these individuals was distributed among the agent's favourites. Also, the agent's favourites would receive their earnings in a lump-sum payment; therefore, they were able to purchase capital goods such as machinery, tractors, vehicles, lumber to build barns, etc.

Peigan Nation

Among the Peigan elders, the comments on such experiences were many and varied, ranging from complaints about incompetent farm instructors and Indian agents to memories about the enforcement of the pass system. Ray Cross Child recalled that "the Indian agent worked against us - agreeing with fences

put up by ranchers," even though these fences were often on
Peigan land. The Peigan never trusted the Indian agents and sus-
pected them of working against their best interests. Elsie Crow
Shoe remembered that the agents were often involved in land
sales. She stated that the "White man never paid for the land
they took on the south side of the reserve." She also thought
that payments for the land went to the agents: "Our land was
sold to immigrants by our agents and governments." Fred North
Peigan echoed these feelings about the Indian agents: "In those
days the Indian agents did a lot of dishonest things to us. They
manipulated us ... As long as the Indian agents were on the reserves, our land was getting smaller."

Indian agents interfered with the Peigan's early success in stock
raising and farming on the reserve. They did this through use
of the permit system, established as part of the Indian Act. Farming at Chipman Creek was flourishing, but as Tom Yellowhorn
said, the permit system was used "to stop [the Peigan] dealing
with outside ranchers." Yellowhorn described how his father had
worked the land as a farmer, but as soon as he was successful,
"his land was divided and he had to move on to another operation." Yellowhorn also remembered that on a number of occasions the Peigan paid for cattle by trading horses, but the cattle
were never delivered.

An Indian agent named Wilson persuaded the Peigan to build
a sawmill to produce the lumber for houses on the reserve.

Yellowhorn told the story of how the Peigan built up a successful cattle operation. At first the cattle were sold to local
ranchers, but the Indian agent began to make decisions for the
Peigan that devastated their land. Many cattle died after being
put through an unusual treatment on the orders of the Indian
agent; not only did many cattle die but the band members had
to pay for the treatment from their own funds. In 1921 Indian
agent Tom Graham threatened the Indians if they did not allow
construction of an irrigation dam. Graham was also involved in
shady land transactions. As Yellowhorn alleged, "After deceitful
negotiations a deal was struck, and the Indians never understood
how much their land was sold for." One of the Indian agent's
assistants, a Métis interpreter named John Bastien, was involved
in negotiating a land surrender that the Peigan had opposed.
Bastien claimed he was working on the Peigan's behalf when

he persisted in trying to persuade them to sign the deal. Other land transactions were simply not recorded, such as the land that George Stafford gave back to the Peigan at Crow Eagle Flats.

Another Indian agent, named Nash, tried to settle a score with some Peigan by lying to the police: "Nash shot his revolver in the air to bring the police to the reserve in order to get Indians in trouble." Nash was also the agent accused by the Peigan of distributing poisoned flour, which led to the death of a number of Peigan.

A number of the Indian agents insisted on heavy labour on the part of the Peigan to satisfy the requirements of the Work for Rations policy then in place. These agents abused the system, for even though rations were supposed to be distributed fairly to those who worked, "children died of starvation from the meagre rations."

It was very difficult to make a go of it on the reserve, and initiative was frustrated at every turn: "It has always been that whatever possessions an Indian had or money earned was always controlled by the Indian agent. The agents always tried to collect from the Indians with money no matter what their personal needs were"; "Agents were known to pocket money themselves from the sale of horses. The Indian agent would lower the price of a horse sale simply to take a cut of the sale for himself. If an Indian had agreed to sell a horse for $250, the agent would lower the sale $200 and pocket the remaining $50. The agent took over and controlled the sale."

Yellowhorn said that many Peigan worked very hard for long hours on the reserve picking rocks and harvesting: "We worked as slaves for the agents – we worked on projects for agents without wages." Sometimes there was no food either. Their agents were able to play favourites by paying some people and not others: "Chiefs had no control over the administration of their bands." It was difficult for Indians to have enough food to allow them to work their own farms. They often had to go to work for neighbouring farmers and ranchers, then feed themselves from this income and return to the reserve to work their own lands. On occasion, land worked by an individual would be sold by the Indian agent without his knowledge, as was the case with Many Chiefs, who lost his land without being informed or consulted. Yellowhorn stated that the reserves "were concentration camps" and, as for the Indian Act, it was really meant to "protect the White man and punish the Indian."

A most poignant story was told by Yellowhorn about a Peigan called Four Horns. This man had worked for two years with his own outfit and had successful crops but "to his disappointment ... the Indian agent wrote out a cheque for him in the amount of $2.80 and told him that the rest had been paid towards his debts." Four Horns gave up farming after this meagre reward.

Trading in animal furs and skins was another activity that the Peigan became involved in to make some money. They sold their beaver skins on the black market to CPR agents, and when the trapping became legal, "the Indian agent took the hides, sold them, and put down in the book to pay the Indians' debt – I was lucky to come out of the agency with two to three dollars for my skins."

The Peigan had vivid memories of the enforcement of the pass system. As Louise English remembered, "In those days you had to get a permit to go to Pincher Creek or Macleod ... They [the government] really had a hold on us ... We could not stay longer than the permit stated." Nick Smith said, "When we finally settled down in the land designated as ours, when we wanted to visit other places we had to go to the Indian agent to get permission. We had to let him know how long we wished to visit. He would then write a permit for us. The saying of the old man was true, that we can't go anywhere we please. We could only stay as long as the permit stated, no longer." Cecile Many Guns remembered that even the neighbouring Bloods needed a pass to visit the Peigan. On one occasion some Bloods who came without a pass were arrested: "They were taken to prison and locked up and sent home in the morning." It was the abuse of power on occasions like this "that made us lose trust in the White man," said Many Guns.

One of the worst stories of blackmail and abuse of power was told by John Yellowhorn. It concerned an Indian agent who denied a chief permission to travel with his son: "One day our Indian agent told Chief Crow Eagle to put his signature on a piece of paper, as his consent was needed to commence with a fence around the reserve. The chief would not sign, stating that the people knew their country. The chief then wanted to take a trip to Montana [with his son] but the agent said the boy could not go unless the chief signed the paper – the chief signed the paper and the boy was allowed to go."

Elder Hilda Yellow Wings remembered being told that the pass system was strictly enforced: "It kept people from finding work outside the reserve. If you were caught without a pass, you were immediately told to return to the reserve, or if you were away for a longer period of time and lost your pass, you had a difficult time to get back into the reserve."

Sometimes meat rations were issued from cattle infected with anthrax. There were also the rations of flour mixed with lime, and the Indian agent told the Indians "to close all the windows tightly and shut everything else tight so that the bread will rise and cook better. As a result the Indians would die of suffocation because of inhaling poison fumes," said Yellow Wings.

Siksika Nation

The record of Indian agents on the Siksika reserve is similar to the litany of problems listed by the Peigan. Indian agents often seemed to be the ones who agitated the most for land surrenders on the Siksika reserve, ostensibly to help the Siksika. Bernard Tailfeathers remembered that in 1912 there was pressure for a land surrender under the promise that money would be used to build homes. George Crowchief remembered the Indian agent saying that they would have to sell the land to get rations.

Abusive and arbitrary treatment of the Siksika by officials on the reserve lies at the core of the story of Scrapings, who killed an Indian agent shortly after the death of his son. His son attended the local school but when he became very sick, Scrapings took him away "because he was not being helped by the ladies at the school." Scrapings was terribly heartbroken when his son died and he sought out the Indian agent Frank Skyner and shot him for reasons that are not entirely clear, though it is known that Skyner had a reputation for mistreating band members. Following the killing, the Siksika were unfairly harassed by the authorities, who thought the band members had aided Scrapings. This was in fact not the case, but the Siksika thought that the Mounties should not have shot Scrapings, especially since he was unarmed.

Jim Black told the story of Charcoal, a Blood whose pursuit

and shooting were seen as unfair and indiscriminate by the Siksika. They felt that the earlier actions of the police had heightened the violence in the area that eventually led to the killing of two policemen and to the tracking down and shooting of Charcoal himself.

Victoria McHugh recalled other restrictions on the Siksika people:

The Indian agent was very strict with us when he gave us permits to visit our relatives in Tsuu T'ina. He would only allow three to five days sometimes but most of the time he would allow us one day. We would catch the train in the morning from Gleichen and return at night. The NWMP would be provided with a list of those that left the reserve and they would check our permits as we got on the train in Calgary. We also had to get a permit to sell our horses, cattle, and grain. We had to ask for a permit from the agent [and] he would tell us to come back in three or four days without giving us a reason to wait. The Indian agent would keep all the cheques and he would give us some of the money. He would say that we owed the rest. We never knew how much we made from our grain proceeds, cattle, and horse sales. We even had to ask for a permit to buy lumber when we were going to build a coffin for our dead. Even at that, the Indian agent would give us barely enough to build a coffin. We had a hard time to fit our children into these boxes.

Stoney Nakoda Nation

Many complaints against government policies were also listed by the Stoneys. Mark Lefthand thought the government withdrew from its "issuance of rations," and Elva Lefthand said that the introduction of restrictions on hunting game contravened treaty assurances that the Stoney could hunt whenever and whatever they wanted: "After the treaty restrictions were imposed ... shooting an eagle would bring a heavy fine." Bill Mclean stated that the church, in collusion with the NWMP and government officials, "tried to put a stop to the Sun Dance ... condemned it."

Among the different tribes, each have their own religion and have their own way of conducting their religion. Different tribes such as the Nakotas, the Blackfoot Confederacy, and the Stoneys have carried on the tradition of the Sun Dance from the past. Before the missionaries came, just as the Bible says, there were prophets; the Creator gifted the Indian people with prophets, also. Through these Indian prophets, knowledge of the Creator and what the Indian people can rely on or call on for help was told.

Now throughout the world there is religion. Every faction of people have their own religion. But all of these different religions all pray to one, the Creator. For the Indian people, the Sun Dance is their religion. It is a wonder how they know of it, but it can only be through the Creator. The Creator showed the Native people how they can rely on the Sun Dance. There were people of divine powers in those days, and through these mediums the message of the Creator was relayed. Through the Indian religion, the Sun Dance, the Native people were a powerful force. The Sun Dance was held each year. In these Sun Dances, they prayed to the Creator and all its creatures, the sun, the wind, the water, and all living things. They prayed so they can have a good life, that the future would be good to them; it was a powerful religion the Indian people were bestowed with. That practice is still alive today. But at one time, the different church denominations tried to put a stop to it. They condemned it. They said the Natives are not praying to God but are praying to the sun and other things. But they could not squash it, because the Creator must have helped the Native people. The church people were told exactly the concept of the Native people's religion; that the Sun Dance is held yearly to pray for the well-being of all God's creation, the sun, the land, and the living things, so that there will be good tidings in the days to come. Because of the philosophy of the Indian religion, I think it is a powerful entity that the Native people have.

Lazarus Wesley further explains the cultural significance of the Sun Dance:

Regarding the Sun Dance, it is a time of acknowledging our blessings and to give thanks. Just like the birds of feather who make their nests in the trees and sing their sweet songs praising the Creator, so do the Indian people. They make a nest in the Sun Dance tree. They think of it as representing the Creator. They see it as a tree of life. It is a family representation and they rejoice at these Sun Dances. They rejoice during the beautiful summer season that they have survived another harsh winter. The Sun Dance was seen in this concept to give thanks and praise the benevolence of the Creator.

It is the same with the sweat lodges, too. The Stoneys have relied on these for spiritual guidance and cleansing. They pray to the Creator. But the government has made fun of our religion, calling us Indian worshippers. Even now some of our members have condemned our religion. Myself I have not reached that stage. God gave the Indian people the gift of the Indian religion so his message can be spread through this medium. Because of that I don't condemn it. When they say there is going to be a Sun Dance, I go there with eagerness. The people are in a joyful mood during these occasions. I see the tree of life as a representation of the son of God and take part in the Sun Dances with a joyful spirit.

Lazarus Wesley identified the issue of the insensitivity Indian agents who interfered in every aspect of reserve life. His grandfather had told him that "agents were imposing restrictions on Stoney cattle." Then the government imposed restrictions on "cutting down trees and creat[ed] laws against the hunt." The enforcement of regulations was constant and penalties were often severe: "When Indians hunted around Macleod they would be herded onto buckboards and taken to jail – their families went without food while they were jailed."

The government never consulted or informed the Stoneys about the creation of the national parks; now they would not be allowed to hunt in these areas, which had always been traditional hunting grounds. Compounding this insult, many campgrounds were established in Stoney hunting territory. Wesley said, "It's getting so we can't even shoot a rabbit." Tom Labelle remembered the promises of assistance in agriculture; the Stoneys were "promised cattle to make a living," but the cattle never arrived. Labelle also objected to the many hunting restrictions the Stoneys had to contend with in making a living. Lily Wesley said the government officials were sympathetic to "White ranchers who didn't like Indians hunting anywhere ... They put pressure on the government to bring in restrictions."

Doris Rollingmud went to the core of the problem when she said that the "treaty rights came along with the signing of the treaty" but soon these rights were taken away, especially the right to hunt and fish: "Rights and laws laid down by White settlers ... eroded treaty agreements" that had been made with the federal government.

Tsuu T'ina Nation

Helen Meguinis remembered that some of the Indian agents were helpful to the Tsuu T'ina, while others were "very nasty." She recalled: "The permit or pass system was strictly enforced by the Indian agents. When we go to take part in religious ceremonies with other tribes, we had to obtain a permit. If we are late in returning, the Indian agent made us work for him for two weeks without pay. The pass system was very degrading for our people. The old people never gained the trust for the Indian agent. There was no trust relationship. The old people felt like they were being treated as children and not as adults."

MISSIONARIES

The role of the missionaries was controversial at the treaty negotiations and it remained so in its wake. In just whose interests were the missionaries acting both at the treaty negotiations and afterwards? Certainly the role of Reverend John McDougall at Blackfoot Crossing is now being questioned from the point of view of the First Nations. While some of the elders might have said "we got along with them" when asked about the priests or ministers, the majority, those with more detailed stories, were less sanguine about the legacy of missionary work on the reserves in the post-treaty era.

Blood Tribe

Among the Bloods the memories are mixed. While Priscilla Bruised Head tersely responded that "we got along with them," Annie Bare Shin Bone said that much of her traditional Blood culture was lost to her: "I never knew anything about traditional culture because I was raised by nuns and priests." She also remembered the hard physical work at the school: along with learning to read and write, Blood children had to do basic chores, houseclean, and learn to garden. When asked about the legacy of the missionaries, Wallace Mountain Horse simply replied, "they tried to teach us about God, which was a concept we already knew about."

Louise Crop Eared Wolf stated, "The missionaries' role enhanced the treaty-making process because they were seen as sacred trustees. Today, however, they are not taken as holy men because of how they treated us and robbed us of our language and culture during the residential school era. They were involved politically when they first came to the Indians and they were always present during the treaty-making process, but today [when] we ask them to help us politically, they always say they cannot be involved politically."

Peigan Nation

Among the Peigan, there were those who had little to say of a critical nature about the missionaries. Nick Smith, for example, recalled that they taught people not to hate each other. But Fred North Peigan stated that at the Catholic schools "all the regulations were enforced and people caught speaking Blackfoot were penalized." Louise English also remembered the treatment in the schools as being severe: "All the blame was in the priest and nuns and staff of the Anglican boarding school. Those days they were too strict with us. Now they know they cannot control us. They started to change things around again."

Hugh Crow Eagle described the problems that developed for the Peigan because of the way the Roman Catholics and Anglicans established their missions in two distinct areas of the reserve: "This created a split among the people, with one part of the reserve being Anglican and the other Roman Catholic. This created a great deal of animosity among the Indians because of the way they were pitted against each other by the churches to the point where young people from each denomination would physically fight one another."

Hilda Yellow Wings said that the missionaries were the first people to lie to the Peigan about the treaty.

Siksika Nation

Jim Black stated that at first the people trusted the missionaries because of their deep religious convictions: "Later on, when they [the Siksika] began to understand a lot more things, we didn't really respect the missionaries or the police." Black remembered that when it came to the issue of land surrenders, the missionaries or ministers were usually pressuring the Siksika to agree to the surrender. This was especially the case in 1910, when "Good Living" (a minister) was strongly in favour of the land surrenders being proposed by the Indian agent.

Stoney Nakoda Nation

The name of John McDougall still evokes strong feelings among the Stoneys. Both Archie Daniels and Lazarus Wesley said that McDougall did not work in the best interests of the Stoneys: "McDougall voiced his own opinion, not that of the Stoneys." Lazarus Wesley went on to state that McDougall never really discussed treaty issues with the Stoneys and that his main purpose both at and after the treaty was to help the government. The Stoneys who had converted to Christianity were pressured by McDougall to help change the minds of those who did not want to sign the treaty. Bill Mclean also said that McDougall paved the way for the treaty among the Stoneys. McDougall, furthermore, was very unsympathetic to the religious practices of traditional Stoney spirituality, especially when it came to the Sun Dance.

Gwen Rider remembered it being said that McDougall was a "cruel person," that he always tried to talk the Stoneys into allowing roads through their lands and "always had his way." Matthew Hunter thought the Stoneys should never have placed their trust in McDougall: "McDougall told us to close our eyes and pray, but when we opened them our land was gone."

Another criticism of the missionaries came from former chief John Snow, who said that the missionaries "did not have the right attitudes to each other." They were intolerant and did not respect the Stoneys: "I have noticed that they think of the Indians as lower-class people. They call us savages referring to animals." "[They] downgraded our culture," Snow went on, and "criticized our religion." McDougall was out for himself, taking his own land first, rather than acting in the interest of the Stoneys; when land questions were at issue the missionaries commonly worked against the best interests of the Stoneys. When Snow tried to explain what the Stoney position at the treaty had been, he was never listened to, but neither was he met with indifference: "I told missionaries [on the reserve today] about treaty agreements, that the government didn't do what it should have done, that Indians have been overpowered – that the White man has been working to overpower the Indian all along ... But the missionaries didn't think [this] was important." As an ordained minister in the United Church of Canada, Snow has successfully conveyed his people's belief in the treaty process to a wide audience in church circles and in the constitutional meetings held across Canada in the early 1990s.

Tsuu T'ina Nation

Some among the Tsuu T'ina thought that the presence of the missionaries had been positive: "They helped set up schools and helped educate Indians," said Lucy Big Plume. But most others disagreed and were anxious to point out the overall negative impact of the missionaries on the Tsuu T'ina. Louise Big Plume said, "They tried to brainwash us into being Christians." Maurice Big Plume noted that while they taught the Tsuu T'ina English and to read from the Bible, "the missionaries looked down on Indian religion ... our relationship with them was not good."

Tom Heavenfire was more forceful in his condemnation: "They rounded up all our young people and put them in boarding schools and they tried to take our culture away." The missionaries were abusive and threatening, which meant that many people were afraid of them and therefore "complied with the laws." Rosie Runner concurred, saying that the "missionaries tried to force religion on Indians and civilize them." But according to Helen Meguinis, the missionaries were not always successful: "They were trying their best to convert the people to Christianity, but a lot of our people never changed. They stuck with their own beliefs, their spirituality." She emphasized that many people never converted; her grandfather, Two Guns, for example, never took a Christian name. Meguinis said that while it was good to learn English, "the missionaries built boarding schools to take our little children away." At the schools the children were forbidden to speak their own language and were only allowed to come home briefly at Christmas, Easter, and for their summer holidays.

Meguinis said that Father Lacombe was the first missionary to come to the Tsuu T'ina. On his visits, he talked about God and arranged for baptisms and marriages. "Later he kept coming back and was baptizing more of our people because George Runner told our people that he only talked about the Creator and was not there to harm them."

SCHOOLS

The school system imposed on the Treaty 7 nations, as well as certain other governmental policies, might be seen as evidence that the Canadian government simply wanted the First Nations people out of the way. The emerging Anglo-Canadian elite was so concerned with its own interests that it was unwilling to make the new institutions and policies work properly to the benefit of the Aboriginal people. Underfunding, incompetent officials, and racial stigma were the issues that the First Nations had to deal with in the post-treaty era.

Not everyone categorically condemned the educational system. Wallace Mountain Horse of the Bloods thought that the "schools taught Indians how to deal with hard times" and that in the past they were better than they are today. But Annie Bare Shin Bone thought that even though the Bloods were taught to read, write, do basic chores, and houseclean, the children were often badly treated. Bonds between parents and children were weakened and even broken because of long periods of separation: "It was just after I left school that I came into contact with my mother, and it was then I realized I never knew Indian culture, traditions, or anything being raised by the nuns and priests."

The Peigan elders had mostly negative memories of the schools. Louise English blamed the government for all the regulations that controlled every aspect of the children's lives. She was critical of the staff as well: "All the blame was in the nuns and priests and staff of the Anglican boarding school. Those days they were too strict with us." Fred North Peigan spoke of how the children lost their connection with their home life: "That this is the only reason me and my grandmother were separated. I was not close to her anymore [physically] because the school was pretty well year-round – only six-week holidays in July and part of August. On Saturday afternoons we were allowed to come home if our parents lived close by. They had very strict rules. If a student did not arrive back at school, he was suspended the next week." The regime was very restrictive – the "White men controlled us." The students were not allowed to speak Blackfoot, and between the ages of seven and eighteen, they spent most of their time in the schools. These children, said Tom Yellowhorn, were sent to school for twelve, thirteen, or fourteen years: "They lost the way of their people ... they'd lost everything and were not qualified to work for the White society ... They were scared to talk to the White people and afraid to talk to their own people because they got criticized by their own people as well." The same issues were mentioned by John Yellowhorn: "On education, the individual was brought away from his reserve, just to take away anything that was left of his Indian ways. He was not taught – he did not know the White man's way of life either. They did not know either way of living; they were really lost. These people who went to school were not allowed to come home during holidays. They were not allowed to go out of the boarding school, so they did not know how the White people were living. They were not allowed to come home, so they did not know how Indians were living."

Hugh Crow Eagle remembered: "In residential school we were not allowed to leave the schoolyard, which seemed like an extension of the 'pass system.' The matrons walked around with their key chains wrapped around their knuckles and if we spoke our own language they hit us over the head with their knuckles."

Elder Hilda Yellow Wings recalled from her own experiences the terrible treatment the children received: "In residential schools they were very cruel to us. They lashed and strapped us all the time. The nuns would call us savages, especially those that could not speak English. During the winter we almost froze in bed because they gave us only one thin blanket to use as a cover. Many of the girls ran away from school because of the way they treated us."

Lily Wesley of the Stoneys likened the schools to orphanages for the way Stoney children were separated from their families: "The White people, thinking they were smart, thought they would teach the Indian children in an environment different than it is now." Tom Heavenfire also remembered this segregation: "Nuns and priests – they rounded up all our young people and put them in boarding schools and tried to take our culture away."

The Tsuu T'ina thought they had been promised an education and a better way of life.

Siksika elder Beatrice Poor Eagle, who attended a Catholic boarding school as a child, stated that "the nuns were very strict with us. We were separated from our families and from the boys. We were forbidden to have any contact with the boys. There were some nuns who treated us well but most of them were very bad. There were White men that were hired to train the boys on the job. They were trained in farming and ranching. They worked the church farms and looked after the cattle, pigs, horses, chickens, turkeys, ducks, and the general upkeep of the church farm."

Victoria McHugh also had negative memories of the boarding school:

The mission school's purpose was to brainwash us. They did a lot of damage to our way of thinking because of the abuse they did upon us. I believe that most of the nuns were sadists. They did not allow us to speak our own language and we had to continue to please them by attending mass all the time. When we received nice gifts or nice things from our parents, the nuns would take them away from us and send them to their relatives in the East. They would say to us that we were performing for the "devil" when we carry our Sun Dance. We were not allowed to pass grade eight. We had to make a request to the Indian agent if we can go past grade eight. I once heard teachers saying that we cannot educate those Indians because they would take our jobs away. I had to take a high school correspondence course.

RESERVE LIFE: "WORK FOR RATIONS"

The government promised the Treaty 7 tribes rations under the terms and benefits listed in the treaty. This straightforward promise was altered by the government when it decided to make the rations contingent on work performed.

Both the Bloods and the Peigan had stories about their food supplies being poisoned by farm instructors. Rosie Red Crow recalled that on the Blood reserve "rations were poisoned with lyme to keep the bugs off." Members of the Siksika described the abuse of power practised by Indian agents who established a system of favouritism in ration distribution. Tom Scalplock said that people were tricked by the agents: "Some people got good equipment and the best farms." Conflict surrounding the issuing of rations led to the killing of Indian agent Skyner of the Siksika reserve.

Tom Yellowhorn said that in spite of the promise of rations the people were always hungry: "Babies died of malnutrition ... People would go to each other's camps in search of food." Some men didn't have the strength to work because they had not been given rations. These provisions of the Indian Act were used to "punish the Indian." John Yellowhorn said that the Work for Rations policy was used to "get even" with some people, as was the case with Indian agent Nash: "This agent did not care for people who did not work. They got rations of meat and bread – after a while rations got fewer and fewer until there were none." If the Indian did the least thing wrong, the rations were withheld. This practice was seen by the First Nations as running counter to what they had been promised. In some cases, on the Siksika reserve, for example, people were even told that they had to sell land to get rations. All kinds of reasons were given to convince the First Nations to surrender the land.

There was extensive poverty and malnutrition, and sometimes people had no food to eat at night. On the Siksika reserve, people were told they would only receive their flour rations if they allowed the CPR to pass through the reserve. Helen Meguinis remembered that up to 1947 on the Tsuu T'ina reserve, they were given rations of flour, sugar, rice, syrup, soap, and baking powder once a month. Also, if the band owned their own cattle, two cows were killed each week and rationed out on Wednesday. In difficult times, "the old people used to go with their lard cans and draw blood from the main artery of the cows and drink it while it was still warm. Some of them took it home to make blood soup with berries. The kidney, liver, tripe, guts, and stomach were also prepared for food."

Beatrice Poor Eagle remembered that people worked hard to keep from starving: "After Sun Dance each year we would go and cut hay for ourselves and also sold it to the White ranchers and coal mines near Bassano. We used those farm implements and harnessed horses that were promised to us through the treaty. We also did a lot of work for White people to make ends meet for the winter. We did farm work like seeding, harvesting, and haying for them. We also did a lot of fencing for them. Most of these men that worked for these White people never received any pay but a cow was butchered for them instead." Poor Eagle said that on the reserve a cow would be butchered Wednesday and rationed out Thursday: "Flour and tea were rationed out at the flour house once a month. Only the old people received beans, sugar, lard, syrup, matches, and tabasco. Up to the 1930s we were still receiving some rations like salt pork and bacon. A few years after, we received food in boxes like bologna and other canned foods. Those that sold hay to the ration house were paid in money. They sold hay all summer to the ration house."

LAND SURRENDERS

Issues relating to the fraudulent surrender of land are raised by all of the First Nations of Treaty 7. Some of the misunderstandings stem from the different interpretations of what was given up in the treaty. The First Nations say that sub-surface rights were never ceded and that they were misled. As Rosie Red Crow said, "Only Canada benefited from mining and minerals." Augustine Yellow Sun noted that the Siksika should have received all of the royalties from oil found on Jimmy Davis's land, but they were given only $40 each. George Crowfoot said that there were oil wells all around the Siksika reserve and oil wells on land surrendered by the Siksika but this did not benefit them. He stated, "Oil and gas were never surrendered." Jack Big Eye said that those looking for gas and oil "are not telling the truth." Only White men made money from the gas and oil under First Nations land. Big Eye also said that the Siksika were tricked into surrendering land in order to raise money to build homes on the reserve. Beatrice Poor Eagle stated, "In 1910 the land around Milo and Arrowood area was leased out for ninety-nine years. We used to get $25 per head as a lease payment but this has long been stopped. In 1911 the Bassano dam was built and I believe it belongs to the Siksika Nation. We only received payment once. It was a lump-sum payment of $500 per head."

Victoria McHugh said that the terms of some surrenders were never properly explained to the Siksika. For example, "We used to have a homestead in Carseland area but now they have moved the fence line in five to six miles." The lease of land in Arrowood and Milo was only achieved after the Indian agent had starved eight councillors who opposed the surrender into submission. McHugh remembered a time when

the Indian agent gave one of the stockmen a parcel of land near Arrowood for his long service to the Indian Affairs Department, but his land was never legally surrendered by the Siksika Nation or agreed to by the chief and council. Another stockman by the name of Campbell Evans was given that parcel of land that we lost by Carseland for his faithful service to Indian Affairs. And still another stockman that retired or was leaving cleaned up the band ranch of everything. Old Jack Winnipeg helped him move in the middle of the night on a garden wagon. The Indian agent did a lot of these things by giving up land that belonged to the Siksika Nation through having councillors sign papers that were later switched to make it look like the chief and council had agreed to give up these lands.

Fraud related to surrenders was also an issue on the Peigan reserve. According to Ray Cross Child, "White people came and fenced out land, then took it over ... The government cheated us." Nick Smith also said that "the government owns land the Peigan thought was theirs." Fraud was also involved in the loss of the Crow Eagle reserve. As Tom Yellowhorn said, "The government took everything and they sure cheated us." The government told the Peigan that they had to fence their lands, but the Peigan refused. As a result, the Peigan lost their land.

Elder Eva Bad Eagle told the following story about land that the Peigan lost:

There was a big cattle rancher by the name of McLean who asked the Indian agent if he could fence off a twelve-by-six-mile area on the Peigan reserve so his cattle will not roam all over the place. The Indian agent agreed and hired some Peigans to fence it off. After a few years the rancher McLean decided to sell out and move on. The Indian agent then asked the Peigans that were outside of this area that they should move inside the fence area. He told them that the area outside the fence did not belong to them anymore. The Peigans still lay claim to this area outside the fence because we never sold it. The area covers ninety-five square miles.

Fraud was also claimed in the way some Whites secured permission to build a road through the Peigan reserve. The road allowance was voted on three times before it was finally passed.

Hugh Crow Eagle outlined a number of instances where the Peigan lost land they believed was theirs. An area around Pincher Creek called Halifax was abandoned by the Peigan after a man was mauled to death by a bull, as traditionally the Peigan vacated areas where people were killed. Later a rancher moved onto these lands and asked the Indian agent to have them fenced off. The Indian agent agreed to this and the labour of local Peigan was used for the task: "The Peigans have never been able to claim this part of their reserve since the Indian agent gave it away."

Elder Paul Smith explained that there was fraud surrounding a number of land transactions. In one case, an Indian agent leased land to a local rancher: "The band enjoyed the lease payments for a while; then the payments stopped coming and the Indian agent told us that the land did not belong to us anymore." Smith attributed a land surrender in 1907 to the fact that none of the Peigan involved had an education: "I strongly believe that the Peigan people did not know what they were giving up when they voted on a referendum to surrender 2,300 acres of land on the north side of the reserve. They did not understand the meaning of surrender at the time because they had no schooling." The Indian agent was influential in getting this land surrender, as was Commissioner Yeoman, who told the Peigan that "the money will be falling from their pockets." "He told the Indians that the money they make from the surrender will buy them a lot of horses and farm equipment." The first referendum did not work because the Indian agent had "cheated on the returns." The next vote was delayed for a year, and during that year the ranchers and farmers continued to pressure the Indian agent to arrange the surrender of the land:

When the time was right, the Indian agent rallied fifty supporters and gave them many promises if they voted yes for the surrender. When he knew that he got their support, he called a referendum for one early morning without giving notice to non-supporters but only to the fifty that were in support of him. There were only ten non-supporters that somehow found out about the referendum. They quickly tried to tell other non-supporters but it was too late by the time they got to them. The vote was 50 to 10 in favour of surrendering the land. The Indian agent treated these supporters very well, while the non-supporters were ignored when they would ask for any type of assistance from the Indian agent. He arranged to have twenty-five acres of land to be broken for farm land for each supporter. From their farm proceeds they were able to buy such things as Democrat horse wagons, sewing machines, furniture, etc.

Elder Hilda Yellow Wings said that the Cypress Hills Ranches asked the Indian agent if they could fence the northern part of the reserve to prevent their cattle from wandering there. The Indian agent gave them permission. Shortly after this area was fenced off, Indian Affairs officials came down to survey the Peigan reserve. When they saw the fence, they assumed it was the boundary and mistakenly surveyed there.

The Stoneys believed that fraudulent representations were made to the Eden Valley people, who thought they were being promised a reserve south of Morleyville at the headwaters of Pekisko Creek and Highweed River. Similarly, the Bighorn people were expecting to establish their own reserve on the Kootenay Plains north of the Morley reserve.

Helen Meguinis of the Tsuu T'ina pointed out the unfairness of a system where "only Canada has benefited by oil, roads, coal, mining, and forestry."

CPR ON THE SIKSIKA RESERVE

The Siksika think that Crowfoot might have been tricked or cheated into agreeing to the surrender of land for the Canadian Pacific Railway right-of-way. Philip Many Bears recalled: "The Queen's negotiators said that they were going to put railroad tracks through the middle of our land only on a temporary basis but it's still here." Exactly what was promised remains vague in the memories of some elders. They said that flour rations were promised and Crowfoot was to get a free pass to travel on the railway in perpetuity. Arthur Yellow Fly thought that the agreement involved "free train" rides for the chiefs "and half-price for the rest of the tribe. Some members of the tribe remained suspicious of Crowfoot, of whom it was said, "He always had money."

SURVEYS

The issue of fraudulent, flawed, and improper surveys, especially with respect to reserve lands, was voiced strongly by both the Peigan and the Stoneys. For the Peigan, the loss of the Crow Eagle reserve was a major issue; it had been "lost to the provincial government," which got all the money from the land. Tom Yellowhorn said that "fences encroached on the surveyed reserve land, then became permanent." Similarly, Mrs Buffalo noted, "Each tribe claimed a tract of land for their own use. But as time went on, these areas claimed by the different head men were reduced by the White man's fences and surveyors."

The survey for the Stoneys was a botched job because of incompetence, negligence, or both. There was from the outset a failure to communicate properly. The Stoneys used natural divisions to describe their lands, while the surveyors were intent on surveying 128 acres for each member of the band. The list of band members had never been complete to start with, nor were the Stoneys ever all together when the surveyors were present. Surveyors came to Morleyville three times to begin the survey according to Bill Mclean:

At the treaty, the Stoneys, as told to me by Chief Bearspaw, were asked which land they selected to keep. Chief Bearspaw told me in response, "We said from the origin of the Jumping Pound Creek to the confluence of the Bow River and from the origin of the Ghost River to the confluence of the Bow River would be the boundaries for our land. The area within these boundaries is the land we select." All the three chiefs [who made treaty] relate this same story. This is what has been told to me by my father [Chief Walking Buffalo]. He personally heard these stories from the chiefs himself and, in turn, related them to me ...

In those days the Stoneys were nomadic people, always travelling, going on hunting trips in separate groups, not banded together. They were scattered all over. They rarely stayed in Morley. They returned to Morley infrequently. They would be away on hunting excursions for long periods of time, sometimes not returning to Morley for a year or even two years.

Then one day, an Indian agent from Sarcee came with surveyors. A grandfather, Chiniquay, was told that men have come to survey the land for the Stoneys. He told the surveyors, "This flat [meaning the land around his house] is what I choose for my land." He apparently thought he was being asked to select his own personal lot. That's John Chiniquay, Chief John Chiniquay, who did that. However, some Stoneys told him that is not what the surveyors meant. They told him when you chiefs made the treaty, you were told then that land will be surveyed for the Stoneys. They are saying which is the land to be surveyed?

Then John Chiniquay said, "Chief Bearspaw and Chief Jacob [Goodstoney] are not here. I will wait for them."

So that time, the Stoneys' land was not surveyed. The surveyors came back a second time but the Stoney chiefs were not back yet. On the third visit, the Stoney chiefs were not back yet. In those days, only some of the Stoneys had been collecting their treaty money [annuity]. When they collected their money, they sign for it. Their numbers [population] were determined by counting those signatures or marks that were made by the payee on the annuity pay list. And using these figures, the size of the reserve was determined.

I believe it was on the basis of 128 acres per person – something in that area. They [surveyors] had been waiting for the chiefs to come back, but since they didn't, they used annuity pay list figures and the reserve size was determined. But almost half of the Stoney population had not been coming back for their annuity.

The areas the chiefs had chosen when the treaty was made using the natural boundaries of the rivers were disregarded. These areas were never taken into account by the surveyors; they only concerned themselves with the "so many acres per head" and the annuity pay list, which was not a complete list.

Lazarus Wesley suggested that the surveyor himself was incompetent: "Mr Patrick was the surveyor. He didn't do a good job." The surveyor did not pay attention to what was said at the treaty, which was that the Stoneys were to get the land bounded by the Ghost River and Jumping Pound Creek. It was said that McDougall had made a map of the area to be surveyed for the Stoneys but had lost it. The surveyor did not come at the convenience of the Stoneys but rather in August and September when there would be the least hindrance for his work. According to Wesley, the Stoneys were not informed that he was coming and were unfamiliar with the straight measurements he was using.

[Our people] didn't know when the surveyor was coming. Just as I said before, they [surveyors] came in the fall, in August and September. Most of the Stoneys weren't here then. During that time of the year the animals are fat, and the Stoneys knowing this were away on hunting trips. My opinion is that the government's men, coming here and finding most of the Stoneys away and not wanting to make a dry run, and possibly fearing not getting paid for not getting anything done, just did a haphazard job. They did this just so they can take something back to their superiors. That is my thinking.

There is no evidence where the Stoneys said, "This is how much land they are going to assign us for our use. Let's say yes to it." The government just arbitrarily assigned the land as it wanted. It never told them "only this area is yours," and the Stoneys didn't say "we only want so much back for ourselves." What the Stoneys said was to name the Ghost River and the Jumping Pound Creek to bound the land they chose. They never employed the straight-line method of measurement as done by the White people. They didn't say so many square miles or so many sections because they didn't know what these terms were.

Others among the Stoneys echoed Mclean's and Wesley's description of the surveyor's incompetence. Bearspaw was on a hunting trip when the surveyor came, and according to Lily Wesley, no one was informed about the survey – the surveyor just showed up: "The Stoneys understood the survey was only temporary." Matthew Hunter said that the "survey was never properly recorded ... Only what the White man wanted was given [to] us." Joe Brown said, "The side of the reserve we chose was never surveyed." Paul Mark also thought that the survey was only temporary, because "everyone was not present." Gordon Labelle said that "the surveyor died before the survey was finished and that the areas the Stoneys chose were not surveyed – Kootenay Plains area was never surveyed for the Stoneys."

Like many of the contentious issues surrounding the circumstances of accepting Treaty 7, misunderstandings and difficulties in communication became evident soon afterwards in the simple act of setting aside reserve lands. According to the written treaty document, the Siksika, Blood, and Tsuu T'ina tribes were to receive one large reserve along the Bow River in the vicinity of Blackfoot Crossing. By the early 1880s the Tsuu T'ina had chosen their existing reserve at Fish Creek and Elbow River, and the Blood Tribe had moved to the junction of the Belly and Oldman rivers. Until 1948 the Stoney nations were living on one reserve at Morley, but they now have satellite reserves at Bighorn Reserve 144A and at Eden Valley Reserve 216.

A classic "bird's-eye" view of Blackfoot Crossing

Such panoramas were typically produced by Victorian artists. Mary Louise Pratt has described such views as representing the colonizer in a position of power, as the "monarch-of-all-I-survey." As in this scene, the land is typically shown as empty, waiting to be made productive, waiting to be settled. When Native inhabitants are shown, they are either distant or sinister and threatening. Victorian viewers of these scenes were thrilled by the opportunities for expanding their empire such panoramas suggested.

Treaty Flats at Blackfoot Crossing, where Treaty 7 was negotiated

Chief Eagle Child of the Bloods

The chiefs portrayed on pages 173–7 attended the treaty making at
Blackfoot Crossing and accepted Treaty 7 on behalf of their people.

Chief Yellow Horse of the Siksika

Chief Running Rabbit of the Siksika

Chief Crow Eagle of the Peigan

Chiefs present at Blackfoot Crossing

Left to right: Sitting on Eagle Tail Feathers, Peigan; Three Bulls, Sik-sika; Crowfoot, Siksika; and Red Crow, Blood.

Blood, Blackfoot, and Peigan chiefs at Ottawa, 1886

First Nation chiefs (left to right): North Axe (North Peigan), Three Bulls (Siksika), Crowfoot (Siksika), Red Crow (Blood), and Onespot (Blood). Father Lacombe is second from right, front row.

Buffalo bones gathered for shipment at Gull Lake, NWT,
ca. 1890s

The slaughter of buffalo was one of the factors that led Plains tribes to
agree to treaties. The Treaty 7 elders say that the commissioners made
commitments to protect the buffalo at the treaty negotiations – promises that they did not keep.

Blood camp near Fort Macleod, June 1898

The people of Treaty 7 continued to camp in areas well beyond their reserves after they agreed to the treaty. The elders say that during the treaty negotiations the commissioners told them they would be able to freely move across their traditional territories.

Blood powwow at NWMP barracks, Fort Macleod, June 1898

Religious and cultural ceremonies were carried on by the Treaty 7 First Nations in spite of the fact that some were banned under the Indian Act. Elders of Treaty 7 were angered that they were not informed in 1877 about the way in which the Indian Act would be used to control their lives. The act had not been mentioned during the negotiations at Blackfoot Crossing.

Crazy Dog Society members dancing, Blackfoot reserve near Cluny,
Alberta, 1920s

Blackfoot Prairie Chicken Society

Stoney pupils at McDougall Orphanage, Morley, Alberta, ca. *1901*

The Stoneys were promised assistance in becoming agriculturalists but the programs established were not adequately funded, and seed and equipment were of poor quality. Little of the reserve land at Morley was suited to agriculture, and Stoney elders point out that missionary John McDougall took the most prime agricultural land for himself.

Roman Catholic mission, Blood reserve, near Stand Off, Alberta,
ca. 1910

St Joseph residential school, Catholic mission near Cluny, Alberta,
ca. 1910

Treaty 7 elders remember that they were promised education but the
mission schools established were not what they expected. Many of
their children died of diseases in the boarding and industrial schools.
The children were taught to turn away from their traditional culture
and adopt the ways of non-Native society. Rarely did their education or
training provide them with off-reserve employment.

Priest, sisters, and schoolchildren at St Joseph residential school, 1900

Stoney pupils at McDougall Orphanage, 1901

Stoney pupils from McDougall Orphanage, ca. 1901

Pupils of St Paul's Anglican boarding school, Blood reserve, 1911

Blood women

The resourcefulness and ingenuity of women in the post-treaty era was crucial in preventing starvation and preserving community. Their work, which included snaring small game and harvesting provisions such as berries and wild turnip, was vital at a time when the buffalo had disappeared and government rations were meagre. In the early years there remained scope for women to practise their gathering economy and strategies, but these opportunities diminished with increased non-Native settlement. Treaty 7 elders said that government officials reneged on promises to share the wealth of the land with those who agreed to the treaty.

PART TWO

The Historical Canon and Elder Evidence

WALTER HILDEBRANDT
WITH SARAH CARTER

CHAPTER FIVE

Treaty 7 in Its Historical and Political Context

INTRODUCTION

Past and present perspectives vie for prominence in the continual debate about what constitutes the history of any event. While the facts of an event remain unaltered, interpretations change and new stories come to light. Such is the case with Treaty 7. The history of Treaty 7, as Treaty 7 people understand it, has always been there, but it has not been part of the mainstream story of Canada. In most historical accounts, Treaty 7 is simply recounted as an event that paved the way to nationhood, making the West safe for settlement by Ontarians and Europeans. But the treaty has a different significance for the Treaty 7 First Nations because in their histories they emphasize issues that have little to do with nation-building. They even disagree with how the Canadian government continues to define its lawful obligations under Treaty 7.

It is only recently that non-Aboriginal Canadians have been willing to listen to what First Nations have to say about their history, and to acknowledge that official histories may have to be changed to accommodate the Aboriginal point of view.

One of the fundamental problems associated with coming to an understanding of Aboriginal-White relations has to do with the fact that Canadian intellectuals generally eschew a colonial framework and scarcely mention imperialism as a factor in the settlement of the West. Told from the point of view of the "victors," or the newcomer settlers, Canadian history emphasizes the perspective of the dominant society. Token recognition is extended to tragedies related to the history of the Aboriginal peoples – the unfortunate disappearance of the buffalo, disease, alcohol – but it is assumed that everything worked out for the best in the long run. Established historians such as Arthur Lower, Donald Creighton, and George Stanley consistently maintain that Canada's Indian policy was honourable, if at times misguided. Intentions were always good. In the long view of Aboriginal-White relations, the "partnership" forged between newcomers and Aboriginal peoples has served both sides well – it was inevitable that Canada's history in the Northwest turned out as it did. The effects of empire-building, according to the establishment historians, has on balance been to the benefit of all concerned in this spread of "civilization." In the words of George Stanley:

The gravest problem presented to the Dominion of Canada by the acquisition and settlement of Rupert's Land and the North-West was the impact of a superior civilization upon the Native Indian Tribes. Again and again, in different places and in different ways, the problem has unfolded itself at the contact of European and savage. Too often the advent of the white man has led to the moral and physical decline of the Native. In Africa, Melanesia and America, the clash of peoples in different stages of development has spelled disaster to the weaker. The European, conscious of his material superiority, is only too contemptuous of the savage, intolerant of his helplessness, ignorant of his mental processes and impatient at his slow assimilation of civilization. The savage, centuries behind in mental and economic development, cannot readily adapt himself to meet the new conditions. He is incapable of bridging the gap of centuries alone and unassisted. Although white penetration into Native territories may be inspired by motives of self-interest, such as trade and settlement, once there, the responsibility of "the white man's burden" is inevitable.[1]

However euphemistically writers like Stanley portray the process, we can no longer ignore colonialism and its imperial context as we write the history of the Canadian West. As cultural critic Edward Said notes:

The global reach of classical nineteenth and early twentieth century European imperialism still casts a considerable shadow over our own times. Hardly any North American, African, European, Latin American, Indian, Caribbean, Australian individual – the list is very long – who is alive today has not been touched by the empires of the past. Britain and France between them controlled immense territories: Canada, Australia, New Zealand, the colonies of North and South America and the Caribbean, large swatches of Africa, the Middle East, the Far East (Britain will hold Hong Kong as a colony until 1997), and the Indian subcontinent in its entirety all these fell under the sway of and in time were liberated from British or French rule.[2]

Imperial powers played a major role not only in physically neutralizing indigenous populations but in creating and sustaining negative images of Aboriginal peoples. The dissemination of these negative images helped those in power justify, to themselves, the removal of Aboriginal peoples from their traditional lands. Said has called this the "struggle over geography": "That struggle is complex and interesting because it is not only about soldiers and cannons but about ideas, about forms, about images and imaginings."[3]

After justifying their right to move into and control new territory, the European powers went wherever they could: "Scarcely a corner of life was left untouched by the facts of empire; the economies were hungry for overseas markets, raw materials, cheap labour, and hugely profitable land, and defense and foreign-policy establishments were more and more committed to maintaining vast tracts of distant territories and large numbers of subjugated people. When the Western powers were not in close, sometimes ruthless competition with one another for more colonies ... they were hard at work settling, surveying, studying, and of course ruling the territories under their jurisdictions."[4]

The Aboriginal people of southern Alberta were not a pool of cheap labour, nor a new market to be exploited, but they did occupy valuable land and stood in the way of those who wanted to exploit coal, oil, and other minerals in and along the Rocky Mountains. The invasions and intrusions of traders, surveyors, and settlers were experienced by the indigenous people as the National Policy became the driving force behind the Canadian expansion into the Northwest. The same forces at work in other parts of the world were at work in the Canadian West. These forces were defined by Said as follows: " 'Imperialism' means the practice, the theory and attitudes of a dominating metropolitan centre ruling a distant territory; 'colonialism,' which is almost always a consequence of imperialism, is the implanting of settlements on distant territories."[5] Imperialism can be exercised in a variety of ways, including force, political collaboration, economic pressure, and social or cultural co-option; it is the process of establishing and maintaining an empire. The accumulation of wealth that invariably takes place is accompanied by productions and portrayals – books, newspapers, visual images – that justify and document the need of the colonizers to dominate the land and make it bountiful in ways that those who originally occupied it have been unable to do. Thus, terms such as "inferior," "subject race," "subordinate people," "dependency," "expansion," and "authority" come into common use by the colonizer.

Those agents of colonialism who exercised power used concepts and languages that gradually became familiar to the colonized and over time became part of the culture of domination. As the agents of empire sought to exploit spices, sugar, slaves, coal, rubber, cotton, opium, tin, gold, oil, and silver, they found it difficult to maintain these huge empires. They needed "immense will and self-confidence even arrogance"[6] in order to rule the indigenous people and convincingly portray them as subordinate, less advanced, and inferior. Thus, a process of "education" began whereby the colonizers tried to persuade the colonized that what the colonizers were doing was right, that they should accept the colonizers' notions of what was best for the lands they were living on. It was, as Stanley put it, the "white man's burden" to persuade the indigenous people that the newcomers' way was the best way. The newcomers promoted the idea of a partnership, but in this partnership the colonizers would try to convince the colonized that what was being done was in their own best interests.

Thus, to understand properly what happened in the Treaty 7 area, one must acknowledge the concepts of imperialism and colonialism, for these concepts shaped the relations between Aboriginal and newcomer, and were behind the forces that permanently changed the landscape and lifestyle of the Aboriginal peoples of the western prairies. The history of Treaty 7 must be broadened to allow the voices of the colonized to be heard.

UNDERSTANDING TREATY 7

The numbered treaties, from 1 to 7, were substantially similar, but each one dealt with particular circumstances and contained distinct clauses. While there can be unanimity on the meaning of certain clauses, in general the texts of the treaties can be interpreted in a variety of ways. It is questionable whether a "mutually understood agreement" was ever arrived at between a people representing a written culture on the one hand and a people representing an essentially oral culture on the other. Indeed, many indigenous cultures throughout the world were at a distinct disadvantage as the nation-states that had been growing since the mid-eighteenth century expanded their interests. In the period from the late eighteenth century to the twentieth century, the world witnessed "the construction of the state in the image and interests of the new middle classes."[7] The expansion of these nation-states saw the subordination of classes, ethnic groups, and races to a dominant class or racial group. The interests of one particular class or group were privileged at the expense of the interests of the others. What emerged in each instance was a so-called national culture that in fact was little more than the culture favoured by those who made up the dominant group or class. By the twentieth century it was clear that the dominant class was the middle class, and its cultural forms and economic interests were favoured. In most nation-states this meant that the culture of the subordinated class, ethnic group, or race was either suppressed or expropriated as nominally part of the "national" culture. National identity and culture were "disseminated throughout the whole of society in several ways, such as the spread of literacy, the 'invention of tradition,' the standardization of 'national' language, the establishment of public education, religious evangelism, promotion of economic individualism."[8] What went hand in hand with the valorizing of a national culture was the diminution of other cultures: "Local, 'unprogressive,' and particularist attitudes and practices, such as minority religion, dialect and minority languages, folk customs and traditions rooted in agrarian economy and so on, were either taken over (or tidied up) as folklore of the 'nation' or discouraged and even prescribed as 'superstitious,' 'barbaric' or 'unprogressive.'"[9]

At times the subordinated groups were described in national

narratives as "noble savages," especially when any threat from them had dissipated. What they learned from their experiences was that it was best to become assimilated within the dominant culture if they hoped to survive. Their real culture was somewhere far in the distant past: "Nostalgia could be indulged, and the 'primitive people' could be safely used as a moral, because they could not or soon would not pose any political, social or cultural problem in their own right and on their own behalf. Meanwhile the middleclass reformers of the early nineteenth century rapidly developed strategies for 'modernizing' these primitive people, along with the lower classes."[10] While the "noble savage" was idealized, the cultural practices of subordinated groups were belittled. This condemnation included "merely oral culture, communalism (if not communism) and sociability, apparently improvident and opportunistic work patterns and domestic economy, 'immoral' sexual practices, a tendency to nomadism if not outright vagabondage, 'superstitions' or false religion and an ad hoc and adaptive attitude to 'improvement' and new technology, an ad hoc practical approach to leadership, work organization and the 'moral economy' and 'irrational' or merely 'traditional' ideas of social land economic justice."[11]

The dominant middle-class society was either unwilling or unable to see Aboriginal culture as a successful and long-term accommodation to its environment. Thus, the dominant culture that emerged was a literate society directed by Christian principles. In the Canadian West, the dominant culture had a specific agenda: "Just as important were ideas of economic self-sufficiency and individualism and settled, disciplined and investment oriented work habits and domestic economy. These would be supported by a middle-class sexual morality and model of domesticity and reinforced by a more routine, 'orderly' and hierarchical pattern of leadership in work and social life; and a market-oriented, competitive attitude to labour and its rewards. Finally there should be acceptance of regular institutions of surveillance, control and policing."[12] The agents of this European culture, which was making its way across North America in a search for wealth, were not always primarily interested in controlling the indigenous populations – at least not at first. Early in the contact period, they needed the expertise and knowledge of indigenous people in order to establish their own position of strength. The need to denigrate and then to convert and civilize the Aboriginal only came once the economic advantages had been secured. Those who at first had been important "partners" were soon to become major impediments to "civilization."

By the time the treaties were being negotiated on the prairies, the Euro-Canadian leadership were confident that they were powerful enough to secure agreements that would allow White settlements to be established and to thrive. Unknown to the Aboriginal leadership, the treaties were to privilege the written culture of the dominant society while denigrating the oral culture of the Aboriginal treaty makers. For this newly emerging middle-class power, the land had to be made "bountiful," and in its estimation the Aboriginal peoples had not succeeded in this. There were no cultivated fields or estates by which Euro-Canadians measured success. In fact, when the treaties were being negotiated, the Aboriginal peoples were viewed as an obstacle to the colonization schemes envisaged for the West by Euro-Canadian elites. The treaties were seen by people like Father Scollen, Reverend McDougall, Colonel Macleod, and Commissioner Laird as expedient means of beginning the process of assimilation through which (they believed) the Aboriginal populations would eventually disappear. It is clear that Canadian officials and religious leaders were preparing the Aboriginal population for the White settlers who they knew would be arriving in large numbers to take over the land. These agents of Euro-Canadian society showed scarcely any ability to appreciate the "communal economy and social practises"[13] of the populations with whom they came into contact. They did not approach the treaty process as equals negotiating with equals but rather as superiors with inferiors. This was a major disadvantage for the Aboriginal leadership, who came to negotiate Treaty 7 in good faith. The attitude of the Canadian treaty makers was paternalistic and condescending – they would do what they thought was best for the Aboriginal peoples, even to the extent of ignoring what the Aboriginal leaders clearly wanted to include in the treaty.

Thus, a major problem with the treaties was that ideologically and culturally the treaty makers for the Crown did not respect the Aboriginal leadership and what it represented: "The white policy-makers' idea of the nature and powers of native chiefs was in part a relic of the earlier political culture of monarchy and court government and the idea that a European monarch was treating a weaker or lesser peer, the chief, in The New World, Africa or Australia."14 They did not respect the authority or legitimacy of the chiefs with whom they were negotiating, and perhaps they never had any intention of honouring what they were negotiating: "The treaties, circumstances and perceptions of the Canadian Government and its officers profoundly altered the political and social organization of the Native people, according to white assumptions and practices that had been formed in North America but they were also informed by models of social structure and relationships developed in Britain. To some extent, at least, the chiefs were made something like a cross between a Highland laird ... [and] an idealized version of the professionalised landed gentleman and the Victorian public school ideal of the gentlemanly public official."15

The Aboriginal leaders were allowed to feel that they were negotiating as equals, but the Euro-Canadians did not respect their culture and they saw their nations as inferior. The Aboriginal leaders could hardly be expected to know that these men they were bargaining with in good faith had little resolution to take seriously the discussions that the Aboriginal leadership solemnized by smoking the pipe.

The power relationship between the Aboriginal government and the Canadian government was not equal, and leaders such as Crowfoot and Red Crow were aware that military force was being used to slaughter indigenous people in the United States. By accommodating the newcomers, the Aboriginal people hoped to work out an arrangement to share the land so that both sides could benefit from living side by side. They could not have known that the newcomers expected more than a commitment to share the land, that in fact they wanted to take what they could, even if it meant disregarding the treaties. The Aboriginal leadership did not know about the cultural attitudes that had long been evolving in Europe, which privileged the culture of one class above that of all others. Anything not European was subordinated, and values that were not middle class were dismissed or ignored. What happened in western Canada in the 1870s was only one incident in the global process of subjugation that was played out wherever colonial fragments of the British Empire took hold. There never was a reconciliation between what was actually discussed at Blackfoot Crossing in September 1877 and what was included in the written legal text of the Treaty 7 document. The territorial imperative of the Crown is still imposed today upon the First Nations of Treaty 7.

CONTEXT OF TREATY 7: SOME CONSIDERATIONS

A problem with understanding Treaty 7 arises out of the way in which it has been described and represented to date. Until very recently the treaty has been explained in the context of nation-building, usually in an academic discourse by male writers who are defending a linear approach. Their chosen form is the essay, which usually presumes a monological or single perspective, with a narrator arbitrarily organizing evidence to produce the Truth – a single unassailable verity. Much of the writing done about Treaty 7 assumes this tone of truth, of finality: that we (Euro-Canadians) are right and their (the Aboriginal peoples') opinions are of no consequence. This position has been allowed to go unchallenged – until only very recently – because few of these authors have considered what Aboriginal people themselves thought or think of the treaty; they either never asked, or when they have, they have selectively asked only certain people. The result has been that areas of the treaty that are clearly problematic have been glossed over and the discourse of those who hold power has allowed authors to ignore difficult issues. The consequence has been to discredit the voices of those who disagree with the "official" government line on what the treaty means.

What is clear is that there is no agreed-upon interpretation of Treaty 7; nor is there agreement on what motivated both sides to agree to the treaty. Studies based on a single perspective have failed to stop the nagging questions about the treaty. Over the years academics have come to the recognition that a dialogic (dual or multiple) perspective is needed to understand historical events such as Treaty 7. What becomes evident when a dialogical approach is used is that on some points there is agreement while on others there is divergence of opinion. One of the crucial differences between the perspectives of the Canadian government and the First Nations is that the government side has privileged the written form of representation, while the First Nations side has relied (and still does) on an oral discourse. Thus, while the Crown thought that what was written down was the final word, the Aboriginal people believed that what was said in the discussions at Blackfoot Crossing was as valid as what was written down.

Problems relating to language are at the very core of the Euro-Canadian's difficulty in understanding the Aboriginal world view. The spoken languages of Aboriginal peoples have been ignored by dominant imperial cultures, and the failure to recognize or acknowledge Aboriginal culture constitutes a form of cultural subjugation. As Sakej Youngblood-Henderson has written: "Everywhere we are born into language, everywhere it binds our consciousness. Its mystery and development reflect our particular habits, those of our linguistic heritage. Our language [or languages] contain the essential ways in which we experience and interact with our culture. Thus, our linguistic understanding [the world view in English] is our map that a particular language creates in order to navigate the larger worldview. These understandings become, then, in some sense, most of the worldview."[16]

Youngblood-Henderson argues that the noun-centred objectifying languages of the Eurocentric world view help users of these languages to reify and classify the world environment. By contrast, Aboriginal languages are verb-centred and reflect an apprehension of the world that is in a constant state of flux or change. Thus, there are very few fixed or rigid objects in the Aboriginal world view: "With the fluidity of semantic-phonemes comprising the verb sounds, every speaker can create new vocabulary 'on the fly,' custom tailored to meet the experience of movement to express the very finest nuances of meanings."[17] Youngblood-Henderson maintains that such different ways of seeing the world mean that these languages cannot be easily translated – that simply translating a word by itself does not relay with it the world view that the language as a whole contains.

The fundamental assumptions underlying European and Aboriginal languages are so radically different that simple translation is impossible. For the Aboriginal, "to see things as permanent is to be confused about everything: an alternative to that understanding is the need to create temporary harmonies through alliances and relationships among all forms and forces – this process is a never-ending source of wonder to the indigenous mind and to other forces who contribute to the harmony."[18]

To ignore Aboriginal languages and to insist on assimilation or "cognitive imperialism" is to deny and destroy the Aboriginal sacred understandings. Youngblood-Henderson concludes that "cultural and cognitive racism must be exposed and resolved. Under modern thought, at least in theory, every language describes the world completely, though each in its own way. The Aboriginal languages and worldviews must be strengthened and developed with their own contexts. Any interference is domination, both cognitively and culturally. Thus every Aboriginal language has the right to exist without conforming to Eurocentric languages or worldviews ... The failure to admit differences in worldview is also domination."[19]

Thus, a fundamental problem continues to exist in the discourse between those who have held power and those who have not or those who have represented a new way of life and the indigenous populations. The table on pages 202–3 presents a breakdown of the way one writer has conceptualized the different world views, the Eurocentric (A) and the Aboriginal (B).

Before exploring this problem further, we must first try to understand the motives of both sides and the policies that the government established in its treaty making, so that we might come to an appreciation of the relations between Aboriginal peoples and the Canadian government. One cannot understand Treaty 7 without placing it in the broader context of government policy – both the government's announced intentions and what the government in fact did.

ARRIVAL OF THE EUROPEANS

Trade for furs was the predominant reason for the presence of agents of European empires in northern North America. The trade for European goods included guns, metal, and dry goods. This trade, conducted mostly by the British and French, had great consequences for the Aboriginal people who became involved in it. In the first decades of the European presence, there was little attention paid to land entitlement because the trade depended on the wide-ranging pursuit of the furs undertaken by Aboriginal people. The issue of who owned or occupied the land

Eurocentric	Aboriginal
– money as "capital"	– nature as "capital"
– quantitative	– qualitative
– domination of nature	– living with nature
– large-scale economic projects that are concentrated	– small-scale economic projects that are spread out
– centralization	– decentralization
– individual creativity is often subverted	– individual creativity is encouraged
– democratic or autocratic decision-making	– consensus decision-making
– alienation from the process of government on a day-to-day level	– active participation in the process of government on a day-to-day level
– power concentrated in the hands of a few	– power broadly based
– strong ethic of direct leadership	– strong ethic of collective leadership
– "economics" as a separate and specialized area best left to "experts"	– "economics" as inseparable from other aspects of daily life
– dehumanization of work	– humanization of work
– workers leave home to travel to a work site	– workers work close to home
– work alienates worker from family units	– work is performed in family
– work emphasizes material gain	– work emphasizes spiritual gain
– individual ownership	– collective ownership
– concern with goods	– concern with services
– work is provided by an external provider	– work is evident, not provided
– work is assigned	– work is selected
– work is time allocation	– work is task allocated
– strict control of time	– flexible time
– hours, minutes, days	– seasons
– linear time	– concentric time
– leisure as an alternative to work (rest time)	– work and leisure as part of the same process
– ethic of competition	– ethic of cooperation
– work-related stresses	– stress associated with external variables
– resources at a distance	– resources close at hand
– urban focus	– rural focus
– mobility of labour	– immobility of labour
– capital intensive	– labour intensive
– economic rigidity	– economic adaptation
– elimination of perceived obstacles to economic "progress"	– willingness to accommodate to changes in economic circumstances
– land/means of production can be owned individually	– land/means of production are held collectively
– legal titles and deeds can be held individually	– no such concept

Eurocentric	Aboriginal
– exclusivity of lands is on personal level and enforced by legal strictures of society	– exclusivity is cultural and enforced by force, one culture by another, but not within cultures
– limits to land and territory are demarcated by manmade monuments	– lands are demarcated only by natural and preexisting
– land is an "economic" resource like any other	– land is the source of life
– land belongs to "us"	– "we" belong to the land
– one major model of economic organization	– many models of economic organization
– economic success is measured quantitatively	– economic success is measured qualitatively
– success measured by accumulation	– success measured by peer review
– economic specialization	– economic generalization
– profound belief that economic change can be imposed from an outside society	– profound belief that economic change can only be acomplished from within society
– structures of society are formalized and rigid	– structures of society are flexible and implied
– formal education away from home	– informal education at home
– "teachers" are outsiders away from home	– "teachers" are family members at home
– ethic of individualism	– ethic of "kin-ism"
– actions reflect upon an individual group	– actions reflect upon a kin or clan
– permanent institutions	– fluidity of institutions
– eccentricity is generally not tolerated	– eccentricity is generally tolerated
– deviance is punished by confinement within society	– deviance is punished by exile from society
– problems are isolated away from society in general	– problems are dealt with at a community level
– parameters of society are at a large supranational level	– parameters of society are at a local level
– coalitions of interests expand to form broad segments of larger self-interest	– ranges of interests are at a local or culture-wide level
– ability to form large and coherent large-scale interest groups	– great differences and inter-tribal enmities are difficult to overcome
– literate traditions	– oral traditions
– preservation of details	– preservation of concepts
– monotheism	– pantheism
– structured religious dogma	– unstructured and fluid animism
– primarily male deities	– male and female deities
– concepts of "god" as "above" earth	– concepts of "god" as "in" and inherently part of the earth.[20]

was thus of little importance, although documents like the Hudson's Bay Company (HBC) charter made the assumption that the enormous territory of Rupert's Land belonged to Britain. But as settlements were established and the colonial presence grew, problems relating to landownership emerged for the European powers. Claims to the land by settlers and by those who wished to exploit its resources brought about the need for Europeans to control and also protect those within their territorial sphere. The need to improve their laws and maintain order became paramount for them. Colonies established by Britain and France grew, and as a result of competition between these two powers, wars erupted in both the Old World and the New. Through a series of treaties between France and Britain that were negotiated at the end of the wars, it became clearer just how the European powers defined their claims in the New World and how they defined themselves in relation to the First Nations of North America.

It was the British who would finally emerge as the most powerful imperial presence in North America; the land they controlled was huge (perhaps even more extensive than they realized at the time) as a result of land acquired through the treaties of Utrecht (1763) and Paris (1813). After the American Revolutionary War of 1776–83, the extent of British influence was again redefined.

Following the defeat of France in North America, the Royal Proclamation of 1763 set a precedent for the way Aboriginal title to the land would be recognized. The proclamation established the provision that land could be purchased only by the Crown and not by individuals. Those lands that had not been purchased by Britain or had not been ceded to Britain were to be considered the lands of the Aboriginal peoples. The Aboriginal peoples' rights to these lands were to be rights of occupancy and not title in fee simple – all this, of course, in accordance with British law. Up to this time, treaties with First Nations had focused on peace and only secondarily on land, but as pressures from settlement increased, the emphasis shifted from peace treaties to land acquisitions.

The Aboriginal leadership believed that they had the right to negotiate what was to happen in the lands they had occupied for hundreds of years. They had the right to expect to be treated as equals by the treaty commissioners because British law had already established that indigenous peoples were to be treated as legitimately holding "title" to the land. This was the direction in which British land law had evolved since the Proclamation of 1763. Among other principles that had been settled since the eighteenth century were the following two: "There was no presumption of Crown title to Aboriginal dominion but only its exclusive right to purchase from the Aboriginal Nation or Tribes and a prohibition of colonial or private acquisition of tribal lands,"[21] and "the Crown had to obtain title to reserved Hunting Grounds from the Indian nation or tribe before any sale or lease of land could be carried out to any British subject ... The *1763 Proclamation* also affirmed the Aboriginal nations and tribes legal right to exclusively regulate the reserved lands and determine the Aboriginal rights to use and enjoy the land through time."[22]

A fiduciary relationship arose out of the legal position of the Crown: "By affirming the royal protection of lands not ceded or purchased in the 1763 Proclamation, the British Sovereign willingly agreed to protect the ancient land tenure of the Mikmaq under its prerogative jurisdiction ... His Majesty thereby established nation-to-nation sale as the only valid method of extinguishing treaty-reserved Aboriginal dominion and converting it to His Majesty's derivative tenure. Until the Crown purchased the land, it had to act as fiduciary and protect the reserved Aboriginal dominion and its ultimate or future interest."[23] This is how the law stood, but in practice the law was not upheld: "Increasingly, the fact that the British colonists either could not maintain, or had no interest in maintaining, the Crown's promises became apparent. The Aboriginal nations soon began to question the British colonial authorities' ability or willingness to support His Majesty's law. They came to understand that British immigrants had different concepts of ownership and rights than either His Majesty or themselves."[24]

British law helped to establish the practice of treaty making that protected the Aboriginal peoples' tenure on their lands: "The Crown did not treat North America as a *res nullius* or *terra nullius* or conquered. It affirmatively acknowledged the territorial sovereignty of the First Nations through the treaties."[25] The Crown was left with legally enforceable fiduciary duties: "Failure of the Crown to perform the obligations would cause the jurisdictional interests over the land to revert to the First Nations."[26]

THE ROBINSON TREATIES

By 1850 Canada West began to desire to exploit the mineral resources north of the Great Lakes. The Robinson Treaties of present-day northwestern Ontario, which set the pattern for the "numbered" treaties of the 1870s in the West, were made to provide access to mineral resources. The commissioner who oversaw the treaties was Benjamin Robinson. In two treaties, he secured title to land that was twice the size negotiated in any other treaty up to that time. Under the Robinson Treaties the government agreed to a number of commitments that would become standard in subsequent treaties. These included annuity payments, assurances that bands would be able to continue to hunt and fish, and the provision of reserve land: "They were negotiated by specially commissioned officers of the Crown to extinguish title to relatively large expanses of territory; they offered existing hunting and fishing rights and promised reserves as well as annuities. All were consistent with the terms of the Proclamation of 1763. All were cheaper means of taking surrenders than the earlier British form, and cheaper still than the American alternative of dictating the terms of treaty after military conquest."[27] The granting of reserves in return for title was seen by Robinson as a cost-saving measure, since (he argued) otherwise the government would need to assume responsibility for the welfare of all people in the territory, which, as he emphasized, was vast.

WESTERN CANADA TREATIES 1-6

The treaties leading up to the making of Treaty 7 give us insight into what motivated the Canadian government to enter into treaties where and when it did. They provide examples of what the government said it was agreeing to and what it in fact did. As the definition of the Canadian "nation" evolved, so did the discussions about just how such an identity could be created.

After the Robinson Treaties, the most obvious territories to prepare for settlement and make accessible for exploration were those to the west. In 1857 the Select Committee of the British House of Commons was established to consider the future of Rupert's Land, as the HBC charter was up for renewal. Discussions were held to determine how this territory could best be governed. It was decided that as there was not yet enough of a colonial presence to govern the territory directly, the land should be taken over bit by bit as the railway moved westward. The major recommendation was that the Red River and Saskatchewan districts should be ceded to the colonies. While the latter recommendation was not then acted upon, it was clear that the idea of a nation "from sea to sea" had found fertile ground in the minds of the colonists who held power in central Canada and in the British Colonial Office.

During the 1860s the idea of a Canadian nation from sea to sea took shape in influential political, intellectual, and business circles. The drive towards nationhood became more urgent as external threats in Canada's hinterland were felt as a result of the American Civil War. In the wake of the war, settlement in the American West grew dramatically and the still-active war economies of the northern states were able to complete railway lines that were to bring in even more White settlers into what had become the mythical "Last Best West." With the American West filling up with settlers from Ireland, there were threats from Fenian activists who on occasion struck at the underbelly of the British Empire with raids north. Canada had to respond to these outside pressures. The Canadian Confederation that had begun with the Maritime provinces, Ontario, and Quebec made promises to British Columbia in 1871 that a railway to link the country physically from coast to coast would be complete in four years. Thus, the stage was set to complete the idea of a Canadian nation that had been envisaged for so long by the political and business leaders of Canada West. One of the primary goals of westward Canadian expansion was to provide an outlet for the overflow of population created by dwindling farm lands of Canada West. In order for the population influx to settle peacefully, the West needed to be made safe for settlement. Central to the goal of creating safe conditions for Ontarian settlers would be the removal of the threat posed by the Aboriginal people inhabiting the territory.

Thus, the colonial government undertook to make treaties with the Aboriginal people who were living on lands most attractive to Ontarian settlers. Beginning with treaties 1 and 2, signed in 1871 at Stone Fort (Lower Fort Garry) and Manitoba Post, the government proceeded westward to secure territory for their National Policy, which entailed settlement in western Canada and the completion of a railroad from Atlantic to Pacific. These two prongs of the National Policy could successfully be dispatched through the relatively painless treaty process. Treaty 3 (1873) of the Lake of the Woods, Treaty 4 of southern Saskatchewan, Treaty 5 in central Manitoba, Treaty 6 of central Saskatchewan and Alberta, and Treaty 7 encompassing southern Alberta were all made along major transportation routes and where farmland was most attractive. Other territories on the north, where settlement was less likely to occur, were left without treaties, there being no urgency to establish access for transportation or to clear the way for settlement.

Manitoba, the first of the stepping stones into the West, had already experienced attempted colonization by the Earl of Selkirk early in the nineteenth century. He purchased land from the Hudson's Bay Company in 1811 to establish a colony of Scottish crofters who were expected to concentrate on farming and were not to compete with the fur-trading monopoly of the HBC. The first groups of settlers arrived in the area in 1812. Lord Selkirk signed a treaty with the local Saulteaux and Cree nations of the Red River District, and through this 1817 document, land was secured for settlement in return for an annual payment of one hundred pounds of tobacco to each nation. The Métis of the Red River settlement were not so obliging and challenged the company's monopoly after the merger of the HBC and the North West Company in 1821.

Resistance to the Canadian presence in Red River grew. Métis discontent was directed against those who, though by far in the minority, were aggressively advocating union with Canada. These opposing points of view culminated in the first Riel Rebellion of 1869-70, which eventually led to the creation of Canada's sixth province. In 1870 Louis Riel and his followers negotiated for the rights of the Métis, and although Métis land and language were supposedly to be guaranteed by the Manitoba Act that resulted from the negotiations, no mention was made of other Aboriginal rights, such as hunting and fishing. The Canadian government only reluctantly agreed to the language rights; it originally had no intention of granting any rights to the Métis of Red River. In fact, over the years it expended considerable energy in attempts to nullify the language provisions of the Manitoba Act. The powerful business leaders of central Canada, however, were anxious enough for western settlement that they were willing to make compromises, especially if it meant that settlement could proceed without further incident. Thus, a pattern was established whereby the government would take an initial, apparently intransigent, position in negotiations and when the negotiations eventually broke down, it would make accommodations, adopting positions with which it had not initially agreed.

A major piece of the final picture of the dream of a West settled by colonists was the addition of Rupert's Land to Canada. In 1870 this land was sold by the Hudson's Bay Company to Canada; the HBC received £300,000 and the right to select one-twentieth of the land that was to be surveyed for settlement across the West. Article 14 of the agreement recognized the rights of the Aboriginal peoples: "Any claims of Indians to compensation for lands required for purposes of settlement shall be disposed of by the Canadian Government; and the company shall be relieved of all responsibility in respect of them."

From the beginning of negotiations of the numbered treaties during the 1870s, the Canadian government showed that it was only willing to pursue its own agenda. It wanted to sign treaties in those areas of the country where major transportation lines had to be established or preserved, such as land for the railway across the fertile belt, the waterway north of Winnipeg in Treaty 5, the route from Edmonton to Pelly River for access to the Klondike gold field in Treaty 8, and the land that would give access to oil at Norman Wells in Treaty 11. The government signed whatever it had to in order to assure the success of its economic and national agenda. It showed far less willingness to live up to the clauses that committed it to assist Aboriginal peoples to adapt to new economies in areas where their dependence on the buffalo was no longer viable. The government cared so little about some treaty negotiations that it only haphazardly recorded the wishes and demands expressed by Aboriginal groups during the negotiations. The treaty commissioners cynically agreed to programs designed to ease the Aboriginal peoples' transition to new economies but obviously without a clear commitment to make these programs work. On the face of it, it seems that they simply wanted Aboriginal groups out of the way, and this they could achieve by gaining their compliance. Once Aboriginal people were outnumbered by the predicted flood of White settlers, they could be ignored or put off without much consequence, which is exactly what happened.

ABORIGINAL AND GOVERNMENT OBJECTIVES IN THE TREATY ERA

In their approach to the treaties, the Aboriginal peoples and the government had different goals and priorities. The Aboriginal leadership had four basic goals. The first was to secure the physical survival of their people, especially in face of the devastation suffered in the wake of disease and disappearing buffalo herds. Secondly and very importantly, they hoped to establish peaceful relations with the colonial government, to establish a relationship of equality between nations, and to create an atmosphere of respect. This was especially important to the Aboriginal leadership in view of the military solution that the Americans had chosen with respect to their "Indian problem." Thirdly, the Aboriginal leadership wanted to ensure their peoples' cultural and spiritual survival as separate and distinct nations; this was to be achieved by keeping their own forms of government and institutions intact. The persistence of some of their cultural and spiritual ceremonies and the preservation of their languages to the present day, in face of government pressures to outlaw them, testify to the importance of cultural survival for the Plains Aboriginal people. The fourth goal of the Aboriginal leadership was to begin a transition to a new way of life, as they knew that they could no longer rely on the buffalo for subsistence. To effect this transition, the leadership hoped to adopt new technologies suitable to economies based on agriculture and stock raising. Many were willing and anxious to participate in both farming and ranching. They also wanted to benefit from educational and health benefits that Canadian society offered. This is clearly evident in certain clauses of the treaties. This last goal was to be achieved by sharing their land with the newcomers, who in return for the use of the land would provide expertise and training so that the Aboriginal people could share in the resource development of their homelands.

Although official accounts of treaty policy suggest that the government alone was responsible for the content of the treaties, more recent scholarship suggests that the government had no plan or comprehensive policy to deal with the Aboriginal peoples of the West. Early histories, based on limited sources, suggest that government treaties in the West evolved out of eighteenth-century British practices and ran parallel to US policies of the nineteenth century and to those successfully implemented in Upper Canada. The other assumption underlying the histories of the prairie treaties is that government policy was "deliberate, wise and benevolent."

Historians John Taylor and John Tobias, however, have argued that most of the content in the treaties that showed any concern with the survival of Aboriginal people in fact came from the people themselves, whether the Saulteaux in Treaty 1 or the Cree in Treaty 6. The government was originally prepared to offer only reserves and annuities, but the Aboriginal negotiators refused to sign such treaties and in fact asked for the inclusion of clauses that would help both their survival and their transition to a new economic livelihood. These requests included hunting and fishing supplies, livestock, as well as implements and machinery for farming.

Thus, the treaties contain some of what the First Nations themselves thought necessary to help them make the transition to a new way of life. Perhaps because the government never shared in this vision, it was completely unwilling to implement the clauses that the Aboriginal peoples insisted be included in the treaties. Insofar as the Aboriginal leaders were able, through hard bargaining, to get their goals into the treaties, the treaties reflect their vision of how the Plains people would survive into the future. Had it not been for their comparatively large numbers at the time of the treaty, one doubts that the government would have acceded to their wishes.

The government hoped that treaties would achieve five main goals. These related mostly to the overarching goal of realizing the "purpose of the Dominion" as expeditiously as possible, and very little to any vision of a future for Aboriginal people. The government's objectives did not reflect in any way a fiduciary relationship with the First Nations. They were almost entirely aimed at the colonizing and developing of the West as quickly as possible. The first goal of the government was to acquire legal title to land that could potentially be used for farming, fishing, and mining and over which the railway was to run. The second aim was to encourage Ontarians and European immigrants to settle the West. The third was to remove Métis and Aboriginal title to the land with as little cost as possible, to avoid both costly military campaigns and costly land settlements. The fourth was to stop American intrusion into Canadian territory and to establish Canadian authority so as not to encourage American expansion into the western territories north of the 49th parallel. The Cypress Hills Massacre of 1873 had proven the vulnerability of southern Saskatchewan and Alberta, and the arrival of Sitting Bull into southern Saskatchewan and the Nez Percé War of 1877 underlined the potential for serious international disputes along the boundary. The fifth goal was to respond to the requests by Aboriginal people for treaties as well as treaty benefits – though it appears that the government did less to develop a consistent policy in this area than in any of the others. In contrast to the encouragement given the Europeans and Ontarians, there was little done to encourage the indigenous populations to take part in the economic development of the West. As noted, it was the Aboriginal people themselves, not the government, that wanted Aboriginal participation in the development of the West.

CANADA'S INDIAN POLICY

Canada's "Indian policy" has been described as being based on the goals of "protection, civilization, and assimilation." Protection of First Nations peoples involved two almost mutually exclusive perceptions of them. The first was a paternalistic view – the Aboriginal people were seen as incapable of dealing with Anglo-Canadian society and therefore were in need of protection from unscrupulous exploitation. The concept has been entrenched in the Indian Act and is also implicit in the reserve system and in other government policies that extend to the present day. The second perception, historically much older, has to do with responsibility and stems from the time when Aboriginal people acted as allies to imperial powers, when their military support was valuable in helping to protect lands occupied by either the French or the English. In the struggle for North America, both the British and French established policies to handle relations with their Aboriginal allies. British policies were concerned with protecting their Aboriginal allies from encroaching White settlement as well as from fraudulent trade practices that were common in the eighteenth century. Superintendents were appointed to take care of Aboriginal issues as well as to distribute payments to Aboriginal allies to ensure their loyalty. Regulations dealing with a variety of matters were passed into law and implemented in the period from 1745 to 1761. These laws were consolidated and incorporated into the Royal Proclamation of 1763. The commitment to protection of allies in the circumstances of eighteenth-century North America dictated that Aboriginal people be treated as though they had the right to the lands they lived on. Thus, the format for subsequent treaties was established during the time when various eastern tribes were greatly valued allies of both the French and British.

Linked to the principle of protection was the idea that Aboriginal people needed to be "civilized" – that is, brought "up" to the level of the Europeans' concept of civilization. The dominant imperial cultures of the time viewed almost anyone they came into contact with in the so-called New World as inferior. Aboriginal people were seen to be low on the cultural evolutionary scale and therefore in need of considerable education to be brought to the level of the European. Pressure for this "civilization" came from primarily Protestant sects that zealously embarked on missions to Christianize/civilize the "brethren" of the New World. It also came from organizations such as the British Aborigines Protection Society, which advocated the protection as well as the civilization of Aboriginal peoples of the New World. "Civilizing" indigenous people through the imposition of European values emerged in Canada as a policy around 1815, and by the 1830s churches had begun to establish missions for Aboriginal people in North America. Thus, the paternalistic policy of protection that was embedded in the legislation of the time was accompanied by a variety of schemes aimed at converting the Aboriginal inhabitants to Christianity and to European cultural values.

After the War of 1812 Aboriginal tribes gradually lost their value as military allies and there was a profound change in Aboriginal policy in British North America. By 1830 a civilian Indian department was created and a whole new approach was adopted: Aboriginal people were to abandon their lifeways in favour of Christianity and adopt a life of agriculture. The chief instrument of this transformation was to be the reserve.

Protective ("civilizing") measures extended to taxation and alcohol, while other matters, such as who would be classified as being "Indian," were decided without any consultation with the various tribes affected by the legislation.

The third goal of British North American Indian policy emerged under the rubric of assimilation. Assimilation as an eventual result of having been "civilized" had always been implicit in the missionary work, but by the decade of the 1860s the need for assimilation was seen as more immediate. More had to be done to indoctrinate Aboriginal people in the ways of European civilization in order for assimilation to occur more quickly. To achieve this end, "An Act to Encourage the Gradual Civilization of the Indians of this Province and to Amend Laws Respecting Indians" (known as the Enfranchisement Act) was passed in 1857. There was now greater pressure to encourage Aboriginal people to turn their backs on their own culture and religion and adopt European values. But paradoxically, while the goal of the 1857 act was to eliminate distinctions between Anglo-Canadians and Aboriginal people, the act in fact entrenched differences by stipulating exactly what an "Indian" was. The act was established to outline the criteria whereby an Aboriginal person could be considered to be fully assimilated and qualified for enfranchisement. The act stipulated that if an "Indian" could be said to read or write English or French, was free of debt, and was of good moral character, he would be entitled to an allotment of twenty hectares on a reserve, and that if in the following year of probation the Indian could be said to be civilized, then that person could be given the franchise. But as John Tobias has summarized the 1857 Enfranchisement Act: "The legislation to remove all legal distinctions between Indians and

Euro-Canadians actually established them. In fact it set the standards for acceptance that many, if not most, white colonials could not meet, for few of them were literate, free of debt and of high moral character. The civilized Indian would have to be more 'civilized' than the Euro-Canadian."[28]

Up to the time of Confederation, protection, according to John Tobias, had been the main objective of the policy relating to Aboriginal peoples in British North America. Through the 1860s, this goal began to be supplanted by the White society's desire to civilize and assimilate its Native populations. An act passed in 1869 consolidated the Indian policy contained in the 1857 legislation and reflected the shift away from protection and towards full assimilation. The wording of the acts themselves showed this shift, from an act that was "for gradual civilization" to an act that was "for gradual enfranchisement" of the "Indian." "Inferior" Aboriginal forms of government were to be replaced by councils elected through provisions of the 1869 act. Canadian government authority was to replace traditional forms of Aboriginal government. Reserves that chose to elect their councils were given specific powers that would not otherwise have been recognized.

Canada embarked on its colonization of its western territories by applying the goals of protection, civilization, and assimilation as it entered into treaties with the prairie tribes. By the time the Canadian government consolidated its position on Indian policy through the Indian Act of 1876, the emphasis was now clearly on the long-term goals of civilization and assimilation. The language of the act was stronger than that of the earlier acts in attacking Aboriginal sexual, marriage, and child-rearing practices. Regulations controlled who could be on reserves and who could cohabit with an "Indian," and restricted the presence of Indian women in public places. The Criminal Code was amended to extend the definition of vagrancy "in order that the western Indian could be kept on the reserve where he might be taught to farm and learn the value of work".[29] The paternalism of the act was evident in its control of every facet of reserve life, from government benefits to cultural ceremonies. Traditional Aboriginal values were to be discredited and replaced by Euro-Canadian concepts of education, religion, economics, politics and property: "The 'Sun Dance,' Potlatches and all 'Give Away' ceremonials were banned because they promoted pagan beliefs and were anathema to the development of a concept of private property."[30]

As in the earlier acts, stipulations for attaining enfranchisement were central to the Indian Act of 1876. A single parcel of land would still be given to an individual who could prove he would use the land as a Euro-Canadian would. It was hoped that reserve residents would all claim their parcels of land as private property and consequently dissolve the reserves entirely. Other methods of enfranchisement were now offered under the revamped act. Not all of the clauses relating to enfranchisement applied to the tribes in the Northwest, who were not seen as having reached the same level of "civilization" as eastern Aboriginal peoples. Authority was vested in the act to give a location ticket to a plot of land* without the necessity of a probationary period to any "Indian" who went to university to become a minister, lawyer, teacher, or doctor. Assimilation by means of teaching the value of private property remained a central goal whose ultimate aim was to eliminate reserves entirely.

In the 1880s the government increased the discretionary powers of local officials to use new amendments to the Indian Act allowing for intervention in political decisions on the reserves. A bureaucracy was created to handle matters related not only to the Indian Act but also to Indian Affairs. Bands were encouraged to participate in the new form of government, which was seen as a necessary step towards complete assimilation: "The elected band council was regarded as the means to destroy the last vestige of the tribal system, the traditional political system."[31]

Schools were the institutions that could best ensure the completion of the process of civilization/assimilation. Since the environment of the reserve was deemed to be detrimental to instilling new values, local schools were not encouraged: "Residential and industrial schools, which removed the children from the detrimental influence of uncivilized parents and Indian traditions, were regarded as better instruments of government

---

* To assist in familiarizing reserve residents with concepts of Canadian society and private property, portions of some reserves were surveyed into individual lots. After a three-year period, if various criteria were met, the ticket holder could be enfranchised and could be given freehold title to that piece of property.

policy."[32] When parents refused to cooperate with the system, the government introduced amendments to empower authorities to make regulations "to commit children to the boarding and industrial schools."[33]

However, many of the programs intended to promote Aboriginal economic development were poorly implemented or underfunded. Indeed, there were fewer provisions in the Indian Act relating to economic development than there were for ways to deal with those reserves that refused to cooperate with the government when it wanted Indian lands alienated for purposes of mineral exploration, rights-of-way for highways and railways, or land leases for neighbouring farmers and ranchers. Vast powers were given to the superintendent general of Indian affairs to alienate land required for non-Aboriginal economic development because "Indians had refused to make surrenders for these purposes in the past."[34] Indeed, the superintendent general could lease reserve lands at his discretion to raise money for reserve residents, even if the band opposed such leases.

Though many Aboriginal people successfully adapted to agriculture in the early reserve years and enthusiastically embraced new technologies designed to establish alternative economies, they did not assimilate in the way Canadian authorities hoped they would. In the years from 1857 to 1920, only 259 "Indians" were enfranchised. Enfranchisement, clearly, was a goal and a process that did not interest reserve residents. Aboriginal reserve residents chose to farm on their own terms and not on those advocated by the authorities. Their initial successes were often undermined by government-imposed restrictions on their right to sell their own produce or purchase the labour-saving machinery necessary to keep them competitive. In addition to this, the Aboriginal farmer or rancher was seen as a threat by his White neighbours, who often complained about competition from the reserve farmers or ranchers. Thus, though Aboriginal people learned to adapt, the reserves did not disappear. Because the Aboriginal people were simply not interested in assimilation as envisaged by the authorities, this part of the policy failed abysmally. However, while skills that could be called the tools for civilization were learned, the real purpose behind the Indian Act was never really to benefit Aboriginal people, but rather to benefit Euro-Canadians. John Milloy summarized the policies of the

Indian Act as follows: "Responsible white authorities, politicians, departmental officials and missionaries were convinced that their duty toward the Indian was, as Superintendent General David Laird declared in 1876 'to prepare him for higher civilization by encouraging him to assume the privileges and responsibilities of full citizenship' and that this could only be achieved through a system of wardship, colonization and tutelage."[35]

The greatest concern of Canadian officials was to develop the West for those incoming residents who shared their own cultural aspirations. The interests of Aboriginal people were only taken seriously by the government when they intersected with or interfered with the government's own goals of developing and creating wealth from the West.

As the Canadian government moved to make the treaties in western Canada, its hidden agenda became more apparent. The Indian Act's goals and policies with respect to prairie Aboriginals were never discussed with western Aboriginal people, especially not with the leadership involved in Treaty 7, who had entered into the treaty the year after the Indian Act of 1876 was passed. David Laird had been minister of the interior when the act was passed, and at that time he had said that the Aboriginal person must be treated either as "a white man or as a minor."[36] The following year, as treaty commissioner for Treaty 7, Laird ostensibly dealt with treaty tribes as equals, as nations, but was evasive in not explaining to Treaty 7 First Nations that the government intended to restrict and control Aboriginal people through the provisions of the Indian Act. The legislative control over treaty people extended to the cultural, political, social, and economic areas of their lives. Treaty 7 people were not told how the Indian Act would serve to dominate their lives completely. In being told they would "be taken care of" when they made the treaty, they had been deceived into thinking the treaty could be relied on to guarantee their rights. The First Nations at Blackfoot Crossing were reassured about their rights as represented in the treaty and agreed to during the negotiations.

There was great confusion for years among the treaty signatories when they found they were regulated by an Indian Act that had never been discussed rather than by the treaty they had entered into. Adding to the confusion was the creation of the Department of Indian Affairs in 1880. The department was given extensive powers to implement new government policies that reached into almost every aspect of Aboriginal life. Furthermore, Parliament did not allocate this costly bureaucracy sufficient funds to implement the programs promised to Aboriginal peoples. Since the legislators felt a greater allegiance to the eastern electorate than to those in the thinly populated prairies, they had little compunction about failing to approve sufficient funds to implement treaty promises. Cabinet ministers or senior civil servants alike often did not recommend the financial budget that was required to fund programs properly.

The Aboriginal leadership wanted to integrate Euro-Canadian forms of education, farming, and ranching with their own cultural traditions. They wanted to benefit from the development of the West on their own terms. They did not simply want Euro-Canadian culture to replace their own ways. They were not informed that the Indian Act would in fact work against the wishes they had expressly made during treaty negotiations. They indeed wanted to benefit from Anglo-Canadian education but not to the detriment of their own ways. They never intended to stop using their own languages and had never imagined that their cultural practices, such as the Sun Dance, would be banned. They wanted their schools to be on reserves and did not want their children to be taken from their homes and families or to be punished for speaking their own languages. The Blackfoot Confederacy, Tsuu T'ina, and Stoney leadership wanted their children to be taught skills that would allow them to participate in the new economy of the West, rather than to be taught obedience or to despise their parents' way of life. Here again regulations of the Indian Act conflicted with treaty promises. Conflicts arose between the Aboriginal leaders, who wanted reserve day schools so that their children would be educated within the Aboriginal community, and the government, who hoped to wean the children away from their parents' way of life and thereby advance the goal of assimilation. The government spent more of its energies on banning Aboriginal cultural practices than it did on educating Aboriginal children in skills that could help them adapt to the Euro-Canadian world that was upon them. The ban on the traditional Aboriginal cultural ceremonies remained in effect until 1951.

THE 1877 PRELUDE: THE EXAMPLE OF TREATY 6

Contrary to popular and established beliefs, it was owing to pressure exerted by Aboriginal people that many of the treaties' provisions were adopted. The Ojibway refused to sign treaties 1 and 2 until clauses assuring them of domestic animals, farm tools, and other equipment were added. In the following years, the Cree on the plains interfered with the geological survey and the construction of telegraph lines until their rights to the land had been recognized. These facts challenge the long-accepted view that the Canadian government was far-sighted in the policies it developed for the West.

Treaty 6, signed the year before the Treaty 7 agreement was reached at Blackfoot Crossing, is an excellent example of the government's role in treaty making: it demonstrates what the government presented, what it promised, and what it in fact did. What is clear is that high on the Cree agenda was the goal of gaining assistance in adapting to an agricultural way of life; this is what the Cree demanded in return for allowing settlers to use the land.

The Cree had a long history of survival and adaptation. In the seventeenth century a branch of the Cree emerged from the woodland forests of the Canadian Shield to become Plains people. They adapted to the fur trade economy of the Northwest in the eighteenth and nineteenth centuries. With the decline of the buffalo, beginning in the 1850s the Cree tried to adapt again by moving into Blackfoot territory where the buffalo were more numerous, but their attempt was thwarted by the powerful Blackfoot tribes. At the Battle of the Belly River in 1870 the Cree were defeated and so was their goal of gaining better access to the diminishing buffalo herds.

The Cree leadership regrouped following this defeat and settled on the strategy of becoming agriculturalists. Increasingly, this became a way of life that many of the leaders recognized as a viable alternative to the buffalo hunt. But the Cree did not entirely give up on the buffalo as a mainstay of their economy. From the 1860s on, they pressured government officials to limit the buffalo hunt to Aboriginal people. Big Bear, who did not sign Treaty 6 until 1882, was a powerful spokesman, and it was he who pressured Treaty Commissioner Alexander Morris to agree to the regulation of the buffalo hunt. A significant number of Cree leaders, including Big Bear, Piapot, and Little Pine, who were committed both to the goal of preserving the buffalo and to making the transition to agriculture, did not sign the treaty because they doubted that the government would honour the treaty agreements. Big Bear in particular was also concerned about the autonomy of the Cree if they signed the treaty. He had said numerous times to government officials that he feared his loss of freedom and that he did not want to become enslaved as an animal with a rope around its neck. Cree oral traditions maintain that these powerful Cree leaders did not sign the treaty because they first wanted to see whether the Canadian government honoured the treaty and they hoped to put pressure on government officials to include additional items. Piapot, for example, only signed the treaty in 1875 (a year after others had signed) after Morris had agreed to consider his additional requests for blacksmithing and carpentry tools, that mills be built, and that instruction be given not only in farming but in other trades as well.

Big Bear and Little Pine continued to resist signing the agreement, hoping that they could form an alliance with other Plains people in order to protect the diminishing buffalo. They hoped that with an alliance they would be able to put their arguments to authorities from a position of strength. Little Pine and Big Bear could already see that even after a few years the government was not living up to its promises. The assistance that had been promised for farming was not forthcoming, and officials were slow in responding to complaints and protests from reserve residents. Big Bear's worst fears were realized when he witnessed starving Cree waiting for equipment and instructors to arrive. The situation grew serious enough that Laird warned government officials in Ottawa that the non-fulfilment of treaty promises was fuelling the flames of discontent among those Cree who had still not signed the treaty.

Unfortunately for Big Bear, he was not able to organize an alliance among prairie tribes to bargain for increased protection of the buffalo. Constant skirmishing among the Cree, Siksika, Peigan, Bloods, and Crow had made this effort impossible. With the hunters of the starving tribes independently pursuing the diminishing herds, the situation was not conducive to securing agreement, even with skilled and determined leadership. The starvation among those who had not signed the treaty became so severe that bands of Cree and Assiniboin returned to Canada from their buffalo hunting forays into the United States to sign adhesions to existing treaties.

Big Bear also failed to unite the Cree bands that had not signed the treaty. He gathered them in the Cypress Hills, hoping to establish a large reserve there, but his plans would be denied by the newly appointed Commissioner Edgar Dewdney, who feared that a large concentration of Cree and Assiniboin in the Cypress Hills could only be dealt with through military confrontation. Dewdney denied rations to these bands and to all those who had not signed the treaty, hoping that starvation would force them to sign on terms he could dictate. He took these steps against the Cree knowing not only that they were "in violation ... of promises made to the Cypress Hills Indians in 1880 and 1881, but also that by refusing to grant reserves on the sites the Indians had selected, he was violating the promises made to the Cree by the Treaty Commissioners in 1874 and 1876 and in the written treaties ... Dewdney wanted to exploit the opportunity presented to him by the hunger crisis and disarmament of the Cree to bring them under the government's control, even if it meant violating the treaties."[37]

By 1882 Big Bear's followers at the Cypress Lake camp, just to the south of Fort Walsh, were in a desperate state. Starving, without rations, they were divided about whether to sign the treaty or not. Big Bear was still reluctant. Piapot had recently complained to him that treaty promises were not being fulfilled and that the Cree on the reserves were losing their autonomy, exactly as Big Bear had feared. Finally, with his followers divided and starving, Big Bear signed an adhesion to Treaty 6. But for Big Bear, signing the treaty did not mean acceptance of Canadian authority. It was only a tactic he undertook to put himself in a position to renegotiate the provisions of the treaty and to pressure the government to negotiate in good faith and to deliver on its promises.

The authorities under Dewdney and Laird recognized the threat posed by a united front of Cree people, and they used the police to enforce the ban on the Sun Dance and to limit large gatherings. In the wake of funding cutbacks for western reserves in 1884, there were a series of assaults against farm instructors who denied rations to the old and infirm. Dewdney knew that starving the "Cree into submission was not the means to control them. He wanted to use coercion."[38] Thus, force was threatened by the NWMP whenever a potential confrontation with authorities arose. Dewdney's new tactics received support from the Indian agents, who encouraged him to "adopt a more coercive policy designed to subjugate the Cree."[39] But the Cree continued, in the face of these tactics, to seek renegotiation of the treaty. In 1884 the Cree leadership met with authorities at Duck Lake to submit a detailed list of treaty violations. They said they had been lied to about support for the transition to an agricultural way of life. They charged officials with bad faith, saying that they "had been deceived by 'sweet promises' designed to cheat them of their heritage and that unless their grievances were remedied by the summer of 1885, they would take whatever measures necessary, short of war, to get redress."[40]

Big Bear's vision of a united front to renegotiate the treaty was interrupted by the events of 1885, specifically the battle at Duck Lake, which marked the start of the Northwest resistance. The Cree and most of the Plains tribes had rejected an alliance with the Métis. They had their own agenda and were planning to meet in 1885 at another council. But even before violence erupted at Duck Lake in March of 1885, Dewdney had decided on a plan to arrest and depose those chiefs who were causing trouble for the department. Dewdney had support from Ottawa to arrest chiefs on charges of inciting insurrection and then to secure long sentences for them from cooperative magistrates. But the fighting in the spring of 1885 gave Dewdney a better excuse for removing influential Cree leaders from their positions of power. Dewdney went out of his way to have both Poundmaker and Big Bear sentenced to long prison terms even though evidence against them during the spring of 1885 was thin and even contrary to the charges against them.

A pass system, introduced in 1885 with the support of Dewdney, restricted Indian movement and brought the Cree alliance under control. Indian agents could prevent large meetings of Cree across a number of reserves by refusing to issue passes to large numbers of Cree. Thus, the legacy of Treaty 6, with its announced intentions of good faith, is in need of revision.

Promises broken, promises made in bad faith, and attempts to prevent free assembly and to discredit legitimate Cree leadership followed in the decade after the treaty was signed. Did the government and its officials act with fairness and with the intention of honouring their legal commitments at Treaty 6?

The record of the Canadian government in dealing with the Cree is thus not one of honourable fair-mindedness and justice as the traditional interpretation portrays. As Dewdney admitted in 1885, ... the treaties' promises and provisions were not being fulfilled and Dewdney himself had taken steps to assure Canadian control over the Cree, which were themselves violations of the treaties. Thus, he had refused to grant the Cree the reserve sites they selected; he had refused to distribute the ammunition and the treaties required. His plans for dealing with the Cree leaders were based on a political use of the legal land judicial system and ultimately he made use of the military, the police and the courts in a political manner to achieve his goals of subjugating the Cree. Only by ignoring these facts can one continue to perpetuate the myth of Canada's just and honourable Indian policy from 1870 to 1885.[41]

THE EFFECTS OF INTERNATIONAL EVENTS ON THE MAKING OF TREATY 7

As the Canadian government moved to make a treaty with the First Nations of southern Alberta, it had more than just national issues to confront. Two significant international events threatened the security and indeed the sovereignty of the Canadian Northwest in the mid-1870s. Tribes of the Lakota and Nez Percé sought refuge in Canada while in flight from the US Army. Both the Lakota under Sitting Bull and the Nez Percé under Chief Joseph fought against American authorities after treaties negotiated in good faith were flagrantly broken by successive American governments.

The Lakota

Beginning in the early 1850s, the Lakota had signed a series of treaties with the US government to keep intruders out of their lands in the Big Horn Mountains and the Black Hills. But from the start, breaches of the treaties were followed by battles, then

by truces, then by more military confrontation. The most flagrant treaty violation was the invasion of Lakota territory by
White miners after gold was discovered in the Black Hills. The
US government unilaterally redrew the boundaries of Lakota reservations, then threatened to forcibly move those who refused
to settle on the new, smaller reservations. The US government
declared that any Lakota not on a reservation by January 31,
1876, would be considered an enemy of the state. A major military campaign was then launched against those Lakota who had
not complied. Marching against the Lakota was a force under
the command of Brigadier General Alfred Terry, with support
from Colonel John Gibbon, General George Crook, as well as
the 7th Calvary of the infamous "Indian fighter" Lieutenant
Colonel George Custer. The strategy of General Terry was to
pursue the Lakota until every avenue of retreat had been closed
off. Unfortunately for Terry, the over-eager George Custer was
determined to attack when the first opportunity arose. On June
26, 1876, Custer, ignoring the advice of his Crow scouts, attacked
2,500 Lakota soldiers with a column of only 215 men. The battle
was over in just hours, leaving Custer and every one of his men
dead on the battlefield. The Lakota, allies of the British in 1812,
moved towards Canada for safety, believing they would be protected by the former British colony.

Sitting Bull soon learned that Canadian authorities did not
welcome their one-time allies with open arms but instead did
all they could to dissuade the Lakota from staying. The presence
of the Lakota along the border produced a number of problems
for Canadian authorities. The Lakota were traditional enemies
of a number of Plains tribes and had fought wars against the
Plains Cree and Saulteaux peoples, as well as against the Bloods,
Peigan, and Siksika of the Blackfoot Confederacy. The buffalo
were becoming increasingly scarce throughout the 1870s, and
the presence of the Lakota heightened tensions, since they relied
on the same herds for food as the Cree, Assiniboin, Saulteaux,
Bloods, Peigan, Siksika, Tsuu T'ina, and Métis on the Canadian
side of the 49th parallel. Thus, the potential for violence existed
among these groups – this in addition to potential incidents that
could pit the Lakota against the US Army and the US Army against
any Canadian tribes that might support the Lakota. The US Army
particularly feared attacks from the Lakota based in Canada, and

American diplomats pressured Canadian authorities to return the Lakota to the United States. Both Canadian and American authorities feared alliances among these disparate tribes, who though once enemies might join together in a large force, posing a major threat to Canadian and American security.

It is clear that Canadian authorities, especially those sent to complete Treaty 7, were worried about potential First Nations alliances with the renowned Lakota, who had enjoyed such impressive military successes against the formidable and experienced US Army. Missionaries John McDougall and Constantine Scollen had already warned authorities in Ottawa about the threat the Blackfoot Confederacy posed for peaceful settlement of the Canadian territories.

Sitting Bull sent out emissaries to meet with various tribes on the Canadian side of the border to talk about forming military alliances. In August of 1877 Crowfoot and Sitting Bull met, shook hands, and exchanged tobacco. A friendship dance followed before the men went their separate ways. Authorities on both sides of the border were alarmed by the meeting. It undoubtedly fuelled their worst fears, that an alliance between these two powerful and militarily experienced nations might become an actuality.

The Nez Percé

While perhaps not as immediate or as threatening for Canadian authorities as the Lakota uprising was, the Nez Percé War of 1877 was a significant international factor in the negotiations leading up to Treaty 7. Like the Lakota, the Nez Percé were victims of treaty violations that led to the formation of a group of non-treaty Nez Percé.

In 1855 the Nez Percé had signed a treaty giving them a substantial parcel of land that straddled the states of Washington and Idaho. By 1863 the reservation had been reduced to a fraction of its original size, mostly as a result of gold discoveries on the land. Approximately one-third of the Nez Percé refused to be confined within the now much smaller reservation, whose boundaries had been unilaterally redrawn, and continued to live outside the reservation but within their traditional lands. This group, under the leadership of Chief Joseph, were now classified as non-treaty Nez Percé.

In 1877 the Nez Percé were given an ultimatum much like that given to Sitting Bull's Lakota. The non-treaty Nez Percé under Chief Joseph finally agreed to move onto the reservation. The plan to move was undertaken even though it was an impossible task to gather all the stock within the thirty-day deadline ordered by General Oliver Howard. When the move was almost complete, three young Nez Percé men decided to seek revenge against settlers who had cheated and killed members of their families. The young men first attacked individual families, then went on a rampage, raiding settlements and killing seventeen people over two days.

The tribe of non-treaty Nez Percé, fearing reprisals, began to retreat. General Howard, in fact, did send troops against them. The army attacked but were routed by the Nez Percé at White Bird Canyon on June 17, 1877. What followed over the next months was a series of battles between the Nez Percé and the US Army as the Nez Percé attempted to elude their pursuers. Remarkably, the Nez Percé, numbering eight hundred and burdened with all of their stock, managed not only to outdistance the army most of the time, but also to engineer a series of brilliant victories, swooping down on the pursuing columns from all directions.

The Nez Percé simply wanted to find a place where the army would leave them alone and where they could be far enough from settlements to avoid further fighting. It was not to be. The ex–Civil War officers, anxious for victories in the field, pursued the Nez Percé relentlessly. From July to October 1877, the Nez Percé moved across numerous ranges in the difficult mountain terrain of Montana – over the Bitterroot Mountains into Yellowstone Park, then north across the Badlands (or Breaks) of central Montana towards the Bear Paw Mountains located just south of the Canadian border. The Nez Percé fought battles at Clearwater, Fort Fizzle, Big Hole, Birch Creek, Camas Meadows, Canyon Creek, Cow Island, and finally the Bear Paw Mountains. Their ultimate destination was Canada.

Of the 800 Nez Percé who began their journey in June, only 431 remained. Of these, 231 surrendered to the US Army. After fighting to a stalemate, the Nez Percé had been assured that they would be allowed to return to their lands, but instead they were taken as prisoners to Fort Leavenworth. Nine years later in 1885, they were finally granted permission to return to their traditional homeland along the Columbia River. Only 200 Nez Percé, with Chief White Bird, ever made it to Canada to join the camp of Sitting Bull at Wood Mountain.

The Impact of the Lakota and Nez Percé in Canadian Territory

The Nez Percé's feat of covering 1,300 miles of difficult terrain while fighting off the US Army greatly affected the Canadian authorities who were about to negotiate Treaty 7. The making of Treaty 7 in September coincided with the Nez Percé moving closer and closer to the Bear Paw Mountains and to the camp of Sitting Bull. The ability of the Nez Percé to avoid defeat was extraordinary.

A Canadian Mountie, James Stanford, who was present at the making of Treaty 7, wrote about his experiences in a letter to his mother in 1877. Stanford related the problem that both Sitting Bull and the Nez Percé War posed for those trying to complete a treaty with five different tribes at Blackfoot Crossing: "The Indians were peaceful at the Treaty but they are raising the devil all around us. The Nez Perces who were fighting across the mountains have left them and are on their way to joining 'Sitting Bull's' camp at Cypress Hills. We get news to day [sic] that the Sioux [Lakota] had burned all the freight and stores left at Cow Island on the Missouri."[42] There was no doubt that Canadian officials expected these events to boost the morale of Treaty 7 peoples. Stanford reported: "Sitting Bull has been sending agents among our Indians to try and get them to join him. Col Macleod and a party have gone to visit his camp. They are friendly towards us so far, but awfully down on the Yankees. Col Macleod is now in Sitting Bull's camp with 19 men and General Crook is coming to meet him to try and make terms of peace with them. He brings an escort of 1100 men and then thinks he is not safe. The Indians have more respect for one red coat than they have for 100 blue ones."

Stanford's letter conveys the great alarm that the NWMP and James Macleod felt about keeping peace in 1877. Threats from both the Nez Percé and the Lakota may well explain why no mention was made of a land surrender during negotiations and why the Treaty 7 peoples were allowed to believe that their demands had all been met. Canadian authorities did not want the kind of trouble that the Americans were having. They wanted to prevent the people in the Treaty 7 area from becoming discontented. Discontented tribes, especially those of the Blackfoot Confederacy, might have led their leaders to talk more seriously with the American tribes that had been so successful in military campaigns against the intimidating US Army. Canadian treaty commissioners were clearly aware of the threat posed by potential alliances between the Treaty 7 nations and Sitting Bull's Lakota and White Bird's Nez Percé, both present on the edge of Treaty 7 territory in the fall of 1877.

CHAPTER SIX

The Text of Treaty 7

The text following contains the articles of the treaty as presented by the treaty commissioners. As is clear from the evidence of the elders, this document does not represent the true spirit and original intent of the treaty that was made at Blackfoot Crossing. The elders say that the treaty as presented to them a year after the negotiations does not contain all of the agreements concluded between the commissioners and chiefs. Many contentious issues concerning the written treaty remain unresolved, especially issues relating to the translation. Many elders have stated that the written treaty they were given was written prior to the arrival of the commissioners, and that agreements made during the negotiations were never incorporated into the final treaty text. The elders feel that much discussion, analysis, and amendment are still required before the written treaty contains the true spirit and original intent of the agreement. In addition to the fundamental issue of whether the treaty represents a land surrender, the elders point to the careless drafting and translation of the treaty.

Elder Louise Crop Eared Wolf* cites examples of gross misrepresentations of names on the treaties as evidence of the incompetence of the translators and those who wrote the treaty. Improper translations and spellings of the Blackfoot names appended to the treaty abound. She identified over eighty errors

---

* Louise Crop Eared Wolf: "My comments regarding all the mispronounced Blackfoot names of chiefs of the Bloods, Blackfoot, and Piegan give enough evidence to show that the interpreter (James Bird) at the Treaty 7 peace-making agreement was not a fluent speaker of

made by the translators. Some of the worst examples include the recording of Crowfoot's name as Chapo-Mexico instead of Issapo-maksika; Chapo-Mexico has no meaning and sounds more like an English word. The name of another leading Siksika elder, Old Sun, was recorded as Matose-Apiw, which is simply incomprehensible in Blackfoot. Stamis-cotocar, for Stami-kso-tokan (Bull Head) of the Tsuu T'ina, again has no meaning in Blackfoot, as there are no "r's" in the Blackfoot language. Natose-onistors is a misrepresentation of Natoso-nista, which was wrongly translated as Medicine Calf instead of Powerful Calf. Takoye-stamix is an incorrect representation for Sakoi-yi-stamik (Last Bull, which was also mistranslated as Fiend Bull). Issokoi-ya-wotanni or Cougar Shield was translated as Sakoye-aowotan, which means Heavy Shield. Crop Eared Wolf points out that this latter translation is an example of a very poor understanding of the language, since even though the words are close in sound – *issokoioyi* for "cougar" and *issokoi* for "heavy" – a real Blackfoot speaker would know the difference. Also Pitah-siksinum, meaning White Eagle, is the wrong spelling and translation of Pitai-siki-namm, which means Black Eagle. Pitah-otsikin, which means "disgusting," was used to represent Pitai-tsi-kinn, which means Eagle Moccasin.

When recording the names of the Stoney chiefs on the treaty documents, the officials used the Cree language and not the Stoney-Siouan language. Chief Jacob Bearspaw is written as Mas-gwa-ah-sid, Cree for Bear's Paw, and Chief Jacob Goodstoney is written as Ki-chi-pwat, the Cree word for Big Stoney. The use of Cree to record Stoney names underlines the claim of the Stoney elders that their chief adviser, Reverend John McDougall, officially representing their position during the negotiations, was not a competent translator. McDougall knew Cree but not the Nakota-Siouan language.

The written treaty text below must therefore be read with the understanding that the Treaty 7 elders see it as something that does not fully represent what was agreed to at Blackfoot Crossing.

---

the Blackfoot language at the time. How could he have accurately explained the articles of the treaty if he was unable to master the Blackfoot terms of the names in Blackfoot. My belief is that our ancestors were not made aware of all the English terms of the treaty."

"THE TREATY WITH THE BLACKFEET; NUMBER SEVEN"

Articles of a Treaty made and concluded this twenty-second day of September, in the year of our Lord one thousand eight hundred and seventy-seven, between Her Most Gracious Majesty the Queen of Great Britain and Ireland, by her Commissioners, the Honorable David Laird, Lieutenant-Governor and Indian Superintendent of the North-West Territories, and James Farquharson McLeod, C.M.G., Commissioner of the North-West Mounted Police, of the one part, and the Blackfeet, Blood, Peigan, Sarcee, Stony, and other Indians, inhabitants of the territory north of the United States boundary line, east of the central range of the Rocky Mountains, and south and west of Treaties Numbers Six and Four, by their head Chiefs and minor Chiefs or Councillors, chosen as hereinafter mentioned, of the other part:

Whereas the Indians inhabiting the said territory, have pursuant to an appointment made by the said Commissioners, been convened at meeting at the "Blackfoot crossing" of the Bow River, to deliberate upon certain matters of interests to Her Most Gracious Majesty, of the one part, and the said Indians of the other;

And whereas the said Indians have been informed by Her Majesty's Commissioners that it is the desire of Her Majesty to open up for settlement, and such other purposes as to Her Majesty may seem meet, a tract of country, bounded and described as hereinafter mentioned, and to obtain the consent thereto of her Indian subjects inhabiting the said tract, and to make a treaty, and arrange with them, so that there may be peace and good will between them and Her Majesty, and between them and Her Majesty's other subjects; and that her Indian people may know and feel assured of what allowance they are to count upon and receive from Her Majesty's bounty and benevolence;

And whereas the Indians of the said tract, duly convened in council, and being requested by her Majesty's Commissioners to present their head Chiefs and minor Chiefs, or Councillors, who shall be authorized, on their behalf, to conduct such negotiations and sign any treaty to be founded thereon, and to become responsible to Her Majesty for the faithful performance by their respective bands of such obligations as should be assumed by them, the said Blackfeet, Blood, Piegan and Sarcee Indians have therefore acknowledged for that purpose, the several head and minor Chiefs, and the said Stony Indians, the

Chiefs and Councillors who have subscribed hereto, that there-
upon in open council the said Commissioners received and acknowledged the head and minor Chiefs and the Chiefs and
Councillors presented for the purpose aforesaid:

And whereas the said Commissioners have proceeded to negotiate a treaty with the said Indians; and the same has been
finally agreed upon and concluded as follows, that is to say: the
Blackfeet, Blood, Piegan, Sarcee, Stony and other Indians inhabiting the district hereinafter more fully described and defined,
do hereby cede, release, surrender, and yield up to the Government of Canada for Her Majesty the Queen and her successors forever, all their rights, titles and privileges whatsoever
to the lands included within the following limits, that is to say:

give up
all rights
and land

Commencing at a point on the international boundary due
south of the western extremity of the Cypress Hills; thence west
along the said boundary to the central range of the Rocky Mountains, or to the boundary of the Province of British Columbia;
thence north-westerly along the said boundary to a point due
west of the source of the main branch of the Red Deer River;
thence south-westerly and southerly following on the boundaries
of the tracts ceded by the Treaties Numbered Six and Four to
the place of commencement; and also all their rights, titles and
privileges whatsoever, to all other lands wherever situated in the
North-West Territories, or in any other portion of the Dominion
of Canada:

To have and to hold the same to Her Majesty the Queen and
her successors forever:

And Her Majesty the Queen hereby agrees with her said Indians, that they shall have right to pursue their vocations of
hunting throughout the tract surrendered as heretofore described, subject to such regulations as may, from time to time,
be made by the Government of the country, acting under the
authority of Her Majesty; and saving and excepting such tracts
as may be required or taken up from time to time for settlement,
mining, trading or other purposes by her Government of Canada, or by any of her Majesty's subjects duly authorized therefor
by the said Government.

subject
to gov
regulations

It is also agreed between Her Majesty and her said Indians
that reserves shall be assigned them of sufficient area to allow
one square mile for each family of five persons, or in that proportion for larger and smaller families, and that said reserves
shall be located as follows, that is to say:

reserves

First – The reserves of the Blackfeet, Blood and Sarcee bands of Indians, shall consist of a belt of land on the north side of the Bow and South Saskatchewan Rivers, of an average width of four miles along said rivers, down stream, commencing at a point on the Bow River twenty miles north-westerly of the "Blackfoot crossing" thereof, and extending to the Red Deer River at its junction with the South Saskatchewan; also for the term of ten years, and no longer, from the date of the concluding of this treaty, when it shall cease to be a portion of said Indian reserves, as fully to all intents and purposes as if it had not at any time been included therein, and without any compensation to individual Indians for improvements, of a similar belt of land on the south side of the Bow and Saskatchewan Rivers of an average width of one mile along said rivers, down stream; commencing at the aforesaid point on the Bow River, and extending to a point one mile west of the coal seam on said river, about five miles below the said "Blackfoot crossing"; beginning again one mile east of the said coal seam and extending to the mouth of Maple Creek at its junction with the South Saskatchewan; and beginning again at the junction of the Bow River with the latter river, and extending on both sides of the South Saskatchewan in an average width on each side thereof of one mile, along said river against the stream, to the junction of the Little Bow River with the latter river, reserving to Her Majesty, as may now or hereafter be required by her for the use of her Indian and other subjects, from all the reserves hereinbefore described, the right to navigate the above mentioned rivers, to land and receive fuel and cargoes on the shores and banks thereof, to build bridges and establish ferries thereon, to use the fords thereof and all the trails leading thereto, and to open such other roads through the said reserves as may appear to Her Majesty's Government of Canada, necessary for the ordinary travel of her Indian and other subjects, due compensation being paid to individual Indians for improvements, when the same may be in any manner encroached upon by such roads.

Secondly – That the reserve of the Piegan band of Indians shall be on the Old Man's River, near the foot of the Porcupine Hills, at a place called "Crow's Creek."

And Thirdly – The reserve of the Stony band of Indians shall be in the vicinity of Morleyville.

In view of the satisfaction of Her Majesty with the recent general good conduct of her said Indians, and in extinguishment of all their past claims, she hereby, through her Commissioners, agrees to make them a present payment of twelve dollars each *annual* in cash to each man, woman, and child of the families here *payment* represented.

Her Majesty also agrees that next year, and annually afterwards forever, she will cause to be paid to the said Indians, in cash, at suitable places and dates, of which the said Indians shall be duly notified, to each Chief, twenty-five dollars, each minor Chief or Councillor (not exceeding fifteen minor Chiefs to the Blackfeet and Blood Indians, and four to the Piegan and Sarcee bands, and five Councillors to the Stony Indian Bands) fifteen dollars, and to every other Indian of whatever age, five dollars; the same, unless there be some exceptional reason, to be paid to the heads of families for those belonging thereto.

Further, Her Majesty agrees that the sum of two thousand dollars shall hereafter every year be expended in the purchase of ammunition for distribution among the said Indians; provided that if at any future time ammunition became comparatively unnecessary for said Indians, her Government, with the consent of said Indians, or any of the bands thereof, may expend the proportion due to such band otherwise for their benefit.

Further, Her Majesty agrees that each head Chief and minor Chief, and each Chief and Councillor duly recognized as such, shall, once in every three years, during the term of their office, receive a suitable suit of clothing, and each head Chief and Stony Chief, in recognition of the closing of the treaty, a suitable medal and flag, and next year, or as soon as convenient, each head Chief, and minor Chief, and Stony Chief shall receive a Winchester rifle.

Further, Her Majesty agrees to pay the salary of such teachers *teachers* to instruct the children of said Indians as to her Government of Canada may seem advisable, when said Indians are settled on their reserves and shall desire teachers.

Further, Her Majesty agrees to supply each head and minor *goods* Chief, and each Stony Chief, for the use of their bands, ten axes, five handsaws, five augers, one grindstone, and the necessary files and whetstones.

And further, Her Majesty agrees that the said Indians shall be supplied as soon as convenient, after any band shall make due application therefor, with the following cattle for raising stock, that is to say: for every family of five persons, and under, two cows; for every family of more than five persons, and less than ten persons, three cows; for every family of over ten persons, four cows; and every head and minor Chief, and every Stony Chief, for the use of their bands, one bull; but if any band desire to cultivate the soil as well as raise stock, each family of such band shall receive one cow less than the above mentioned number, and in lieu thereof, when settled on their reserves and prepared to break up the soil, two hoes, one spade, one scythe, and two hay forks, and for every three families, one plough and one harrow, and for each band, enough potatoes, barley, oats, and wheat (if such seeds be suited for the locality of their reserves) to plant the land actually broken up. All the aforesaid articles to be given, once for all, for the encouragement of the practice of agriculture among the Indians.

And the undersigned Blackfeet, Blood, Piegan and Sarcee head Chiefs and minor Chiefs, and Stony Chiefs and Councillors, on their own behalf and on behalf of all other Indians inhabiting the tract within ceded do hereby solemnly promise and engage to strictly observe this treaty, and also to conduct and behave themselves as good and loyal subjects of Her Majesty the Queen. They promise and engage that they will, in all respects, obey and abide by the law, that they will maintain peace and good order between each other and between themselves and other tribes of Indians, and between themselves and others of Her Majesty's subjects, whether Indians, Half breeds or whites, now inhabiting, or hereafter to inhabit, any part of the said ceded tract; and that they will not molest the person or property of any inhabitant of such ceded tract, or the property of Her Majesty the Queen, or interfere with or trouble any person, passing or travelling through the said tract or any part thereof, and that they will assist the officers of Her Majesty in bringing to justice and punishment any Indian offending against the stipulations of this treaty, or infringing the laws in force in the country so ceded.

In witness whereof Her Majesty's said Commissioners, and the said Indian head and minor Chiefs, and Stony Chiefs and Councillors, have hereunto subscribed and set their hands, at the "Blackfoot crossing" of the Bow River, the day and year herein first above written.

(Signed)   DAVID LAIRD,
Gov. of N.-W. T., and Special Indian Commissioner.

JAMES F. McLEOD,
  Lieut.-Colonel, Com. N.-W.M.P.,
  and Special Indian Commissioner
CHAPO-MEXICO (or Crowfoot),   His x mark
  Head Chief of the South Blackfeet.
MATOSE-APIW (or Old Sun),   " x "
  Head Chief of the North Blackfeet.
STAMISCOTOCAR (or Bull Head),   " x "
  Head Chief of the Sarcees.
MEKASTO (or Red Crow),   " x "
  Head Chief of the South Bloods.
NATOSE-ONISTORS (or Medicine Calf).   " x "
POKAPIW-OTOIAN (or Bad Head).   " x "
SOTENAH (or Rainy Chief),   " x "
  Head Chief of the North Bloods.
TAKOYE-STAMIX (or Fiend Bull).   " x "
AKKA-KITCIPIMIW-OTAS (or Many
  Spotted Horses).   " x "
ATTISTAH-MACAN (or Running Rabbit).   " x "
PITAH-PEKIS (or Eagle Rib).   " x "
SAKOYE-AOTAN (or Heavy Shield),   " x "
  Head Chief of the Middle Blackfeet.
ZOATZE-TAPITAPIW (or Setting on
  an Eagle Tail).   His x mark
  Head Chief of the North Piegans.
AKKA-MAKKOYE (or Many Swans).   " x "
APENAKO-SAPOP (or Morning Plume).   " x "
*MAS-GWA-AH-SID (or Bear's Paw).   " x "
*CHE-NE-KA (or John).   " x "
*KI-CIII-ГWOT (or Jacob).   " ӿ "
STAMIX-OSOK (or Bull Backfat).   " x "
EMITAH-APISKINNE (or White Striped Dog). " x "
MATAPI-KOMOTZIW (or the Captive
  or Stolen Person).   " x "
APAWAWAKOSOW (or White Antelope).   " x "
MAKOYE-KIN (or Wolf Collar).   " x "
AYE-STIPIS-SIMAT (or Heavily Whipped).   " x "
KISSOUM (or Day Light).   " x "
PITAH-OTOCAN (or Eagle Head).   " x "
APAW-STAMIX (or Weasel Bull).   " x "

---

* Stony Chiefs.

Onistah-pokah (or White Calf).	His x mark
Netah-kitei-pi-mew (or Only Spot).	" x "
Akak-otos (or Many Horses).	" x "
Stokimatis (or The Drum).	" x "
Pitah-annes (or Eagle Robe).	" x "
Pitah-otsikin (or Eagle Shoe).	" x "
Stamix-ota-ka-piw (or Bull Turn Round).	" x "
Maste-Pitah (or Crow Eagle).	" x "
†James Dixon.	" x "
†Abraham Kechepwot.	" x "
†Patrick Kechepwot.	" x "
†George Moy-any-men.	" x "
†George Crawlor.	" x "
Ekas-kine (or Low Horn).	" x "
Kayo-okosis (or Bear Shield).	" x "
Ponokah-stamix (or Bull Elk).	" x "
Omaksi Sapop (or Big Plume).	" x "
Onistah (or Calf Robe).	" x "
Pitah-siksinum (or White Eagle).	" x "
Apaw-onistaw (or Weasel Calf).	" x "
Attista-haes (or Rabbit Carrier).	" x "
Pitah (or Eagle).	" x "
Pitah-onistah (or Eagle White Calf).	" x "
Kaye-tapo (or Going to Bear).	" x "

Signed by the Chiefs and Councillors within named in presence of the following witnesses, the same having been first explained by James Bird, Interpreter.

(Signed)   A.G. Irvine, *Ass't Com., N.-W.M.P.*
J. McDougall, *Missionary.*
Jean L'Heureux.
W. Winder.
T.N.F. Crozier, *Inspectors.*
E. Dalrymple Clark, *Lieut. and Adjutant. N.-W.M.P.*
A. Shurtliff,
C.E. Dening,
W.D. Antrobus, *Sub-Inspectors.*
Frank Norman, *Staff Constable.*

---

† Stony Councillors.

MARY J. MacLEOD.

JULIA WINDER.

JULIA SHURTLIFF.

E. HARDISTY.

A. McDOUGALL.

E.A. BARRETT.

CONSTANTINE SCOLLEN, *Priest,* witness to signatures of
    Stonixosak and those following.

CHARLES E. CONRAD.

THOS. J. BOGG.

CHAPTER SEVEN

A Narrative of Events at Blackfoot Crossing, September 1877

In September of 1877 commissioners representing the Dominion of Canada and chiefs of the Siksika, Peigan, Blood, Tsuu T'ina, and Stoney nations met to negotiate Treaty 7. The territory encompassed approximately fifty thousand square miles of southern Alberta. The treaty was completed after four days of uncertain and difficult negotiations. For the Canadian government, Treaty 7 was the last of the numbered treaties that secured the southern prairies for settlement and enabled the peaceful completion of the transcontinental Canadian Pacific Railway (CPR).

Negotiations for the final treaty did not occur over only those four days in September. There had been meetings and discussions about the treaty for a number of years before it was actually completed. Missionaries such as George and John McDougall had been relaying government messages about the treaty to the Treaty 7 nations as had NWMP Commissioner James Macleod. The First Nations as well had been discussing the treaty. In the autumn of 1875 the member tribes of the Blackfoot Confederacy met in a general council in the Hand Hills to define the issues that were important to them. The issues so defined were incorporated in a petition prepared by Jean L'Heureux. This petition was given to the chief negotiator for the government, Lieutenant-Governor Alexander Morris.

The Blackfoot had already been assured by Commissioner James Macleod that their lands would not be taken without a full discussion of the issues at a general council. The main concerns of the Blackfoot were the presence of Cree and Métis hunters on their lands and the disappearing buffalo. The Blackfoot tribes were not so concerned about the presence of the NWMP or missionaries but were clearly worried about the invasion of their country by people who would never have been there if the Blackfoot had not given the Mounties their promise to stop tribal warfare. Now Cree and Métis hunters were in their midst shooting the buffalo with impunity.

The 1875 petition outlining their concerns as recorded by L'Heureux was only delivered to the commissioners in the following year. It is not clear whether the Blackfoot were anxious to enter into a treaty; what is certain is that they were concerned about retaining their traditional territories. Certainly McDougall and other missionaries were pressing for a treaty, and it seems that the treaty commissioners interpreted the petition of 1875 as an indication that the Blackfoot were willing to enter into a treaty as soon as possible. The treaty commissioners received the petition from the Blackfoot too late in 1876 to be able to do anything about it in that year, but they agreed to meet with the tribes the next fall.

In August 1877 the government appointed Lieutenant-Governor David Laird and Superintendent James Macleod as commissioners for Treaty 7. The first meetings were scheduled to be held at Fort Macleod, but when the Siksika decided that they did not want to meet at a White man's fort, the location was changed to Blackfoot Crossing. The change in venue did not sit well with the Peigan and Bloods, who preferred to meet closer to their traditional hunting grounds. A number of the Blood chiefs said they would not attend the negotiations at Blackfoot Crossing.

From the beginning there were problems over who represented the five nations and the many tribes and bands that made up these nations. The Stoneys, for example, had always had three distinctly separate bands and in fact were represented by a leader from each of these factions. There was less of a problem for the Tsuu T'ina, who were the most homogeneous tribe both in language and leadership. The biggest problem concerned the leadership of the Blackfoot Confederacy. The Blackfoot system of governing did not include an overall leader; rather the leadership varied depending on what circumstances were at hand. Crowfoot was favoured by the government officials because of his commitment to peace and diplomacy, and they dealt with him as though he were the chief for the entire Blackfoot Confederacy. However, it is not clear that the Blackfoot themselves thought of Crowfoot as the overall leader, especially when other chiefs such as Rainy Chief and Red Crow had much larger followings and greater influence.

The tribes and the Canadian officials agreed to meet in mid-September 1877. The government officials arrived on September 16 to find the Stoneys, Tsuu T'ina, and Siksika but very few Peigan and no Bloods. The First Nations had been meeting to smoke the pipe and talk among themselves. The commissioners arranged to hold a meeting on September 17 with those present. At this meeting it was agreed that negotiations would be put off for two days, allowing time for the Bloods and the rest of the Peigan to arrive. Laird offered flour, tea, sugar, and beef to those assembled, stating that acceptance of these rations would not be seen as a tacit agreement to the treaty. Crowfoot refused the rations, believing the bargaining position of the First Nations might be compromised if they accepted gifts before an agreement had been reached. He did not want to feel indebted to the government commissioners before bargaining had even begun.

On Wednesday the 19th the commissioners and the leaders of the tribes met again, though not all the Blood or Peigan leaders had yet arrived. The commissioners were accompanied by an honour guard, and Laird made a speech in general terms about how the Great Spirit had made the "white" and "red" men brothers and how they should take each other by the hand and how the Great Mother loved all her children. Laird stressed the achievement of the government in halting the whiskey trade and how laws had been passed to save the buffalo from extinction. Laird then went on to give the reasons why the Aboriginal people should sign the treaty, emphasizing that in a few years the buffalo would be gone and that the government wished that ranching and grain farming would become their new way of life. He also said that annuity payments would be part of any agreement.

The Blackfoot, Tsuu T'ina, and Stoneys then withdrew to discuss the offer. It is not known how all the groups responded to the initial offer, but it is known that among the Blackfoot some favoured the treaty while others were opposed. The Blackfoot met in the lodge of Heavy Shield, whose brother, Old Sun, announced that he was too old to make a decision on this issue and that he wished to defer to Crowfoot. The only chief in favour of immediate acceptance was Eagle Child, the leader of the Many Children band. Other chiefs, such as Eagle Rib of the Skunks band, threatened to leave the negotiations if they could not get better terms from the treaty commissioners. Crowfoot was generally in favour of the treaty but could not make a decision without consulting Red Crow, chief of the Bloods. Crowfoot therefore decided that no agreement could be finalized without Red Crow's presence.

On Thursday September 20 the groups met again and Laird clarified a number of issues, including hunting and fishing rights, which had been debated the previous day. The chiefs were reassured that they were free to hunt anywhere on their lands as long as they did not interfere with settlers. They were told they could sell timber and coal from their lands at fair prices. But no decision could be reached that day without the presence of Red Crow. A major speech was made by one of the Bloods present, Medicine Calf. He reiterated the point made in the Blackfoot petition of 1875 that the Bloods wanted the Cree and Métis kept off their land. Medicine Calf then went on to give the commissioners some sense of the experience the Blackfoot had had with past treaty agreements:

The Great Spirit sent the white men across the great waters to carry out His (the Great Spirit's) ends. The Great Spirit, and not the Great Mother, gave us this land. The Great Mother sent Stamixotokan (Col. Macleod) and the Police to put an end to the traffic in fire water. I can sleep now safely. Before the arrival of the Police, when I laid my head down at night, every sound frightened me; my sleep was broken; now I can sleep sound and am not afraid. The Great Mother sent you to this country, and we hope she will be good to us for many years. I hope and expect to get plenty; we think we will not get so much as the Indians receive from the Americans on the other side; they get large presents of flour, sugar, tea and blankets; the next year it was only half the quantity, and the following years it grew less and less, and now they give only a handful of flour. We want to get fifty dollars for the chiefs and thirty dollars each for all the others, men, women and children, and we want the same every year for the future. We want to be paid for all the timber that the Police and whites have used since they first came to our country. If it continues to be used as it is, there will soon be no firewood left for the Indians. I hope, Great Father, that you will give us all this that we ask.[1]

This was a major speech by one who had signed the Lame Bull Treaty of 1855 with the US government. It reflected not only the sense that much would have to be given in return for use of the land but also the great frustration that the Blackfoot had experienced with other treaties. Laird responded to Medicine Calf's words with ridicule and disdain, saying that the Blackfoot should pay the government for driving out the whiskey traders rather than that the police should pay for timber they had used. But Laird did assure those gathered that the law for the protection of the buffalo would be effective and that rations to the tribes would increase as their numbers grew. He emphasized again that their right to hunt would be preserved, as would be their right to sell the timber on their reserves.

Not all the leaders were as suspicious of the treaty as Medicine Calf. Chief Jacob Bearspaw of the Stoneys, who had initially been opposed, stated on this day that he was pleased with the treaty's promises of money and provisions. The day ended with the Blackfoot, Tsuu T'ina, and Stoneys breaking up into their councils, where heated discussions ensued. It was not clear that an agreement could be reached, and Laird himself feared the collapse of the negotiations.

A major shift in the negotiations occurred when Red Crow arrived with his large band on the evening of Thursday the 21st. Crowfoot immediately met with Red Crow and explained the treaty (as he understood it) to him. The next day Red Crow discussed the terms with his other chiefs. Crowfoot, unsure of the situation, went to seek the advice of an elder by the name of Pemmican. There was great tension in the camp and great uncertainty about what was at issue and what should be done. It is not clear that all terms of the treaty were properly understood by both sides, but the issue for Crowfoot and Pemmican appears to have been a general concern about the future and not necessarily the specifics of the treaty. There was concern about the buffalo and about their people's survival. The quandary of Pemmican, expressed in his words to Crowfoot, seemed much like that of Big Bear:

I want to hold you back because I am at the edge of a bank. My life is at its end. I hold you back because your life henceforth will be different from what it has been. Buffalo makes your body strong. What you will eat from this money will have your people buried all over these hills. You will be tied down, you will not wander the plains, the whites will take your land and fill it. You won't have your own free will; the whites will lead you by the halter. That is why I say don't sign. But my life is old, so sign, if you want to. Go ahead and make the treaty.[2]

Crowfoot's decision to agree to a treaty was not made any easier by the elders' advice, but it was made easier when Red Crow announced on the morning of September 21 that he would agree to a treaty if the Siksika did. The Blood chiefs were not in full agreement (Medicine Calf, Many Spotted Horses, and White Calf were among the chiefs who were opposed to the treaty), and thus Red Crow's endorsement was not overwhelming. But by this time there was a growing consensus among the Stoneys, Tsuu T'ina, and Peigan in favour of acceptance. Certainly, by the 21st, after Laird had made specific promises, more were in favour of the treaty than opposed.

After having conferred with all the tribes, Crowfoot came forward to give his decision to the commissioners:

While I speak, be kind and patient. I have to speak for my people, who are numerous, and who rely upon me to follow the course which in the future will tend to their good. The Plains are large and wide. We are the children of the plains, it is our home, and the buffalo has been our food always. I hope you look upon the Blackfeet, Blood and Sarcees as your children now, and that you will be indulgent and charitable to them. They all expected me to speak now for them, and I trust the Great Spirit will put into their breasts to be a good people – into the minds of the men, women and children, and their future generations. The advice given me and my people has proved to be very good. If the police had not come to the country, where would we all be now? Bad men and whiskey were killing us so fast that very few, indeed, would have been left today. The police have protected us as the feathers of the bird protect it from the frosts of winter. I wish them all good, and I trust that all our hearts will increase in goodness from this time forward. I am satisfied I will sign the treaty.[3]

Medicine Calf, who had been one of the strongest opponents of the treaty, spoke to give his agreement and state that he would be part of the treaty. Then Red Crow said, "Three years ago, when the police first came to the country, I met and shook hands with Stamixotokon [Col. Macleod] at Pelly River. Since that time he made me many promises. He kept them all – not one of them was ever broken. Everything the police have done has been good. I entirely trust Stamixotokon, and will leave everything to him. I will sign with Crowfoot."[4]

Old Sun then expressed the hope that the "sweet promises" would be made good:

Crowfoot speaks well. We were summoned to meet the Great Mother's chiefs here, and we would not disappoint them. We have come and will sign the treaty. During the past Crowfoot has been called by us our Great Father. The Great Mother's Chief [Governor Laird] will now be our Great Father. Everything you say appears to be very good, and I hope you will give us all we ask – cattle, money, tobacco, guns and axes, and that you will not let the white man use poison on the prairies. It kills horse and buffalo as well as wolves, and it may kill men. We ourselves can kill wolves and set traps for them. We all agree with Crowfoot.[5]

Following the speeches, Laird informed the chiefs that the treaty would be drawn up for signing and in the meantime he wanted each of the nations to indicate where they would take their land. Only the Siksika, Stoneys, and Peigan chose land immediately. The Tsuu T'ina and Bloods did not seem much interested, if indeed they understood what was being asked of them. They went along with Crowfoot's idea that they all take a reserve at Blackfoot Crossing along the Bow River. Crowfoot hoped that having this many tribes together would put them in a strong position to confront the government in the future. Later, the Tsuu T'ina moved further west to Nose Hill and the Bloods took land west and south of Stand Off. The Stoneys, according to the treaty wording, were to take a reserve around Morleyville, but it is most certain that they did not intend that all three of their bands occupy the same reserve.

On September 22 the treaty was signed and the final speeches were made. Crowfoot, whose name was put first by the treaty commissioners, came forward and gave a brief statement: "Great Father! Take pity on me with regard to my country, with regard to the mountains, the hills and the valleys; with regard to the prairies, to all the animals that inhabit them, and do not take them from myself and children forever."[6]

The last major speech was made by Colonel Macleod:

The Chiefs all here know what I said to them three years ago, when the police first came to the country – that nothing would be taken away from them without their own consent. You all see today that what I told you then was true. I also told you that the Mounted Police were your friends, and would not wrong you or see you wronged in any way. This also you see is true. The police will continue to be your friends, and be always glad to see you. On your part you must keep the Queen's laws, and give every information to them in order that you may see the laws obeyed and offenders punished. You may still look to me as your friend, and at any time when I can do anything for your welfare, I shall only be too happy to do so. You say that I have always kept my promises. As surely as my past promises have been kept, so surely shall those made by the Commissioners be carried out in the future. If they were broken I would be ashamed to meet you or look you in the face; but every promise will be solemnly fulfilled as certainly as the sun now shines down upon us from the heavens. I shall always remember the kind manner in which you have spoken today of me.[7]

The treaty agreement was made possible not only because many of the tribes present trusted Colonel Macleod but also because of the commissioners' many promises and their solemn oaths to honour them. As the leaders smoked the pipe to seal the agreement, there must have been many among them who had doubts about the fulfilment of the promises. Indeed, it was not long before Macleod, the very man they trusted most, would begin to talk about the impossibility of enforcing two of the major points that the Blackfoot, Tsuu T'ina, and Stoneys thought they had secured from the treaty commissioners: that the Cree and Métis would be kept off their lands and that the buffalo would be preserved.

CHAPTER EIGHT

Analysis of Firsthand Accounts by Government Officials

COMMISSIONER ALEXANDER MORRIS

Officially Indian Commissioner Alexander Morris stated that the treaties were offered to the Aboriginal peoples of the Northwest to accept or reject. He said that he did not have the authority to negotiate any major changes to them, emphasizing that on the main issues the treaties were a "take it or leave it" deal.

This is more or less the position taken by historian George Stanley, who has emphasized the point that the government tried to do the best for the First Nations of that time and that the Aboriginal peoples were not really capable of understanding what was going on. Stanley maintains that the treaties were imposed by a benevolent government that had no other choice open to it. He argues that the assumption that the treaties were negotiated between equal and consenting parties is false with regard to the prairie tribes: "The natives seldom understood the full implication of the contract. The disparity in power and interests between the signatories reduced the treaties to mere grants of such terms as the weaker people might accept without active resistance, and such treaties were, accordingly, rather the preparative and apology for disputes than securities for peace."[1]

But what Morris said formally at the treaties (and what Stanley has argued subsequently) does not stand up to the considerable evidence showing that there was substantial negotiation and that some, though by no means all, of the conditions stipulated by Aboriginal negotiators were in fact included in the written terms of the treaties. David Hall, for example, has shown that the government did not have a comprehensive, well-thought-through approach to the treaties and that because of this it had to respond to many requests at Treaty 1 that it had not been prepared for. As a result of the many requests by the Saulteaux, the officials had to go back to Ottawa to ask for permission to include the specific provisions; they then returned to the negotiations with approval for many of the items.

Even Commissioner Morris, who officially told each of the Aboriginal groups that he was powerless to include new items in the treaties, wrote in correspondence to the minister of the interior: "There is moreover, no cast iron form of Treaty which can be imposed on these people."[2] After being censured for making too many concessions to the Aboriginal negotiators, Morris vigorously defended his record: "I would call your attention to the fact that in dealing with the Indian people, the Commissioners, away from all opportunity of obtaining advice, must act at times largely on their own responsibility, and deal with emergencies which arise."[3] Morris went on to say that he "encountered on all occasions, difficulties which the Commission overcame but which they were able to deal with, only by assuming responsibility and at the moment without hesitation, making stipulation to obviate the failure of the Treaties."[4] Morris pointed out that the Canadian tribes were very knowledgable about the more liberal terms granted to American Indians. He warned of the very real possibility of war and of threats to telegraph and survey parties in the West from Aboriginal groups who were not satisfied with what they had signed. With respect to the treaty agreed to in Manitoba in 1875, Morris reminded Ottawa officials: "I asked and obtained authority to promise these Indians, a Treaty, with the most tranquilizing effect. In the next place I have to remind you, that in the interval, war broke out, between Americans and the Sioux, in a region of the United States, not far from our frontier."[5] In describing the famine clause negotiations for Treaty 6, Morris said, "The Indians fully understood the effect of the promises of the Commissioner, and its extent, and abandoned their demand for daily food – although they know that rations were given in the United States."[6] The tone of much of Morris's letter suggests that in each circumstance the commissioners needed to do whatever was necessary to "tranquilize" the prairie Aboriginal populations. The urgency of getting a treaty signed meant that it was important to agree to some requests so that other more controversial parts of the treaty could be downplayed or perhaps not even mentioned.

Morris, though he was not at Treaty 7, did indicate in his letter to the minister of the interior that flexibility would need to be exercised to secure a treaty in southern Alberta: "The only Indians remaining to be treated with are the Blackfeet. I do not think that the terms granted to the Crees will appreciably affect their action, the more so as I am of the opinion that the terms of a treaty with the Blackfeet must be adapted to their circumstances, and vary considerably from the Treaties already concluded."[7]

Contrary to Morris's official position in the actual negotiations (that the numbered treaties were basically the same), it is clear that the treaties did differ from one another. Of Treaty 5 and negotiations in general, Morris wrote:

The provisions of Treaty No. 5 are far less onerous, than any of the other treaties because the circumstances are different. I would further state, that, when, in the year 1873, I proceeded to the North West Angle to make a treaty, after two previous failures, I felt that the terms of the Treaty would largely shape those that were to follow. I had confidential instructions then, while at Fort Carlton, I was unfettered in that way. I spent twelve days in endeavouring to come to an understanding with the Indians, and at length succeeded, having the satisfaction of knowing that I had fixed the rate of annuities within the limit of my instruction, at a scale, which has since governed, in all the other Treaties, and which has thereby resulted in a very large saving to the Dominion.[8]

COMMISSIONER DAVID LAIRD

After attending at Treaty 6, David Laird, now the lieutenant-governor of the North-West Territories, made the journey to Fort Macleod to act as a commissioner for Treaty 7; he was to serve in this capacity along with Colonel James Macleod. Interestingly, in his report on the treaty process to government officials in Battleford, Laird's first observation concerned the businesses that had been established at Fort Macleod: "In the village I found some excellent stores, supplies with almost every article."[9] Laird then remarked on the fact that the land between the Bow and Oldman rivers had great potential for grazing and that on his arrival he had noticed several successful crops, including grain and vegetables. Laird was next most favourably impressed with the coal that was being mined only a short distance from the fort: "Coal is used from the Belly River, at a place some twenty miles distant from Fort Macleod. I was told by the proprietor of the shop that the coal answers tolerably well for blacksmithing purposes, and in the fort it is extensively used for fuel. It burns nearly as well in a stove as some varieties of Pictou coal."[10]

By Tuesday September 18 the Blood chief Red Crow had not yet arrived, although Laird mentioned that an agreement had been made to meet with the Siksika on the next afternoon. At the Wednesday meeting the chiefs were told that provisions of flour, tea, sugar, tobacco, and beef were available and that accepting the provisions did not commit them to signing the treaty. On Thursday Laird met the chiefs again and explained two points: first, "that by the Canadian Law their reserves could not be taken from them, occupied or sold without their consent"; and second, "that their hunting over the open prairie would not be interfered with, so long as they did not molest the settlers and others in the country."[11]

At the end of the Thursday meeting, Crowfoot and Eagle Tail, along with the Stoney leaders, told Laird they would not speak again till the next day. One of the Bloods, Medicine Calf, did speak, saying that the North-West Mounted Police owed them for the wood they had taken; he asked that each chief be given $50 for the wood and that collectively the others be given $70. At this point Laird felt he had to respond to Medicine Calf, for unless he did, the incident might be interpreted as giving an advantage to the Aboriginal side. He told the chief that if he respected the NWMP for protecting his people, then it was "unreasonable" to ask the government to "pay a large gratuity to each Indian for the little wood their benefactors had used." Laird then concluded: "On the contrary, I said if there should be any pay in the matter it ought to come from the indians to the Queen for sending them the police."[12] Laird then heard a "hearty" laugh from Crowfoot and the other chiefs, which he chose to interpret as being at the expense of Medicine Calf for his outrageous request. It is more likely, as Hugh Dempsey has explained, that they were laughing at Laird for his outrageous suggestion that the Blackfoot pay for the protection that the police were offering them.

As Red Crow had arrived at Blackfoot Crossing on the Thursday evening, there was representation by leaders of each nation for the Friday meeting, when the treaty was to be signed. Laird had assured each tribe that the representatives that they put forward would be acknowledged and recognized as chiefs by the commissioners. Jean L'Heureux assisted by fixing the corresponding names to the X's on the treaty document.

Laird stated in his report that following the signing ceremony he was met by a deputation of Métis who asked that the ordinance restricting the buffalo hunt not be enforced in the coming winter. The Métis also made a request for assistance in agriculture, which Laird said he would pass on to Ottawa. With regard to the buffalo ordinance, Laird replied, "I told them that the notice having been short, the law would not be strictly enforced for the first winter."[13] This statement was in direct contravention of what he had only a few hours earlier told the Treaty 7 leadership – that he would use the NWMP to protect the buffalo. In fact, it was primarily this promise that persuaded Red Crow to accept Treaty 7. Later that day each First Nation explained what land it would take and the chiefs described the areas where they would reside.

In his account, Laird sketched out the week's events. On Monday, payments, flags, medals, and uniforms were distributed. On Tuesday, he finalized an agreement with Bobtail's Cree. On Wednesday he was invited by the Blackfoot to a meeting at which speeches were made thanking the commissioners. Later that day he "drove to the coal source about five miles east of Blackfoot Crossing."[14]

The concluding remarks in Laird's report leave room for doubt about his commitment to protect the buffalo. While he had allowed certain measures for the protection of the buffalo to be discussed, he expressed the belief that the buffalo would soon disappear in any case "and that further protection would be needless."[15] Then in the next sentence, Laird wrote (perhaps ironically): "At any rate by that time the Indians hope to have herds of domestic cattle."[16] Thus, it appears that Laird agreed to demands that he never had any intention of seeing enforced. He certainly did not include the demands in writing. In fact, Laird seemed most proud of the role that he played in "keeping down the costs." He made promises that required no expenditures and offered to provide cattle, a less expensive commitment than agricultural instruction: "Their delivery to the Indians will cost an inconsiderable sum, the total expense of supplying the articles promised to this treaty will, I am convinced, cost less than those under either Treaty No. 4 or No. 6."[17]

It is now apparent that there were great misunderstandings about certain issues that were discussed, since the First Nations chiefs believed that they were all to benefit from the promises made to them. In his report to the department, Laird described how the promises might be seen as excessive, but he carefully explained that the government's obligations were not as great as it might at first appear: "The articles promised in addition to the money payments may to some appear excessive. The Stoneys are the only Indians adhering to this treaty who desire agricultural implements and seed. The promises, therefore, respecting these things may be understood as merely applicable to that tribe. The Blackfeet and Bloods asked for nothing of this kind; they preferred cattle, and the Commissioners being fully of the opinion that such were likely to be much more serviceable to them than seed and implements, encouraged them in their request."[18]

Clearly, the government's promise to provide a transition to an agricultural way of life, by providing instruction, tools, and implements, was an especially shallow one considering that costs could be cut if the Blackfoot could be persuaded that they would be better off if they were given cattle and took up ranching as a way of life.

What is questionable as well is Laird's position with regard to the land the nations were to choose. Could the First Nations at Blackfoot Crossing have known that all they would be provided with after a survey would be a small tract of land, especially as they had been allowed to describe vast territories for their claim? No wonder the First Nations agreed to the treaty without hesitation. The government clearly did not explain how small the reserves would be.

Finally – and perhaps the greatest deception of all – there is no evidence to indicate that the issue of ceding or surrendering the land was ever raised by the commissioners in the discussions. Though the written treaty was clear enough on this point, there is also no record that the entire treaty was ever read to the five First Nations assembled at Blackfoot Crossing. If this issue had been raised in their language, it would have been opposed by the leadership of these nations, who would have trusted (wrongly) the commissioners to include in the written treaty all of the items that had been discussed. Ironically, Laird's report on the treaty process ends as follows: "Copies of the treaty printed on parchment should be forwarded to Fort Macleod in good time to be delivered to each Head and Minor Chief at next year's payment of annuities."[19] It is unclear whether this was ever done.

When he began his negotiations at Blackfoot Crossing, Laird was afraid of the response of the Blackfoot Confederacy to the government proposals. In light of this, it is no wonder that he was unwilling to tell them the whole truth. Laird had read Father Scollen's briefing notes describing the Blackfoot as being wary of the White man's tendency to cheat them. Scollen had warned that

the Blackfoot are extremely jealous of what they consider their country, and never allowed any white men, half-breeds, or Crees to remain in it for any length of time; the only reason that they never drove the Americans off, apart from their love for whiskey, was their dread of the Henry rifle ... they have an awful dread of the future. They think that the police are in the country not only to keep out whiskey traders, but also to protect white people against them, and that this country will gradually be taken from them without any ceremony. This I can certify, for although they may not say so to others yet they do not hide it from me.[20]

Scollen also warned at the end of his letter, which was intended to inform the commissioners about the state of the country, that the Lakota were sending a deputation to the Blackfoot to form an alliance with them against "all the white people in the country."[21] Furthermore, in September 1877 the ongoing Nez Percé

War had the potential to create further international troubles for Canadian authorities.

It is possible that Laird's apprehensions about the prospect of making a treaty with such dangerous tribes of "Natives" led him to decide against raising "surrender" issues for consideration. He knew these would be divisive. When the commissioners tried to talk of restricting hunting rights on the first day of negotiations, they were vigorously opposed and had to back off this issue. In light of this, there would surely have been resistance to any discussion about ceding, releasing, surrendering, or yielding up the land. What the Aboriginal leadership believed was that they were agreeing to share the land. To give up the land was unconstitutional for any of the First Nations present.

McDougall, Scollen, and other Whites in the territory all warned about the urgency of making treaty with the tribes of southern Alberta. Scollen himself described how the tribes had been regaining their strength in the years after the whiskey traders were driven out, so the fears that they might become a powerful force once again may have been present in the minds of the Whites who were pressing for a treaty to be made in this territory.

Certainly Laird's account of the treaty is most remarkable for what he does *not* mention rather than for what he does.

FATHER CONSTANTINE SCOLLEN

Some of the most revealing evidence on Treaty 7 was left behind by Father Scollen, OMI. The two most important documents are the letter he wrote in 1876 to inform the treaty commissioners concerning the state of the Aboriginal peoples in southern Alberta and a letter he wrote in 1879 in which he outlined the condition of the Treaty 7 nations just a few years after they had made the treaty.

Scollen's Letter of 1876 for the Treaty Commissioners

Scollen's letter of 1876 combines an apparent concern for the Treaty 7 First Nations with a paternalistic disdain for "their thirst for blood and their other barbarous passions [that] were constantly fired to the highest pitch frenzy."[22] These unwarranted and misleading comments were made of the Blackfoot rather than of the Cree, who, according to Scollen, had always regarded the "whiteman as a friend, or to use their own language, as a brother."[23] The Blackfoot were described (ethnocentrically) as sullen, superstitious, and dangerous – as people to be feared, who were threatening and needed to be brought under control. Even though throughout the 1870s it was just as often the Cree who attacked the Blackfoot, the Blackfoot were the ones portrayed as more warlike. And even though the religious beliefs of the two Plains tribes were similar, the Blackfoot were depicted as being more unreasonably sunk in dangerous superstitions: "They have regarded the white man as a demi-god, far superior to themselves in intelligence, capable of doing them good or evil, according as he might be well or ill-disposed towards them, unscrupulous in his dealings with others, and consequently a person to be flattered, feared and shunned, and even injured, whenever this could be done with impunity."[24]

Scollen, who had moved from working among the Cree some years earlier to working among the Blackfoot, may have had his own reasons for wanting a treaty concluded with the tribes. For him, it would have been of great relief to know that the tribes of the Blackfoot, Stoney, and Tsuu T'ina could be "settled" on reserves. This mission of "civilizing" would be made much easier if their movements were controlled and laws were enforced to make them comply with familiar codes of behaviour. Scollen may have tried to exaggerate the threat posed by the southern tribes in order to encourage the Canadian authorities to establish a more prominent presence in the area. He may have promoted the potential of the land for ranching and agriculture, perhaps even drawn attention to the high quality of coal present, in order to heighten the government's interest in the area. The consequence of this would be to speed up the process of making the territory safe for White settlers. He was clearly as much concerned for the White settlers of the area as he was for the tribes among whom he was attempting to win converts to Christianity when he wrote that settlers are "anxious that a treaty be made as soon as possible, so that they may know what portions of land they can hold without fear of being molested."[25]

But it is not clear that the tribes of the territory wanted a treaty that would resemble treaties 1–6. In fact, at a meeting held in the Hand Hills in 1875 the Blackfoot spoke about the need to keep settlers and the Métis out of their territory. They were, however, concerned about the dwindling buffalo herds, and they wanted to stay on the land and use it in the way they always had. The meeting at the Hand Hills, as recorded by Jean L'Heureux, showed that the goals that the Blackfoot wanted addressed were far different from those that the treaty makers were attempting to get the tribes to accept.

Both Scollen and McDougall likely knew about the Blackfoot resistance to land surrender issues, and the missionaries therefore probably sent warnings to the commissioners about the potential for disagreement. This may be why the land surrender was never raised for discussion and was only written into the treaty after the discussions and negotiations. What seems evident for Treaty 7 is that the various tribes appreciated the work of the NWMP, who had rid the territory of whiskey trading, and that in the wake of this they were regaining their strength. McDougall and Scollen made it appear that the First Nations were anxious to conclude a treaty when in fact, as they had stated in the council memorandum of 1875, what they wanted to do was to keep out settlers and preserve the buffalo.

Scollen's 1876 letter is not without concern for the well-being of the tribes of the territory. Possibly embellishing to some extent, he described the effects of alcohol that flowed like "streams from the Rocky Mountains." The whiskey trade was devastating "and hundreds of poor indians fell victims to the white man's craving for money, some poisoned, some frozen to death whilst in the state of intoxication, and many shot down by American bullets."[26] Alongside whiskey was the horrific toll taken as a result of smallpox, "which told upon the Blackfoot with a terrible effect, destroying between six and eight hundred of them."[27] Together, alcohol and smallpox wrought further destruction: "They endeavoured to drown their grief in the poisonous beverage. They sold their robes and horses by the hundreds for it and began killing one another, so that in a short time they were divided into several small parties, afraid to meet."[28]

Scollen, with evident concern, wrote: "It was painful for me to see the state of poverty to which they had been reduced. Formerly they had been the most opulent indians in the country, and now they were clothed in rags, without horses and without guns."[29]

After the NWMP arrived to save their numbers, as Scollen wrote, the disposition of the tribes began to change: "During the last two years I have calculated that they have bought two thousand horses to replace those they had given up for whiskey."[30] But Scollen warned that even though they were grateful to the police for protecting them and driving out the whiskey traders, "underneath this friendship remains hidden some of the dread which they always had of the white man's intention to cheat them; and here, excellent Governor, I will state my reasons for believing that a treaty should be concluded with them also at the earliest possible date."[31]

Scollen's letter of 1876 to the commissioners is both sympathetic to and disdainful of the First Nations people, and it reflects a hidden agenda – "that a treaty should be concluded with them at the earliest possible date."[32]

Scollen's Letter to Major Irvine, 1879

If Scollen's letter in 1876 warning the treaty commissioners was a veiled plea to establish Canadian legal and administrative authority, then his letter of 1879 to Irvine is an example of how seriously Canadian Indian policy was failing. In this letter Scollen expressed great concern over the conditions in which the Treaty 7 First Nations found themselves only two years after the treaty was made:

I have now been acquainted sixteen years with the Blackfoot. I have seen them in all their places – in the days of prosperity and opulence; when their braves mustered double the numbers they muster now: when they were entire masters of the immense prairies from Benton to Edmonton and the terror of their enemies on every side, North, South, East and West. I have seen them in those days mourn the loss of numerous relatives fallen in deadly combat against the foes. I have seen them later on, when reduced to the last stage of poverty and disorganization from the effects of intoxicating liquor, but through all these stages I have never seen them so depressed as they are now; I have never seen them before in want of food; last winter for the first time have they really suffered the pangs of hunger, and for the first time in my life have I seen a Blackfoot brave withdraw from his lodge that he might not listen to his crying children when he had not meat to give them. Such, Dear Sir, has been the state of the Blackfoot Indians last winter. They have suffered fearfully from hunger. Two poor women on Elk River, fell victims to the scourge, a thing never heard of before amongst the Blackfoot. Many sustained life by eating the flesh of poisoned wolves. Some have lived on dogs; and I have known others to live several days on nothing else but old bones which they gathered and broke up, where with to make a kind of soup.[33]

The poverty, Scollen wrote, had the result of forcing the Treaty 7 people to steal cattle to stave off starvation:

White-men, farmers are becoming disgusted. There is now at Fort Mac-leod, an industrious hard working man from Calgary on his way across the line. He is leaving the country after working hard all last summer and raising a magnificent crop, he could get no market for his produce; and the Indians have been robbing him all winter. If things continue without a change, others will do the same. Men will be thinking of driving their stock across the line for security, as many Indians are now thinking of crossing it in order to get something to eat from the American Agents. It is an undeniable fact that there is in the country a money-making monopoly. The members of this monopoly will, of course, put up with a great deal, in order to hold their grasp, but the poor hard working man, the bone and sinew of the land, will not be inclined to linger where there is no security for his property.[34]

The blame for this situation was placed squarely on the government for failing to live up to its treaty promises. Scollen was particularly angry with Lieutenant-Governor Laird, to whom he had written requesting ploughs and seed to assist in establishing some subsistence agriculture: "With this help I intended in spring to work with the Indians on their reserve at the Crossing, and put in twenty five or thirty acres of potatoes. The Indians would all willingly have worked with me, and in the fall, would be able to enjoy the fruits of their own labour. This would en-courage them for next year, and others would join in with them, and so the government would see a great good done amongst them with very little expense."[35] But in response to Scollen's request, Laird had replied that he was not an Indian agent and that he could not agree to such a request without looking into it. Scollen responded: "Is it not strange that the Dominion Government who can endow a man with power to hang another for murder, has not endowed the Lieut. Governor with power to grant so paltry a thing as the above, which might be the means of saving a few indians from starvation."[36]

Then Scollen described the consequences of not delivering on the treaty promises:

The Peigan indian, according to the treaty are entitled to farming implements and seed, and now is the time they should be using them – yet they have received neither, nor had their reserve even been surveyed. Surely this is too much procrastination at a time when indians are in extreme want. It will now be another year before the Peigans can use their farming implements; and when they do get them, I suppose they will be useless flimsy ploughs without colters etc. Such as have been sent to the Stoney indians, whereas they ought to be furnished some good strong breaking ploughs, hoes etc. Such as one would suppose the government paid for.[37]

Perhaps the most interesting part of the whole letter is what Scollen wrote about what the Blackfoot and Stoney thought they had agreed to at Treaty 7. He indicated that the First Nations did not believe they were agreeing to a land surrender and thus provides further evidence that the issue of "cede, surrender, release and yield up" had never been discussed. Scollen wrote that the Treaty 7 First Nations entered the treaty because "they had always been treated kindly by the authorities, and did not wish to offend them."[38] He continued: "Although they had many doubts in their mind as to the meaning of the treaty ... they hoped that it simply meant to furnish them with plenty of food and clothing, and particularly the former every time they stood in need of them."[39]

On the issue of whether the real intent of Treaty 7 was ever understood by the Aboriginal peoples who were party to it, Scollen's answer was unequivocal: "Now, in the van of my statements stands this all important question, which to my mind is the pivot on which all others revolve. Did these indians, or do they now, understand the real nature of the treaty made between the government and themselves in 1877? My answer to this question is unhesitatingly negative, and I stand prepared to substantiate this proposition."[40] It seems apparent that when Scollen referred to "the real nature of the treaty," he meant the surrender of land. It seems equally clear that the First Nations of Treaty 7 had not understood that a land surrender was at the heart of the treaty. This had never been discussed. They saw the treaty as meaning that they would be furnished with "plenty of food and clothing ..." in return for sharing the land. Giving away land was not possible; it would have been unconstitutional.

Scollen's letter is interesting as well for what it tells us about the representatives of the Canadian government. He had a particularly dim view of Lieutenant-Governor Laird, who felt no commitment to live up to the promises that he himself had made to the Aboriginal peoples of Treaty 7. Laird's refusal to respond to Scollen's request for ploughs and seed shows that men like Laird did not live up to what they said at the treaty and may have deliberately deceived the Aboriginal leadership at Blackfoot Crossing in other ways as well. It was the government that broke the treaty only months after the agreement. The government slipped the land surrender clause (the most crucial part of the treaty) into the written treaty after the fact and then did not deliver on its promises. It could certainly be argued that Laird negotiated the treaty for the purpose of getting the tribes onto reserves and under the authority of Canadian laws and administration so that they would not stand as obstacles to the White settlers who were soon, Laird hoped, to flood the area.

REVEREND JOHN McDOUGALL

John McDougall's role in the Treaty 7 negotiations remains shrouded in controversy. In the multitude of books McDougall wrote over the years about his mission work in the Northwest, he said very little about Treaty 7 or his role in the negotiations. What we do know is that McDougall received a commission from the Canadian government in 1874 to travel throughout the Northwest to explain to the tribes who would eventually enter into Treaty 7 what the role of the NWMP would be when they arrived in the foothills. In his own writings, McDougall described the great concern he had for the First Nations he worked among, and he emphasized his mission work rather than the work he did for the government in persuading the prairie tribes to conclude the treaty. He congratulated himself as being loved by the people he worked among, although evidence from the Stoney elders casts doubt on the sterling reputation that McDougall gave himself.

Never one to be modest, McDougall saw himself in the vanguard of civilization and viewed his role as the representative of the government to the tribes as no less than "John the 'Baptist' of the new regime of law and order and government."[41] Shortly after receiving his commission, McDougall met with the Stoney chiefs to deliver the government message. He then proceeded to meet with Crowfoot of the Siksika at Crowfoot Creek: "In a short time the big lodge was full of chiefs and leading men. Through my interpreter, I told them of the coming of the mounted force across the plains and the purpose of their coming. Tribal war was to be suppressed and whiskey trading and horse stealing and all crimes were to be done away with. I exalted British justice and made much of the quality of men in the eyes of the law and most keenly and patiently those men listened to my story."[42] According to McDougall, his representations were well received:

When I was done, Crowfoot took my hand and placed it on his heart and said, "My brother your words make me glad. I listened to them not only with my ears but with my heart also. In the coming of the long knives, with their firewater and their quick-shooting guns, we are weak, and our people have been woefully slain and impoverished. You say this will be stopped. We are glad to have it stopped. We want peace. What you tell us about this strong power, which will govern with good law and treat the Indian the same as the white man, makes us glad to hear. My brother, I believe you, and am thankful." Old Sun and all the rest present gave assent to what Crowfoot had spoken.[43]

Chief Crow-that-Makes-the-Large-Footprint also spoke for the Siksika:

If left to ourselves we are gone. The whiskey brought among us by our traders is fast killing us off and we are powerless before the evil – totally unable to resist the temptation to drink when brought in contact with the whiteman's water. We are also unable to pitch anywhere that the trader cannot follow us. Our horses buffalo robes and other articles of trade go for whiskey. A large number of our people have killed one another and perished in various ways under the influence and now that we hear of our great mother sending her soldiers into our country for our good we are glad.[44]

McDougall continued on his assignment, meeting with Blood, Tsuu T'ina, and other Siksika bands before submitting his report for the season in October 1874.

This commission that McDougall undertook for the government had been requested by representatives of the Hudson's Bay Company for a number of years. Employees of the HBC who knew the Blackfoot tribes well were concerned about potential clashes between the North-West Mounted Police and the Siksika, Bloods, and Peigan, who had always guarded their territory against intruders. These HBC men knew that it was very unlikely that the Blackfoot would give up their land. The Canadian government took the warnings seriously, and Minister of Justice A.A. Dorian established the commission. Through the chief factors at Fort Edmonton and Fort Ellice, Dorian authorized the employment of missionaries of various denominations to relay to the tribes of the region the message that the NWMP intended to protect the local population from American whiskey traders. Dorian further authorized the distribution of "gifts": "Presents not exceeding $2500.00 should be entrusted to the care of these gentlemen for the purpose of distribution among the Indians in any interviews they may have with them."[45]

McDougall never revealed how the money was distributed, but it is clear that the authority given to him to distribute gifts put him in a position of influence among those who received these payments. McDougall used these occasions to speak about the future and to explain to the various tribes that the Whites would be arriving in large numbers "to flood the land." McDougall, who himself was anxious to have the Stoneys settle in one place, was a great advocate of the treaties and was probably responsible for instilling a fear of the future in many of the tribes that he visited. Many tribes were close to starvation, and the gifts he distributed no doubt made them more willing to listen to his message. Some among the Blackfoot, Tsuu T'ina, and Stoney leadership must have been suspicious of the money given out, wondering whether there would be strings attached. The reluctance to accept rations during the first few days at Blackfoot Crossing might well have been linked to this concern about what would be expected in return. Clearly, in 1874 McDougall was acting as the agent of a government so concerned about the threat from the prairie tribes that it would use money to keep them peaceful and perhaps keep them from forming military alliances with the nearby Lakota of Sitting Bull or the Nez Percé of White Bird.

In 1875 McDougall again met with Blackfoot tribes, this time to talk about the treaties. During these meetings he again presented the position of the Canadian government to Crowfoot. As Hugh Dempsey writes, "McDougall explained in detail what had happened to the Indians in other parts of Canada. Treaties had been signed, lands set aside, the rights of the Indians respected."[46] McDougall told them that justice would be given equally to everyone and the country would be "settled." Dempsey suggests that Crowfoot understood McDougall's message: "This was Crowfoot's first intimation of a Canadian treaty and he seemed satisfied. He knew his tribe could not always hold its hunting grounds against the advancing white civilization but was worried that a settlement might not be made."[47]

McDougall, as his writings show, felt concern for the Stoneys and the other Aboriginal peoples he worked among, but his work as an agent of the government put him in a conflict of interest. Furthermore, he consistently seemed to put his own interests ahead of the interests of the people he worked among. This is no more clearly shown than in John Snow's history of the Stoney people, in which he describes McDougall's vested interest in bargaining for only one reserve for the Stoneys, even though their traditional territory ranged widely and even beyond the boundaries set by Treaty 7:

Although the Stoneys did not realize it, Treaty Seven meant that we would receive only one reserve, which was to be located at Morleyville. But at the time of the treaty negotiations, Chief Goodstoney expected to receive a similar reserve in the Bighorn-Kootenay Plains area for his people who lived there before the treaty was agreed to and Chief Bearspaw expected to receive land for his band south of Morley. This was done for the different Blackfoot bands, who received reserve lands at Gleichen, Cardston and Brocket; our Chiefs expected the same consideration for their three bands of our tribe. We now know and realize that John McDougall had a personal interest in having one large reserve established at Morleyville; the church was there, the hay fields were nearby and a small area was under cultivation. It was apparently his feeling that the church could not continue effectively Christianizing my people if we did not all settle on one reserve.[48]

It has furthermore been shown that McDougall made his own land claim at Morley before he undertook to help the Stoneys. The land he chose for himself turned out to be better land for farming than the land surveyed for the Stoneys.

The literature McDougall left behind describing the treaty process stands in stark contrast to what the Stoney elders now say. Stoney elders insist that McDougall did not speak for the people he lived among; rather he spoke with enthusiasm for the way of life that the newcomers would bring to the Northwest. McDougall's writing shows his contempt for much of the Aboriginal life he observed. As historian Sarah Carter has written, McDougall and his generation

had enormous admiration for the technological achievements of their own society and found the Indians woefully backward in comparison. Indians appeared oblivious to the whiteman's crusade to subdue nature, their religion was an affront to the missionaries' central beliefs and what they perceived as the Indians' cruel indifference to women was offensive to the virtues of domestic affection and the home, which they cherished. Contemporary readers of these stirring missionary accounts were left with the overall impression that the Indian was a member of a feeble, backward race, living in a world of ignorance, superstition and cruelty. It would have been difficult to escape the conclusion that the vast, rich lands occupied by the Indians should be settled by a stronger, more industrious race of men. Missionary publications provided information that justified and sanctioned the appropriation of Indian land and authorized the establishment of a society based on social inequality.[49]

Even though McDougall claimed to admire hunting, trapping, and the outdoor life, he never wavered from seeing the Aboriginal way of life as inferior. His passages on the life of "the pagan brethren" are as strident as those of other missionaries of the day. Methodist missionaries such as McDougall gained energy for their work from the idea that they were playing a great part in the march of "progress." McDougall believed that "the North American Indian" stood in the way of this march of progress and that "civilization" would replace superstition with reason: "When the missionaries contrasted their civilization with that of the Indians, they saw the development clearly as one of progress. This commitment to an ideal of progress compelled the missionaries to view the Indian as historically anterior and culturally and morally inferior."[50]

The evidence of the Aboriginal peoples' inferiority was that there were no farms or cities, as the Europeans would define them, to indicate "civilization." There was no private property or literature; nothing was being done to "subdue the earth" as the Christian clarion call had announced. There was also no provision for the future. McDougall found idleness to be a great bane of Aboriginal society, but their religion was the target of his most aggressive attacks. Christianity offered "light," while the pagan beliefs of the Stoneys were portrayed as shrouded in darkness: "McDougall made it quite clear why the Indians' religion must be banished. The Indians' religion was inextricably linked to their moral, material and mental backwardness. It was a cause of the Indians' inability to gain some measure of control over their environment."[51]

It would be an understatement to say that McDougall had little respect for the people he sought to convert to Christianity. In his view, only by joining the tide of progress could they share the glorious future that enlightened guardians such as himself offered them. In many ways McDougall's writings suggest that there was little room for Aboriginal people in his vision of the future; rather he saw his own people as being dominant in the future. He felt that by converting the Stoneys he was making a contribution to the glorious future he envisioned. When he visited a dam site at Horse Shoe Falls in 1911, he believed he saw evidence that his dream had been realized:

Truly, all this marvellous brains and nature, cement and steel – verily a strong combination and stronger still, the great God in His Mighty purpose for His own child, man ... Doubtless there are more which some day will be developed. In the meanwhile, last Friday I stood on the edge of the dam below the present power plant and the huge dam above it and was thankful for this realization of my vision – thirty-eight years and a month to wait – but what are these periods in the presence of the huge problem now given men that they should subjugate this big Dominion for the glory of God and the blessing and comfort of man?[52]

Notwithstanding his high-sounding and virtuous ideals, McDougall's career is blemished by his duplicitous behaviour towards the Stoney people. In a number of instances he was in a conflict of interest, as he was, as already noted, when he claimed land at Morley before the land set aside for the Stoneys had even been properly surveyed. In 1891, long before leasing and surrender of reserve land was common, McDougall wrote a letter to Indian Commissioner Hayter Reed asking him for a grazing lease on the Stoney reserve. Reed rejected McDougall's request, arguing that this could not possibly be in the best interests of the Stoneys. McDougall disagreed: "That part of the reserve was never any benefit to the Indians until I fenced it but rather a loss for the settlers [who] used to run their cattle in between the river and railroad and by using it will not in any way deprive the Indians but be a source of revenue and a protection to the reserve."[53] Reed responded: "I had a talk with the Minister today about you obtaining part of the Stoney Reserve under a grazing lease but he felt, that although he would like to oblige you, he would be offering a dangerous precedent and that great pressure might be brought to obtain portions of other reserves looked upon as most desirable for grazing purposes."[54]

McDougall functioned as a kind of informer for the authorities, as on the occasion when he provided information to Colonel Macleod of the NWMP about the activities of traders in the territory. As evidence that McDougall's work was appreciated by the authorities, Laird, in 1877, sent him a cheque in the amount of $25, "as a small acknowledgment of your services in translating for the Stoneys."[55] This money was sent in a letter in which Laird also thanked McDougall for his role in pacifying those Stoneys who were most dissatisfied with the treaty provisions, especially the "gift" of ammunition that turned out to be unsuitable for their guns.

In summation, McDougall seems to have been far more than the selfless missionary bent on converting the Stoneys to Christianity. What his books leave out is that he was also a paid government agent providing authorities with important information and a man not averse to accepting political patronage. It also appears that he was frequently in a position of serving competing interests, his own among them. Unlike Father Scollen, who genuinely cared for the Bloods he worked among, McDougall seems to have been to some extent self-serving.

THE OFFICIAL HISTORY OF THE NWMP

The observations of the events at Blackfoot Crossing made by members of the NWMP are in substance similar to Commissioner Laird's official report, which was printed in the *Sessional Papers* of Canada. However, they differ in emphasis from Laird's account in that they tend to be more ethnocentric and self-serving. The Aboriginal viewpoint is presented as much more obviously inferior or "savage," while the government position is represented as being the most eminently reasonable one. The analysis below is a summary of viewpoints expressed in the official history of the NWMP (John Peter Turner's *The North-West Mounted Police, 1873-1893*, published in 1950), which was based largely on the writings of NWMP officers Cecil Denny, Sam Steele, William Parker, and James Macleod, who had all been present at the treaty signing.

Turner's account of what happened at Blackfoot Crossing begins on a dramatic and self-congratulatory note: "In glittering contrast to the melancholy story from south of the international boundary, an event, probably the most important thus far in the transitional period of Western Canada, was staged in late summer on the banks of the Bow River some 60 miles east of Fort Calgary."[56] The treaty, according to this history, was about adjusting "by mutual arrangements the primitive to the modern."[57] Of course, the heroes are the treaty commissioners who persevere under daunting obstacles, bringing civilization into a country whose Aboriginal way of life is obviously inferior. The police are presented as important agents to help "relegate to the past the redman's claims to his jealously-held hunting-grounds."[58]

This history continues to perpetuate myths that have long been thrown into question, even by official government evidence. It describes Jerry Potts, for example, as a "tactful guide and interpreter who had firmly established himself in the Mounted Police service as an intermediary of rare talent."[59] Crowfoot is presented as the chief whose "word prevailed," even though it is probable that the most powerful chief at the time of the treaty was Red Crow and that all First Nations discussed the treaty agreement prior to its conclusion. The ethnocentricity and bravado of the NWMP account is probably no where better expressed than in the following words: "This was to be the last brilliant pageant of a prehistoric race – the last great gathering in Canada of Stone-Age man. To many it was obvious the west would never see its like again."[60]

The account then goes on to state that during the first days of the negotiations the commissioners told the First Nations that "the land reserves to be allotted could not be taken from them and their liberty of hunting over the prairie would continue as long as they molested no one."[61] Of course, the trusted position of the police force is given full recognition as a major factor in the success of the treaty: "The influence of the scarlet-coated riders was magical – the Force was regarded as the friend of all. Native esteem was strong for Commissioner Macleod; and though danger lurked, no one doubted that the police represented the Great Mother's authority fairly and squarely ... Here at Blackfoot Crossing was a scene to please the eyes of tolerance and humanity – utter savagery bowing to a new order proffered fearlessly and honestly. The entire Blackfoot Confederacy had been weaned from its original barbarism by Macleod and his command."[62]

This history then describes Laird's offer to the First Nations peoples:

The Great Spirit had made all things; the Great White Mother (Queen Victoria) ruled over the country; the white man was a friend to his red brother; the White Mother loved all her children and wished them good; she would punish both alike for wickedness; the buffalo would soon disappear, and assistance would be given to the Indians to raise cattle and grain. Money would be paid to them every year. The chiefs would get clothes, a silver medal and a flag. Reserves of land would be set aside for the red brethren, one to each division of the confederacy, where no others would be permitted to encroach. If required roads would be built; cattle and potatoes would be provided; ammunition would be issued each year. Instructors would be supplied to teach the redman's children.[63]

While Crowfoot is singled out as the "noble savage" who understood what the others did not, Medicine Calf is portrayed as hindering "proceedings with stupid and irrelevant remarks and questions."[64] After a general review of the negotiations, similar to Laird's account, this thoroughly uncritical history concludes with a statement that attempts to perpetuate the myth of Canada's honourable Indian policy: "In any comparison between methods followed on either side of the international boundary, an unbiased view must at least acknowledge that Canada had gained valuable experience by the breaking-down of various Indian treaties in the United States. Aside from this the Canadian treaties had no relation whatever to those south of the border. Entirely different policies were pursued, and Canada's record in her occupation of the plains by the Mounted Police was something of which Canadians could be proud."[65]

HUDSON'S BAY COMPANY TRADER RICHARD HARDISTY

Accompanying the entourage of the treaty commission was a large contingent of merchants who hoped to take advantage of the treaty money that was to be paid to the signatories of Treaty 7, the amount to be a substantial $52,954. One of these was the HBC trader Richard Hardisty, brother-in-law of John McDougall. Hardisty's eye-witness account is brief and similar in most respects to Laird's official report. There are, however, interesting details in his version of the events. He observed, for example, that Crowfoot was not necessarily the main chief for all the First Nations present. In describing the last day of the negotiations, Hardisty recalled:

The meeting of the chiefs was to take place at 10 a.m. My father and John McDougall were aware of the fact that many of the war chiefs were opposed to the treaty. The young bucks were with them in opposition. Word had come to them that the U.S.A. was not living up to treaties made with their brothers across the line. There was no doubt of Crowfoot's sincerity and friendship. He was, however, not a war chief, although head chief of the Blackfoot, he was only camp chief, consequently was not a hero, as he had never won fame as a fighter, holding his position through force of eloquence.[66]

It is noteworthy that an HBC man would understand Crowfoot's status in relation to the other groups present in a way that other officials at the time failed or refused to do.

The other significant observation made by Hardisty is that the First Nations leaders and the commissioners smoked the pipe on commencement of the treaty negotiations: "From somewhere, unnoticed till that moment, a dignified and stately figure walked to the centre in front of the commissioners' tents (the commissioners being already seated) followed by two other figures. One spread a robe on the ground. The leader, Crowfoot, sat down. A stone pipe was filled and lighted. Crowfoot took one puff and the pipe was then passed to Governor Laird, who also took a puff. The conference was now open and in time the treaty was drawn and signed."[67] This was a significant event for the First Nations, who on smoking the pipe would proceed to negotiate solemnly and in good faith.

CHAPTER NINE

A Study of the Accounts of Treaty 7 by Hugh Dempsey

Hugh Dempsey is the most authoritative author to have examined Treaty 7 to date. His major works on Crowfoot of the Siksika and Red Crow of the Bloods have given us insight into what motivated those leaders to agree to Treaty 7. The strength of Dempsey's work is that he is knowledgable about the culture of the Blackfoot Confederacy and is sensitive to the perspective of the Aboriginal people who signed Treaty 7. In his studies he has used both oral interviews and informants as well as comprehensive primary and secondary material. Dempsey discusses Treaty 7 within the genre of biography, which he uses to frame his history. Biography focuses on character and circumstance, and Dempsey's biographies of Crowfoot and Red Crow do this with great success, perhaps allowing us to understand the motivations of the Siksika and Blood peoples more easily than those of the Peigan, Tsuu T'ina, and Stoney peoples.

Dempsey does not seriously question the motivation of the Canadian authorities and largely takes what they said at face value. Did they have a hidden agenda, as some of the material seems to indicate? Was the issue of the land surrender ever discussed? What else was promised to the First Nations at the treaty but never written down? How were issues such as sharing the land discussed or disputed? Were the First Nations at Blackfoot Crossing misled to the extent that they were allowed to believe anything they wanted about the treaty, so long as they signed it? Dempsey suggests there was a general meeting of minds between the two sides at Blackfoot Crossing but was this really the case? Can we take the promises made by Laird, Macleod, and McDougall at face value? Is there reason to question the significance of the disparity between what they said and what they subsequently did? What was the significance of Laird saying one thing to the Métis about protecting the buffalo and another thing to the First Nations at Blackfoot Crossing? Or of Macleod saying he would protect the buffalo and the next year doing nothing about it? Or of McDougall being more concerned about getting title to his own land than in determining what land the Stoneys were entitled to? Or of Laird promising ploughs and seed but demonstrating little willingness to do anything about delivery?

CROWFOOT

Hugh Dempsey's book *Crowfoot: Chief of the Blackfoot* is a classic biography of a significant Aboriginal leader and sheds much light on what happened at Blackfoot Crossing. Dempsey's narrative of the events provides details of the meetings that Crowfoot had with Canadian officials in the years just prior to the signing of Treaty 7.

One of the most significant of these meetings was with John McDougall in the summer of 1874. McDougall had been sent out to meet with the Blackfoot nations to inform them of the coming of the NWMP. He was also to inform the Aboriginal leadership about the treaties that were being signed in the Northwest. The meeting between Crowfoot and McDougall took place in the heart of Blackfoot country on Crowfoot Creek. McDougall explained to Crowfoot that the Mounties were coming and that this police force would be enforcing British concepts of justice. The NWMP would be enforcing laws that would apply to everyone equally. Most importantly, the Mounties were being sent out to put a stop to the whiskey trade by driving the traders out of the territories. Crowfoot was pleased with this and responded with his own speech, saying he was glad that the whiskey had stopped flowing and that his people were no longer being indiscriminately shot. He expressed his gratitude for the peace that had been established.[1]

Crowfoot told McDougall that he would see to it that the Mounties were assured of a peaceful reception from the Blackfoot peoples. In the short time the Mounties were in the territory, Crowfoot expressed his appreciation for the way the law was enforced and the way the whiskey trade was discouraged.

In December of 1874 Crowfoot met with Colonel Macleod at Fort Macleod and asked him to hold a general assembly at which the colonel could explain the intentions of the Mounties in the territory. At the assembly, Macleod addressed the chiefs, telling them that there would be one law for everyone, that both White and Aboriginal would be punished equally for breaking the law. As he concluded his statement, "there was a nod of approval among the chiefs when he said that they had not come to steal the land from the Indians, but only to protect the people who were in it."[2] For the time, the issue of land entitlement had been put to rest by Macleod. Crowfoot and Macleod shook hands and both sides went away feeling that they had come to an understanding of what the role of the police would be. Crowfoot, particularly, accepted British-Canadian law and justice and did much to help the police enforce the law concerning horse stealing, often intervening himself to return stolen horses.

In the summer of 1875 Crowfoot again met with John McDougall. Crowfoot explained that generally he was pleased with the work of the Mounties in the territories, as this was allowing his people to recover and rebuild. However, he raised concerns about the dwindling buffalo herds and the increasing number of White and Métis on Blackfoot lands. It was at this meeting that Crowfoot was first informed about the treaty being planned for the Blackfoot territories, that "in due time the treaties would be made and a settled condition created in this country wherein justice would be given to all."[3] Shortly after this, Crowfoot met with Major-General Selby-Smith and asked him what the Canadian intentions were for Blackfoot territories. In a general reply about the effects that treaties would have, Selby-Smith reassured Crowfoot that "his government's objective was to deal fairly with all tribes in her Majesty's domain and to extend uniform justice to the Indians of the plains."[4]

As a result of these meetings with McDougall, Macleod, and Selby-Smith, Crowfoot called a meeting of the Siksika, Bloods, and Peigan. After discussions, a petition was drawn up and given to the commanding officer at Fort Calgary to be delivered to the lieutenant-governor of the North-West Territories, Alexander Morris. The petition, which had been transcribed by Jean L'Heureux, was signed by the chiefs present and reads as follows:

Petition of the Chokitapix or Blackfeet Indian Chiefs to Lieut. Governer Morris, President of the Council for the North West Territories: –

Humbly sheweth: –
1. That at a general Council of the Nation held by respective tribe of Blackfeet, Bloods and Peigans in the Fall of 1875, it was decided to draw the attention of your honourable Council of the North West to the following facts, viz–
2. That in the Winter of 1871 a message of Lieut. Governor Archibald was forwarded to us on the Saskatchewan by Mr. I.W. Christie, a Member of your honourable Council, and the contents of said message was duly communicated to all your petitioners.
3. That we understood said message to promise us that the Government, or the white man, would not take the Indian lands without a Council of Her Majesty's Indian Commissioner and the respective Chiefs of the Nation.
4. That the white men have already taken the best location and built houses in any place they pleased in our "hunting grounds."
5. That the Half-breeds and Cree Indians in large Camps are hunting Buffalo, both Summer and Winter in the very centre of our lands.
6. That the land is pretty well taken up by white men now and no Indian Commissioner has visited us yet.
7. That we pray for an Indian Commissioner to visit us at the Hand Hills, Red Deer River, this year and let us know the time that he will visit us, so that we could hold a Council with him, for putting a stop to the invasion of our Country, till our Treaty be made with the Government.
8. That we are perfectly willing the Mounted Police and the Missionary should remain in the Country, for we are much indebted to them for important services.
9. That we feel perfectly confident that the representative of Our Great Mother, Her Majesty the Queen, will do prompt Justice to her Indian children.

Praying that the Ottawa Government will grant us our Petition, or do in the matter what to you and your Honourable Council of the North West may seem meet; –

Your Petitioners Remain, Your Excellency's Humble Servants.[5]

The Blackfoot were thus setting out their own agenda for negotiating with the government. Clearly, it was their intention that any agreement with the Crown would only be acceptable if the conditions outlined were met. In 1876, while Morris was negotiating with the Cree, the Blackfoot attempted to send a delegation to discuss the details of their petition with him but they were unable to reach the Saskatchewan territory. Instead, McDougall and Scollen took their message to the commissioners and returned with the news that the commissioners intended to meet with the Blackfoot the next summer to talk about a treaty. There were mixed feelings among the Blackfoot. Some were pleased with this news, while others, especially those who had signed American treaties and had seen them go unfulfilled, were not optimistic about the wisdom of signing a treaty. The Blackfoot's 1875 petition had been the approach that all had favoured for the time being; it was considered a "condition precedent" for the signing of any treaty.

The arrival of the Lakota on Canadian soil in 1876 gave the government a major reason to get a treaty signed with the Blackfoot as soon as possible. Sitting Bull had already asked the Blackfoot to join a campaign against Canadian and American forces, but this had been refused. Crowfoot and Sitting Bull met face-to-face in 1877. After exchanging tobacco and smoking the pipe, they made the agreement to live peacefully with one another without disturbing the Canadian authorities. A friendship dance followed and then both Crowfoot and Sitting Bull returned to their respective camps.

Another factor pressuring the government to proceed quickly with the treaty was the threat of an international incident should the Nez Percé, who were fighting the US Army, reach Canada and request refugee status.

The fear that these tribes might unite at some future time spurred the Canadian government to get a treaty signed while the Blackfoot and the government were still on good terms. The Blackfoot, meanwhile, were waiting for the government's response to their petition of 1875. Dempsey's narrative mentions all of these facts, but he leaves the impression that what happened at Blackfoot Crossing was inevitable – that Crowfoot was driven to sign because of his bleak view at the future, which he expressed numerous times, and that both sides did what was reasonable in the circumstances to get the treaty signed.

Dempsey's account diverges from that of the Blackfoot elders on the issue of what motivated the actions of the government negotiators, especially with regard to the question of land surrender. Although the facts that Dempsey presents lead one to conclude that the government suppressed any discussion of the land surrender just to get the Blackfoot to sign the treaty, he does not come to this conclusion himself. Dempsey does not fully explore the fact that there is no evidence that land surrender was discussed or that the treaty was ever read in its entirety to the Treaty 7 leaders. Speeches made by all of the government authorities reassured the Aboriginal leaders that they had nothing to be apprehensive about, that "they would be taken care of." When Laird made the suggestion that hunting rights might be curtailed in the future, he was immediately shouted down by the Treaty 7 leadership, this on the first day of negotiations. It must then have been clear to Laird, Macleod, McDougall, and Scollen that the leaders had no intention of giving an inch on issues relating to what they could do on their lands and that any discussions along these lines might lead to a breakdown in the treaty negotiations. All they could do was emphasize the bounty that the Queen offered in return for the First Nations' agreement to peace. It is remarkable that all the speeches made by the officials representing the government focused on what the government was promising the Aboriginal peoples rather than on what the First Nations would be giving up.

In light of the fact that the Treaty 7 elders so adamantly disagreed with the notion that the treaty was essentially a land surrender, they must have had other ideas about what happened at Blackfoot Crossing. Is it possible that the Blackfoot, for example, thought that the government was essentially agreeing to the points made in their petition of 1875? The Aboriginal leadership seemed satisfied after the treaty was signed that they could continue to use the land as they always had and that newcomers would be free to "use" some of the land.

At the end of his chapter on the treaty signed at Blackfoot Crossing, Dempsey remains vague about what was agreed to. In citing Scollen's letter of 1879, in which Scollen had said the "Indian" did not understand the treaty, Dempsey comments: "The interpreters were incapable of explaining the terms of the treaty and could not deal with such matters as land tenure surrenders and reserves."[6] With this, he indicates that such major issues were in fact not understood. But Dempsey then seems to let the government officials off the hook when he asks: "At the same time, how could any interpreter explain to a nomadic Indian that 128 acres of prairie would be his?"[7]

Dempsey skirts around the issue of whether the treaty was understood by the Treaty 7 leadership as a peace treaty, stating that Crowfoot might have had an understanding of the treaty that was different from that of the other leaders at Blackfoot Crossing: "Only Crowfoot understood the treaty in his own way. To him, it was simply a pact of faith between the Indian and the white man."[8] Then Dempsey concludes on a note of inevitability about the whole treaty process: "The buffalo were disappearing and the settlers were coming in; nothing could stop them. But the Mounted Police had proven to be honourable representatives of the Queen and now the treaty would give the Blackfoot all the protection and help they would need for years to come."[9] It is difficult to reconcile the optimistic tone of this summation with the letter Scollen wrote just two years after the treaty was signed, in which he expressed great disappointment with the non-fulfilment of the treaty promises.

Crowfoot is of particular value in our attempt to understand Treaty 7, as it provides the most reliable description of the role that Crowfoot played in the negotiations. Crowfoot was a key negotiator, though his role may have been misrepresented by government officials who knew him. Other chiefs at Blackfoot Crossing were as powerful as Crowfoot, even more powerful, but by being chosen as the person to speak for the Blackfoot, Crowfoot appeared to some to be the main leader, a role, as Dempsey indicates, that Crowfoot did little to dispel.

In his analysis of Treaty 7, Dempsey does little to delve into the "spirit and intent" of the treaty as the Blackfoot have understood it. He might have given more attention to the fact that most of the evidence shows that the treaty was sold to the Treaty

7 leadership as a peace treaty, not as a land surrender, and to the possibility that the Aboriginal leadership was deliberately misled by the treaty commissioners.

RED CROW

In *Red Crow: Warrior Chief*, Dempsey provides more evidence than he did in *Crowfoot* (written eight years earlier) that what was signed at Treaty 7 was not understood in the same way by each side. Dempsey shows that Red Crow of the Bloods had his own agenda, different from both Crowfoot's and that of the Canadian authorities. At no time did Red Crow want to "give up the land for nothing."[10] It is clear, as Dempsey outlines the details of the problems faced by the Bloods, that the Bloods were not especially anxious to sign a treaty, certainly not as anxious as McDougall and Scollen claimed. What they wanted was to have intrusions into their territory halted and to have the buffalo protected.

As in *Crowfoot*, however, Dempsey is unwilling to attribute any blame for the failure of the two sides to understand the treaty in the same way. Dempsey sees no deliberate manipulation of the situation either by the missionaries or the treaty commissioners. He suggests that, in the final analysis, it was all just a big misunderstanding, but he does little to examine what motivations might have produced the misunderstanding – nor is he concerned about where the onus rested to make the contents of the treaty clear. However, Dempsey does agree that the Bloods did not believe that they were signing a land surrender.

Dempsey begins his section on Red Crow and the treaties by indicating that the Bloods had no knowledge of the treaty process until 1875 and that John McDougall likely did not inform the Bloods of the arrival of the NWMP in 1874, but rather gave that information only to the Stoneys: "It is likely that he contacted only his own docile Stoneys and the neighbouring Blackfoot who were camped on the Bow River."[11] Dempsey suggests that the Bloods remained suspicious of the intentions of the Mounties, since they wanted to keep any intruders out of their territory. The Peigan were the first to meet with Macleod after the Mounties arrived. Bull Head, their chief, gave Macleod permission to establish his post for one winter and also gave the police permission to cut wood for their own use for the winter. By November 1874 the Bloods had also met Macleod and were assured by him that the police were not there to take their land but only to remove whiskey traders from the territory. Macleod gained the respect of the Treaty 7 Aboriginal leadership, but the tone he used to describe this accomplishment suggests that he was bemused by having achieved it so easily:

Upon being introduced, they all shake hands and invariably express their delight at meeting me. They then sit down and my interpreter lights and hands the chief a pipe, which he smokes for a few seconds, and then passes to the others, and all remain silent to hear what I have to say.

I then explain to them what the Government has sent this force into the country for, and endeavour to give them a general idea of the laws that will be enforced, telling them that not only the white men, but Indians will be punished for breaking them, and impressing upon them that they need not fear being punished for doing what they do not know is wrong.

I then tell them also that we have not come to take their land from them (an intimation they all receive with a great pleasure), but that when the Government wants to speak to them about this matter, their great men will be sent to speak to them and that they will know the intention of the Government before anything is done.

The chief then stands up and shakes hands with every one and makes a speech, expresses his great delight at our arrival, tells us how they were being robbed and ruined by the whiskey traders; that their horses robes, and women were taken from them; that their young men were continually engaged in drunken riots, and numbers of them shot; that their horses were gradually decreasing in numbers, and that before long they would not have enough to chase the buffalo, and would have no means of procuring food – that all this was now changed, and as one old chief expressed, suiting the action to his words, "Before you came the Indian crept along, now he is not afraid to walk erect."[12]

Many other chiefs also gave speeches expressing their appreciation for the job the police had done in bringing peace to the territory.

Red Crow, though he also appreciated the presence of the police, was concerned about them because they had made it possible for the Métis and the Cree to come into Blood territory without fear of being attacked and driven off. The Métis, in particular, had established settlements in Blackfoot territory after the NWMP arrived. It was this fact that most alarmed the Blackfoot and it was this issue that was central to their petition to the government in 1875. In this petition, written by Jean L'Heureux, the Blackfoot reminded the government that "the white man will not take the Indian lands without a Council of Her Majesty's Indian Commissioner and the respective Indian Chiefs."[13]

Written in the summer of 1875, the petition did not reach the commissioners until 1876 and at that time the government agreed to meet with the Blackfoot the next summer. Many of the Blackfoot were stronger now that the whiskey traders had gone but they were still concerned about the buffalo. The leaders met with Macleod in 1874, threatening to attack the Métis and Cree if they were not kept out of their territory. Macleod said there was nothing he could do, that he had been promised that regulations were to be put in place to protect the buffalo but that this had not yet been done. Macleod described the frustration of the Bloods:

Before our arrival here, the acknowledged hunting grounds of the Blackfoot extended from Red Deer River south by Cypress Hills to the boundary line and went to the Rocky Mountains. He was at war with the Crees, Half-breeds, Sioux and Assiniboine and others who were continually endeavouring to press in upon his country. Now that we have come into his country, he finds that from all sides his old enemies, who he dare not attack, are under our protection pressing in upon him. A great number, notably the half-breeds whom he considers his worst enemies, are armed with the breech-loader which they procure at Fort Garry, and he has to compete with those who are armed with a better rifle than his.[14]

The Blackfoot were gravely concerned; they did not want to give up their land by signing treaties like those that had been signed in the United States. The supplies promised in those treaties had at first been plentiful, then had gradually dwindled until they were discontinued entirely. In the end the American treaties were almost worthless. The Blackfoot complained to Macleod, who told them that all he could do was write to Ottawa and keep them informed. He advised the Blackfoot not to take matters into their own hands. Dempsey concludes that unlike the Cree, who wanted to get whatever they could in order to start farming, the Blackfoot wanted people off their land: "When all the factors were taken into consideration, the Blackfoot were not anxious for a treaty."[15]

The Bloods were especially reluctant to be involved with any treaty process. Red Crow appreciated the NWMP but was less enthusiastic when he heard that the treaty commissioners were coming. He was neither as friendly with the Whites nor as concerned about the future as Crowfoot was. He was especially disappointed when the treaty site was moved to Blackfoot Crossing from his preferred site of Fort Macleod. Red Crow, with a large contingent of Bloods, was slow to join the other tribes at Blackfoot Crossing, arriving four days after the date the negotiations were to have begun.

The Blood position as articulated by Medicine Calf was threefold: to secure the Blood ancestral grounds, to receive compensation for territories already lost to White settlement, and to be wary of promises that might trick the Bloods into "giving up their land for nothing." Medicine Calf wanted the Mounties to pay for the wood they had used since their arrival in 1874. Laird discussed his requests and told him that instead the tribes should be paying the government for the protection the police were giving them. When the Blackfoot broke into laughter, Laird thought they were laughing at Medicine Calf but more likely they were laughing at his own suggestion.

Dempsey describes Red Crow as "proud and independent" but compares him unfavourably with Crowfoot, who Dempsey claims was far-sighted in realizing "that his people would soon need the protection and help of the Queen if they were to survive after the buffalo were gone."[16] Dempsey suggests that Red Crow and his people did not have the foresight to envision a life beyond the treaties: "It was simply beyond their comprehension."[17] If Red Crow did not understand the talk about reserves and land surrenders, however, it might have been because they had never been properly explained to him. In 1876 Laird, Macleod, Scollen, and McDougall had been especially concerned about an alliance between the Blackfoot and Sitting Bull's Lakota, and it is unlikely that after Red Crow spoke about not giving up land for nothing, they would explain exactly what was going on.

Macleod concluded his words at Blackfoot Crossing by alluding to the respect he had gained among the tribes over the years. He continued to ride this wave of respect and took full advantage of his popularity: "You say that I have always kept my promises. As surely as my past promises have been kept, so surely shall those made up by the Commissioners be carried out in the future. If they were broken, I would be ashamed to meet you or look you in the face; but every promise will be solemnly fulfilled as certainly as the sun now shines down upon us from the heavens."[18]

It remains uncertain, however, whether at Blackfoot Crossing Macleod did his best to explain what the reserve system meant and what land would be set aside for each First Nation. Each leader was asked which territories were theirs and each chief described large tracts of land. Nothing was said to them when they explained what the boundaries of their territories were. Obviously they did not think there would be restrictions on their movements over the land they described. What the Blackfoot, Stoneys, and Tsuu T'ina really wanted was land over which they would be free to hunt. It seems clear that the objectives of the two sides never meshed.

In *Red Crow*, Dempsey departs from his position in *Crowfoot* in that he is more willing to say that the government came to Blackfoot Crossing with a written treaty that it did not intend to alter and that the commissioners made promises they knew they could not keep. Dempsey falls short of calling the government's negotiating tactics "bad faith" but he almost suggests as much:

The treaty was signed, not after serious negotiations, nor with any spirit of compromise. Governor Laird had come to the session with the treaty in his pocket. The Indians, too, had come with their demands in readiness. When they parted company, the commissioners had a document which said the Blackfoot had surrendered their lands. The chiefs, on the other hand, believed they had been promised protection for the buffalo herds and treaty money for allowing the white man to come into their ancestral grounds. Yet neither side really understood what they had given away. To Laird, buffalo preservation and firewood compensation were minor considerations, not to be taken seriously. To the chiefs, the selling of land and the allotment of reserves was beyond their comprehension.[19]

The final sentence remains somewhat contentious. If the government and its commissioners came to Blackfoot Crossing to bargain in bad faith, making promises they could not and/or would not keep, then it seems strange to suggest the treaty was beyond the comprehension of the Treaty 7 First Nations. The Aboriginal leadership were sophisticated enough to understand many difficult issues, but could they be expected to understand issues and a treaty that were never fully explained to them? It appears that it was not so much that they did not understand the treaty but that the clauses and consequences of the treaty were intentionally left vague and unexplained. In the final analysis, the government, as Dempsey points out, never intended to protect the buffalo or to keep invaders out. Even Scollen concluded that Laird had never intended to honour the treaty and had refused to send supplies he had promised. Only a year after the treaty was signed, Red Crow lost respect for Macleod when he saw that Macleod had no intention of living up to the promises he had made. Dempsey, in *Red Crow* as in *Crowfoot*, ends his section on the treaty by saying that for the First Nations the signing of the treaty had been a "simple act of faith."[20]

In conclusion, it seems clear that if Red Crow acted in good faith, then the government commissioners did not. Furthermore, the general perception of Commissioner Macleod's role is in need of revision. It ought to be emphasized not only how quickly he gained the trust of the Aboriginal people for clearing the land of whiskey traders, but also how quickly he lost that trust when he failed to live up to the promises he had so piously and perhaps cynically made at Blackfoot Crossing. In history books, too much pride is taken in listing the promises that were kept; in the interests of fairness and accuracy, the promises that were not kept should also be listed.

"TREATY RESEARCH REPORT: TREATY SEVEN"

In 1987 Dempsey produced a research report on Treaty 7 for the Department of Indian Affairs and Northern Development. Titled "Treaty Research Report: Treaty Seven," this article-length analysis summarizes and amalgamates the material contained in *Crowfoot* and *Red Crow*. Here, as in his books, Dempsey generally attributes honourable motives to Laird, Macleod, Scollen, and McDougall. As for the First Nations' side, he suggests that the tribes were unable or "incapable" of understanding the treaty. Consistent with his other writing, Dempsey attributes the "success" of Treaty 7 to the presence and reputation of Colonel Macleod.

After summarizing events leading up to the "negotiations" of Treaty 7, Dempsey begins to explicate the government position on the treaty. In this report, unlike in his books, Dempsey does not explain that Sitting Bull's presence and the threat from the Nez Percé were factors in the treaty negotiations, even though the ever-growing number of Lakota arriving in Canada in 1876 were clearly seen as a major threat to Canada's security. Laird and Macleod knew that any alliance between the powerful First Nations could seriously undermine the newcomer settlements in the Northwest. Dempsey admits that many chiefs were reluctant to sign the treaty and leaves the issue without further comment. However, it is important to note that the Canadian authorities wanted to introduce rules that would help to control Aboriginal populations. Obviously, the government side, anxious for a treaty, would not introduce divisive issues into the negotiations and may have been content to win the agreement of the Aboriginal leadership at any cost.

It is clear that the Canadian government moved to sign treaties in the nineteenth century only in those areas that were important for development. As in the United States, treaties were seen as a means to an end. It seems that the government's intentions were to move into the Northwest and establish its presence as soon as possible in order to allow for access to the rich pasture lands described by missionaries and scientists, as well as to mineral resources, particularly the coal that Laird had described as being as good as the coal in Pictou County.

Although he acknowledges that the Treaty 7 leaders misunderstood the treaty, Dempsey does not explore the reasons why this was so. It is possible, for example, as mentioned earlier, that the government simply did not raise the issue of "surrender, release, cede or yield up" because it knew that this would be unacceptable to the First Nations of southern Alberta. The elders from the five First Nations that signed the treaty did not think that they had signed a land surrender, and there is no evidence

that the treaty was ever read out in its entirety to those assembled. When Dempsey says that Laird explained the key features of the treaty, he is assuming that this is in fact what happened. Laird took considerable flak when he suggested that there
could be restrictions placed on the hunting rights of First Nations
people – so much flak that he had to back down from this issue.
Is it not possible that he refrained from describing what the reserve system would be like because this might have irretrievably
alienated the Aboriginal leadership? Dempsey's claim, therefore,
that the First Nations were incapable of understanding the issues
of the treaty discussions misses the point; in fact, it might be
nearer the point to say that the main issues were never properly
explained and that the consequences of the reserve system were
left vague.

It is clear, furthermore, that the Treaty 7 leadership thought
that the treaty would include issues related to the Blackfoot petition of 1875 that had been discussed in the negotiations. A
number of these issues were not mentioned in the treaty. Again,
this suggests that the words of the treaty commissioners should
not simply be taken at face value. What seemed more important
to Laird than including the wishes of the Aboriginal leadership
in the treaty was saving money for the Canadian government.
It is evident that both Laird and Macleod made promises about
protecting the buffalo that they had no intention of honouring.
Another issue of central concern for the Blackfoot was keeping
the Cree and Métis out of their land, which Macleod and Laird
simply stated could not be done.

The government officials clearly let it be assumed that after
the treaty was made there was to be no disruption of the life
that the First Nations had lived up to that time. And, in fact,
at first their way of life did not seem to have changed in any
significant way; they continued to hunt and subsist as they had
always done. The reason that the First Nations might not have
said more on the issue of land reserves is that they understood
they would be free to hunt as they always had – and therefore
to live as they always had. The commissioners did nothing to
dissuade them from this belief. The First Nations had been promised so much – annuities, education, "to be taken care of" – surely
they had no reason to believe their freedom would be restricted.
Dempsey's failure to explore the government's reasons for not

explaining the treaty fully makes this section the weakest part of his report.

Dempsey's section on the Indian perspective is stronger. Here he is on firmer ground as he examines the First Nations' reasons for signing the treaty. Dempsey admits that the nations at Blackfoot Crossing probably did not understand key sections of the treaty. In the section on land tenure, he states that the tribes "had no recognition of land tenure for the individual and it is questionable whether such ownership was recognized on a tribal basis ... rather than ownership, the Indians considered themselves as having the rights to occupancy."[21] The Blackfoot had always controlled their lands, and those who wished to pass through their territory had to seek permission and even had to pay for using the land. It has become more evident that it was this kind of use that the First Nations at Blackfoot Crossing thought they were agreeing to when they accepted the treaty. The Treaty 7 elders clearly stated that they were willing to allow use of the land; they had not agreed to surrender it. Dempsey appears to acknowledge this when, with regard to the American treaties, he writes: "They were simply allowing the Americans to occupy a portion of their land, just as they had when they had permitted traders to become established."[22]

Dempsey explains that Medicine Calf, for example, demonstrated his belief that the police were simply being allowed to "use" the land, but that they should pay the Blackfoot for this privilege and for the wood they used. The Blackfoot did not believe that the NWMP had any legitimate right to be at Fort Macleod without Blackfoot permission. It was the right of the Blackfoot to lease out the land to the NWMP, not the other way around. Dempsey explains this:

Nowhere is there a clear statement that the Blackfoot were knowingly prepared to give away their entire hunting grounds and there is nothing in their prior experience which would make such an action comprehensible to them ... Accordingly, when the announcement was made in 1877 that the Queen's government wished to meet with them to make a treaty, the news caused neither surprise nor concern. It was likely perceived as a gathering, whereby friendship with the Mounties would be affirmed, promises made to live in peace and if they were lucky, that action would be taken to curb incursions of the white traders and enemy hunters.[23]

The elders of Treaty 7 would have concurred almost to the word with Dempsey's assessment. To them, Treaty 7 was a peace treaty. They did not mind "sharing" the land with the newcomers, they did not mind the Mounties and the missionaries, and they did not mind all the promises of the Queen's bounty that they were to get in return. There had been no thought, or perhaps even discussion, of land surrender. As Dempsey suggests, it is unlikely that the treaty was a particularly big issue for the First Nations; this might be illustrated by the fact that the keeper of the tribal calender for the Bloods, Father of Many Children, chose to refer to 1877 as the year "when we had a bad spring," not as the year the treaty was made.[24]

Dempsey also indicates that the First Nations might have found the many promises made to them a compelling reason to sign the treaty. Another attractive incentive could have been the many items brought to Blackfoot Crossing by the regional merchants who were waiting to market their wares to the tribes once they were enriched with treaty money. Monetary incentives were certainly a tactic used throughout the British Empire to persuade people to sign treaties.

Dempsey raises the issue of the inadequate job done by the interpreters at Blackfoot Crossing, an issue that was raised by elders from all of the five First Nations. There is no doubt that the interpretation was poor, and it should be remembered that this might have been to the advantage of the government officials.

In summarizing Dempsey's report, it should be reiterated that its strength is its discussion of issues relating to the Aboriginal perspectives of the treaty. Many of Dempsey's conclusions are similar to or the same as those of the elders of the five First Nations. His analysis of the government perspective is less successful, as he does not fully examine what was potentially at issue for the government.

It is also evident that Dempsey is stronger in speaking about the Blackfoot tribes than about the Stoneys or the Tsuu T'ina. The elders of all the nations highlighted the significance of a "peace treaty" and spoke eloquently on this issue. Dempsey, however, underestimates the importance of peace to the five nations, especially to the Stoneys, and the significance of ending not only the violence associated with the whiskey trade but also the tribal wars that had traditionally occupied them, particularly the Stoneys' ongoing conflicts with the Cree.

As he did in his books on Crowfoot and Red Crow, in this research report Dempsey overestimates the importance of Macleod's reputation in the Blackfoot's decision to sign the treaty. Aboriginal leaders signed the treaty because of what they thought was in it – promises of peace, money, education, cattle, agricultural assistance, hunting and fishing rights, protection of the buffalo – not because they trusted Macleod. There is no doubt that the role of the Mounties and Macleod in freeing the country of whiskey traders was appreciated, but Dempsey's emphasis on Macleod ignores the goals that Aboriginal leaders clearly had in mind when they agreed to allow newcomers to share the land. That they could continue to hunt freely and would be taken care of by the Queen were considered the big promises; the Treaty 7 elders more frequently mentioned these as the reasons they had signed the treaty than they did the role of Macleod.

The motivation of the Aboriginal leadership and their understanding of what they were signing must be given a more prominent place on the stage if we are to fully understand why they agreed to sign Treaty 7. Stoneys such as Bearspaw were not simply and uncritically under the influence of McDougall; leaders such as Red Crow were not in submissive awe of Macleod, even though they appreciated the friendship of the Mounties, at least in the early years. Their own understanding of the treaty may have been different from the government's, but details aside, to them their birthright to the land on which they had lived for hundreds of years lay at the heart of the "spirit and intent" of Treaty 7.

Dempsey further writes in his summary that "the tribes had little comprehension of what they were signing but they did so because of their trust in the Mounted Police as representatives of the Queen."[25] It might be more accurate to say that they had their own understanding of the treaty as expressed by their elders. They thought that their grievances and interests would be discussed and then addressed in the treaty. Macleod lost his favoured position with Red Crow the year immediately following the treaty when Red Crow saw that he had no intention of honouring the treaty.

Immediately after negotiating the treaty, Laird left Blackfoot Crossing to examine a nearby coal seam. He had been impressed with the coal he had seen at Fort Macleod, and that he should so quickly take this action shows where his interests lay. Laird was primarily concerned with the potential riches that the territory offered White settlers. Like many of their generation, Laird and Macleod believed that Aboriginal people were not fully developing the potential of the land and that it was Euro-Canadians who should assume this task. It was this vision of Empire that gave Canadian officials the confidence and inspiration to negotiate with the First Nations. Dempsey does not consider the context of colonialism as it relates to Treaty 7 but instead portrays what happened at Blackfoot Crossing as an inevitable fact of history. The colonial context is evident, however, in the fact that the promises made at Blackfoot Crossing were not kept and that representatives of the Canadian government did not work to fulfil their commitments to the Aboriginal peoples in good faith. Once the government authorities had their treaty in hand, they turned their full attention to making the Northwest attractive to the kind of settlers that they wanted to take over the land.

CHAPTER TEN

A Study of the Siksika by
Lucien and Jane Hanks

A valuable study of the Siksika is *Tribe under Trust*, written by
Lucien and Jane Hanks. This work is of particular significance
because it is based on interviews conducted in the 1930s and
1940s with many Siksika elders. Many of these interviews are
in the Glenbow-Alberta Archives. There is not a great deal of
information specifically on Treaty 7, as it was not the focus of
the study, but some material does touch on issues relating to
Treaty 7.

The Hankses suggest that Treaty 7 was considered a dangerous
treaty to negotiate because the Blackfoot tribes would frequently
attack White travellers who attempted to pass through their territory. Even as late as 1870 members of the Blackfoot Confederacy planned to attack Fort Edmonton. This aggressive behaviour made it clear that the negotiations that commissioners Laird
and Macleod were to undertake would be both difficult and dangerous. Even though the talks would be precarious, they were
considered necessary because of pressure from settlers who were
anxious to move into the territory. The Hankses suggest that
there were four reasons for the success of the treaty negotiations:
"(1) the character of Chief Crowfoot; (2) his appreciation of white
strength and his tendency to accede to white demands; (3) the
conception of the treaty on the part of the Indians; (4) the pressures of the moment of signing."[1]

The Hankses emphasize that the relationship between Crowfoot and Father Lacombe was an important factor in the signing
of Treaty 7. Lacombe has been recognized as having been a friend
of the Siksika. He had been given the name "Kind Hearted Per-

son" after he had selflessly taken care of Siksika who had been wounded following an attack by the Cree in 1865. The Siksika believed him to be a powerful man, no doubt partly because they thought that he had demonstrated the power to withstand bullets during the Cree attack. Consequently, Lacombe was highly respected by the Siksika and treated as a man of great spiritual power. He had displayed both kindness and generosity towards the Siksika, two qualities that they valued and looked for in their own leaders. Crowfoot himself is said to have "attempted to carry into practice certain Christian like ideals"[2] because of his respect for Lacombe. He would ask members of his tribe to return "stolen" horses, and this was seen by the Hankses as the main evidence of Lacombe's influence on the Siksika chief: "Horses captured from this tribe [the Cree] were ordered by Crowfoot to be returned, even though this assumption of authority defied all Blackfoot precedents. It was only when Crowfoot attempted to enforce this practice with those of equal status that his orders were sometimes ignored."[3]

The authors emphasize that there were many pressures on the tribes of Treaty 7 to come to an agreement with the treaty commissioners. The coming railway, the whiskey trade, prospective settlers, and the disappearance of the buffalo were all significant factors. The Aboriginal leadership, Crowfoot especially, were believed to have been told by missionaries and the NWMP that in any military confrontation between Whites and Aboriginals "the red man had little chance of survival."[4] It was also clear that the White man had better guns, such as repeating rifles, while most Natives had only powder and ball muskets. But most importantly for Crowfoot was the fact that Lacombe was seen as above reproach – as was Macleod, who was respected for ridding the territory of the whiskey trade.

Crowfoot had always favoured Whites, according to Lucien and Jane Hanks, but the Whites also favoured Crowfoot:

They [the Whites] thought every group of people had a titular political head, a social structure with some ultimate, responsible person to lead and coerce. They did not percieve that Blackfoot leadership consisted, not of one head-chief, but of a fluctuating number of chiefs of small autonomous bands. They demanded someone who could speak for the entire tribe. The Blackfoot accorded Crowfoot the role of negotiator without complaint. A man of Crowfoot's experience in dealing with whites was, naturally, given the job automatically. So Crowfoot became a crucial figure for the first treaty, but the Blackfoot never considered him a leader authorized to make decisions on their behalf and responsible for tribal conduct.[5]

The Hankses maintain that "the significance of the terms of the treaty was probably never very clear to the Indians. Governor Laird's 'presentation address' emphasized the wishes of the 'Good Queen Mother' for peace among her children and dwelt on the benefits of rations and the yearly annuity."[6] The tribes present at Blackfoot Crossing were told that they would be free to hunt buffalo on the lands ceded, and as this was to their liking, they were put at ease with the treaty generally. But the authors emphasize that it is unlikely that the treaty was properly understood. They doubt that even a skilled translator such as L'Heureux would have been able to fully explain the treaty to the Blackfoot tribes: "In the first place, disposal of land was completely foreign to the Blackfoot. Though horses and tipis could be sold, land was not property in the same sense. Moreover, Governor Laird was greeted by the chiefs with flowery speeches of welcome which, as printed in eastern newspapers, do not sound like the terse forthrightness of most Blackfoot speeches. The known doubts that were in the minds of many, as told sixty years later by their sons and grandsons, fully bespeak a lack of understanding of what 'ceding' meant."[7]

From the Blackfoot perspective the treaty meant four things: that they would give up warfare against the Cree and other traditional enemies; that they would be allowed to continue to hunt; that each member would be given a small annual payment as well as cattle and farming tools; and that each chief would get a medal, money, a uniform, and a Winchester rifle.

Lucien and Jane Hanks, however, note that the Siksika did not know that they were being asked to surrender "rights, titles and privileges" to their lands: "It was beyond their remotest dream that they should give up the Indian life ... They expected rather that life would continue in much the same way with the added benefits of sums of money coming to them every year. During the summer they would continue to range with the buffalo over vast areas, and in the winter they could return to this friendly spot for money to buy goods from the traders."[8]

The authors argue that many of the chiefs at Blackfoot Crossing were influenced by "immediate considerations rather than remoter consequences of signing treaty."[9] They suggest that the pressures of negotiations weighed heavily on Crowfoot: "Crowfoot seemed to sense that signing it [the treaty] meant subjugation to the whites and an end to the wars that had made the Blackfoot respected on the plains."[10] While most of his followers thought that they would be able to go on living as they always had, Crowfoot, because of his contact with agents of the newcomer society, was only too well aware of possible consequences of the treaty. Nevertheless, misunderstandings, confusion, and the momentum of the ceremony itself led to a smoother and quicker conclusion than most had predicted. Opposition to the treaty (as it was understood) was not strong: "Possibly, had there been tangible support from his friends to resist the whites, he [Crowfoot] might have refused the treaty. Button Chief [Medicine Calf] of the Bloods seemed to be the only one who asked for more money ... The Stoneys were all willing. The agonized Crowfoot was left alone in his tipi to make the decision."[11]

Lucien and Jane Hanks say that an important gesture that Crowfoot made in his acceptance speech was left unrecorded. Crowfoot is said to have plucked a feather from his eagle-wing fan and given it to Commissioner Laird with the words: "Keep us like this feather forever, keep us like a pampered child."[12] Crowfoot expected to be treated kindly by the Whites, perhaps to be pitied by them, and certainly "to be taken care of." The Hankses say that the swift success of the negotiations came as a surprise to the Whites, that in the eyes of the Canadian officials Laird and Macleod "had won an easy victory."[13] The authors do not believe that most tribes understood what was in store for them. As for the newcomers, a huge new territory had been opened up: "The Whites were very well satisfied with their accomplishment; they had subdued the most war-like tribe of the northern plains. They were oblivious of the internal complications that were shortly to arise because of the selection of the chiefs."[14]

Lucien and Jane Hanks's work is important in that it reiterates what others like Father Scollen had said at the time of the signing of the treaty – that the treaty was not really understood to have been a land surrender by the Blackfoot tribes. The version of the treaty signing described by these authors also supports the argument that the treaty commissioners, intimidated by the Blackfoot tribes' reputation as powerful warriors, may have deliberately misled the Treaty 7 tribes by not mentioning a "land surrender." The Hankses say that peace, rather than surrender, was the issue emphasized by Laird. Their version of the role played by Crowfoot adds a new dimension to our understanding of the quandary that Crowfoot found himself in at the Blackfoot Crossing negotiations. The Hankses suggest that he was not betraying his own people as some have thought, but rather that he might have found it difficult to explain to the other leaders just how the newcomers would change the landscape when they arrived. Few understood what Lacombe and others meant when they said that the land would be "flooded with new settlers." Few would know that the consequences of this colonization would mean restricted hunting, especially since assurances of unrestricted hunting had persuaded many of the chiefs to sign Treaty 7.

The weakness of the Hankses' study is that in using primarily Siksika informants, they have not been able to explain the treaty process from the point of view of the other four nations that signed Treaty 7.

CHAPTER ELEVEN

Academic Arguments and Discussions on the Treaties Generally and Treaty 7 Specifically

INTRODUCTION

The numbered treaties were one component of Canada's federal strategy for the Northwest. They have been presented by some historians as one stage in the necessary preparation of the prairies for settlement. Historians generally attribute the peaceful history of the Canadian prairies, in comparison to the situation in the United States, to the work of the North-West Mounted Police and to government policies that were implemented after real negotiations and not at the point of a gun. Canada is viewed as having had a just and honourable Indian policy, and the treaties are claimed to be evidence of this. Donald Creighton sees the treaties as part of the orderly process of the movement westward that was planned and directed by the Canadian government. In Canada, the power of the state preceded western settlement, unlike in the United States, where the law followed settlement. Long before settlement in the Canadian West, the police, surveyors, government officials, and treaties paved the way, so that newcomers would be protected and controlled.

An older and more traditional point of view emphasizes that the Aboriginal peoples were passive victims of a brutal exploitation and that they had little or no understanding of what the treaties signified. There are different shades of opinion within this point of view, the most prominent found in George F.G. Stanley's *The Birth of Western Canada: A History of the Riel Rebellions.* Stanley says that the treaties were not "sacred covenants" but rather tragic misunderstandings. He argues that they were not negotiated in the proper sense and that Aboriginal peoples never understood what was happening; they were like children compared to the powerful Europeans. Stanley's work, published in the 1930s, set the stage for subsequent interpretations.

Some writers see the treaties as an empty form imposed by the conqueror on the conquered. Like Stanley, they stress that the treaties were not negotiated in the proper sense, that the Aboriginal peoples were not treated as equal bargaining partners, that they were illiterate and had had to rely on biased interpreters and on the often questionable advice of missionaries. It is argued that these arrangements were forced upon the Aboriginal peoples. They could only refuse or accept the treaties, and no accommodation was made for their demands.

Those who argue this point of view say that the Aboriginal peoples were given no advance notice of the so-called negotiations, that the nature and purpose of the talks were not adequately explained, and that the tribes could not possibly have had any legal understanding of what they were agreeing to. Furthermore, Aboriginal peoples had no concept of private property. Their notion of property encompassed common property whose resources were used by everyone. Since they did not understand actual ownership of property or the trade of real estate, they could not have understood the treaties.

This is more or less the argument Howard Adams presents in *Prison of Grass* (1975). He stresses that the treaties served the purpose of colonization. They legitimized the imprisonment (on reserves) of Aboriginal peoples by White people who were supported by police and soldiers. In return, the First Nations peoples received almost nothing. True negotiations were not possible, as power was unequally distributed: officials from Ottawa bargained in their own language with the backing of state power, with the support of Parliament, and with legal mechanisms familiar to them, while the Aboriginal peoples were divided among themselves and economically dependent or broken. Adams writes: "To most Indians who were forced to attend these spectacles it was an agonizing experience of final surrender to the colonizer."[1] They could not disagree with forms that were dictated to them, and the treaties appeared to give legal sanction to Aboriginal subjugation. The real reason for the treaties was to acquire Aboriginal land. In conclusion, Adams suggests that the treaties are worthless.

Harold Cardinal, on the other hand, argues in his book *The Unjust Society* that "to the Indians of Canada, the treaties represent an Indian Magna Carta. The treaties are important to us, because we entered into these negotiations with faith, with hope for a better life with honour ... The Indians entered into the treaty negotiations as honourable men who came to deal as equals with the Queen's representatives. Our leaders at that time thought they were dealing with an equally honourable people. Our leaders pledged themselves, their people and their heirs to honour what was done then."[2] Cardinal states that Aboriginal leaders were not beggars with nothing to offer in return for the rights they expected – they had their land. To the Aboriginal peoples, the treaties marked the beginning of a contractual relationship whereby the Queen and the federal government committed themselves to lasting responsibilities for the Aboriginal peoples in return for the land. Cardinal stresses that the treaty documents recognize first and foremost that the First Nations had aboriginal rights; otherwise there would have been nothing to negotiate. Cardinal says that for the Aboriginal peoples the treaties are a sacred, honourable agreement between themselves and the Canadian government that cannot be abrogated at the whim of its leaders.

Another position on the treaties presented by academics is that Aboriginal peoples understood only too well what was happening to them – they were not weak tools or passive victims, but made the best of a difficult situation and negotiated the best deal they could for their land, notwithstanding the clear imbalance of power. Jean Friesen writes that in the negotiations for treaties 1–6 the Aboriginal leaders displayed an awareness of their situation. They had an important role in shaping the treaties and were able to obtain more than they were originally offered. In fact, they were responsible for introducing most of the important treaty items that allowed for the development of alternative economies. Friesen stresses that Aboriginal leaders were aware that this was a land sale on an enormous scale: "They may not have been able to influence the commissioners as extensively as they desired; but within the political and diplomatic framework they were presented with, they maneuvered, stalled, cheated, compared offers, and with some success played upon the commissioners' desire to win their friendship and peaceful acceptance of white intrusion into their lands."[3]

Friesen's argument emphasizes that the Aboriginal peoples in the Northwest in particular had a lengthy history of negotiating treaties with other Aboriginal groups and with Europeans. They negotiated for such things as access to trade routes or to resources, the exchange of prisoners, or peace. These negotiations took place over many days and were conducted with much oral flourish and ceremony, not unlike those with government officials at Treaty 7.

Over two centuries of relations with newcomers, Aboriginal people evolved an ideology and practices that served them in their meetings and negotiations with European strangers. New approaches were blended with their own traditions, such as reciprocity, gift giving, and exchange.

Friesen notes that there were different kinds of negotiations. Aboriginal peoples' treaties with fur traders, for example, were different from treaties they made with governments. The treaties with fur traders were agreements made at annual meetings and they could be renegotiated or changed as circumstances warranted. Treaties also involved yearly tribal meetings in which there were renewed declarations of friendship and mutual obligation. Relationships were viewed as familial and were often based on kinship ties.

John Tobias agrees with much of what Jean Friesen argues. In demonstrating his point that the numbered treaties were not simply imposed by the government, he describes how Aboriginal people were able to influence the timing of the treaties. There is also evidence that the federal government did not necessarily have any intention of proceeding with the treaties. Tobias argues that the Plains people were very much aware of what was happening to them. They knew that their means of subsistence was dwindling and that Canada was intending to claim their land. They were worried that the land might simply be taken from them without compensation. This argument suggests that it was Aboriginal people who initiated the treaty-making process, that they pressured the authorities to deal with them and their concern for the future. In Manitoba, Yellow Quill's band of Saulteaux turned back settlers who wished to go beyond Portage, insisting that a treaty be made with them. Plains Cree interfered with the geological survey and prevented construction of telegraph lines through their territory to make their point that the government had to deal with the Cree when it came to Cree land. Tobias states that Aboriginal people knew very well what was happening across the border and they were determined not to allow settlement or use of their land until their rights had been clearly recognized.

It would take hard bargaining for treaty agreements to be made across Canada, for Aboriginal people had the clear sense that the land was theirs. Their chiefs said the following: "This is what we think, that the Great Spirit has planted us on this ground where we are, as you were where you came from. We think where we are is our property"; and "The sound of the rustling of gold under my feet where I stand. We have a rich country. It is the Great Spirit who gave us this. Where we stand is the Indians' property and belongs to them."4 In return for allowing the Whites to use the land, the Aboriginal peoples asked for many things, and it was frequently only through protracted negotiations that agreements were reached. Because the negotiations were hard, government negotiators used a variety of tactics. One of these tactics was to attempt to break down united fronts that opposed the treaty. Aboriginal opinion was not always monolithic; there were many interests and factions – some wanted to reject the terms, while others were willing to listen to and accept government arguments. Once the government officials had a few of the Aboriginal people on their side, they threatened to settle with them alone and exclude the hard-liners. This would have left those who did not sign without the financial benefits. In many cases, such tactics were successful.

A major question is still debated today – did the Aboriginal leaders really understand the concept of a land sale? Some, like Stanley and Adams, argue that they could not. Others suggest that they understood only that they would be sharing the land. Jean Friesen's research led her to conclude that Aboriginal people were aware of what a land sale meant.

The First Nations did not, in Friesen's view, sell the resources of the land. They believed that they had only allowed access to resources. They certainly believed they could hunt and fish as they always had. It was assurances on this issue and promises of economic assistance and education that convinced them to sign the treaties. They believed that negotiations relating to other matters would be ongoing.

What emerges from a look at the analytical literature on the treaties is that there are at least two major interpretations of the nature of the Aboriginal/White relationship established by the treaties. In the treaties, the government negotiators used a paternalistic and archaic language to describe the responsibilities of the government towards the Aboriginal peoples. Metaphors were used extensively in the proceedings to explain abstract concepts. There were references to the Great Mother and to her children who would be taken care of. The government and courts have interpreted these references narrowly – that is, that the Queen had only limited, specific responsibilities towards the First Nations. Groups such as the Cree, however, have a different understanding. In their society the child has autonomy and freedom from the parents but the parents are obligated to provide aid in time of need. The Cree felt they had been guaranteed autonomy and could reasonably expect the government – not necessarily the Queen – to assist them to acquire it. "By basing their claim on how the Indian would understand the metaphor of a parent-child relationship or Great Mother, the contemporary Indian demand for autonomy can be said to be a treaty right."[5]

These are some of the complications involved in the task of trying to define and understand treaty rights. Contemporary Aboriginal leaders try to interpret how they think their ancestors might have understood the metaphors that were used and emphasize the importance that these metaphors play in understanding the "spirit and intent" of the treaties.

Education is a right guaranteed in the treaties according to Aboriginal elders. They believe that the education rights negotiated at the treaties assured them free education at all levels and in perpetuity in return for the use of the land by newcomers.

The elders also emphasize that they did not give up subsurface rights to the land. The word "land" in Cree or Blackfoot has a totally different meaning than it has in English. "Land" in Cree requires many prefixes before it can properly be understood and its precise meaning known. The Cree and Blackfoot both thought that they were allowing newcomers to come onto

Indian land for one purpose only and that was to farm, and that White settlers would only use the land that was needed for farming. They believed this to be the case because they were repeatedly told that the land would not be taken away from them, and that their livelihood and way of life would remain unaltered.

ACADEMIC ANALYSIS

There has been little specific academic analysis of Treaty 7. However, in a number of studies published either in academic journals or essay collections, academic historians have touched on issues that apply generally to the numbered treaties 1–7. Several of these studies provide significant insight into what happened at Treaty 7. Much of the analysis remains tendentious for two reasons. First, the perspective of the Treaty 7 First Nations is absent either because documentation was not available to the authors or it was not sought. (The interviews that are contained in Part 1 have helped to rectify this situation.) The second reason is that Treaty 7 differs in a number of important ways from treaties 1–6. Jean Friesen in her article "Magnificent Gifts," for example, does not even attempt to include Treaty 7 in her analysis because of these differences. The distinguishing features of Treaty 7 hinge on the fact that, of all the First Nations that signed treaties, the Treaty 7 nations had the least contact with Euro-Canadian authorities. This meant that they had different expectations of the treaties than those who signed treaties 1–6, who had become familiar with Euro-Canadians, especially through the fur trade. Contact with American treaty makers was more common to the experience of Treaty 7 First Nations. They did not have sustained contact with the Northwest fur trade and its annual rendez-vous tradition, which was a kind of annual negotiation of mutual obligations. Furthermore, real problems arose because of faulty translation or no translation at all, which was especially the case for the Tsuu T'ina, Stoneys, and to some extent the Blackfoot. As well, while the purposes of the first six treaties were understood, there were conceptual differences over just what Treaty 7 was about: was it a peace treaty or a land surrender? While the First Nations of treaties 1–6 had pressured governments into signing treaties, the same may not be the case with regard to Treaty 7. The Treaty 7 leadership certainly wanted to be on friendly terms with the Euro-Canadians and accept gifts for sharing the land, but they would not have wanted to participate in a land surrender, even if this were agreed to by the other First Nations, and would never have pressured for a treaty of this nature.

The commissioners at Treaty 7 were different from those at Treaty 6 and the earlier treaties. Just how Commissioner David Laird managed to obtain the Aboriginal leadership's agreement to Treaty 7 remains contentious; these people had a tradition of signing peace treaties but not major land surrenders that would put them on reserves that were much smaller than anything they had previously known.

With all these differences, therefore, it is not clear how relevant some of the insights of the academic historians are to the peculiar circumstances of Treaty 7. Nevertheless, points made in each of the articles shed some light on the main question of how the treaties are to be understood.

JOHN TAYLOR

The only article that directly analyses Treaty 7 is John Taylor's "Two Views on the Meaning of Treaty Six and Seven." Taylor begins by stating that he does not believe a common understanding was reached by the two sides at the treaty signing, but he is less sure of just where the two sides differed. Taylor emphasizes that the government position is clearly contained in the text of the treaty but that "we do not know to what extent the meaning of the treaty texts was communicated to the Indians. Written accounts of the treaty negotiations concentrate almost entirely on what the Indian parties would receive, barely mentioning what was to be given up by them."[6]

Taylor states that after Confederation it became important for the Canadian government to sign treaties if for "no other reason than that the Indians could seriously hamper its plans for the Northwest."[7] But from the beginning, starting with Treaty 1, the written treaties did not contain everything discussed and agreed upon: "Archival evidence makes it clear that the government had intended giving only reserves and annuities, the provisions for schools and agricultural aid must have been introduced into the negotiations by the Indians."[8] The government proceeded across the West to make treaties only as territory was required for settlement or to gain access to resources, such as coal. Taylor points out that one of the major problems in the negotiations conducted by Lieutenant-Governor Morris (treaties 3–6) was that Morris did not understand the importance or sacredness of the pipe-stem (or medicine pipe) ceremony. For Aboriginal people, only truth could be spoken by all taking part in this ceremony. Morris, however, saw the ceremony as simply picturesque. For him, only the signed document at the end of negotiations was important, but for the First Nations, everything that was said once the pipe was smoked would be considered part of the agreement. Once the pipe had been smoked, a spirit of trust and friendship was established, and as a result it was the "spirit and intent" of all the discussions that constituted the agreement, not just the signed document: "On the Indian side, the atmosphere of alliance and friendship had already been expressed through the pipe-stem ceremony. Whatever specific provisions might be put in the treaty, they could hardly be inconsistent with the spirit in which both Indians and Her Majesty's representative had come together on this solemn occasion."[9]

With reference to Treaty 7, Taylor reiterates the point that up to the 1870s the Blackfoot Confederacy had remained on the fringes of the major British fur trade networks. The Blackfoot had more contact with American traders, especially through the buffalo robe and whiskey trade of the 1860s. Because of their reliance on the buffalo robe trade, the tribes of southern Alberta viewed with alarm the diminishing herds, a situation that worsened dramatically as each year passed. The arrival of the Lakota into Canadian territory further exacerbated the problem, as now increased numbers had to live off these herds.

Morris was aware of these problems and of the threat that the Blackfoot posed for the peaceful settlement of newcomers. He strongly recommended against delays in signing a treaty for southern Alberta. Now that the North-West Mounted Police had put an end to the whiskey trade, the strengthened tribes might pose a threat to settlement. Morris indicated that a treaty was required as soon as possible to preserve "the present friendly disposition of these Tribes."[10] He was already aware that the Blackfoot did not want Métis and Cree buffalo hunters to intrude into their traditional hunting territories. As well, both Father

Scollen and Reverend McDougall were strongly pressing for a treaty.

Taylor reviews the actual negotiations and concludes, very much like Hugh Dempsey, that only through extensive discussions did all the tribes agree to sign. Again considerable credit for this is given to the NWMP's and Macleod's friendship with the tribes. Taylor then points to the significant differences between treaties 6 and 7, the latter having no famine clause or medicine chest, but rather promises of ammunition and cattle: "With these exceptions, the familiar terms of previous treaties reappeared in almost the same language."[11]

On the important issue of how well the treaties were understood by the First Nations, Taylor makes two important points. He shows that no one was sent out to explain the nature of the treaties ahead of time. For Treaty 7, John McDougall was sent out to give the news that a treaty was to be made, but he was not told to explain anything: "There is no indication that McDougall attempted to explain the meaning of a land surrender or that any other missionary did so."[12]

The second major point that Taylor makes is that "there is no recorded evidence that the commissioners attempted at the treaty negotiations to explain what they meant by a surrender."[13] The First Nations were told that settlers were coming, that buffalo were disappearing, and that it was desirable that they live in peace with those newcomers about to arrive. This message, says Taylor, "is in sharp contrast to the prominence and explicit detail of the surrender clauses of the treaty texts."[14] Once again the focus during treaty discussions was on what the Indians would receive and not on the fact that they would be giving up their land.

It is clear from the testimony of the elders and also from documentary evidence that has come to light since the time of the treaty signing that the First Nations did not want to give up their rights to timber resources or to animals, birds, and fish. Furthermore, evidence provided by the elders shows that the First Nations never intended to give up sub-surface rights; rather they had specifically stated that they would only allow newcomers to share the land to the depth of a plough. These points are in direct contradiction to what was written in the treaty. Indeed, what was contained in the treaty became contentious shortly after the treaty was signed and remains so today. Thus, today there are still widely divergent views on what constitutes the "spirit and intent" of the treaty. Taylor concludes his analysis with the following: "Unfortunately, we are dependent on inference from inadequate evidence for much of the Indian viewpoint. It appears that government and Indian began from different assumptions, and that there was little attempt on the part of government either to understand the Indian viewpoint or to convey its own to the Indian people. Under these circumstances, it is hardly surprising that Indian interpretations of the treaties do not conform to those of the government, or that there are some variations in the viewpoints of Indian people themselves on the meaning of their treaties."[15]

Taylor's analysis is in agreement with many of the substantive points made by the Treaty 7 elders. There is major agreement over the fact that the First Nations were never told that the treaty meant that their land would be surrendered or that they would be unable to retain control over sub-surface materials or forge rights to the birds, animals, and fish of their lands. The terms of the written treaty were not recognizable to the First Nations, whose descendants still claim that issues that were agreed on were not put in the treaty. The government either deliberately misled them or did not fully explain its position. Taylor's analysis, even though not fully substantiated by an Aboriginal perspective, does substantially corroborate the evidence given by the elders of Treaty 7.

CANADA'S POST-TREATY RELATIONSHIP WITH THE FIRST NATIONS – A FIDUCIARY POSITION OR TUTELAGE?

In signing treaties with Canada's Aboriginal peoples, the government assumed obligations that included a fiduciary responsibility to guarantee the promises the Crown had made to the Aboriginal peoples it treated with. The government also agreed to protect treaty rights as constitutionally guaranteed rights and not just as contractual obligations. Finally, Canada agreed that "the competition between incoming commercial or individual interests against a constitutionally protected Aboriginal right has to be decided on the basis of meeting the Aboriginal right first;

and in the accommodation of the Aboriginal right, government must err towards the maximum reasonable benefit as originally promised."[16] These principles have been more recently affirmed by section 35 of the Constitution Act and by a series of court cases, including the *Sparrow, Simon, Soui, Guerin,* and *Horseman* cases. However, Canada's federal government has not always taken its fiduciary responsibilities seriously, and it was only in 1974 that it established the Office of Native Claims to speed up hearings to settle outstanding grievances and disagreements regarding land claims.

The Aboriginal peoples of Treaty 7 were not listened to seriously from 1877 to the 1970s, and throughout this period considerable damage was done through Canadians' lack of response to issues raised by Aboriginal groups. Instead of straightforwardly upholding its fiduciary responsibilities for the First Nations, the government dealt with Aboriginal groups as a tutor would with pupils. This paternalistic attitude produced problems in that the government was less concerned with assuring the legal rights guaranteed to Aboriginal people than with overseeing lifestyle changes that officials felt Aboriginal people would have to make if they were to succeed in Canadian society. Thus, there was not a true fiduciary relationship; instead the government passed regulatory legislation without consultation with Aboriginal groups: "The tutelage that Canadian Indians have experienced has been based neither upon a contractual agreement nor a negotiated understanding but upon the power of one side to regulate the behaviour of the other in accordance with a set of unilaterally selected purposes."[17] The system of tutelage was established on the premise that the European was culturally superior to the Aboriginal. This resulted in a shared attitude among officials, from the prime minister down to Indian agents and farm instructors, that debased Aboriginal culture: "This constructed theory of Indian 'inferiority' provided the rationale for the unilateral assumption of control over Indian lands, resources and way of life."[18]

Thus, with regard to Treaty 7, government officials were not prepared to listen to what the Aboriginal leadership said; rather they did what they thought was best – perhaps even to the extent of putting items in the treaty that they considered more in the interests of the Aboriginal people than what had actually been negotiated and agreed to.

Despite considerable evidence of the prevalence of the system of tutelage, the goal of the system has consistently been downplayed. The control over the Aboriginal populations that enabled newcomers to exploit resources to create wealth for themselves has rarely been articulated: "Each new generation of tutelage agents has been convinced of the morality of its undertakings and the practical need of Indians for the particular 'gifts' that they on behalf of Canadian society, have sought to give Aboriginal people. Tutelage has never been presented by tutors as self-interested compulsion or exploitation; they invariably define their activities as charitable benevolence."[19]

The voices of Aboriginal people have simply been ignored: "Indians as members of a social and political category, continue to be regarded as incapable of knowing what is in their best interests and how to achieve it."[20] Certainly Treaty 7 demonstrates that the leaders were not listened to and that control of mineral and other resources was assumed to be better left to the newcomers. The Aboriginal people's integrity and ability to make decisions to properly exploit their environment were continuously attacked. The main thrust of such attacks served not to protect their rights but rather to bring about a "swift alienation of Native people from their land and resources."[21]

Rather than serving to protect Aboriginal populations so that they could affirm their identity and realize their potential, the laws and regulations enslaved those on reserves: "In the same way that workhouses under the English Poor Laws were intentionally places of shame, humiliation and banishment from moral community, so too have Indian reserves served to signify the moral boundaries and the preferred values of the civil society constructed in Canada ... In order for tutelage to achieve these ideological, political and material purposes it must destroy aboriginality and create dependence. Given Indian unwillingness to accept the over-all premise of tutelage, their compliance had frequently been forced."[22]

Officially, Canadian representatives were responsible for protecting the agreements with Aboriginal groups, but the history of unfulfilled agreements suggests that their promise to be protectors was a shallow one indeed. By comparison, the elders' position on the treaties is as credible now as it has ever been.

MUTUAL OBLIGATIONS AND TREATY 7

To Canadian officials, the treaties were a means to put an end, "once and for all," to aboriginal right and title to the land. But as Jean Friesen has argued, this "once and for all" interpretation of the treaty ignores much of what the negotiations meant to Aboriginal peoples.

Aboriginal leaders had long been involved in ceremonies with Europeans to secure peace, economic survival, and a favoured status in trading relations. For some groups, the treaties were seen as a further stage in a process that would continue to assure them peace and security. Friesen argues that Europeans did not understand the history of the ceremonies that had been an integral part of European-Aboriginal relations: "It is clear that they [Europeans] did not understand the significance of the social contract the Indians were making."[23]

The Aboriginal peoples saw the treaties as documents that marked the beginning of a relationship of mutual obligation. Across the lands of the numbered treaties, it is evident that Aboriginal leaders thought they would share the land with newcomers in return for the promise made on behalf of the Queen "to grant me where-with to make my living"[24] – that is, "promises of kinship, annuity, economic assistance and clothing."[25]

The Aboriginal peoples were generous in granting Ontarians, Icelanders, and Germans access to the fish and game resources that would allow them to survive in the early years: "Yet it was these settler governments that initiated the process of restricting access to game for Indians, in violation of the promises and assurances given at the treaties. The Dominion government, the trustee of Indian land and interests, found it easier in the end to restrain Indians than it did to challenge provincial governments or federal departmental bureaucracies."[26]

Kinship obligations were inherent in the metaphors used by the treaty negotiators, especially when they referred to the Great Mother who was to take care of her children. Exchanges were made solemn by ceremonies of pipe smoking that established kinship relations:

Indeed without this kinship tie there were no terms through which to negotiate an exchange. Brothers, mothers, brothers-in-law, cousins and fathers all had particular kinship responsibilities in resource-sharing, marriage, education and mutual assistance in emergencies. The commissioners are called Brothers who represent the Queen but who are nevertheless in the same position relative to Her Majesty as her Indian "children." When the governor general, the Marquis of Lorne, visited the west in the 1880s, he was greeted by the Indians as Brother-in-law for he had married the Great Mother's daughter. In the fur trade alliances, the factor had been addressed as Father, for he served in one sense as provider and supplier. Similarly, to take the hand of the Great White Mother indicated that one accepted that the Queen would "clothe" the Indians – that is, that protection and material wants were part of what was being offered whether or not it was written in such precise terms. In using such language, the treaty commissioners were accepting an implied moral responsibility of greater proportions than they realized.[27]

The treaties were negotiated as "sacred contracts made with much hesitation on our part,"[28] said an Ojibway chief. Still, they were seen as a framework of mutual obligations for continuing economic and diplomatic relations with the European newcomers – "closer to the idea of Dominion-provincial relations than to the once-and-for-all interpretation applied later."[29]

Friesen summarizes the status of the treaty rights that were guaranteed to those who signed the numbered treaties by suggesting that the government has never understood its responsibilities and has underestimated the "spirit and intent" of the treaty as understood by the Aboriginal peoples:

In Indian political thought the treaties represented continuing political and economic relations of "mutual" obligation. But in the decades after the conclusion of the treaties the burden of ensuring that these obligations be kept fell to the Indians. Their frequent requests by letter, petition and deputation for fulfilment of promises filled the department's archives and led government agents to regard the Indians as chronic complainers and so to treat their demands in the words of the deputy superintendent general, as only "Indian Talk." To Indians, disillusioned with the government's unilateral interpretations, increasingly confined in their economic opportunities and ruled by a federal Indian

Act to which they had never consented, the treaties came to be seen in the words of a Saskatchewan chief as merely "Sweet Promises."[30]

The First Nations felt that the mutual obligations that began with their agreements with the HBC, which allowed them various strategies for survival, extended to their treaties with the federal government. Historians John Tobias, Jean Friesen, and Sarah Carter have shown that for a time the government seemed willing to acknowledge responsibility for the subsistence of Aboriginal people by granting fishing and hunting guarantees as well as assistance in agriculture. This, however, came to an end in the late nineteenth century when the government unilaterally stopped honouring its treaty obligations. The Aboriginal peoples had been clear about sharing their land for the benefit of others, but as Friesen writes, reciprocity was what the First Nations expected: "The full response of the Canadian government has taken longer to emerge and the betrayal of the spirit and letter of those treaties has been masked by the rhetoric of Her Majesty's 'civilizing' mission."[31]

Sarah Carter has documented the litany of broken promises in present-day southern Saskatchewan with regard to agricultural assistance that had long been promised to prairie tribes. Despite the government's obligations, officials blamed the Aboriginal farmers for early failures in agriculture and deflected any suggestion that their own inaction was to blame:

It was in the interests of the government to deny that there was starvation in the North-West. Such reports could damage the reputation of the West, which the Department of Interior promoted as a land of prosperity and plenty. Hungry Indians were presented as authors of their own misfortune. They were regarded in much the same way as were the destitute farmers of the American Great Plains who suffered grasshopper plagues in 1873–78. Although the farmers were victims of natural disaster, they were treated with suspicion and contempt by public officials, who blamed them for creating their own problems through idleness. Legislators of the day believed the remedy was to teach farmers to help themselves and to adopt habits of hard work, determination and sobriety.[32]

Instead of delivering the goods promised or honouring the starvation clause, the government began to argue that its assistance was bad for the Aboriginal farmer: "It was thought that if they offered relief, the state would be rewarding pauperism, encouraging dependence and creating a permanent class of needy. Instead the farmers required advice, encouragement and moral suasion. Similarly, the starving Indians of the North-West did not have the means to improve their condition and yet the legitimacy of their need was questioned. Relief was viewed as demoralizing and dangerous. Poverty was attributed to individual human conduct, not to its systemic causes."[33]

The authorities viewed the Aboriginal farmers' requests that the government honour the treaties as new items that had not been included in the treaties: "Officials saw the treaty as a 'covenant' between the Indians and government; therefore, it was impossible to comply with demands."[34]

Consequently, as the conflict between government officials and Aboriginal farmers intensified, the government did less and less to fulfil its promises and blamed Aboriginal farmers more and more for the failure of agriculture on the reserves:

The result of these early years of administration was an erosion in the spirit of amity and entente with which the venture might have been more successfully approached. The gulf of understanding between Indian and department officials widened and deepened as both sides began to regard the other with fear, distrust and aversion. The Indians had reason to feel they had been deceived and led along a path that had ended in betrayal. Their irritation and anxiety were increased by hunger and an uncertain future. Department officials began to blame the Indians for their misfortunes and to view their spokesmen as trouble makers, incapable of telling the truth. They perceived the items promised to the Indians in their treaties as gratuities or government charity, rather than as payments for the land the Indians had ceded.[35]

WRITTEN WORK BY TREATY 7 ELDERS
LOUISE CROP EARED WOLF, JOHN SNOW, AND BEN CALF ROBE

Louise Crop Eared Wolf, an elder among the Bloods, and John Snow, a leader of the Stoneys, have written significant (though regrettably little-used) accounts of how Treaty 7 was viewed by the First Nations at Blackfoot Crossing. A memoir has also been published by Ben Calf Robe.

Louise Crop Eared Wolf

In the academic studies of the treaties, there are few references to written accounts such as the one by Louise Crop Eared Wolf. Crop Eared Wolf is a member of the third generation of Bloods since the signing of the treaty, and the story she tells had been passed down to her from previous generations. According to this story, the spirit and intent of the treaty was "to share our lands with the Queen's people in exchange for a number of rights."[36]

Of greatest significance to the Bloods, says Crop Eared Wolf, was Governor Laird's promise that "the Government will hold you on the palm of its hand as a downy feather to protect you and look out for your best interest."[37] This was a powerful metaphor for the Bloods, who were told that this would last forever or "as long as the sun shines, as long as the rivers flow, as long as the grass grows and as long as the mountains stand."[38]

Laird's promise holds great importance to this day: "The Government made an Oath in the presence of the four sacred powers of the Deity. They say that the spirits of the Above and the spirits of the Earth are the witnesses to our Sacred Peace Treaty. No other powers will stand in the way of doing away with our treaty. It was said that the treaty promises of the Government were sealed by the smoking of the Sacred Pipe which was the traditional way of binding an agreement."[39]

To the Bloods, the treaty was the coming together of two nations to agree to peace, and the peace was sealed by smoking the pipe and exchanging gifts – smoking the pipe is similar to the non-Natives' practice of swearing on the Bible. Such a treaty is understood as creating "a good and lasting relationship or friendship between two nations who at one time were at war with each other."[40] The Bloods had already made treaties with the Crow, Lakota, and Cree in the 1860s and 1870s.

Crop Eared Wolf says that the Bloods had their own system of government prior to the arrival of Europeans. "Traditional Indian law" consisted of customs, education, counselling, child rearing, and policing. Health care was based on a knowledge of herbs, roots, plants, and barks. These were used to treat various illnesses. The Bloods were a very spiritual people who valued respectability, spirituality, honesty, and generosity above all else. The arts of weaving with quills and sewing with beads were esteemed, as was the art of singing the many songs of the various societies.

There was great respect for Mother Earth. All of nature was held sacred, especially the Sun "because they were aware that there exists some power beyond that bright sun at whose brilliance we can never stare for a length of time without getting temporarily blinded by its rays."[41] The Bloods believed that "the Creator had given to all living things and living beings an equal right to live on the Earth; therefore, they thought it strange that some should possess more than others, so every member of the tribe shared alike both in good times and in hard times."[42] It was of great importance to the Bloods to live close to nature. "By 1880," says Crop Eared Wolf, "three years after the signing of Treaty Number Seven, was the end of an era of freedom and at living close to nature. Our people were made to live in square wooden boxes; they could not build their homes round like a circle. The circle was very important to our people; the earth is round, so is the sun and the moon. We made our tipis in a circular shape, our fireplace is circular in shape, the camp is in a circle."[43]

Crop Eared Wolf simply does not believe that the Blackfoot Peigan, Bloods, Tsuu T'ina, and Stoneys agreed to "cede, release and surrender" the land. She states that their ancestors would not have given up the land, since it was not theirs to give up: "Their respect for the land is so great that they would not dig up the ground for herbs or roots for medicinal purposes, without asking the Creator for permission for their use and they always put an offering of tobacco on the ground."[44]

Crop Eared Wolf concludes by telling the story of Red Crow: "It was said that at one time he was addressing an official from Ottawa when he took a clump of grass in one hand and a clump of dirt in the other hand. He returned the dirt to the ground saying we will never sell the Earth, Our Mother Earth; the grass he said he would share."[45]

Crop Eared Wolf also writes that the elders always said that their people did not give up the minerals and that none of the elders could remember it said that anyone agreed to "cede, release and surrender the land."[46]

The elders know about Treaty 7, says Crop Eared Wolf, and are coming forward to help the youth "to awaken the Federal Government to its Trust and Responsibility to the Indian people."[47]

John Snow

John Snow has produced an article and a book that together provide a comprehensive perspective on the signing of Treaty 7. Snow's history book, published in 1977, is a most valuable work because it provides a context for the Aboriginal point of view. Unfortunately, this work has not been used widely by authors who have written on the treaties.

Snow begins his analysis of Treaty 7 by discussing problems that the Canadian officials in particular had in understanding Aboriginal law: "The treaty commissioners performed their assigned tasks often times unaware of the full meaning of aboriginal law and title, without knowledge of our language and without benefit of the most elementary background as to our history, culture and way of life. Many of our present day problems derive from the consequent confusion, misunderstanding and apprehensions which surrounded the signing of the treaties."[48] The misunderstandings have been compounded by the fact that one society communicated using oral traditions, while the other communicated (especially for its legal agenda) using a written discourse. Snow points out that oral and written laws of both cultures should be used to arbitrate differences of interpretation in the treaty. The dominant English legal tradition has excluded Aboriginal law from consideration. This has consistently been to the detriment of the Treaty 7 First Nations. Snow writes: "I am sure that government representatives at the negotiations were well aware that in the future only the written statement contained in the documents would be honoured and upheld in the courts if there were any disputes. (This is now true. Only a narrow and literal interpretation of the treaties, in most cases, is upheld in court today.) But my people, who had an oral tradition and had honoured verbal agreements in the past, thought that the government would also honour what was spoken during the treaty making."[49] These were the fundamental problems that have never been fully debated or considered by those who write about the treaties.

Snow is convinced that the Aboriginal peoples at Blackfoot Crossing understood that they were making a peace treaty and nothing more. Offering his most definitive evidence, Snow quotes from a Stoney, Peter Wesley, whose Cree-speaking mother was at Blackfoot Crossing:

On the morrow the Chief asked him [Lieutenant-Governor Laird] what was the real meaning of this proposal? The answer was, "To make peace between us. We will have friendship when and where we ever meet. I am asking you to put your rifle down in exchange for a peace treaty. The money I am just about to give you is for this purpose. Not to kill each other. And furthermore, I am not going to take over your land, but I am willing to pay you money if you put down your rifle and make peace with me, this is what I mean." This was the answer given by the Lieutenant Governor. So that was how peace was made and that is the way it was. Nothing besides peace-making was talked about. The Chief had been told that he could still use his land in the same manner as before and there would be no interruption either, these were the final words put forth by the Governor through the interpreter. My mother talked and understood Cree very well. That was why my mother understood all the conversations held between the Governor and the Chiefs.[50]

Snow suggests that Treaty 7 people were deliberately misled by officials such as John McDougall who had a vested interest in the outcome of the treaty: "... this misunderstanding was intentionally allowed by the government because it was to its advantage to extinguish title to Indian land quickly as possible."[51] The government officials created a legal situation that was never understood by the Treaty 7 people and that allowed them to survey the land and then control the movement of Aboriginal people:

If my forefathers had known what this would mean to our people: the disappearance of the buffalo and diminishing other game, the restrictive game laws, the ploughing and fencing off of all lands, more whiteman's diseases, attacks on our religion, culture and way of life, the continual

eroding of our treaty rights; if they could have foreseen the creation
of provincial parks, natural areas, wilderness areas, the building of dams,
the flooding of traditional hunting areas, they would never have signed
Treaty 7. But they relied on what the missionaries said, "The Queen's
government will honour the promises in the treaties."[52]

Snow points to salient issues that prompted the government
to seek the treaty. A major concern was the presence of Sitting
Bull's Lakota and the possibility that the Lakota might succeed
in persuading other prairie tribes to form a united front against
the Canadian officials. The government was therefore unlikely
to raise divisive issues in the negotiations, being "anxious to win
the confidence of my people on its side of the border by concluding a treaty and reassuring them of its peaceful intentions."[53]
Similar pressures existed in British Columbia, where the federal
government feared fighting between Aboriginal tribes and White
settlers. This threat of violence made paramount the need to
control and neutralize the Aboriginal people who were perceived
as being such a threat.

Snow says it might have been more appropriate for his people
to have signed Treaty 6 than Treaty 7, since much of their land
lay in the Treaty 6 area. Unlike other Plains tribes, the Stoneys
thought they would be able to continue to survive by hunting,
trapping, fishing, and gathering plants on their traditional lands.
They were not interested in agriculture, and it was McDougall
who wanted to discourage nomadic behaviour and who pressed
for terms concerning agriculture. Snow argues that the government officials were more interested in pacifying the Blackfoot
Confederacy than they were in dealing with the Stoneys, whom
they did not perceive as a threat to settlers. The Stoneys were
also out of the way of settlement and did not block the development of mineral resources such as coal.

Snow also demonstrates that McDougall was a major hindrance to the Stoneys when he negotiated on their behalf. Controversial issues were consequently never fully explained to the
Stoneys, and McDougall did not try to put forward arguments
concerning the Kootenay Plains people (who wanted their own
reserve north of Morley) because he hoped that all the Stoneys
would come to settle at Morley, where he could more easily
preach to them. When McDougall was asked what the territory
of the Stoneys consisted of, he simply identified territory in the

vicinity of Morley, even though the range of Stoney territory was much larger and the make-up of the Stoney people far from homogeneous.

Snow also puts at issue the possibility that Crowfoot may not have been the leader authorized to speak for the Blackfoot. The Stoney system of leadership was often ignored as well. Snow emphasizes that leaders who came from areas outside the Treaty 7 boundaries were never properly consulted about their traditional areas of occupation. The government's failure to identify the proper leaders of various groups of Stoneys continued to create problems, especially when it came to the surveys. Surveyors frequently consulted the leader of one band assuming that the leader spoke for all the others, and this led to insufficient territory being surveyed for the Stoneys. McDougall did little to correct the misconceptions of the surveyors and was pleased to have the Stoneys all in one place.

Ben Calf Robe

A short published memoir of what happened at Treaty 7 was left behind by the highly respected Siksika elder Ben Calf Robe (1890–1979). Calf Robe was the elder chosen to say prayers and give blessings for the huge gathering assembled to commemorate the one-hundredth anniversary of the making of Treaty 7 at Blackfoot Crossing. The Queen was represented at the time by Prince Charles. Calf Robe was also holder of the medicine pipe bundle and worked for a number of years as an interpreter for the RCMP. During the 1930s he was chief of the Siksika, and in 1942 he was one of the founding fathers of the Indian Association of Alberta.

Ben Calf Robe's father, Weasel Calf, was one of the Siksika chiefs who negotiated Treaty 7. What Calf Robe remembered most clearly is that the treaty was not a land surrender: "What I heard from the Old People about this treaty is that it was a peace treaty. They agreed to make peace, but they didn't say anything about selling the land. The treaty papers have a lot about giving up our lands, but the Old People didn't know anything about it. That is what I heard them saying, when I was young."[54]

Like the elders interviewed in the 1980s, Calf Robe placed much of the blame for the misunderstanding relating to the treaty on poor translation: "They blamed the interpreter – he was a half-breed who only knew a few words of Blackfoot ... there should have been interpreters who knew the Blackfoot language and the Blackfoot customs."[55] Another problem was that what leaders said during the treaty process was not properly recorded: "You see, when there is an important council meeting, like this treaty ... all the head men – the chiefs and Elders – stand up and say what they think. But none of their words were written down with the treaty papers ... their words were not recorded."[56]

The authority of the Queen as a provider and protector was invoked to persuade the First Nations to agree to the treaty. Calf Robe said that the many promises made on behalf of the Queen clinched the First Nations' agreement to the treaty:

The way the Old People told me about it, the head of the government group was called Tall White Man (Lt. Gov. David Laird). He said he was speaking for the Queen of England, who was the boss of Canada. We call her the Chief Woman. Tall White Man said, "your Mother, the Chief Woman, wants you to put down your guns and your sharp weapons and to end your wars. She wants you to settle down in one place so you will sleep good and you will be able to raise your children. This one with the Long Robes will care for your children, and he will teach them. And this one with the Red Coat will put you in jail if you steal anymore [sic] horses or drink anymore [sic] liquor. And he will put those in jail that steal horses from you or try to sell you liquor."

These are the things that the Old People said they agreed to. There was no mention to sell land; or to sell what is underneath the land; or to sell the mountains, trees, lakes, rivers, and rocks. And we didn't say to sell the animals that travel on the land – the ones that we eat – or the birds that fly, or the fish that swim. The Old People didn't get asked to sell these things. They were told, "the Queen will be like your mother, and she will take care of you until the Sun stops shining, the mountains disappear, the rivers stop flowing, and the grass stops growing."[57]

POSTSCRIPT: THE MEMORANDUM OF R.N. WILSON

One document written in the post-treaty era that squarely challenges the "honourable record" of the federal government in its handling of First Nations issues is the memorandum of R.N. Wilson, who served as Indian agent for the Bloods and Peigan from 1898 to 1911. It documents the litany of broken treaty promises and the disgraceful administration of Aboriginal affairs. It is valuable in that it is, like Scollen's letter to Irvine in 1879, written by an employee of the government; it cannot simply be dismissed as a complaint by one of the aggrieved First Nations. It tells a dismal story indeed, one that was likely repeated on the other reserves in Treaty 7.

One of the major features of Treaty 7 that distinguished it from the previous numbered treaties was the commitment by the government to assist with the development of ranching on the reserves. The Bloods developed a very successful and viable ranching industry. By the first decades of the twentieth century the Bloods had a herd of four thousand of the finest beef cattle and a large herd of over three thousand horses. Their haying operations were also successful, and by the war years they were able to harvest up to ten thousand tons of hay and successful grain crops as well. Remarkably, however, the federal government, the Indian agents, and surrounding ranchers began to pursue a deliberate policy to arrest the development of the Bloods' growing cattle operation.

It is clear that local ranchers had a vested interest in sustaining the ration system on the local reserves. They sold a considerable amount of meat to local Indian agents to feed the Aboriginal population on the reserves. A successful Aboriginal cattle operation would of course mean the end of such sales. This was true of many of the large ranches of southern Alberta. Thus, Aboriginal farming and ranching were deliberately obstructed, especially at the end of the First World War. Prodded by the local ranchers, the politicians proposed that returned veterans be given lands that were said to be lying unproductive:

A crisis has arisen which justifies the Government in doing things autocratically, if necessary. The Government can do things today that it could not do before and probably will never be able to do again. An announcement that the Government proposed to deal finally with these Indian Reserves and in this manner would be hailed with delight by practically every resident in Western Canada. It would also seem most appropriate that the returned soldiers should be settled on what are unquestionably the very best vacant lands in the West. In the face of a national necessity, such as this, shallow sentiment or Indian obstinacy should not be permitted to influence the Government's action in this great welfare undertaking. The Indian can be handsomely compensated and will, in the end, be much better off with his individual holding than roaming over enormous undeveloped areas of highly valuable lands, now needed urgently for national purposes.[58]

Conveniently, seizing reserve land would solve two problems: returned veterans could be settled on choice land and the local ranchers would no longer be threatened by the Bloods' successful cattle operations.

Many coercive and disreputable tactics were used to secure the surrender of reserve lands that were so necessary for the burgeoning cattle industry. Reserve residents who opposed the land surrenders were threatened with discontinued rations as well as with exclusion from any profits that might be made from land sales. Supporters of surrenders, on the other hand, were enticed with promises of rations and cash windfalls. Those opposed to land surrenders were thus officially blacklisted. In addition, land that had been leased to Aboriginal people who participated in the Greater Production Campaign to help the war effort was reclaimed when the war ended. Fraudulent documents were used to try to secure land surrenders, and reserve land that had been cultivated by reserve residents was seized outright and leased to neighbouring ranchers. Police were used to intimidate reserve residents. Sections of the Indian Act were applied so as to disrupt the work of reserve residents on the cattle operations, hindering their ability to purchase materials and equipment or sell their cattle and produce. Wilson writes: "Previous to 1919 such routine duties as roundup work, with expenses paid from locally raised funds, were performed as matter of course in their proper season without the necessity of obtaining special authority from Ottawa but following the disorganization of the Department incidental to the so-called 'Greater Production' activities, the then Agent at the Blood states that he received orders not to incur any expenses whatever exceeding $10.00 without special permission from Regina."[59] Because the reserve residents could not borrow the money needed for treating cattle disease, for the harvest, for the round-up, and so on, the cattle operations became inefficient and began to suffocate. Hay was left unharvested or unsold; cattle that could not be branded or whose brands were not recorded were lost; horses that could not be stabled died. The list of calamities goes on. Some have argued that Wilson's memorandum is not reliable evidence, that he had become a disgruntled employee after being relieved of his duties as Indian agent on the Blood reserve. This might be a damaging charge were it not for the fact that Wilson's documentation of the destruction of reserve cattle operations is corroborated by the Blood elders' descriptions of what happened on their reserve. As well, elders on the other Treaty 7 reserves have described similar acts of coercion, intimidation, and fraud on the part of Indian agents.

An examination of the relations between the Treaty 7 First Nations and the government in the first half of the twentieth century clearly shows that the Canadian government willingly and stridently violated central principles of the treaty it had signed only a few decades earlier. Were it not for the continued protests and resistance of reserve residents, the Aboriginal reserve lands would surely have been lost in face of the numerous tactics employed by the federal government to gain surrenders of treaty lands. It must have been difficult for reserve residents to reconcile the "sweet promises" and "magnificent gifts" that had been offered with the astonishing behaviour of government officials intent on destroying the very industries that they had agreed to establish for the First Nations. It must have left many Aboriginal leaders wondering whether the government had acted in good faith when it signed the treaty, or whether it had done what was necessary to get the First Nations onto reserves where they could be restricted and controlled.

CONCLUSION

The evidence given by Treaty 7 elders from the time the treaty was signed in 1877 to the present has not changed. In the oral histories passed down from generation to generation, their understanding of what happened at Blackfoot Crossing remains consistent. According to the research, this is true whether elders were interviewed in the nineteenth century, in the 1920s, the 1930s, the 1960s, or the 1990s. The elders have said that Treaty

7 was a peace treaty; none of them recalled any mention of a land surrender. They remembered that they would be "taken care of," that they would be given an education and provided with medical care and annuity payments. They remembered promising that they would "share" the land with the newcomers and in return they would be provided with the benefits that the new society could offer them, such as assistance in agriculture and ranching.

The elders remembered that issues that were important to them had been discussed at the treaty negotiations but left out of the treaty itself, such as the government's commitment to protect the buffalo, the basis of their economy. They did not remember giving up their rights to sub-surface minerals, only that they would allow the newcomers to use the land for agriculture to the depth of a plough blade. The elders remembered that there were translation difficulties at the treaty negotiations and that many issues were left unexplained or vague. Present-day elders believe that this was done purposefully so that the Treaty 7 people would be misled into believing they were signing a peace treaty when all along the government was hiding the main clause from their attention, which was that they were surrendering the land.

None of the elders recalled discussing any issues having to do with a land surrender. What they remembered was being given the freedom to continue to fish and hunt and gather as they always had and to choose the lands on which they would live. They thought that they would be allowed to live on the large expanses of land that they had described to the treaty commissioners. They did not know that they would eventually be given relatively small parcels of land to live on, land that was often unsuited to the alternative agricultural economies that had been promised to them.

The present-day elders feel that their people were betrayed by missionaries, treaty commissioners, government officials, and even the NWMP, all of whom were initially welcomed and trusted. They feel that treaty promises have too often been broken. The Treaty 7 elders remembered smoking the pipe to bless and solemnize a treaty that was to enable them to live in peace and harmony. By smoking the pipe of friendship they did not need to know all the details (some of which were subsequently used against them) of the treaty. Once the pipe had been smoked, they believed that they would be "taken care of" and that their lives would be enriched by the government's "magnificent gifts" and "sweet promises."

What the elders have said about Treaty 7 is substantially corroborated by a number of historians and academics. Only a few support the official government position on Treaty 7. To various degrees the academic analysis suggests that the elders are correct in saying that Treaty 7 was presented to them as a peace treaty rather than a land surrender. The academic arguments support the position that the Aboriginal people of Treaty 7 were either deliberately or unintentionally deceived. It does not appear either from evidence given at the time of the treaty or from subsequent analysis that a land surrender was agreed to or explained.

Treaty 7 people did not misunderstand what was said to them at the treaty negotiations. They were told that this was a peace treaty and that they would be "taken care of." Only later did they discover the actual terms of the written treaty. The academic authors who agree, to various degrees, with this interpretation include John Taylor, John Tobias, Jean Friesen, Doug Sprague, Richard Price, Noel Dyck, Hugh Dempsey, and Sarah Carter. But perhaps most telling are the opinions that Father Scollen expressed about the treaty. He was at Blackfoot Crossing, and he worked among the Blackfoot both before and after the signing. He agreed with the elders that the land surrender aspect of Treaty 7 had never been explained to them and, perhaps even more serious, that Treaty Commissioner Laird had never intended to keep the promises that he made to the Aboriginal peoples at Blackfoot Crossing. The claim that the Canadian government bargained in good faith is no longer acceptable; the evidence to the contrary is too great. It is clear that the Treaty 7 people were not told the whole truth, either by the commissioners or the translators. The degree of the deception is more difficult to determine. Was it deliberate, was it fraud, or was it merely a sin of omission? The treaty commissioners might have allowed the Aboriginal leaders to believe that "sharing the land" – which the chiefs were willing to agree to – was the same as a "land surrender" – which the government was determined to achieve.

What cannot be questioned is the fact that the treaty was not honoured by the government. The non-performance on treaty promises was so flagrant that even supporters of the government such as Father Scollen were offended. As a consequence, the First Nations of Treaty 7 began to petition the government to honour all of the promises that the elders remembered being made to them. They continue to press for justice to this day.

CHAPTER TWELVE

The Value of the Elders' Historical Testimony

Until very recently, Canadian historians have relied on written documents as the main sources of evidence. In the western European tradition, written records and official documents were thought to be more verifiable than the spoken word and, therefore, more reliable. In national histories, the stories of those whose lives were recorded in writing were part of the nation's narrative, while the stories of those peoples and classes who left behind no such documentary record were marginalized or ignored.

Those who hold cultural power also control the form through which history is told; for example, they might give legitimacy to history presented in the form of an essay but not to history as told in a story or an epic poem. Those who hold cultural power also control who tells the story. In the case of many First Nations, "their" history would be told by non-Aboriginal historians who routinely ignored the original form and intent of the Aboriginal history. Non-Native historians searched for facts in the Aboriginal oral histories, often missing the main point of the telling of a story and often ignoring the context in which a story was being told.

While it is obvious that oral and written documentation may reveal different kinds of evidence, it is not the case that one is better or more reliable than the other. Documentary evidence may be more focused on the narrative of the text and on the facts contained in it. Oral traditions, on the other hand, may reveal more about the significance of the speaker and the place to which a particular story relates. The esteem in which an elder who tells a story is held may outweigh particular facts used in the telling of the story. Furthermore, Aboriginal stories are often directly connected to specific places in the landscape of a tribe's territory. The telling of these stories is frequently left to people who have connections with that particular landscape through family or clan membership. Thus, great significance is attached to those who have knowledge both about stories and about the place where the events in the stories happened. Genealogy, context, and the right of a particular clan member to tell a story thus combine to be as significant as the facts of a particular oral historical narrative. Some stories, for example, need to be absorbed over many tellings before the significance of the message as it relates to the social context provided by the teller and the occasion can be understood; such stories cannot be superficially analysed for meaning. Oral testimony cannot be sifted for "facts" alone; the importance of the speaker and the forum must be appreciated as well. This does not diminish the legitimacy or truth value of an oral history but simply means it must be understood for what it can tell us. Written histories often hide their real purpose and create an illusion of objectivity by avoiding an up-front reference to the significance of the speaker or the ideological context of the message. In an oral history these components of the narrative are self-evident.

As Aboriginal people demand the right to tell their own history, it becomes increasingly evident that the teller of the history is as important as the facts. The oral and the written forms must be seen as two equally legitimate ways to construct history.

The privileged position enjoyed by a scholarly tradition based on written evidence is, however, dying hard. In the 1991 land-claim case of the Gitksan-Wet'suwet'en, Justice MacEachern of the British Columbia Supreme Court denied the First Nations' oral traditions equal footing with the written histories of the western European tradition. Anthropologist Julie Cruikshank points out that Justice MacEachern's decision provides "a powerful example of the unequal weight accorded to different narratives. The inescapable lesson seems to be that removing oral tradition from a context where it has self-evident power, and performing it in a context where it is open to evaluation by the state, poses enormous problems for serious understanding of its historical value."[1] MacEachern rejected the legitimacy of the

Gitksan-Wet'suwet'en oral traditions in spite of the fact that their validity was explained to the court by a variety of historians, archaeologists, anthropologists, and linguists.

Compounding this devaluing of the legitimacy of oral traditions has been the problem of "cultural amnesia" prevalent in the dominant newcomer society. Published versions of oral history have long been available to academic historians but rarely have they been included in national narratives. Because the First Nations peoples have been economically and socially marginalized, their history has been ignored. Euro-Canadian society for many decades has denied the existence of the many smaller nations throughout our country, but these communities have not gone away. Indeed, First Nations peoples are increasingly demanding to be heard. Listening to them, writes Julie Cruikshank, might eventually be to our benefit: "If we discuss or overlook the historical contributions of small-scale societies, we risk losing evidence of human diversity and of alternative solutions to complex human problems."[2] Oral traditions should be used to complement the facts that can be proven from the written record so that the history of First Nations peoples can be fully represented.

Oral History of the Treaty 7 First Nations

The oral history of the Treaty 7 First Nations has been recorded and passed on in a variety of ways. First and foremost, the oral history continues to survive in its traditional forms through the stories that are carried by various societies on reserves. Many stories have been lost but many have survived, and the bundles from these societies contain items to which many important stories are attached.

The First Nations themselves have conducted interviews over the years, and these have been recorded on audio- and videotapes. In some cases, oral interviews were used in support of specific land claims, such as the interviews conducted by the Stoneys with regard to the Kootenay Plains claim at the Bighorn Stoney reserve. A number of the Treaty 7 First Nations have also carried out general interview programs with elders to assist in preserving language, history, and culture.

In the 1970s the Alberta Treaty and Aboriginal Rights Research Centre in Edmonton interviewed a number of elders on issues specifically related to Treaty 7. Some of these interviews have been used in this volume.

The oral history presented in this study was a result of a treaty review process begun by the Treaty 7 Tribal Council in 1991. The aim was to gather the "collective memory" of the Treaty 7 elders and, in so doing, determine what the "spirit and intent" of Treaty 7 encompassed. Treaty 7 elders have always maintained that what was included in the written treaty did not include all that was discussed and agreed to. It was therefore imperative to establish clearly what the elders of the five First Nations remembered.

PART THREE

Biographies of Elders, Interviewers, Translators, and Researchers

The Blood Tribe

PAUL RUSSELL (1902–1976)
Born March 17, 1902, Old Agency
Father: Jim Russell
Paul was born on the Blood reserve. He signed up with the armed forces as a teenager to fight in the First World War, but he began to go blind in one eye and could not go overseas. He was, however, stationed at the air base located in Fort Macleod as a labourer. When the war ended, Paul moved back to the Cardston area and worked at various jobs, such as ranch hand, seasonal field harvester, and feedlot operator.

Paul and his wife, Annette, had seven boys and two girls. His advice remains embedded in the minds of his children today: "Live a life of honesty and truthfulness, it is the only way of life."

CHARLIE ("GEORGE") COMING SINGER (1909–1981)
Clan: Tall Trees
Father: Kills From Afar
Mother: Coming Singer
George's parents died during his younger years, and he lived with relatives in Browning, Montana, and in Canada. However, most of his life was spent on the Blood reserve.

George, like most young men in his day, worked as a ranch hand, seasonal harvest labourer, and general labourer. He may very well have been one of the first to go south into Washington State to pick apples.

Although Charlie was his legal name, he liked the name "George" and used it for himself, so much that "Charlie" was forgotten.

George remained a bachelor all his life. He died on December 23, 1981, after complications set in after a stroke. He was laid to rest at the Stand Off Cemetery.

ADAM DELANEY
Born January 3, 1930
Parents: John and May Delaney
Adam worked for the Blood Band Ranch during the late 1950s and early 1960s. He moved to the United States in 1963 where he worked in the construction field. He returned to Canada in 1966 and lived in Calgary. In 1972, Adam became the leader of the Horn Society and remained its leader for fifteen years.

In the past few years, Adam has been working for Kainai Corrections as well as for the Federal Parole Board.

BILL HEAVY RUNNER
Born June 7, 1922
Grandparents: White Bean and White Eagle Woman
Bill was born on the Blood reserve on June 7, 1922. His parents were Red Boy and Many Sacrifices, but he was raised by his grandparents.

Bill became a member of the Horn Society at an early age and later in life joined the Crazy Dog Society. During the 1960s and 1970s, Bill hosted a radio program called "Blackfoot Radio," aired throughout southern Alberta.

In recent years Bill's health has kept him near home. However, he is always ready to sit and talk with whoever visits.

PETE STANDING ALONE
Born June 18, 1928 (?)
In his early teens, at fifteen, Pete ventured out on his own to look for work in the United States. He worked in the oil refinery industry on and off for ten years. He worked in areas of North Dakota, Nebraska, Texas, and elsewhere.

During the late 1970s, Pete was elected to the council of the Blood Tribe and served three terms as tribal councillor. In 1977, he was given the honour of making a saddle for the Prince of Wales and presenting it to him.

Pete remains active in the community and in governing matters.

LOUISE CROP EARED WOLF SAKOWAHTOMAKHA
Born July 21, 1922
Father: (Paul Tallman) Spitai-Kawan
Mother: (Mary Davis) Sa-ko-yi-sino-pa-ki
"My parents were very traditional. My father was born in 1874 (Lone Fighter's clan). My mother was born in 1878 (Fish Eater's clan). My informants are my uncle, Morning Bird, and his wife, both older than my parents.

"As a child I was exposed to a lot of storytelling in our home from members of extended families, when family unity was still very prevalent. Some of my father's friends and relations who I remember used to come to our home were Black Horse and his wife, Beautiful Coup Woman; Cross Child and his wife; Shot Close and his wife, Calf Woman; Po'na/Shot Both Sides and his wife, Long Time Pipe Woman; Calling Last and his wife, Kommayi; Good Striker and To-wai-pi-yi or Oaka."

Louise has nine children, eighteen grandchildren, and three great-grandsons. She and her husband, Joe, recently celebrated their fiftieth wedding anniversary. Louise was employed as a teacher's aide and guidance counsellor in the local education system for a number of years and also served on council.

Since her retirement she has remained active in community affairs and currently serves on a number committees. She is involved in various community projects such as the Kainai Corrections Society, Red Crow College, and Blood Tribe Education.

Louise is a strong supporter of language retention and cultural preservation and is personally involved in that area.

FRED GLADSTONE
Born April 7, 1918
Father: James Gladstone
Mother: Jane Healy
Fred was the oldest child born to James and Jane (née Healy) Gladstone. According to his parents, Fred was born on April 3

but the birth records state April 7. Fred's father, a non-Native, was adopted into the Blood Tribe and married a full-Blood woman, Jane Healy. James Gladstone became the first Treaty Indian to be appointed to the Canadian Senate.

Fred was educated at the St Paul's residential school for about eight or nine years. When he left school, he married Edith, who came from Saskatchewan. They had a small trucking business, a farm, and a ranch operation.

As a young man, Fred used to accompany his father, who was then the president of the Indian Association of Alberta (IAA). They met with many of the elders of the time to talk about different Indian political matters. Fred followed in his father's footsteps by getting involved in the IAA. He served eight years as a Blood councillor under the lifetime system.

Fred stressed that Treaty Indians should continue to fight for our treaty rights.

DICK NICE CUTTER (deceased)
Born June 10, 1907
Dick Nice Cutter was born on the Blood reserve on June 10, 1907. When he lost his parents at the age of five, Dick boarded at the St Paul's residential school. He excelled in English and literature and enjoyed reading in his spare time. He was a hard-working young man, doing various chores around the school. When he left school in 1928, Dick married Anna Hunt (deceased).

Dick spent over thirty years working off the reserve to support his family. He worked in the coal mines near Lethbridge and took various farm labour jobs in Carmangay, Medicine Hat, Milo, and Bow Island. He was the foreman at a seed-cleaning plant in Lethbridge until it shut down. Then he worked at the Lilydale plant until he reached retirement age.

Dick was a member of the Horn Society, Skinny Horse Society, and Eagle Society. In his younger days, he listened to many elders and he shared with the interviewers for this project the information and knowledge he had gained over the years.

ROSIE RED CROW
Born July 15, 1916
Father: Aloysius Crop Eared Wolf
Mother: Teresa Crop Eared Wolf

"I was born in Stand Off. I was born at the Sun Dance. My father and mother were married in 1912. Our home was built in 1912–13; it was on the edge here in Stand Off. We were given our treaty money there; I don't know how many years we were given the treaty money there. There were large gatherings [rodeos] at our home. People would set up camp near our home. I went to school, I was ten years old, I hurt my back, I was still very young. I did not stay at the school very long; for two years I stayed at home. When I was sixteen years old, I went back to school."

ANNIE BARE SHIN BONE
Born August 11, 1918
"I was about six years old when my parents separated. My mother left my dad. My father just came out of Dunbow school; he thought it best that I go to residential school. My grandmother was the one that raised me. I was brought to the missionary school; from there I hardly left school and we moved up to St Mary's – 1926 we moved out to St Mary's school. Those big grain tank boxes and teams of horses – that's what we moved up. We all moved to St Mary's school and that's where I spent all my life until 1935. The year 1935 was when I finished school, but summers I stayed in school. I hardly ever knew my mother. It was just after I left school that I came in contact with my mother. I never knew Indian culture traditions or anything, being raised by nuns and priests. It was just after I left school, I got married with my first husband and then we stayed with my grandmother, the old lady that raised me. She married – his name was Mark Wolf Child. She remarried after I went to school and that's where we were living. They always invited people. They always had gatherings, every day inviting all the other elders. There's always a big gathering at their house, the elders. And that's when I heard about the treaties. Blackfoot Crossing, that was where Crowfoot was, and Red Crow.

WALLACE MOUNTAIN HORSE
Born February 28, 1927, Moses Lake
Father: Joe Mountain Horse
Mother: Taking Home Sacrifice
"My dad's Indian name was Owl's Head. That's the name I've

got right now, I'm recognized by this name. My father was in
the First World War – a war veteran. When he came back, that's
when I was born. He got a fairly good education at the time,
I guess. He was one of the first students of the first Anglican
school that was established here on this reserve at the beginning
of the century. He was a spokesman for the lifetime chiefs, Chief
and Council, and met the federal government officials that came
around telling us how we should live our lives during that time.
I have that sense in me that I should carry out the footsteps
that my dad wanted to try and do for his people. When he came
back successfully from that First World War, he continued to
help his people on the Blood reserve – politically in the sense
of speaking for the Chief and Council. I had a pretty good understanding as I was growing what I should like when I go about
my business as a person – knowledge. This is what I am continually working on right now – still I have lots of concern for
my people, not just this reserve – right across Canada. I have
political experience and I'm a politically minded person. I would
like to see lots of things established for Native people across
Canada with the present people that came about when Chris-
topher Columbus discovered this country. It is really important
to understand the international rights of all nations all over the
world, and to know how to use them."

PRISCILLA BRUISED HEAD
Born May 23, 1916
Father: Percy Creighton
Mother: Jessie Tail Feathers
"My father and mother were legally married. They raised me
in the right way. I was about five years old when I began to
help them out. Since at that time there was no such thing as
free labour, we all had to work for our own living. I was raised
with that kind of work. I was about six when my father was
raising our own crops. I would get up really early (my parents
woke me up). I would run out to the field and chase the horses
in. After I had them watered, then I would bring them in. I
would help my mum out at the house. I was about nine, almost
that age, when I went to school. All my life I was taught almost
everything. Older people loved my father. They would camp near
our home, and they would tell us about many things. Dan Weasel

Moccasin's mother and father and his father's close relatives would stay with us. They would tell many things about the good life, what is good. When the two-year election came about, I ran in the election, I did not know I was in the race when they counted the ballots. I came in third and that's how I joined the council. I served on council for ten years. My life was not too bad. I took care in how I conducted my life. In 1960 there were some old ladies who gave me work every day. I would pray that people would come to me, and when they did I would paint their faces and do what I can so that the Indian way of life will persevere on the reserve. Today the reason why I live alone, I pray, I want things to be good. My son is going to school – weekends he comes home, he stays with me. Others come in to check on me."

WILTON GOODSTRIKER
Born Cardston, Alberta
Father: Rufus Goodstriker
Mother: Marion Goodstriker

Wilton Goodstriker was born in Cardston, Alberta, and raised on the Blood reserve. Wilton's dedication has been both intellectual and spiritual. His knowledge of the Kainaiwa traditional way of life was passed down to him from his grandfathers and spiritual advisers. Wilton is the son of the former head chief Rufus Goodstriker and the late Marion Goodstriker.

Wilton began his education at St Mary's residential school on the Blood reserve, completing his graduate year in Calgary. He attended the University of British Columbia and the University of Lethbridge. In 1968 he joined the Calgary police force, serving for about four years. He then worked with the Native Counselling Services Association (NCSA), first as a court worker and then as an assistant director. In 1978 he decided it was time to come home. Through his involvement with law work, Wilton established the Blood Tribe Protection Services on the Blood reserve in 1976. He then held the position of executive director for the Blood Tribe for four years. Wilton and his wife, Evelyn (née Goodwill), raised four children, Nadine, Jason, Chris, and Josh, and one grandchild, Tyler. Wilton's ability to deal with the social and political issues that Kainaiwa is faced with proves his integrity and dedication to the promise of a better future.

INTERVIEWERS AND TRANSLATORS

JACKIE RED CROW

Jackie Red Crow received her education in all three reserve schools: St Mary's, St Paul's, and Stand Off. She is a fluent speaker of Blackfoot and worked for the Indian News Media for thirteen years.

Jackie resides on the Blood reserve, where she is now employed with the Blood Tribe Administration. She was involved in the second phase of the interviews and did all her own translations.

HENRY BIG THROAT

Henry Big Throat received his first years of education at St Mary's residential school. He received his BA in sociology and is currently employed by the Red Crow Community College, Kainai. Henry is a fluent speaker of Blackfoot and now resides on the Blood reserve. He assisted with the last and final phase of the research.

DENNIS FIRST RIDER

Dennis First Rider received his early years of education at St Mary's residential school. He recently returned from the University of Regina and is currently living on the Blood reserve.

Dennis is a fluent speaker of Blackfoot and is currently on contract with the Blood Tribe Administration. He assisted with the collection and compilation of the elders' biographies.

SANDRA ABERDEEN

Sandra Aberdeen graduated from St Mary's high school in 1983 and subsequently attended college and university. She is now completing her studies in social work.

Sandra has been employed as an interpretative guide supervisor at Head Smashed In Buffalo Jump Interpretative Centre, as an instructional assistant at Lethbridge Community College, and as a research assistant for the Blood Tribe Administration.

She has lived most of her life on the Blood reserve. She speaks and understands the Blackfoot language and was involved in the first phase of the research.

The Peigan Nation

FRED NORTH PEIGAN
Born October 9, 1921
Father: Victor North Peigan
Mother: Nora North Peigan
Fred was born on the Peigan reserve and was raised by his grand-parents following the native custom. He spent most of his time with them when he was a small child, but was enrolled at the age of seven in the St Cyprian residential school. He attended this school until he was eighteen years old.

In the early part of his life, he and his family lived at the east end of the reserve. When tragedy struck twice, the family decided to move closer to the community of Brocket in 1945. Since the time he married and was awarded a home, he has lived in Brocket.

As a young man, he worked at seasonal and part-time employment. Later he could no longer work because of physical handicaps, though he continued to actively support his church. He was called on to be one of the elder advisers in the controversial *Lone Fighter* v. *the Province* case.

DAVIS CROW EAGLE
Born November 4, 1941
Davis Crow Eagle was born and raised on the Peigan reserve. He was enrolled in school at a very late age, since the boarding schools were filled to capacity at that time and he had to wait for a day school to be built and opened in the 1950s. Unfortunately, he only attended school for a very short time.

He joined the army cadets in his teens and went on to serve

with the reserve army. In later years he attended numerous training programs offered by the Peigan administration. He was on the police force servicing the Peigan people and was an ambulance driver for the Peigan reserve. He was also involved in many other programs, having to do with employment or otherwise.

JOE CROWSHOE
Born January 3, 1909
Father: Willy Crowshoe (Deer Chief)
Mother: Annie Buffalo
Key informants – Grassy Water, Annie Buffalo, Mrs Many Guns
Sun Dance (Peigan) ceremonialist
Thunder medicine bundle ceremonialist
Spiritual elder for the Peigan Nation
Honorary Doctor of Law, the University of Calgary/Order of Canada Recipient
Hereditary band council

RAY CROSS CHILD
Born July 18, 1926
Though now a member of the Peigan tribe, Ray Cross Child was born on the Blood reserve. He grew up there and was educated at the reserve's boarding school.

Ray spent a great deal of his time off the reserve as a young man. For many years he was employed in places such as Fort Macleod, Magrath, and the United States. Through his marriage, he changed his tribal membership and became a Peigan. Since then, he has remained with the Peigan.

LOUISE ENGLISH
Born December 31, 1932
Louise English was born and raised on the Peigan reserve. She received her education at the Sacred Heart Residential School, a boarding school that was situated on the Peigan reserve.

She has served on the band council and has actively supported numerous programs on and off the reserve. She has travelled to many areas of the country to promote First Nations interests and assist in whatever way she could. Because of her strong beliefs, she has made several trips to Lac St Anne in northern Alberta.

WIDOW ELSIE CROW SHOE
Born June 4, 1927
Elsie Crow Shoe was born and raised on the Peigan reserve. She is fluent in the Blackfoot language and familiar with Blackfoot culture and traditions. As a young person, she was enrolled in a boarding school, but a Euro-Canadian education was not one of her primary objectives. In her upbringing on the reserve, she had received the teachings of the Native, the Blackfoot. This influence was dominant and she has maintained this way of life to date.

She was the wife of a head chief for approximately twenty years and was a remarkable role model. She belongs to the Short Pipe Medicine Bundle Society and the Brave Dog Society. Added to this, she actively participates in many other Blackfoot ceremonies and rituals.

NICK SMITH
Born September 25, 1920
Nick Smith was born and raised on the Peigan reserve. He has never left it and did not receive any formal education. His knowledge and wisdom are credited to his traditional Blackfoot upbringing. He worked at part-time and seasonal employment on the reserve.

He married Agnes Crow Eagle. They had seven children and now have fifty grandchildren and nineteen great-grandchildren. He and Agnes took in foster children for many years. Recently Nick became a widower.

He is now an active member of the elder program in the community. The teachings he received from past elders he now gratefully shares with us.

REGGIE CROW SHOE
Born 1951
Red Book Project Manager
Cultural Renewal Project
Raised in the Ninamska tradition, Reggie Crow Shoe has been active in the Cecil Horn Society. The thunder medicine pipe bundle was transferred to Reggie from Browning, Montana, in 1974. He is still a member of the Ninamska Society. In 1985 he put

up a Sun Dance. He has also worked with Alberta Culture on historic sites, using the training he received from past Ninamska members. He attends the University of Calgary and the University of Lethbridge.

EVA BAD EAGLE
Eva was married to Raymond Bad Eagle and both were prominent elders. Eva was especially active in elder organizations and societies.

SALLY PROVOST
Father: Little Moustache
Mother: Black Bear
Sally's parents were both well-known elders. Sally was active in agricultural organizations and was known for her fine bead work. Her husband, Charlie Provost Sr, was a war veteran, a prominent farmer, and active in agricultural circles. Charlie was also an important and influential storyteller. He was a popular man and people liked to gather around him to hear his stories.

WALTER BASTIEN
Walter was both a lifetime councillor and an elected councillor. He served approximately twenty-eight years on council and was active in the Indian Association of Alberta. Walter was knowledgable about the history surrounding Treaty 7 and was very involved in the cultural affairs of his community.

EDDIE BAD EAGLE
Eddie was able to pass on the stories of his father, Pat Bad Eagle, who had great knowledge of the Peigan culture. Pat Bad Eagle was a rancher, a strong traditionalist, and a rodeo enthusiast. He served on council in the 1970s, was a Sun Dance ceremony sponsor, and was very influential both politically and culturally.

CECILE (GRASSY WATER) MANY
   GUNS
TOM YELLOWHORN
ANNIE BUFFALO

JACK CROW
JAMES SMALL LEGS
MR AND MRS JACK CROW SR
TOM BIG SMOKE
ALLAN PRAIRIE CHICKEN
JOE CROW SHOE SR
MR AND MRS BILLY STRIKES
   WITH A GUN
TOM BULL PEN
BEN WHITE COW
PAUL SMITH

The two groups above were elders interviewed prior to the present project. The first group was interviewed in the 1970s and the second in the 1980s

The elders in the first group directly knew some of the people who had made Treaty 7. Cecile Many Guns' grandfather White Striped Dog marked Treaty 7; Annie Buffalo's parents were both present at Treaty 7; Tom Yellowhorn's mother, Mrs Little Leaf, was the sister of Chief Red Crow; and Jack Crow's mother and father were both present at Blackfoot Crossing in 1877.

Davis Crow Eagle, Floyd Smith, and Hugh Crow Eagle gave me (Walter Hildebrandt) information on these elders, whom they preferred to describe as a group. Most of these elders spoke little or no English. It was emphasized that they were traditionalists and among them were spiritually powerful people and skilled linguists. Their knowledge was deep.

Davis, Floyd, and Hugh indicated that two significant observations could be made about these two groups of elders. The first was that they understood the value of living in peace. They remembered that peace was said to have been the most important aspect of Treaty 7. Treaty 7 to them had been a deeply spiritual and solemn moment, a time when the tribes had gathered and had agreed to live in peace, not only with the Crown, but with the other tribes present. The elders said that they have never broken this promise and since that time have never risen against the Crown or against any of the other tribes. The smoking of the pipe at Blackfoot Crossing *after* (not before) the treaty was finalized was an indication of how seriously and solemnly their ancestors had taken the agreement. The second observation is that they spoke from the heart. Although most of them did not know English and were not interested in legal or technical matters, they understood that the true intent and original meaning of the treaty was that all those present should live in peace and that the bounty of the land should be shared with the newcomers.

INTERVIEWERS

JOHNNY SMITH

Johnny was well informed about his people's history through his father, Tom Yellowhorn, who was very knowledgable about Peigan culture. Johnny worked as an interviewer in the 1970s.

HUGH CROW EAGLE

Hugh received his early education at Sacred Heart boarding school on the Peigan reserve and then attended high school in Edmonton. He has served three terms as an elected councillor and has done considerable community work over the years. His father, Robert, was very knowledgable about Blackfoot culture, and his mother, Theresa, whose maiden name is Born With a Tooth, was related to Chief Sitting on Eagle Tail Feathers, who made Treaty 7 as the leader of the Peigan in 1877.

Hugh is an experienced interviewer, translator, and linguist. He was greatly influenced by his parents, who were strong traditionalists. Hugh has spent much time over the years learning from medicine men and healers. The important cultural and spiritual leaders he learned from included Crowflag, Big Face Chief, Nathan Many Fingers, Coldweather, and One Gun.

The Siksika Nation

LILLY MANY BEARS
Born May 14, 1928
Father: Fred Stud Horse
Mother: Maggie Stablast
Lilly went to school at Old Sun residential school, where she finished grade 7. In those days the students had to leave school when the Indian agents told them to, and they were then expected to marry. In school the girls were taught cooking, sewing, and other skills that would help them make a good home.

Lilly's godfather, Earl Calf Child, taught her many things about the Blackfoot culture. She participated in the Sun Dance alongside her parents and grandparents, seeing firsthand the ceremonies performed on these occasions. Though not a member of any society, she could take part in these ceremonies because her parents were members.

PHILIP MANY BEARS
Born April 20, 1925
Father: Lyndon Many Bears
Mother: Dorothy (Akotsipiksakis)
Philip attended Crowfoot residential school and made it to grade 4. Philip has been a member of the Prairie Chicken, Crazy Dog, Horn, and Deer societies since the days of the Sun Dance, but today he does not participate as regularly as he once did because of ill health and the decline of the societies themselves. Now he only attends the Elders Retreat, which is held each spring.

NICHOLAS BREAKER
Born May 2, 1965
Father: Nicholas Breaker
Mother: Marie Breaker (*née* Pretty Young Man)
Nicholas is the grandson of the late traditional chief Leo Young-
man and Alma (Crow Chief) Youngman. His paternal grandpar-
ents were Fred Breaker and Ada (Turning Robe) Breaker. Ni-
cholas's grandparents on both sides were active in the Siksika
Nation societies, having memberships in the Horn, Prairie
Chicken, Crazy Dog, and Deer societies. Within recent years
Nicholas himself was initiated into the Prairie Chicken and Crazy
Dog societies. Nicholas attended Crowfoot Indian day school and
graduated from grade 12. He has been active in doing research
alongside his grandfather Leo Youngman and has learned many
things from his research.

ARTHUR LITTLE LIGHT
Born February 12, 1917
Father: Peter Little Light
Mother: Nellie Little Light
Mother's Father: Stump
Peter's Mother: Issomiyaki
Arthur attended Old Sun residential school, which was located
in the North Camp Flats, and went up to grade 6. He was not
a member of any society. Arthur worked for the bank housing
for fifteen years. After he retired, he attended powwows all over
the country as a dancer. He worked all his life for the Siksika
people.

ROY AYOUNGMAN
Born July 4, 1931
Father: Anthony Ayoungman
Mother: Rosie Ayoungman (*née* Yellow Fly)
Grandparents: Anthony Crow Shoe, Close Range (paternal); Yel-
low Fly, Spotted Butterfly (maternal)
Roy attended Old Sun boarding school and went up to grade
8. He did not hold any society membership. Roy was a rancher
and ran a horse and cattle operation. He was a rodeo competitor
and also owned his own rodeo stock which was used for the

rodeos. In the years 1956 and 1957 he sat on the band council, one of the younger band councillors at the time. He was one of the first members of the All Indian Rodeo Association and helped develop the guidelines for the association.

GEORGE STABLAST
Born May 28, 1928
Father: Louis Running Rabbit
Mother: Miss Crane Bear
Grandparents: Eugene Stablast (paternal); Berrie Woman (maternal)
George attended Old Sun boarding school and went up to grade 4. He held no membership in any society. George is an artist and was involved with the Calgary Stampede in the 1960s (Indian Village).

JOSEPHINE WEASEL HEAD
Born March 30, 1922
Father: Mark Spring Chief
Mother: Louise Black
Grandfather: Francis Wolf Shoe
Josephine attended Crowfoot boarding school and went up to grade 7. She was involved with the Calgary Stampede in the 1960s (Indian Village).

FRANK TURNING ROBE
Born October 28, 1925
Frank attended Old Sun boarding school but cannot recall what grade he reached before he was taken out of school by his parents for some reason. He made his home in the west end of the reserve. He holds no membership in any society but is a strong believer in the ways of the Siksika people. He attended the Sun Dances but only as an observer. Frank sat on council in the late 1980s.

EARL CALF CHILD
Born 1898
Father: Joe Calf Child
Earl attended the first Anglican boarding school located in the North Camp Flats, reaching grade 12. He was a translator for

the Siksika people and the Indian agents employed by Indian
Affairs. He played an active political role in the reserve administration. He held a seat on the council.

AUGUSTINE YELLOW SUN
Born 1898
Father: Many Shots
Mother: Akiiya
Augustine attended the Anglican residential school.

JOE POOR EAGLE
Born June 2, 1907
Father: George Stanley
Mother: Curly Hair (later married Bob Poor Eagle)
Joe was born in the Cypress Hills and later moved to Maple
Creek, Saskatchewan. After his mother married Bob Poor Eagle,
the family moved to the Blackfoot reserve. Joe ran five Sun Dan-
ces, which proves that he held a membership in the Horn Society.
He attended St Joseph's residential school which is now known
as Crowfoot School. Joe was an active participant in rodeos and
worked on his ranch until his passing.

ALMA PRETTY YOUNG MAN
Born May 6, 1927
Father: George Crow Chief
Mother: Delores Sitting Eagle
Grandparents: Good Eagle (paternal); Bear Robe (maternal)
Alma attended Crowfoot boarding school and went up to grade
8. She married the late Leo Pretty Young Man. They were (and
she still is) active with the Indian Village at the Calgary Stampede. Beginning in 1962 the couple worked at ranching and farming. They were also involved in the horseracing business. Alma
is a member of the Buffalo Woman's Society.

STEVE MANY FIRES
Born November 15, 1915
Father: Tom Many Fires
Mother: Eagle Woman
Grandfather: Eagle Rib
Steve attended St Joseph boarding school (Crowfoot School) and

went up to grade 8. He played hockey and participated in the rodeos. He also attended many powwows all over the country, performing as a singer and dancer.

JIM BLACK
Born August 1893
Father: Black One
Mother: Rain Woman
Jim attended Crowfoot School.

FRANCIS BLACK
Born 1903
Father: Black One
Mother: Rain Woman
Francis attended Crowfoot School.

JACK BIG EYE
Born 1904
Parent: Nato aimonisi
Jack did not attend school and was not a member of any society. He was known for his knowledge of the Siksika history and spoke very highly of his people. He firmly believed that the Siksika were a strong body of people.

ALLAN WOLFLEG SR
Born October 18, 1941
Father: Mark Wolfleg
Mother: Mary Margaret Little Chief
Grandparents: Joseph Little Chief and Jane Eagle Rib (maternal); Wolfleg and Einimaki (Catch Woman) (paternal)
Allan attended Old Sun boarding school and went up to grade 11. He later continued his education at Jasper Place in Edmonton. He is an active member of the Prairie Chicken Society. Allan's great-grandfather Eagle Rib was one of the original signers of Treaty 7. In 1977 Allan coordinated a re-enactment of the treaty signing. In attendance was Prince Charles, the great-grandson of Queen Victoria, who had been on the throne in 1877. Allan is a historian and is known for his knowledge of Siksika history. He was brought up by his grandparents and participated in many Sun Dances alongside them.

MARGARET BAD BOY
Born March 10, 1900
Parents: Three Suns; Nitainiki (Lone Killer)
Margaret married Dick Bad Boy. She did not attend school but
has lived in the Shouldice area of the reserve all her life. She
helped her husband farm their land and also helped with their
herd of five hundred cattle and their horses. She is a member
of the Motoki (Buffalo Woman's Society). She raised many of
the reserve's children because she did not have any of her own.

JULIA WRIGHT
Born May 12, 1925
Father: Max Three Suns
Mother: Jane Trying to Fly (related to Old Sun)
Grandparents: Three Suns (Bernadette); Trying to Fly (Small
Woman)
Julia attended Crowfoot School and went up to grade 6. In those
days they were taught in a different way; the girls were trained
to be homemakers. Julia has two pipe bundles and is an active
member of the Buffalo Woman's Society. She has twelve brothers
and sisters.

HENRY SUN WALK
Born May 17, 1914
Henry has been a farmer all his life and has attended many pow-
wows. He was a singer and dancer. He attended Crowfoot
School, reaching grade 6. He mentioned that he learned more
English when he was working than when he was in school.

REVEREND ARTHUR AYOUNGMAN SR
Born August 7, 1919
Father and grandfather: Maistoitsikin (Crowshoe)
Arthur was born on the Siksika Nation reserve into the clan
called "Saayiiks." Like others his age, he spoke only Siksika as
a youngster and spent many hours with family and clan elders.
He attended Old Sun school, the Anglican residential school on
the reserve. Upon leaving school he married Nora Waterchief.
Their ten children, who all spoke Siksika fluently as their first
language, were taught to be proud of their heritage. Arthur has
always actively participated in Siksika cultural activities and was
at one time leader of the Prairie Chicken Society.

Arthur recalls many of the elders' stories – for example, he was told, and shown, where the western boundary of the Siksika Nation reserve should have been. Arthur was elected to several terms on the Siksika Chief and Council and ran for chief a couple of times. When he was only twenty-five years old, he was selected by some Siksika elders to be hereditary chief; however, his own clan elders advised him to wait for a few years.

Joe Crowfoot, a former chief of the tribe, passed on to Arthur the tipi owned by Chief Crowfoot, signatory to Treaty 7. In the elaborate tipi-transfer ceremony, Joe indicated that he and his wife had selected Arthur to receive the tipi because of his fine character and ability to relate well to all people. They knew that the tipi would be well taken care of and that it would be given a rightful prominent place in encampments for all to see as a reminder of the proud Siksika heritage.

Arthur is well known for his gentleness and kindness and often volunteers to help individuals and organizations. He eventually became a lay reader, deacon, and then priest.

ADRIAN SOLWAY
Born March 26, 1953
Father: Adam Solway
Mother: Rosie Medicine Shield
Adrian attended Crowfoot School for most of his school years. He helped his father with the ranching and farming and is still working with cattle at this time. He married Cheryl Smith and has four children.

BERNARD TAILFEATHERS
Born March 25, 1913
Bernard went to school on the reserve but later left to attend Bible school in the United States. When he returned, he was very active in this religion until his passing. He holds no membership in any society.

INTERVIEWER AND TRANSLATOR

NICK BREAKER JR
Nick completed the interviews of the Siksika elders and also did the translations.

The Stoney (Bearspaw) Nation

WILLIAM (BILL) MCLEAN
Born December 1, 1920
Father: George Mclean (Chief Walking Buffalo)
Bill Mclean is a respected elder among the Stoney Nakoda First nations at Morley, Alberta. He is highly thought of for his wisdom, knowledge, and leadership. He comes from a family of respected leaders going back to the pre-treaty period.

George Mclean, Bill's father, was present as a boy of seven at the making of Treaty 7 in 1877. George received his elementary education at the Morley orphanage school and then transferred to the Red Deer Industrial School when he was sixteen years old. Later he attended St John's College in Winnipeg. After two or three years he returned to the West and worked for the RCMP in Calgary, but disliking the duties, he left the force and went to work as a blacksmith before returning to his people. Soon afterwards Chief Jacob Bearspaw, who had helped make Treaty 7, asked him to act as an interpreter for the Stoney council, which he agreed to do. He married shortly thereafter and served as a councillor from 1907 to 1912, becoming chief in 1913, when Chief Moses Bearspaw died. Moses Bearspaw was the son of Jacob Bearspaw; the chieftainship had been passed on to Moses in 1903 when his father died. As an interpreter and leader, George Mclean knew firsthand the true and original intent of Treaty 7. This oral history he passed on to his eldest son, William (Bill).

In terms of the oral history of Treaty 7, Bill's maternal side also had noteworthy relatives. His great-grandmother was Mrs

John Chiniquay, the wife of Chief Chiniquay, who accepted the treaty for the Chiniki Nation. Chief Chiniquay had a son and two daughters, one being Bill's grandmother. Chief Chiniquay's other daughter was married to George Crawler. George had a younger brother called Hector Crawler, who was Bill's maternal grandfather. In other words, the Crawler brothers each married one of Chiniquay's daughters.

The brothers had both held positions in council at one time or other for the Chiniki band. George Crawler served as a councillor at the signing of Treaty 7 and remained a councillor until his death in 1897. Hector served as a councillor from 1906 to 1919 and as a chief from 1922 to 1932.

The aforementioned people in particular, as well as others, all had knowledge of the spirit and intent of Treaty 7. This knowledge was passed on from generation to generation and eventually to Bill Mclean.

Bill's father, George, was known worldwide as "Chief Walking Buffalo." Beginning in the 1950s until his death in 1967, Walking Buffalo travelled the globe on behalf of the moral rearmament movement that promoted world peace. His biography, *Tatanga Mani*, was written by Grant McEwan.

Bill Mclean served as chief and councilor at one time or other over the past years. In the years 1960–65 he was a councillor for the Bearspaw Nation. He was chief in 1967–68, 1971–73, and 1975–78.

LAZARUS WESLEY
Born February 12, 1916, Morley, Alberta
Lazarus Wesley is a respected elder and a vigorous advocate of treaty rights. He spent his younger years on the Stoney reserve at Morley and at Bighorn, where his family often camped. In his youth he followed the traditional hunting trails along the eastern slopes and was taught the traditional ways of his people. He received some formal education at the Morley residential school.

Lazarus is the grandson of Peter Wesley, who was chief of the Wesley Nation from 1903 to 1935. Peter was well known among the Stoneys and the White people of his time for his proficiency as a big game hunter. He was given the name "Ta Otha," meaning great huntsman or game killer. The White people called him "Moose Killer," a misnomer, a mistranslation of "Ta Otha." Because of his dissatisfaction with the way the government was treating his people, Peter led his clan up north in the 1890s to their traditional territory on the Kootenay Plains where the Bighorn reserve is now located.

Peter was present at the making of Treaty 7. He was a younger cousin of Chief Jacob Bearspaw, leader of the Bearspaw Nation. According to Nakoda custom, offspring whose fathers are brothers or whose mothers are sisters are termed brothers or sisters, and Peter and Jacob were such. The two were said to be close, and they referred to each other as "brother." They were especially close at the Treaty 7 gathering, exercising their horses daily in anticipation of a possible outbreak of war.

The stories Peter had about the treaty were passed down through the generations to Lazarus. Lazarus is looked upon today as a person who is knowledgable about Stoney history, culture, and customs. Lazarus served as a Bearspaw band councillor for the years 1960–62 and 1964–68. He is a highly respected orator and lay preacher in the United Church of Canada.

DOROTHY RIDER
Born June 22, 1921, Morley, Alberta
Dorothy Rider was born in Morley and grew up mostly in the Morley area. Although based in Morley, her family had frequently travelled along the foothills from the Kootenay Plains to Waterton Lakes National Park. Her mother died when she was three years old, so her older sister raised her. Dorothy attended residential school for nine years, until she turned sixteen.

Dorothy's knowledge of Treaty 7 comes from various sources but her main informant was her father, Enoch Rider. The stories Enoch passed on to his daughter came from his father, Paul Rider. Paul had been present at the treaty making and had heard what Chief Bearspaw had said. Later on, in 1906, Paul became a councillor for the Bearspaw band, but only for a brief time. He died in 1907.

Jonas Rider was another person whose knowledge of the treaty was passed down to Dorothy. He was the son of Paul Rider's older brother. He too had served as a councillor, from 1919 to 1956.

Dorothy also heard stories from her cousin Julia Amos, whose father was Moses Bearspaw. Moses took over the chieftainship in 1904 after his father, Jacob Bearspaw, passed away. He was the Bearspaw chief until his death in 1912.

Dorothy's aunt, Peggy Bearspaw, her father's sister, was married to David Bearspaw. David was a son of Chief Jacob Bearspaw. He too took over the chieftainship when it was his time. He was chief from 1917 until his death in 1956. When he died, his son, John Bearspaw, cousin to Dorothy, took over as chief. John was the last hereditary chief before the election system came into place in 1957.

Stoney Nakoda (Wesley) Nation

ELDERS

LOU CRAWLER, SR
Born April 15, 1911, Morley, Alberta
Father: George Crawler
Grandfather: George Crawler (minor chief at Treaty 7)
Lou has resided in Morley all of his life. He was raised by his father from the time he was four years old, when his mother passed away. He was educated at the boarding school in Morley and grew up to be a familiar political figure around Morley. He was elected as a band councillor in the 1950s and was very instrumental in the affairs of local government. His political status and knowledge came from his famous forefathers, who were instrumental in the making of Treaty 7.

Lou's father was George Crawler, and his grandfather was the George Crawler who signed the Treaty 7 document. His paternal grandmother's father was John Chiniquay, the Chiniki chief who accepted treaty in 1877. Lou learned firsthand about the spirit and intent of Treaty 7 through the oral history of the Chiniki Nakoda Nation.

DORIS ROLLINGMUD (ROLLING IN MUD)
Born May 25, 1932, Morley, Alberta
Parents: George and Georgia Rolling in Mud
Doris was raised on the Stoney reserve at Morley from birth, and she grew up in the midst of Stoney traditionalism. She received some education from the Morley residential school as far as grade 5. Her parents were George and Georgia Rolling in Mud; her paternal grandparents were Isaac and Mary Ann Rol-

ling in Mud; and her maternal grandparents were John and Leah Hunter. These forefathers were recognized as respected clan leaders in their time. She received a wealth of information on the treaties from her father and her late aunt Mary Jane Chiniquay, whose husband was Moses Chiniquay, a descendant of Chief John Chiniquay, who accepted Treaty 7.

MATTHEW HUNTER
Born September 15, 1907

Matthew Hunter was born on the Stoney reserve to Jean (*née* Patrick) and Elijah Hunter and has resided in Morley all his life. Matthew had a sister (Sophia Ear) and a brother (Albert Bearspaw), both now deceased. Matthew's maternal grandparents were Emma House and John Bearspaw. Matthew doesn't remember much about his paternal grandparents, only that Elijah Hunter's father was known as "Ya me Utha" or "Hunter." Matthew's maternal grandparents were the elders who gave him information about the treaty and Stoney history. As far as he knows, none of his relatives or ancestors held political office.

Matthew's maternal grandparents were people who knew and practised Indian medicine. They were blessed with a gift of healing through this knowledge. They gathered a wide variety of medicinal herbs and roots which they used to cure illnesses. This knowledge of Indian medicine allowed them to help others, and when the influenza epidemic of the 1920s hit the Stoney people, they were able to save some lives.

Matthew went to day school for three years, from age thirteen to sixteen, which was around 1920–23. He was going to be sent to school in Red Deer, Alberta, but his grandmother Emma wouldn't allow it. After this he was put in the Morley residential school, but the school let him go after he repeatedly skipped classes. Matthew used to enter rodeo events such as steer-riding, saddle-bronco, and bareback. He was also a jockey, winning some of the horseraces in which he participated.

When Matthew was eighteen years old, he married Agnes Wesley. They had four children (Roy, Laurier, Violet, and Veronica Hunter), all still living. He was with Agnes until 1945, when she died of tuberculosis. Matthew married his second wife, Elizabeth Twoyoungmen, in 1947 and is still with her. They had eleven children altogether.

When Matthew was twenty years old, he obtained his "A" licence, which allowed him to earn a living as a truck driver. He also got a chauffeur's licence, which he kept for fifteen years. This would have allowed him to drive a limousine or taxicab. He also used to work in the Seebe General Store. Matthew was a councillor for the Wesley band for two consecutive terms, from 1962 to 1965. While in council he helped to negotiate a land lease to a YMCA group, who based their summer camp where the present Nakoda Lodge is located. He also helped to secure housing funds for band members. In those days, the band usually held council meetings once a month and the council members were paid an hororarium of $100 per meeting.

Matthew was also a church participant and sang in the United Church choir at Morley. When he was a child, his mother, Jean, used to play the organ or piano at church. She had gone to school and had acquired a little bit of education, learning to speak English fairly well, something most of the Stoney women couldn't do. Matthew's half-sister Anna Twoyoungmen had a grade 6 education, which was considered a high level at that time (the 1940s). Matthew used to sing at powwows and special ceremonies and he also participated in the Sun Dance. He would be picked to be the announcer or caller at such ceremonies. In recent years, as an elder, Matthew has put up four Sun Dances. He once owned a peace pipe, a rattle, and an eagle whistle but lost everything when his house burned down in 1994. His maternal grandparents owned a medicine bundle, but when they passed away, it was burned and the knowledge died with the owners.

CLARICE KOOTENAY
Born December 12, 1944, Morley, Alberta
Clarice is representative of the young adults interviewed who have both a special knowledge of Treaty 7 and a postsecondary education. She was born at her parents' home in Morley on her grandfather's homestead. She spent her first five years at Morley and the next five or so at the Dick Gardner Ranch, where her father worked. The ranch is south of Longview, Alberta, close to the Eden Valley reserve.

Clarice grew up hearing stories of the treaty from her late grandfather, George Mclean (Walking Buffalo), who had extensive knowledge of the treaty (see Bill Mclean's biography). Clarice also heard stories from her mother, Mary Kootenay, and her aunties Florence Dixon and the late Elizabeth Bearspaw. Florence Dixon is the wife of the late Paul Dixon Sr, who was from the James Dixon clan. James Dixon, whose stories were passed on to his descendants, including Paul's generation, was a signatory at Treaty 7 as a councillor for the Dixon band (Eden Valley). Elizabeth was the wife of the late Johnny Bearspaw, the last hereditary chief of the Bearspaw band. His grandfather was Chief Jacob Bearspaw. Clarice's uncle Bill Mclean is also a source of Stoney history.

Clarice also heard a lot of stories about Treaty 7 from elders who are not with us anymore. In the early 1970s she worked in the Stoney Cultural Education Program when it first started. Part of the program involved interviewing the elders of that time, and this work allowed her the enviable privilege of learning from them.

Clarice's father, the late Joe Kootenay Jr, was a Bearspaw band councillor from 1957 to 1961.

ROSEANNE TWOYOUNGMEN
Born October 12, 1935, Morley, Alberta

Roseanne Twoyoungmen was born in Morley and grew up there, but she also spent some of her young years at the Eden Valley reserve. She comes from a family that knows the stories of Treaty 7, for her ancestors were present at the treaty making. Her mother died when she was seven months old, so her paternal grandparents, John and Flora Salter, looked after her. Soon after, her late aunt, Jenny Salter, took her in and raised her.

John Salter was a step-grandfather of Roseanne's, as her biological grandfather had passed away. John was a good storykeeper and storyteller who was present at the treaty as a young boy. He had never forgotten either what he had seen at the historic event or the stories he had heard from his parents, and he passed these on to succeeding generations, which included his daughter Jenny and step-granddaughter Roseanne.

Roseanne's biological paternal relatives also had stories of the treaty. Her great-grandfather, Thomas Twoyoungmen, had been present at the treaty making. Her grandmother, Flora, had married into the Twoyoungmen clan. Her first husband was a son of Thomas's, also called Thomas Twoyoungmen. Although the

first Thomas was not a political figure, he was very much part
of the Stoney presence at Treaty 7. There were stories about
his uncanny knowledge of horses and his participation in the
horse trading after the treaty was signed.

Roseanne's father, Tom Twoyoungmen, was a councillor for
the Bearspaw band from 1961 to 1963 and a chief from 1963
to 1966 and 1968 to 1971.

LILY WESLEY
Born March 13, 1921, Morley, Alberta
(Married to Lazarus Wesley)
Lily Wesley was born and raised in Morley, obtaining her formal
education at the Morley residential school. She was raised in
the traditional way of life and is an adamant believer in what
her forefathers taught her. She is very knowledgable, having
learned from two prominent families, the Bearspaw clan from
her mother's side and the Wildman family from her father's. She
heard stories of the treaty from her paternal grandfather, Daniel
Wildman Sr, who was at the treaty. Daniel was part Cree and
part Métis and therefore had knowledge of the English language.

Daniel stated that a lot of what the First Nations chiefs understood at Treaty 7 was never written down. He said that each
time a White person spoke, a lot of time was taken writing down
his words, but when the chiefs spoke, very little time was given
to writing. Since he had a command of the English language,
he knew that only a very little of what the chiefs said was written
down, that only a few of their words were acknowledged. This
information is corroborated by Bert Wildman, a grandson of Daniel Wildman Sr and twin brother to Lily.

Lily's father, Daniel Wildman Jr, was a Chiniki band councillor
from 1920 until his resignation in 1933. He was also a chief
for the band in 1959–60.

ARCHIE DANIELS
Born February 14, 1918
Archie is a Bearspaw band member and has been a resident of
Eden Valley reserve since its inception in 1948. He was born
in the foothills. Because his father was a member of the "Jimmy
Dixon Band" (see Mark Lefthand's biography, below), Archie
grew up in the Pekisko area, in the proximity of Longview, Al-

berta. However, during his early childhood years he attended the Morley residential school in the school months, but always went back south in the summer to be with his father, Paul Daniels, who worked at the 44 Ranch in the Pekisko area.

The primary sources of information on the treaty for Archie were his father and his aunt. His mother had died when he was two years old, so his aunt looked after him until his father remarried.

A relative of Archie's acquired some renown at the treaty making. This was Jimmy Jock Bird, the interpreter hired by the government to replace Jerry Potts. However, information about him is scarce. As Archie puts it, "He was a half-breed, a Métis" who moved around extensively, eventually settling in Havre, Montana, and dying there in the 1930s. He was the older brother of Archie's maternal grandmother.

Archie worked as a Bearspaw band researcher during the 1970s on the oral history project initiated by TARR (Treaty and Aboriginal Rights Research), and was able to talk to elders who knew about Stoney history and the treaty making. He thus received a wealth of information from the Stoney elders, some of whom have passed on.

MARK LEFTHAND
Born March 25, 1898, foothills of southern Alberta
At the time of writing (January 1996), Mark Lefthand is the oldest living Stoney band member. He has been a resident of the Eden Valley reserve since its inception. Originally a private ranch, Eden Valley was granted reserve status in 1948.

Stoney oral history tells us that the Nakoda people were nomadic. Several groups or clans constantly migrated throughout the foothills, some staying away from the Morley area for years and others making the journey to Morley an annual trek. One of the most notable groups was the one led by James Dixon. (As a Bearspaw councillor, Dixon was one of the signatories of Treaty 7 for the Stoney Nation.) This band was referred as the "Pekisko Group" or the "Jimmy Dixon Band" by the authorities who dealt with them in the early post-treaty era. Mark's family belonged to this clan.

The clan's favourite territory was the area along the Highwood River and Pekisko Creek in what is now southern Alberta (near

Longview). Thus, the term "Pekisko Group" was attached to
them. Since this clan was, in terms of relations, closest to the
Bearspaw clan, it was included with that band at the making
of the treaty. After the treaty, its members were, in a sense,
forced to move to Morley, away from their traditional territory.

Because of the Dixon clan's move to Morley, Mark spent some
of his earlier years at or closer to the Bow Valley. However,
as time went by, hardships were experienced in the Morley area.
As a consequence of this – and because they still longed for
their habitual region – in the 1930s members of the clan decided
to leave Morley permanently. They moved back to the land of
their forefathers, land which they were used to. They had over
the years, even after the treaty, continually trekked back to hunt,
spending a good portion of the year in that country.

Even though the original leaders of the treaty era had passed
away, the leaders of the 1940s worked hard to acquire land for
the group. The Eden Valley reserve was eventually established
in 1948 and added to in subsequent years.

Mark's primary source of information about the spirit and intent of Treaty 7 was his father, Ezra Lefthand. Ezra, as a boy
of fifteen, witnessed the historic event. He was therefore able
to give firsthand accounts of what he himself had observed and
heard, as well as what his parents, Mr and Mrs John Lefthand,
had told him about the Stoney understanding of the treaty. In
turn, Mark passes these stories to succeeding generations.

JOE BROWN TWOYOUNGMEN
Born June 6, 1922, Morley, Alberta
Joe was the first born of his family and had five siblings: Elizabeth
(Matthew) Hunter, Christine (Felix) Poucette, Mary Twoyoung-
men, Helen Twoyoungmen, and Hazel (Tom) Hunter, who passed
away in the early eighties. Joe Brown's maternal grandparents
were Mr and Mrs George Poucette; George's Stoney name was
Mi schen. Joe Brown's paternal grandparents were Mr and Mrs
Joe Dixon Twoyoungmen; this Joe Dixon Twoyoungmen's
mother was Aggie Bigstoney, a Stoney woman who married a
non-status Indian from north of Edmonton whose last name was
Brown. After she had given birth to Joe Dixon Twoyoungmen
(Joe Brown's grandfather), Aggie Bigstoney came back to Morley
and married a Stoney man named Dixon. Aggie married a third

time, and this husband, named Twoyoungmen, adopted her son Joe. This is how Joe Brown Twoyoungmen got his name, although the last name Dixon was dropped.

Joe Brown's maternal great-grandfather was Jonas Goodstoney. Jonas was the leader who told him everything about Treaty 7 at Blackfoot Crossing. As a young man Jonas was at the treaty making in 1877 with his father Jacob Goodstoney, chief of the Wesley Nation at the time. Jonas told Joe that the Stoney men who were present at the treaty making were chosen by the Stoney people to be their leaders and to represent them at the treaty meeting. Chief Jacob Goodstoney died in 1885 and the chieftainship passed to his son Jonas, who remained in office until 1903.

Joe Brown said Joe Dixon Twoyoungmen was a medicine man who knew all about herbs, roots, and plants and could treat certain illnesses. This is the grandfather who taught Joe all he knows about Indian medicine today.

Joe Brown worked as a band constable back in the late fifties and early sixties. He also held political office as a councillor for the Wesley band for one term, from 1978 to 1979. Joe is now retired and lives on an old age pension, as his health is not too good.

GORDON CECIL
Born April 27, 1912
Parents: Mr and Mrs Sammy Cecil
Gordon Cecil was born in the White Rabbit Creek area near the Kootenay Plains. He married Evelyne Bigstoney and they had ten children; five are still living and five died as children. His paternal grandfather was Noah Cecil and his maternal grandfather was Silas Abraham from the Kootenay Plains area, after whom Abraham Lake is named.

Noah Cecil is the elder who told Gordon about the treaty making. Sammy (Gordon's father) and Noah were the Stoney interpreters at Blackfoot Crossing, along with the missionaries. Noah was originally a Cree from the Saddle Lake reserve but he moved to the Morley area with the Methodist missionaries George and John McDougall. No one in the Cecil family ever held political office until Irby Cecil, Gordon's son, was elected a councillor for the Wesley Nation.

Gordon Cecil was taught about Indian medicine, and he treated people in the traditional way of healing. His wife, Evelyne Cecil, also knew about Indian medicine. Evelyne was the granddaughter of Chief Jacob Goodstoney, who accepted the treaty. Amos Big-stoney was her uncle. Amos was a councillor from 1902 to 1935 and then served as chief from 1935 to 1938.

In the 1930s Gordon, along with a few other Stoney youths, went to school in Edmonton, where he completed grade 8. Gordon passed away on March 9, 1992, having survived his wife by exactly three years.

GEORGE EAR
Born March 13, 1910
Father: Jonas Ear
Mother: Sarah (*née* Twoyoungmen)
George Ear was born on the Stoney reserve, the second of thirteen children, though only seven grew up to be adults. Out of the seven that lived to be elders, only Elsie (Ear) Jimmy-John Lefthand is still living. The rest passed away in the 1980s and 1990s. George's great-grandfather was a spiritually gifted Stoney warrior named No-Ear-Holes, and he had three sons who were also spiritually gifted warriors. The Stoney and Christian names of the three sons were White Buffalo Calf Robe – George Ear (Jonas Ear and his sons were from this clan); Wolf-Comes-Into-View – Mark Ear (Paul Mark and his son belong to this clan); and Red Bear – Peter Ear (Moses Ear, Bill Ear, and Wallace Ear belong to this clan). The spirit guide of White Buffalo Calf Robe (George's grandfather) was the White Buffalo Calf. White Buffalo Calf Robe later became a peacemaker. He and some missionaries helped to keep the Cree from Hobbema from joining the Riel Resistance. He also was a councillor for the Wesley band for one term. His wife, George's grandmother, was Lelah Ear.

George's maternal grandparents were Thomas and Louise Twoyoungmen. All of George's ancestors were Nakoda Stoneys except his paternal grandmother, who was a northern Wood Stoney from Duffield. George has two daughters and three sons; the youngest and the oldest sons passed away in 1976 and 1986. The remaining son, Lawrence Ear, and the two daughters, Madeline Dixon and Virgina Ear, are still living. After George's first wife, Sophia, died in 1968, he married a Stoney woman named

Lily Poucette. George's grandfather George is the elder who told him about Treaty 7. George and his dad and brothers never held political office, although George was nominated as a councillor, losing by only a few votes back in 1969.

George went to school in Edmonton during the 1930s with other Stoney youths. He was there for a few years and completed grade 6.

None of George's relatives were medicine men or women. His family was more involved in Christianity than in Native religion. George was the elder adviser with the Stoney Cultural Education Program (SCEP) in the 1970s, and in the 1980s he and his son Lawrence compiled a Stoney dictionary and list of Stoney place names. He was a trusted adviser to his Chief and Council in his last years. He passed away on May 16, 1994, after suffering a stroke. On the day of his funeral, three wolves were observed sitting on the hill overlooking the Wesley band cemetery. The family regarded these as the spirits of his great uncles and grandfather, showing their respect and coming to get their great-grandson.

LAWRENCE EAR
Born May 4, 1938
Father: George Ear
Mother: Sophia (*née* Hunter)
Lawrence was born on the Stoney reserve and is a member of the Wesley band. Lawrence has two sisters, Madeline Dixon and Virginia Ear, who are still living, but his younger and older brother died in 1976 and 1986 respectively. Lawrence's paternal ancestors were No-Ear-Holes and No-Ear-Holes' sons, White Buffalo Calf Robe, Wolf-Comes-Into-View, and Red Bear (see George Ear's biography). His paternal grandfather was Jonas Ear.

Lawrence attended school in Morley, where he finished grade 9, and in 1960 he married Josephine Adams from Eden Valley. They have two daughters and four sons but one boy died as a baby. Lawrence's wife died in 1974 and he has not remarried since. Lawrence took some college courses at Mount Royal College in 1970. He also attended Lethbridge Community College in the mid-1970s. He worked for the Stoney Oral History Program and interviewed elders and band members to gather information for the Kootenay Plains land claims when the Big Horn dam was built in 1970–72. Lawrence also worked for the SCEP program during the 1970s. During the 1980s Lawrence worked with his father, George Ear, on compiling a Stoney dictionary and a list of Stoney place names.

In the early 1980s Lawrence began to lose interest in everything, and he has kept going downhill spiritually and emotionally, especially since 1984, when his father suffered a stroke.

ELVA LEFTHAND
Born November 18, 1928

Elva was born in the foothills and is a resident of the Eden Valley reserve, as her ancestors belonged to the Jimmy Dixon Band (see Mark Lefthand's biography). Thus, she is a lifetime Bearspaw band member. Even though she received some formal education at the Morley residential school, she firmly believes the stories the elders told her. Her stories of Treaty 7 came from her father, George Lefthand, who received knowledge of the treaty from his father, Frenchie (possibly a nickname), who was at the treaty making. Her grandfather was called "Frenchie" because he had some Métis blood in him. Elva's other main source of information was her maternal grandmother, Jean Aberneezer (at the time of writing her maiden name could not be obtained), who was thirteen years old at the time of the treaty. Jean described to her descendants what she had witnessed at the treaty gathering and also gave accounts of what had been told to her by her parents.

TOM LABELLE
Born March 21, 1895, Hobbema, Alberta

Tom, a Cree, married a Stoney woman around 1935 and was then inducted into the Stoney Nation. His wife, Elsie Hunter, had been married to his brother Scotty, who died. He had two sons and a daughter from a previous marriage and these three children also became Stoney members.

Tom's father was Louie Labelle but his mother is unknown. Tom joined the army in 1915 and was active in the First World War. He was taught the ways of the Stoney people by his father-in-law, John Hunter Sr. His three children were named Johnny, Peter, and Clara, all of whom grew up on the Stoney reserve.

CARL SIMEON

Born February 15, 1928, Morley, Alberta
Parents: Tom and Francis Simeon
Carl has lived in Morley all of his life. His paternal grandparents were John and Mary Jane Simeon. His maternal grandparents were John and Patsy; however, their last name is unknown. Carl was a very active member of his tribe, involved in trades like carpentry, in which he was certified. He was also a Chiniki councillor for a number of years and was successful in many of his endeavours.

GEORGIE MARK

Born October 10, 1930, Stoney reserve
Georgie was adopted by a well-known and respected Stoney couple, Jake and Mary Jane Twoyoungmen, when she was a child. Jake, who was chief of the Chiniki band from 1933 to 1960, was a prominent political figure for the Chiniki Nation. He gained the rank and title of a warrior for his notable career as a true leader of his band. He was also a third-generation descendant of councillor George Twoyoungmen (1877–98), who adopted Treaty 7. Georgie's natural parents were Morley and Mary Jane Twoyoungmen. Mary Jane's father was Chief Tom Chiniquay (1912–21), a son of Chief John Chiniquay (1877–1906). Georgie attended the Morley school as far as grade 7 and later married John Mark. She managed the Stoney handicraft shop for over twenty years, and she and her husband have gained a great deal of respect from the Stoney people.

GWEN RIDER

Born November 5, 1934, Morley, Alberta
Gwen was born and raised on the Stoney reserve and attended school in Morley, completing grade 8. Her paternal grandparents were Jimmy and Sarah Rider, and her maternal grandparents were Adeline Soldier and Tom Powderface. Gwen was always pretty much aware of what was going on in the Stoney community. She obtained a wealth of information from her common-law husband, Lou Crawler Sr, and from the late George Crawler, regarding the Treaty 7 proceedings.

EUNICE MARK
Born March 6, 1907, Morley, Alberta
Eunice Mark is a highly respected elder and one of a very few surviving elders who were born in the early 1900s. Eunice is a true descendant – the granddaughter – of Chief John Chiniquay, who accepted Treaty 7. Her father was Tom Chiniquay. Eunice is a traditional woman who has learned the traditional way of teaching and the original Stoney women's philosophy of life. She has been a member of the Stoney Nation from the time of her birth. Since she was very young, she has participated in cultural activities such as the Calgary Stampede, Banff Indian Days, and other Indian events throughout western Canada and parts of the northern United States. In her younger days she was a very skilful rider and horsewoman, long before barrel racing became popular on the Stoney reserve. Eunice is also a strong believer in the spiritual values of the ceremonial Sun Dance and the sweat lodges. As an elder she carries a knowledge of Indian medicine, passed down to her from her forefathers.

DELLA SOLDIER
Born June 6, 1922, Stoney reserve
Parents: George and Annie Soldier
Della is a member of the Chiniki Nation and has resided in Morley all her life. Her paternal grandparents were Jacob and Jennie Soldier, and her maternal grandparents, Jonas and Mary Goodstoney. Della's grandfather Jonas Goodstoney was eighteen years old when the Treaty 7 First Nations met with Queen Victoria's representatives regarding treaty agreements. Della is a descendant of Jacob Goodstoney, who accepted the treaty.

MILDRED SIMEON
Born July 19, 1917, near Oldman River, Alberta
Parents: Joe and Mary Kootenay
Mildred grew up in Morley, although she was born near the Oldman River. Her paternal grandparents were Paul David and Mary Jane Dixon. Paul David was a Kootenay Indian and Mary Jane Dixon was a Stoney member. Mildred attended the Morley residential school for eight years. She was very active in her community and was also knowledgable about Stoney traditions.

PAUL MARK
Born April 3, 1903, Stoney reserve
Paul is a respected elder of the Stoney Nation and has been active
in both cultural and political affairs. Throughout his life, he has
been very involved in cultural activities such as the Banff Indian
Days and cultural exchanges. His father was John Mark but his
grandparents are unknown. Paul is a recognized stateman from
the Stoney Nation's perspective.

GORDON LABELLE
Born December 19, 1922, Stoney reserve
Father: Scotty Labelle
Mother: Elsie Hunter
Gordon has lived in Morley all of his life. His maternal grandparents were John and Leah Hunter. His paternal grandfather
was Louie Labelle but his paternal grandmother is unknown.
Gordon's father, Scotty, was a non-Stoney member when he died
in the 1920s. Gordon's mother, Elsie, married Tom Labelle, Scotty's brother. Gordon is half-Cree and half-Stoney, but he grew
up on the Stoney reserve as a member of the tribe.

RESEARCHERS AND INTERPRETERS

MADELINE DIXON
Madeline Dixon was born in Morley, Alberta, on January 16,
1944. Madeline's parents were Sophia (*née* Hunter) and George
Ear, members of the Wesley Nation. Madeline attended junior
and senior high school in Cochrane and Calgary, Alberta. She
took one year of business school (1966) in Calgary and then
worked as a clerk/receptionist at Indian Health Services in Calgary (1967). Madeline worked as a receptionist, secretary, and
typist for the Stoney Tribal Administration from 1969 to 1972.
Madeline got married and moved to the Eden Valley reserve,
where she lived between 1972 and 1983. She had two children.
    In 1983 Madeline moved back to Morley to work at the Morley
Community School. From 1986 to 1993 she took university and
college courses through Athabasca University and the University
of Calgary and business administration courses through Mount
Royal College. She joined the Treaty 7 Task Force in 1994 as
the Wesley Nation researcher and continues to work on land

claims, treaty rights, and developing oral history curriculum materials for the Morley Community School

LAWRENCE TWOYOUNGMEN

Lawrence Twoyoungmen was born March 11, 1932, at Morley, Alberta. Raised and educated on the Stoney reserve at Morley, Lawrence attended the Morley residential school. He was a member of the Stoney Police Commission for over twenty years (1972–92) and served as interpreter for the respected elders William (Willie) Goodstoney (a descendant of Jacob Goodstoney, chief at Treaty 7) and Jake Rabbit (a long-serving councillor for the Wesley band). Lawrence has served on many committees and was an adviser on constitutional issues from 1981 to 1992. His knowledge of the treaties comes from his grandfather, George Crawler, and other elders, such as the late Peter Wesley from the Bighorn reserve.

WILFRED FOX

Wilfred Fox was born in a tent on the Stoney reserve at Morley on May 6, 1934. His parents were Joseph (Joe) Red Fox (d. 1978) and Nancy Twoyoungmen (d. 1945).

Wilfred's main information on Treaty 7 came from his grandparents Mark Twoyoungmen and Flora Soldier. Flora was seven years old when the treaty was made in 1877. Mark's brother was Jonas Twoyoungmen, who served as a chief (1906–11) and whose son Jake Twoyoungmen was chief of the Chiniki band from 1933 to 1960. An important observer at the treaty was James ("Jimmy") Jacob, who at the age of eighteen served as a NWMP scout and a bodyguard for the Stoney chiefs at Blackfoot Crossing. Jimmy Jacob died in the 1940s, very old and blind, but he shared his stories with Wilfred and his cousins Moses and Lazarus Wesley.

JOHN SNOW SR

John Snow was born on the Stoney reserve at Morley on January 31, 1933, during the Great Depression. He attended the Morley residential school and then graduated with a high school certificate and a diploma in ministry work from Cook Christian Training School in Phoenix, Arizona. In 1963 he graduated from St Stephen's Theological College, Edmonton, and was ordained in the United Church of Canada. He ministered in Arizona, Saskatchewan, and Alberta. He was elected chief of the Wesley (Nakoda) band in December 1968 and served until December 1992. He was honoured with an honorary doctorate of law (1981) from the University of Calgary and a doctor of divinity degree (1986) from Cook Theological College, Arizona.

John's father, Tom Snow, was chief of the Wesley band during the 1950s and his grandfather has also been chief. Other members of his family – his uncles and cousins – have served as chiefs and councillors for several generations.

John Snow has been active in research, lecturing, and writing on the treaties and on Native heritage and culture. He started the Treaty and Aboriginal Rights Research (TARR) department of the Indian Association of Alberta in 1970 and directed the Stoney Oral History Program. He contributed to written works such as "Citizens Plus" (Red Paper 1970) and "The Right to Be Indian" during the constitutional discussions during the 1980s. He continues to serve in a leadership advisory role in the elders committee of the Assembly of First Nations (AFN). In his book *These Mountains Are Our Sacred Places* (Toronto, 1977), he reflected on traditional Stoney philosophy, heritage, and religious practices and shared his deep knowledge of the oral history and politics of his people. The book was published in the centenary year of Treaty 7.

John Snow was instrumental in organizing the North American Indian Ecumenical Conference, a continent-wide Native spiritual movement, which was hosted by the Stoney Nakoda Nation from 1971 to 1989. He started the Stoney Cultural Education Program in 1972 and the Stoney Wilderness Centre in 1973 to promote a wilderness camping experience in an environment based on Indian culture. He has served on many boards and committees, including the IAA, the Alberta Indian Education Centre, the University of Calgary Senate, the executive committee of the All Chiefs Conferences, the Indian Ecumenical Conference (chairman, 1971–89), the Stoney Education Authority (chairman, 1986–92), the All Tribes Presbytery for United Church of Canada (chairman, 1988–95), and the Indian Resource Council and Indian Energy Corporation (board member, 1987–92).

John Snow has been equally effective in negotiating large land-claim settlements with federal and provincial governments, and he concluded historic agreements with multinational corporations for resource development. He is at home with Indian spiritual people at traditional gatherings and comfortable as well with business leaders in the corporate boardrooms of Canada. He is a sought-after lecturer and guest speaker for community, church, professional, and academic groups nationally and internationally. He has been interviewed on numerous occasions on local, regional, and national radio and television programs.

Chief Snow's success is attributed to the ease with which he accommodates the various cultural differences and interests of Canadian society. It is this adaptability that allows him to achieve understanding and trust between Indian and non-Indian societies, making positive solutions possible.

PETER WESLEY and KILLIAN WILDMAN

In 1971 the Stoney Nakoda Nation started the Oral History Program. Stoney elders were interviewed on Stoney history, land claims, and treaty rights. Two elders, now deceased, who spoke about the spirit and intent of Treaty 7 were Peter Wesley (Walking Facing the Wind) and Killian Wildman. They were interviewed at their homes on the Bighorn (Kista Wapta) reserve near the Kootenay Plains.

Peter Wesley was born on the Kootenay Plains by the North Saskatchewan River on July 2, 1893, to Mark and Elizah Wesley. His uncle, also named Peter Wesley (though his Indian name was Ta Otha – Moosekiller), was chief from 1903 to 1935. Peter (Walking Facing the Wind) learned about the events at Treaty 7 from his mother, who spoke the Cree language and understood the conversations held between the treaty commissioners and the chiefs. Peter made his living from trapping, hunting, and raising horses and cattle. He knew many stories about the history of his people, Stoney place names, Stoney trails throughout the Rocky Mountains, and traditional campsites. Peter was also a keeper of ancient traditional ceremonies. He passed away on June 9, 1989, and now rests in the Kootenay Plains cemetery.

Killian Wildman was born on the Bighorn reserve on May 25, 1905, and died on April 3, 1995. He lived a good life hunting and trapping in the Kootenay Plains and the surrounding mountain valleys. He helped to round up wild horses and break them for riding. He was respected for his helpful spirit and voluntary work, especially in sharing food for the community Christmas feast. His knowledge of traditional customs was acknowledged by political leaders who sought his advise on many issues. His spirit rests in the Kootenay Plains cemetery.

IAN GETTY

Ian Getty was born in 1947 in India, where his father was a Baptist missionary until he returned to Canada with his family in 1952. Raised in Ontario and after 1958 in Alberta, Ian developed an awareness of the social, economic, and political state of the Treaty 7 nations. Ian received his MA in history from the University of Calgary (1970), writing his thesis on the evangelical work of the Church Missionary Society (Anglican) among the Blackfoot (Siksika) and Blood (Kainai) people in the 1880s and 1890s. He later completed three years of doctoral studies at McMaster University (Hamilton) and is writing his doctoral thesis on the social and political history of the Stoney Nakoda people of southern Alberta.

Ian began his career in the 1970s as a historical consultant, working for Parks Canada, the Indian Association of Alberta's TARR program, and, most consistently, the Stoney Nakoda Nation at Morley, Alberta. He has served as the coordinator and director of many reserve programs, such as the Oral History Program (1970–72), the Stoney Cultural Education Program (1972–76), the Nakoda Institute (1980–90), and the Stoney Tribal Administration research department (since 1990).

He has co-edited two books in the field of Native studies, *One Century Later: Western Canadian Reserve Indians Since Treaty 7* (University of British Columbia Press, 1978) and *As Long as the Sun Shines and Water Flows* (University of British Columbia Press, 1983). Periodically since 1974 he has been a sessional instructor and guest lecturer at the University of Calgary, University of Lethbridge, University of Regina, Athabasca University, and other schools and colleges.

Ian's contribution to the Treaty 7 interpretation project was based on his considerable academic research and his years of firsthand experience with First Nations peoples, listening to the elders speak on treaty rights and constitutional issues at work-shops, conferences, field trips, and think tanks.

TOM TWOYOUNGMEN

Tom Twoyoungmen worked as the Bearspaw Nation's inter-viewer and translator for the Treaty 7 project since its inception in 1991. Born at Morley on November 26, 1948, he grew up in Morley, where he completed junior high school. He later com-pleted senior high school in Calgary through the Calgary Adult Education system. After high school he took courses in man-agement studies at the Southern Alberta Institute of Technology (SAIT) and the University of Calgary.

Tom's great-grandfather was Chief Jacob Bearspaw, who made treaty for his nation. Tom worked in various fields, but the sig-nificant jobs he held with the Stoney Tribal Administration were as a planner in the planning and development department and as a manager of Central Registry.

Currently he is employed as a researcher for the Bearspaw Stoney Nation. He is also a committee member on the constit-utional development board for the Stoney Nation. He served as a board member on the Treaty 7 Business Development Board in 1995.

LLOYD (BUDDY) WESLEY

Buddy was born in Morley on February 27, 1950, and grew up on the Stoney reserve. His parents were Peter and Winnifred Wesley and his paternal grandparents were Moses and Mary Wesley. His great-grandfather was Peter Wesley of the Bighorn reserve, and his maternal grandparents were Carl and Leah Si-meon. He received his education at the Morley residential school up to grade 9 and took upgrading at the Stoney Eagle Point classrooms. He worked for SCEP as a printshop layout technician in the late 1970s. He subsequently worked as a guide for the Stoney Wilderness Centre, a ranch hand, and a security guard for Stoney Medicine Lodge. He joined the Treaty 7 Interpretation Task Force in 1991 as a Chiniki researcher.

The Tsuu T'ina Nation

HILDA BIG CROW
Born June 17, 1909
Clan: Many Horses
Hilda received her education at boarding school. Through her marriage to George Big Crow she became a member of the Old Sarcee's band and remains an active member of the Many Horses band. Hilda is holder of the very prestigious Eagle Staff, which was handed down to her by Jane Many Swans. Jane and her husband, Tom Many Horses, were very influential in cultural and spiritual matters among the Tsuu T'ina. Tom was one of the Headmen who made Treaty 7 alongside Chief Bull Head. He was holder of the pipe bundle and owner of many stories relating to the culture and history of the Tsuu T'ina, many of which he passed on to Hilda.

Hilda was involved in establishing the first Friendship Centre with Grace Johnson and was the first member of the Sarcee Homemakers.

DICK BIG PLUME
Born October 13, 1902
Clan: Big Plume
Dick was born on the reserve, the son of Jack Big Plume. He was educated at the Sarcee Agency Missionary School and became a respected farmer and rancher. Dick was chief of the Tsuu T'ina Nation from 1962 to 1972 and was also a hereditary chief. He was a rodeo enthusiast who competed in rodeos across Canada and the United States and a member of the Tall Hat Society.

LUCY BIG PLUME
Born February 10, 1910
Clan: Onespot
Lucy went to school at the Roman Catholic school of Dunbow, where she completed grade 10. She married Dick Big Plume and lived at the west end of the reserve. She was active in the Calgary Stampede and in the early stages of the establishment of the Calgary Friendship Centre.

MAURICE BIG PLUME (1929–1995)
Born December 21, 1929
Clan: Big Plume
Maurice was the son of Chief Joe Big Plume. He was born and educated on the reserve at Agency House Missionary School. A strong traditionalist, he was actively involved in the spiritual ceremonies of the tribe and was also a practising Anglican. He became a prosperous farmer and rancher on the reserve.

TOM HEAVENFIRE
Born June 23, 1942
Tom's great-grandfather was Tom Heavenfire, an influential cultural and spiritual leader of the Tsuu T'ina who fought next to Chief Bull Head before the making of Treaty 7 and was one of Bull Head's spiritual leaders. Tom's maternal grandfather, David Onespot, a very respected and knowledgable member of the Tsuu T'ina who died in 1968 at the age of 105, passed on many stories about Treaty 7 to Tom. David Onespot was a boy at the time Treaty 7 was made but he remembered the threatening presence of the North-West Mounted Police and their cannons, which were pointed down at the Treaty Flats while the treaty negotiations were in progress.

Tom is a pipe carrier and spiritual leader involved in holding seat lodges and leading spiritual and cultural ceremonies. He is a leader of the traditional powwow. Tom was a member of the Intergovernmental Affairs Committee in 1993–94 and was instrumental in helping to establish the child welfare program on the reserve. He still teaches the Tsuu T'ina language at Chula Elementary School and since 1980 has been active in the alcohol and drug abuse program on the reserve. He served on the Tribal

Police Force from 1973 to 1978 and then from 1986 to 1990. Presently he works with the Tsuu T'ina-Stoney Corrections Society as head of the spiritual and cultural program as well as being a board member.

HELEN MEGUINIS
Born October 1, 1924
Clan: Big Plume/Crow Chief
Helen is one of the most respected and knowledgable members of the Tsuu T'ina. She is the granddaughter of Two Guns, who was twelve years old at the time Treaty 7 was made. He was a brother to Tom Heavenfire, who was also present at the treaty ceremony, and was holder of the beaver bundle. Two Guns remembered that the attitude of the negotiations was "scary" and that the NWMP were threatening and ready to attack from hidden positions behind Cannon Hill. Helen remembers the stories of Two Guns passed on to her by her parents, Anthony and Mabel Dodginghorse, who were respected cultural and spiritual leaders among the Tsuu T'ina. Helen has taken a personal interest in the history of the Tsuu T'ina and at an early age would sit and listen carefully to knowledgable elders such as Mary Onespot, Edward Onespot, Stanley Big Plume, Willie Littlebear, and George Heavenfire.

Helen's dedication to preserving Tsuu T'ina culture motivated her to establish a local museum. The museum, begun with the help of Roy Whitney, became a place where the elders met to tell their stories. Helen trained at the Glenbow Museum and worked at the reserve museum from 1981 to 1990. She still serves on its board of directors. She is a strong supporter of traditional spiritual ceremonies and is also an active member of the Roman Catholic Church.

Helen, with her mother, Mabel, has played an active role in preserving the Tsuu T'ina language. Both spent many hours in the 1970s working with Dr Cook, a linguist at the University of Calgary, to record the language on tape and to establish a written form of it. In 1992 Helen received a national award for the preservation of aboriginal languages from the Assembly of First Nations. She was made a senator by the Indian Association of Alberta for Treaty 7 in 1990 and was honoured to have met and spoken with the Queen. She remains active in the politics and social life on the reserve and is a member of provincial boards of Education and of the Family and Child Services.

EDWARD ONESPOT (GINGOLD) (1907–1995)
Born June 13, 1907
Clan: Onespot
Edward was recognized as one of the most flamboyant members of the Tsuu T'ina nation. He was born into the Onespot clan that was part of the Old Sarcee band and was the son of the influential David Onespot. Edward was educated at the Anglican boarding school, which he attended to grade 10. He was a rodeo enthusiast, who, together with Jim Starlight, travelled to Brisbane, Australia, to compete.

CLARABELLE PIPESTEM
Born September 8, 1918
Clarabelle was born on the reserve and received her education to grade 10 at the Agency Missionary House. She married Narcisse Pipestem, who was a strong traditionalist. She is the daughter of the highly respected Chief Joe Big Plume. Clarabelle is still active in spiritual and cultural societies and is dedicated to passing on the traditional ways to her grandchildren.

ROSE RUNNER
Born January 24, 1915
Clan: Otter
Rose Runner is a respected and knowledgable elder who attended Agency Missionary School up to grade 10. She is a member of the Old Sarcee's band and married into the Big Belly clan through her late husband, George Big Belly (Runner).

Notes

CHAPTER FIVE

1 Stanley, *The Birth of Western Canada*, 194.
2 Said, *Culture and Imperialism*, 5–6.
3 Ibid., 7.
4 Ibid., 8.
5 Ibid., 9.
6 Ibid., 11.
7 Kelly, "Class, Race and Cultural Revolution," 19.
8 Ibid., 20.
9 Ibid., 21.
10 Ibid.
11 Ibid.
12 Ibid., 22.
13 Ibid., 24.
14 Ibid., 35.
15 Ibid., 36.
16 Youngblood-Henderson, "Governing the Implicate Order," 3.
17 Ibid., 8.
18 Ibid., 9
19 Ibid., 19.
20 Goehring, *Indigenous People of the World*, 53–6.
21 Youngblood-Henderson, "Land in British Legal Thought," 203.
22 Ibid., 204.
23 Ibid., 208.
24 Ibid.
25 Ibid., 214.
26 Ibid., 217.
27 Sprague, "Canada's Treaties with Aboriginal People," 7.
28 Tobias, "Protection, Civilization, Assimilation," 130.
29 Ibid., 132.
30 Ibid., 135.
31 Ibid.
32 Ibid., 136.
33 Ibid.
34 Ibid., 137.
35 Milloy, "The Early Indian Acts," 152.
36 Chalmers, *Laird of the West*, 99.
37 Tobias, "Canada's Subjugation of the Plains Cree," 232.
38 Tobias, "Protection," 224.
39 Ibid.
40 Ibid., 225.

41 Ibid., 232.
42 Stanford to his mother, October 10, 1877, K. Ross Toole Collection, Conrad/Campbell Manuscript #185, Box 6, file 2, State Archives, Missoula, Montana.

CHAPTER SEVEN

1 Morris, *The Treaties of Canada*, 270.
2 Quoted in Dempsey, *Crowfoot*, 102.
3 Morris, *The Treaties of Canada*, 272.
4 Ibid., 273.
5 Ibid., 272–3.
6 Ibid., 272.
7 Ibid., 274–5.

CHAPTER EIGHT

1 Stanley, *The Birth of Western Canada*, 213.
2 Hall, "'A Serene Atmosphere'? Treaty 1 Revisited."
3 Provincial Archives of Manitoba (PAM), Alexander Morris Papers, MG 12, B2, #251, Morris to minister of interior, March 27, 1877.
4 Ibid.
5 Ibid.
6 Ibid.
7 Ibid.
8 Ibid.
9 Morris, *The Treaties of Canada*, 255.
10 Ibid.
11 Ibid., 257.
12 Ibid., 258.
13 Ibid., 259.
14 Ibid., 260.
15 Ibid., 262.
16 Ibid.
17 Ibid., 261.
18 Ibid., 262.
19 Ibid.
20 Ibid., 249.
21 Ibid.
22 Letter from Father Constantine Scollen to the Governor of Manitoba, September 8, 1876, quoted in Morris, *Treaties of Canada*, 249.
23 Ibid., 247.
24 Ibid., 248.
25 Ibid.
26 Ibid.
27 Ibid., 249.
28 Ibid.
29 Ibid., 248.
30 Ibid.
31 Ibid., 249.
32 Ibid.
33 National Archives of Canada (NA), Indian Affairs, RG 10, vol. 3695, file 14, 942, Scollen to Irvine, April 13, 1879.
34 Ibid.

35 Ibid.
36 Ibid.
37 Ibid.
38 Ibid.
39 Ibid.
40 Ibid.
41 McDougall, *On Western Trades in the Early Seventies*, 174.
42 Ibid., 185.
43 Ibid., 186.
44 PAM, Morris Papers, MG 12, B1, file 901, Jones Graham to Morris, October 20, 1874.
45 PAM, Morris Papers, MG 12, B1, file 754, Dorian to Hardisty, May 20, 1874.
46 Dempsey, *Crowfoot*, 82.
47 Ibid., 82.
48 Snow, *These Mountains Are Our Sacred Places*, 35.
49 Carter, "The Missionaries' Indian," 28.
50 Ibid., 32.

51 Ibid., 37.
52 Ibid., 42.
53 NA, Hayter Reed Papers, MG 29, file 106, vol. 17, Reed to McDougall, July 22, 1892.
54 Ibid.
55 Saskatchewan Archives Board, Laird Papers, GR 186, Laird to McDougall, December 7, 1877.
56 Turner, *The North-West Mounted Police*, 344.
57 Ibid.
58 Ibid.
59 Ibid., 347.
60 Ibid.
61 Ibid.
62 Ibid., 348.
63 Ibid., 350.
64 Ibid., 351.
65 Ibid., 356.
66 Haristy, "The Blackfoot Treaty," 21.
67 Ibid.

CHAPTER NINE

1 Dempsey, *Crowfoot*, 78.
2 Ibid., 80.
3 Ibid., 81.
4 Ibid., 82.
5 PAM, Morris Papers, MG 12, B1, file 1265, 1875.
6 Dempsey, *Crowfoot*, 106.
7 Ibid.
8 Ibid.
9 Ibid., 107.
10 Dempsey, *Red Crow*, 95.
11 Ibid., 82.
12 Ibid., 83.
13 Ibid., 86.

14 Ibid., 88.
15 Ibid.
16 Ibid., 96.
17 Ibid., 97.
18 Ibid., 101.
19 Ibid., 101–2.
20 Ibid., 102.
21 Dempsey, "Treaty Research Report," 35.
22 Ibid., 36.
23 Ibid., 37.
24 Ibid., 38.
25 Ibid., iii.

CHAPTER TEN

1 Hanks, *Tribe under Trust*, 7.
2 Ibid., 8.
3 Ibid., 9.
4 Ibid.
5 Ibid., 10.
6 Ibid.
7 Ibid., 11.
8 Ibid.
9 Ibid., 12.
10 Ibid., 13.
11 Ibid.
12 Ibid.
13 Ibid.
14 Ibid., 14.

CHAPTER ELEVEN

1 Adams, *Prison of Grass*, 67.
2 Cardinal, *The Unjust Society*, 28.
3 Friesen, "Magnificent Gifts," 42–3.
4 Quoted in ibid., 45.
5 Tobias, "The Origins of the Treaty Rights Movement in Saskatchewan," 242.
6 Taylor, "Two Views on the Meaning of Treaties Six and Seven," 9.
7 Ibid., 9.
8 Ibid., 15.
9 Ibid., 19
10 Ibid., 26.
11 Ibid., 39.
12 Ibid., 40.
13 Ibid.
14 Ibid.
15 Ibid., 44–5.
16 Sprague, "Canada's Treaties with Aboriginal People," 23.
17 Dyck, *What Is the Indian "Problem,"* 24.
18 Ibid., 25.
19 Ibid., 26.
20 Ibid., 28.
21 Ibid., 29.
22 Ibid., 30.
23 Friesen, "Magnificent Gifts," 49.
24 Ibid.
25 Ibid.
26 Ibid., 50.
27 Ibid., 47.
28 Ibid.
29 Ibid., 51.
30 Ibid.
31 Friesen, "Grant Me Wherewith to Make My Living," 153.
32 Carter, *Lost Harvests*, 72.
33 Ibid.
34 Ibid., 74.
35 Ibid., 76.
36 Crop Eared Wolf, "Signing of Treaty 7," 7.
37 Ibid., 1.
38 Ibid.
39 Ibid.
40 Ibid., 2.
41 Ibid.
42 Ibid., 4.
43 Ibid., 5.

44 Ibid., 6.
45 Ibid.
46 Ibid.
47 Ibid.
48 Snow, *These Mountains Are Our Sacred Places*, 28.
49 Ibid.
50 Ibid., 29.
51 Ibid., 30.
52 Ibid., 31.

53 Ibid.
54 Calf Robe, *Siksika*, 21.
55 Ibid.
56 Ibid.
57 Ibid.
58 Peterson, *Wake Up, Canada!* 183–4.
59 Wilson, "Our Betrayed Words," 12.

CHAPTER TWELVE

1 Cruikshank, "Oral Tradition and Oral History," 413.

2 Ibid., 416.

Bibliography

MANUSCRIPT SOURCES

National Archives of Canada (NA), Ottawa
  MG 29: Hayter Reed Papers
  RG 10: Indian and Northern Affairs
        Deputy Superintendent's Letterbook

Provincial Archives of Alberta
  Oblates de Marie Immaculate
  Lacombe Papers
  Scollen Papers

Provincial Archives of Manitoba (PAM)
  MG 12: Alexander Morris Papers

Saskatchewan Archives Board
  Reverend J.A. Mackay Papers
  Laird Papers

Hudson's Bay Company Archives, Winnipeg

PRINTED DOCUMENTS AND REPORTS

Canada. Department of Indian Affairs. Annual reports.
Canada. House of Commons. *Sessional Papers*.
Canada. North-West Mounted Police. Reports.

BOOKS AND ARTICLES

Abel, Kerry, and Jean Friesen, eds. *Aboriginal Resource Use in Canada: Historical and Legal Aspects*. Winnipeg: University of Manitoba Press, 1991.

Adams, Howard. *Prison of Grass: Canada from the Native Point of View*. Toronto: New Press, 1975.

Arthur, George W.; Michael Wilson; and Richard Forbis. *The Relationship of Bison to the Indians of the Great Plains*. Ottawa: Parks Canada, 1975.

Asch, Michael. *Home and Native Land: Aboriginal Rights and the Canadian Constitution*. Toronto: Methuen, 1984.

Barron, F.L., and James B. Waldram, eds. *1885 and After: Native Society in Transition*. Regina: Canadian Plains Research Centre, University of Regina, 1986.

Bonnichsen, Robson, and Stuart J. Baldwin. *Cypress Hills Ethnohistory and Ecology*. Edmonton: Alberta Culture, Historical Resources Division, 1978.

Brink, Jack, et al. *Final Report of the 1983 Field Season at Head-Smashed-In-Buffalo Jump*. Edmonton: Archaeological Survey of Alberta No. 1, 1985.

Brink, Jack, and Bob Dawe. *Final Report of the 1985 and 1986 Field Season at Head-Smashed-In-Buffalo Jump*. Edmonton: Archaeological Survey of Alberta No. 16, 1989.

Calf Robe, Ben, with Adolf and Beverly Hungry Wolf. *Siksika: A Blackfoot Legacy*. Invermere: Good Medicine Books, 1979.

Cardinal, Harold. *The Rebirth of Canada's Indians*. Edmonton: Hurtig, 1977.

– *The Unjust Society: The Tragedy of Canada's Indians*. Edmonton: Hurtig, 1969.

Carter, Sarah A. "Agriculture and Agitation on the Oak Reserve, 1875–1895." *Manitoba History* 6, no. 2 (1983): 2–9.

– "Controlling Indian Movement: The Pass System." *NeWest Review*, May 1985, 8–9.

– *Lost Harvests: Prairie Indian Reserve Farmers and Government Policy*. Montreal and Kingston: McGill-Queen's University Press, 1990.

– "The Missionaries' Indian: The Publications of John McDougall, John Maclean and Egerton Ryerson Young." *Prairie Forum* 9, no. 1 (1984): 27–44.

– "Two Acres and a Cow: Peasant Farming for the Indians of the Northwest, 1889–1897." *Canadian Historical Review* 70, no. 1 (1989): 27–52.

Chalmers, John. *Laird of the West*. Calgary: Detselig, 1981.

Clark, Bruce A. *Native Liberty, Crown Sovereignty*. Montreal and Kingston: McGill-Queen's University Press, 1990.

Crop Eared Wolf, Louise. "Signing of Treaty No. 7," *Kainai News* 1, no. 4 (May 15, 1968): 7.

Cruikshank, Julie. "Oral Tradition and Oral History: Reviewing Some Issues." *Canadian Historical Review* 75, no. 3 (September 1994).

Daugherty, William. *Maritime Indian Treaties in Perspective*. Ottawa: Indian and Northern Affairs Canada, 1983.

Dempsey, Hugh A. *Big Bear: The End of Freedom*. Vancouver: Douglas & McIntyre, 1984.

– *Crowfoot: Chief of the Blackfeet*. Edmonton: Hurtig, 1972.

– *Indian Tribes of Alberta*. Calgary: Glenbow-Alberta Institute, 1986.

– *Red Crow: Warrior Chief*. Saskatoon: Western Producer Prairie Books, 1980.

– "Treaty Research Report: Treaty 7." Prepared for the Department of Indian Affairs, Ottawa, 1987.

Denig, Edwin Thompson. *Five Indian Tribes of the Upper Missouri: Sioux, Arickaras, Assiniboines, Crees, Crows*. Norman: University of Oklahoma Press, 1961.

Dickason, Olive. *Canada's First Nations*. Toronto: McClelland and Stewart, 1992.

Dyck, Noel. *What Is the Indian "Problem": Tutelage and Resistance in Canadian Indian Administration*. St John's: Institute of Social and Economic Research, 1991.

Erasmus, Peter. *Buffalo Days and Nights*. Calgary: Glenbow-Alberta Institute, 1976.

Ewers, John C. *The Blackfeet, Raiders on the Northwestern Plains*. Norman: University of Oklahoma Press, 1958.

– , ed. *Five Indian Tribes of the Upper Missouri*. Norman: University of Oklahoma Press, 1961.

– , ed. *The Horse in Blackfoot Indian Culture*. Washington, DC: Smithsonian Institute, 1955.

Friesen, Jean. "Grant Me Wherewith to Make My Living." In *Aboriginal Resource Use in Canada*, edited by Kerry Abel and Jean Friesen. Winnipeg: University of Manitoba Press, 1991.

– "Magnificent Gifts: The Treaties of Canada with the Indians of the Northwest 1869–70." *Transactions of the Royal Society of Canada*, series 5, vol. 1 (1986), 41–51.

Getty, Ian A.L., and Antoine S. Lussier, eds. *As Long as the Sun Shines and Water Flows*. Vancouver: University of British Columbia Press, 1983.

Getty, Ian A.L., and Donald B. Smith, eds. *One Century Later: Western Canadian Reserve Indians Since Treaty 7.* Vancouver: University of British Columbia Press, 1978.

Goehring, Brian. *Indigenous People of the World.* Saskatoon: Purich Publishing, 1993.

Goldfrank, Esther S. *Changing Configurations in the Social Organization of a Blackfeet Tribe during the Reserve Period (The Blood of Alberta, Canada).* New York: J.J. Augustin, 1945.

Hall, David J. "'A Serene Atmosphere'? Treaty 1 Revisited." *Canadian Journal of Native Studies* 4, no. 2 (1984): 321–58.

Hanks, L.M. Jr., and J.R. Hanks. *Tribe under Trust: A Study of the Blackfoot Reserve in Alberta.* Toronto: University of Toronto Press, 1950.

Hardisty, Richard. "The Blackfoot Treaty: An Eyewitness Account." *Calgary Herald*, November 18, 1933, 21.

Harper, Alan G. "Canada's Indian Administration: Basic Concepts and Objectives." *América Indigena* 5, no. 2 (1945): 119–32.

Harris, R. Cole, ed. *Historical Atlas of Canada I.* Toronto: University of Toronto Press, 1987.

Helgason, Gail. *The First Albertans: An Archaeological Search.* Edmonton: Lone Pine, 1987.

Jenness, Diamond. *The Sarcee Indians of Alberta.* Ottawa: King's Printer, 1938.

Johnston, Alexander, comp. *The Battle at Belly River: Stories of the Last Great Indian Battle.* Lethbridge: Lethbridge Branch of the Historical Society of Alberta, 1966.

Kelly, Gary. "Class, Race, and Cultural Revolution: Treaties and the Making of Western Canada." *Alberta* 1, no. 2 (1993): 19.

Lewis, John C. *The Blackfeet.* Norman: University of Oklahoma Press, 1958.

– *The Horse in Blackfoot Indian Culture.* Washington, DC: Smithsonian Institution, 1955.

Lewis, Oscar. *The Effects of White Contact upon Blackfoot Culture with Special References to the Fur Trade.* Monographs of the American Ethnological Society, no. 6. New York, 1942.

L'Heureux, Jean. "Ethnological Notes on the Astronomical Customs and Religious Ideas of the Chokitapia of Blackfeet Indians, Canada." *Journal of the Anthropological Institute* 15 (1986): 301–4.

Little Bear, Leroy; Menno Boldt; and J. Anthony Long, eds. *Pathways to Self-Determination: Canadian Indians and the Canadian State.* Toronto: University of Toronto Press, 1984.

Lowie, Robert H. *Indians of the Plains*. New York: McGraw-Hill, 1954.

Mandelbaum, David G. *The Plains Cree: An Ethnographic, Historical and Comparative Study*. Regina: Canadian Plains Research Centre, 1979.

McDougall, John. *On Western Trades in the Early Seventies: Frontier Pioneer Life in the Canadian Northwest*. Toronto: Briggs, 1911.

Milloy, John S. "The Early Indian Acts: Developmental Strategy and Constitutional Change." In *Sweet Promises*, edited by J.R. Miller, 145–54. Toronto: University of Toronto Press, 1991.

– *The Plains Cree: Trade, Diplomacy, and War, 1790–1870*. Winnipeg: University of Manitoba Press, 1988.

Morris, Alexander. *The Treaties of Canada with the Indians of Manitoba and the North-West Territories*. 1880. Reprint, Saskatoon: Fifth House, 1991.

Peterson, C.W. *Wake Up, Canada! Reflections on Vital National Issues*. Edmonton: University of Alberta Press, 1989.

Price, Richard, ed. *The Spirit of Alberta Indian Treaties*. Edmonton: Pica Pica Press, 1987.

Purich, Donald. *Our Land: Native Rights in Canada*. Toronto: Lorimer, 1986.

Ray, Arthur J. *Indians in the Fur Trade: Their Role as Trappers, Hunters, and Middlemen in the Lands Southwest of Hudson Bay 1660–1870*. Toronto: University of Toronto Press, 1974.

Roe, Frank Gilbert. *The North American Buffalo*. 1951. Reprint, Toronto: University of Toronto Press, 1970.

Said, Edward. *Culture and Imperialism*. New York: Alfred A. Knopf, 1993.

– *Orientalism*. New York: Pantheon Books, 1978.

Sharp, Paul F. *Whoop-Up Country: The Canadian-American West, 1865–1885*. Minneapolis: University of Minnesota Press, 1955.

Slattery, Brian. *Ancestral Lands, Alien Laws: Judicial Perspectives on Aboriginal Title*. Saskatoon: University of Saskatchewan Law Centre, 1983.

Snow, John. *These Mountains Are Our Sacred Places: The Story of the Stoney Indians*. Toronto: Samuel Stevens, 1977.

Sprague, Douglas. "Canada's Treaties with Aboriginal People." Unpublished paper, University of Manitoba Canadian Legal History Project, 1991.

Stanley, George F.G. *The Birth of Western Canada: A History of the Riel Rebellion*. 1936. Reprint, Toronto: University of Toronto Press, 1960.

Taylor, John. "Two Views on the Meaning of Treaties Six and Seven." In *The Spirit of the Alberta Treaties*, edited by Richard Price. Edmonton: Pica Pica Press, 1986.

Tobias, John L. "Canada's Subjugation of the Plains Cree, 1879–1885." In *Sweet Promises*, edited by J.R. Miller. Toronto: University of Toronto Press, 1991.

– "Indian Reserves in Western Canada: Indian Homesteads or Devices for Assimilation." In *Approaches to Native History in Canada*, edited by D.A. Muise, 89–103. Ottawa: National Museums of Canada, 1976.

– "The Origins of the Treaty Rights Movement in Saskatchewan." In *1885 and After: Native Society in Transition*, edited by F.L. Barron and J.B. Waldram, 241–52. Regina: Canadian Plains Research Centre, 1986.

– "Protection, Civilization, Assimilation: An Outline History of Canada's Indian Policy." In *Sweet Promises*, edited by J.R. Miller. Toronto: University of Toronto Press, 1991.

Turner, John Peter. *The North-West Mounted Police, 1873–1893*. Ottawa: King's Printer, 1950.

Walker, James W. St G. "The Canadian Indian in Historical Writing." In Canadian Historical Association, *Historical Papers*, 1971, 21–51.

Wessel, Thomas R. "Agriculture on the Reservations: The Case of the Blackfeet, 1885–1935." *Journal of the West* 18, no. 4 (1979): 17–25.

Wilson, Robert N. *Our Betrayed Words*. Ottawa: privately published, 1921.

Youngblood-Henderson, Sakej. "Governing the Implicate Order: Self-Government and the Linguistic Development of Aboriginal Communities." Unpublished paper, 1993.

– "Land in British Legal Thought." Unpublished manuscript prepared for the Royal Commission on Aboriginal Affairs, 1994.

Index